INTIMACY AND POWER IN THE OLD SOUTH

NEW STUDIES IN AMERICAN INTELLECTUAL
AND CULTURAL HISTORY

Thomas Bender, Consulting Editor

INTIMACY AND POWER IN THE OLD SOUTH

Ritual in the Lives of the Planters

STEVEN M. STOWE

The Johns Hopkins University Press

BALTIMORE AND LONDON

This book has been brought to publication
with the generous assistance of the Andrew W. Mellon Foundation.

The Johns Hopkins University Press
701 West 40th Street
Baltimore, Maryland 21211
The Johns Hopkins Press Ltd., London

The paper used in this publication meets
the minimum requirements of American National
Standard for Information Sciences—Permanence
of Paper for Printed Library Materials,
ANSI Z39.48–1984.

Library of Congress Cataloging-in-Publication Data

Stowe, Steven M., 1946–
Intimacy and power in the old South.

(New studies in American intellectual and cultural
history)
Bibliography: p.
Includes index.
1. Plantation owners—Southern States—History—
19th century. 2. Southern States—Social life and
customs—1775–1865. 3. Southern States—Civilization—1775–1865. I. Title. II. Series.
F213.S865   1987   976'.03'0880621   86-20885
ISBN 0-8018-3388-4 (alk. paper)

For my mother
JOANN McCRAY STOWE
and
for the memory of my father
MAC SHERIDAN STOWE

CONTENTS

PREFACE

Like many students of the South, I am not a southerner. Southerners sometimes remind me of this, although just being "at the South," as the old phrase had it, is to feel the tug of difference in many ways. This present study has less to do with what this difference can be said to mean than with how a certain group of southerners made meaning for themselves. An early, and unformed, appreciation of southern meanings was grasped in a literary way. A youth in California, I stumbled upon the classics: Wolfe, Faulkner, O'Connor, Warren. I read them for the way they joined passion to plainness and made something more complex. Wolfe's ghosts and Faulkner's honeysuckle soon got mixed up with W. J. Cash's confrontations with the complexity of southern temperament and mind. His combination of journalistic squint and wide-eyed cultural gaze sized up the complexity while never getting quite free of it. This seemed pretty close to the center of what was remarkable about being southern.

The late 1960s, a time which many of us thought of as a kind of intellectual great awakening, led me to graduate school. Here my literary enjoyment was shaped into a historical curiosity about the South as an American place and yet a place of its own devising. It was during this time that this present study took its particular form, first as an interest in how slavery organized the encounter between whites and blacks, and ultimately as a study of the interior lives of certain planter families. I chose to study upper class whites for reasons that still strike me as good ones. The history of black southerners was emerging with exciting clarity, but the history of those who would be masters still seemed caught up in older, mythic terms. The intentions and sensibilities attributed to the planters by apologists and critics alike seemed to me to be impossibly thin and unrealistically bright. A look at the manuscript diaries of Mary Boykin Chesnut and Edmund Ruffin suggested that the planters were far more grandiose, angry, humorous, and vexed than I had considered and convinced me that we had only just begun to understand how they perceived themselves and their culture. Looking at family letters convinced me of this all the more. The planters saw the contradictions and felt the tensions in their lives frequently much more clearly than historians allowed. How might this self-awareness be described? How far might we go in reconstructing the intellectual and emotional world of these people?

My route to addressing such questions continued to follow the map of the planters' letters and diaries. I looked closely at what they said about their lives in private, to their lovers and families, and to themselves, as I sought to discover how these intimate understandings reappeared in the public rituals that proclaimed their social power. The voices of the planters, therefore, fill this study. Although their terms are not precisely ours, their struggles to know themselves resemble our efforts to know them. Though they often tried to avoid it, they were led again and again, like us, toward the full complexity of their lives.

It is a happy thing at the end of a long project to recall the many people who helped further it, and to be able to thank them. My greatest intellectual debt is to William R. Taylor. Even though he has looked away from the Old South to the modern city, his critical vigor and warm support over the years have been indispensable. Fred Weinstein, too, will remember the beginnings of this study and see his hand in it. Thomas Bender gave me new perspective on the book as a whole, and many particular insights. Michael O'Brien's deep knowledge of intellectual life in the South helped me to think about the intersection of lives and letters.

John Demos and other members of the National Endowment for the Humanities summer seminar in psychology and history led me to question my sources and formulate my argument, as did participants in the conference on intellectual life in antebellum Charleston. Also challenging in a helpful way were the members of the symposium on the South at Georgia Southern College. My colleagues in the history department at New York University were an unfailingly supportive and stimulating group who helped in countless ways, and I am grateful, too, to the NYU symposium on gender and culture and to the New York Institute for the Humanities Biography Seminar for opportunities to present pieces of my work.

Many others have given generously to making this study a better one, whether through extended, episodic conversations or close, written comment. Peter Williams and Jim Terry were there at the beginning, heard me out, and heard me out again. Also in the earlier going, Edward Countryman, Ellen Rothman, Regina Morantz-Sanchez, Anthony Rotundo, Kathleen Dalton, and Peter Filene provided food for thought. Nearer to completion, Randall Miller, Sydney Nathans, Carl Degler, Dennis Klein, Jane Censer, Jackson Lears, C. Vann Woodward, Drew Faust, Bertram Wyatt-Brown, Laurence Vesey, and Michael Starr all contributed in ways that helped renew my effort or redirect my thinking. My colleagues in the Department of Humanities at the Pennsylvania State University have been willing listeners and able critics in the course of final revisions. At the Johns Hopkins University Press, senior social sciences editor Henry Tom has somehow managed to be both patient and demanding, for which I am grateful. Jean Toll's careful copyediting and Nancy West's seeing the book through production also made working with the Press a pleasure.

The staffs of many fine libraries directed my search through families' lives and rituals, most importantly at the Southern Historical Collection at the University of North Carolina, Chapel Hill, the Perkins Library at Duke University, the Beinecke Library at Yale University, the New York Public Library, the Library of Congress, and the South Carolina Department of Archives and History. Allen Stokes, manuscript librarian at the South Caroliniana Library, University of South Carolina, has my special appreciation for his wide knowledge and consistent helpfulness. Virginia Lingle and other members of the interlibrary loan staff at the George T. Harrell Library, Milton S. Hershey Medical Center, Pennsylvania State University, supplied me with much-needed references in the later stages. My thanks, too, to Laurie Guida for her typing of the first draft, and especially to Alice Lundquist for her thoroughness and good humor in typing all of the other drafts.

My wife, Lisa Gershkoff-Stowe, has given me much love and good advice. She will be happy to see this book on the shelf, mostly because she has always encouraged me to take a sighting, make a decision, and move on. Whatever is on the next horizon, she and Benjamin will be there, too.

INTRODUCTION

This book is about the cultural life of elite southern planters in pre–Civil War America. These men and women have remained singularly visible in American life in spite of their remoteness in time, the losses of war, and shifts in historical writing. The legendary image of this group is part of its uniqueness. Probably no other American class has so regularly appeared across so wide a span of culture: the planters of the Old South populate fiction and history, theater and song, talltale and object lesson. They are anything but gone with the wind. And probably no other elite in American history was in fact so open to dramatic triumph or defeat, so self-consciously influential in their region yet increasingly pinioned by the contradictions in their political goals, in their family expectations, in their racial assumptions and sexual definitions, and in the desiderata at the center of their consciousness. This book explores the quality of the planters' consciousness. It is an attempt to describe a shared mentality that lies between observable behavior, on the one hand, and formal systems of thought, on the other, in order to show how the planters made sense of both behavior and intellect.[1]

Myth and irony are powerful forces to be reckoned with in this undertaking. Even in their own time, the planters became a symbol of a great American difficulty: how to unite folk piety and rootless power, locale and ambition, into a worldview suitable for modern times. As it turned out, black slavery and white secession had nothing to do with modern times. Civil war and black Americans' struggle for social and political autonomy shattered the planters' hope for a great "southron" empire, a sunny realm of harmony, learning, and enterprise. But the mythic image of a cavalier culture was not shattered. It became embodied as a Lost Cause and admired by many as a once-and-future wholeness, an alternative to the waste and fragmentation of northern industrial capitalism. The facets of the myth were many—white racial dominance, agricultural self-sufficiency, public spirit and grace, rural innocence—and combined in many ways. It was resistant to change, as myths are; it protected ideals but smothered criticism, even curiosity, among its believers. For historians and other critics of the South who worked to detach history from the myth, and thereby reclaim a sense of cause, effect, and the foundations of change, irony became the tool. Not a single irony, but many were discovered in southern history, all seeming to derive from the fact that in losing a war for independence, white southerners experienced what other Americans had not. For the southerner, "history had happened" in a way most Americans had never known, and what had seemed to be "the eccentric position of the South in the nation" was revealed, ironically, as America's eccentric place in the history of nations.[2]

Yet in showing how southern history might teach us something new about the American experience, and in revealing how southern myth diverged from history, the ironic point of view oddly sidestepped a full examination of planter-class culture. Just as the myth had replayed moonlight-magnolia-and-the-darkies motifs which removed us from what life actually was like for the master class, preventing us from measuring the impact of mastery on the masters, so the ironic vision, too, was based on a kind of distance. Intent on the incongruity of what was supposed to be and what happened, the ironist frequently is not interested in what life was like before the fall. Sometimes myth and irony explore the ground with the same language, the same stock of images that indicate how much each owes to the other. One antebellum observer, admiring the "Southerner," wrote of how "he is liberal in his feelings, high-minded, a warm and generous friend but a malignant and bitter enemy. . . . He is generous to a fault with his property." A late twentieth-century historian, critical of the slaveowning class, nonetheless produced a similar assessment: "They were tough, proud, and arrogant; liberal-spirited in all that did not touch their honor; gracious and courteous; generous and kind; quick to anger and extraordinarily cruel."[3]

What frequently is absent from both the mythic and ironic points of view is extended testimony from the planters about themselves; their voices and their words. The rich historiography of the Old South is remarkable in the way it frequently describes only briefly the ordinary habits, beliefs, and preoccupations of the elite, on the way to somewhere else. Many of the best studies of plantation society look at "the plantation" as the source of attitudes and actions, rather than at the self-descriptions of the planters themselves. Similarly, the long tradition of studying the mind of the South largely concerns the relative merit of southern thought and whether it was backward compared to northern thought, rather than the place of formal thinking in the daily cultural life of the master class. We see the novels and the proslavery essays, but not the people reading them; the arguments but not the needs, the ideas but not the consciousness, the mastery but not the doubt. Slavery studies, whether of the white institution or the slave community, have given us glimpses of the planter-slaveowner as variously an idle patriarch, a straining capitalist, a canny labor boss, or a one-dimensional "significant other." But here, too, despite the illumination of the material and institutional world of the planters, the sense of their culture is piecemeal because their own voices are muted.[4]

Retrieving those voices and interpreting what they said is the problem, and at the beginning of my research I simply read entire collections of letters in order to see how the planters explained themselves to themselves when, so to say, they were alone. Though I was not sure what I wanted to find, I was certain that to look at the planters' own self-assessments, their own expectations of each other, would be to dig under myth and slip past irony to the common sense of their time and place. The years in which most of the evidence in this study originated, 1820 to 1860, included the height of this culture, and the area of the South covered here—Virginia, the Carolinas, Georgia—was the seat of elite power and tradition. The subjects of this study, too, fall under the traditional index of membership in planterdom: ownership of twenty or more slaves, a somewhat arbitrary number but one that certainly was sufficient to give an individual or family an opportunity for the wealth that was the source of political power, educational advantage, marital choice, and control of commodities and information essential to elite standing. But material conditions do not, of course, simply "cause" a person's self-awareness or a group's characteristic ways of thinking and acting. As an increasingly embattled minority, the planter elite might be expected to have been quietly acquisitive rather than aggressively, even grandiosely, masterful as many of its members were. Their showy, complicated style of leadership, therefore, is as important a measure of elite standing as their wealth, and this study gives attention to makers of their ideology—teachers, clergymen, politicians, authors—who harvested from raw wealth the reasons for legitimate social dominance.[5]

Legitimacy and dominance made up the knot that the planters had to keep tight if they were to survive, and, as they steadily came to understand by the 1830s, if their survival was to have the strength of tradition. It was not enough to dominate others by force. Dominating by persuasion instead would imply that others chose to submit. But of course it made no sense at all for one's authority to be legitimate if one could not dominate others; there was no future for a slaveholder who held to his legitimacy as only a matter of principle. The plan of this book closely mirrors the means the planters invented to meet this central problem. Part One concerns three rituals that condensed and elevated key social events to their full cultural significance. All three organized, replayed—and played with—themes of authority, sexuality, and kinship. These were the "relations of life" which gave savor to reflection, drama to action, and terror to loss. The focus in Part One is on formal maps of cultural experience and on a shared intellectual and emotional terrain that made someone "typical" of a dominant class. Part Two takes the themes developed in Part One and shifts the focus to the lives of three elite families, those of a planter and jurist, a slaveowning Presbyterian minister, and a sea island planter and congressman. Here attention is drawn to the texture of satisfaction and duty in particular lives, and the aim is to suggest how collective rituals were embraced or resisted and, finally, shaped to the routines and novelties of everyday life. All three family narratives reveal decisions and actions that imply formal thought, but bend it in ways that allow us to see how culture took its path.

Because this book's thesis concerns the quality of a people's consciousness and thus reflects mostly on social continuity, some familiar themes in southern history (a history we think of in terms of upheaval) will, I hope, appear in a new light. I have attempted to characterize the essential cohesiveness of the elite's world while not suggesting that change was impossible. Clearly it was not, and in looking at the interdependence of cultural factors in the planters' rituals and routines I have also attempted to show (aided by others' work on the eighteenth century) which beliefs and preoccupations were most important to the potential for long-term change. The *conditions* for change were embedded in the social continuity looked at here, and if the years 1820 to 1860 did not witness radical breaks in the planters' cultural life, they did see the further elaboration of the distinctive consciousness that this book explores.

Indeed, with respect to classic themes in southern historiography, it is part of this book's thesis that the typical antebellum periodization is not so important for thinking about culture as it has been for the study of more swiftly changing phenomena, such as politics. What has impressed me is that even with the growing sectional strain in these years, of which ordinary planters increasingly were aware, the elite's belief remained strong that the adhesions of southron life would hold. Family relations and personal life loomed larger for most planters than the advancing national crisis, just as family letters remained thick with personal events and trust in God's future despite crisis and loss. Similarly, I have been struck with how seldom these letters make mention of black people, even familiar, personal servants. I had expected slaves to be much more in evidence, but they simply were not, and therefore I make only peripheral mention of blacks in this book. The conclusion I draw is that the proximity of certain black individuals to the white elite should not in the least imply intimacy. My findings complement those of students of black history who have found an essential cultural division between the races. The black as a figure in white discourse was a creation of the postbellum years no less in family life than in imaginative literature. Finally, historians of the South usually feel obligated to talk about its distinctiveness with respect to the North. I hope to contribute to this classic counterpoint, but this book does not undertake a regional comparison. Enough fine scholarship exists to make some comparison possible, however, and I note sectional differences throughout these pages. My view of the planters' life does not argue for a separate southern culture but does support a thesis of a significant southern emphasis in certain key aspects of upper-class American life. The distinctiveness I have found may be likened to southern idiom and accent in the language: even though southerners like other Americans spoke English, it misses the point to leave it at this; it is the variation that tugs at our interest, not the sameness. And these pages will further the argument for a significant southern variation on antebellum American family life and mentality.[6]

The themes in this southern variation are the principal thesis here, themes of a people's awareness that inextricably tied forms of expression to certain sustaining beliefs. In part, these beliefs reflected the differences between southern society and the increasingly privatized, market-oriented, sentimental, urban society growing to the North. The planters were on a cusp and saw the risks of wholly belonging to either version of America. I have listened as carefully as I can to the voices of the planters in order to locate these beliefs in the flux of their daily lives. The documents do not do it alone, of course, and decisions have been made, selections justified. As J. G. A. Pocock has pointed out, selecting the level of meaning in a historical document is necessary (whether or not we know we are doing it) because "an utterance may, at any moment in its career, have more than one meaning and participate in more than one history; we are merely responding to the obligation to choose, and declare our choice of, that history which we feel competent to tell." And so it is with my view of the planters' most inclusive, cherished beliefs. The first of these was that sex and gender (not race or class) was the most satisfying explanation for human values and action. The southern elite, I will argue, held to values for each sex shared by other well-to-do Americans but perceived them as being different in the South, more weighted and extreme. In particular, the definition of family and gender duties, the meaning of sexuality, and the expectation of intimacy all were carried by a formal discourse which more sharply divided, even alienated, female from male. Second, a clear hierarchal scheme of value and belief in family life and society was not only evident in planter mentality, but celebrated. The planters conceived of their fundamental codes and purposes as a ranked order, a pattern of tiers on which they relied not only as a matter of tactics or necessity, but also as a matter of delight. Third, elite culture supported a kind of authority (whether in the sexual relation, political decision making, or parenting) which allowed the planters to conflate the personal with the social. In their daily affairs and in the rituals that elevated them, the elite acted to join personal self-esteem closely to a sense of a wider social stability. An entire class's power was thus legitimated by an individual's living a "good" life, and, conversely, neither accolades nor threats touched the social order without touching self-esteem. Finally, I will suggest how the planters' consciousness oriented them to showy displays of their beliefs, leading them to find a kind of substance in the show and to rely upon appearances. Much of the time they knew that they did this, played at it, and enjoyed it. But, less consciously, they also linked appearance to the essence of personal relationships, raising serious struggles for themselves of mastery and doubt, authority and intimacy, which were at the heart of their relations of life.[7]

INTIMACY AND POWER IN THE OLD SOUTH

RITUAL

Between Indulgence and Control

The family establishes the duties and satisfactions that not only mark people as individuals but also make them members of the group. The planters' private correspondence and the advice books, novels, and other commentary they relied upon to help shape their family life contain overwhelming evidence of the work required to make personal relations yield both individual happiness and group authority. Part One explores certain rituals that organized and explained much of this work. These rituals promised to join individuals to whatever was truly important in worldly life, and through them the family emerged as both the reality and the metaphor which oriented the planters to that hope. The term *ritual* may suggest strange scenes of torchlight and coronation, but it need not be so. Ritual does involve, however, a unique heightening of ordinary experience, creating a sense of being outside normal place and time. Ritual challenges and refreshes by transforming business-as-usual into something unusual. Ritual underscores transitions in social and personal life by playing upon a dramatic tension between self-indulgence and self-control. The focus on ritual here, moreover, illuminates a kind of paradox in the history of culture: a ritual regulated the shared rhythms of a people's experience over time even as it lent extraordinary intensity to each individual's life. Participating in ritual (even, at times, resisting it), one became personally exalted and yet more attuned to the rich conventions of social life, more sensitive to one's own typicality.[1]

Part One characterizes three rituals—the affair of honor, courtship, and the coming of age at adolescence—through which the planters explored the meaning of worthiness, sexuality, and knowledge. To

some extent, this focus must turn aside the historian's traditional interest in the sequence of events in order to give full attention to their
setting. The premise is that we can better understand "what happened"
to the planters by looking at what typically *happens* when their values
and perceptions became illuminated by ritual. Ritual suggests a complexity and detail—all that the planters felt about their world, the quality of air and light, the feel of fabric and touch, the tone of voice, gesture, and movement—that are now lost. A threshold to the vanished
world remains in language, however, and because the planters themselves had strong convictions about the power of language, it is a valuable one. The point of view taken here, simply, is that language, especially in the context of ritual, not only communicates information but
also is a kind of behavior. Language can be shown to be causal, while at
the same time providing the very terms of cause, effect, and meaning.
The forms and usages of language, therefore, require close attention. As
Nancy Struever has observed of Vico, "He asked us neither to focus
myopically on the words themselves in some affective present, nor to
look beyond and through the grid of language to the events of the past.
Rather, he insisted that we focus on the grid itself."[2] The various forms
of written discourse so consciously valued by the elite (letter, moral
prescription, fiction, legal brief, essay) themselves comprise a kind of
cultural grammar that defined a sense of who might (or must) communicate with whom, when and in what situations words were essential, what alternatives in expression were appropriate or not, and how
various genres tied into one another. Once we explore this structure,
the context of the planters' standards and expectations, their choices,
and the way they told themselves stories, all reflect brightly upon their
cultural order of things.

Language constrains the people who invent and use it, something
evident in that not just anything is possible in a people's speech and
writing. The planters followed certain forms in the name of correctness
or pleasure. Nonelites, especially slaves, were excluded from the ability
to master particular forms of discourse. Elite children were taught the
use of language with explicit attention to the social order and to family
continuity. Attention to limits was at the heart of the social intercourse
that supported planter dominance: political talk among men followed
conventions of deference and equality; courtship letters showed controlled usages of language, paper, and handwriting; an affair of honor
could not proceed without strict adherence to linguistic form. Moreover, these and other kinds of expression were joined to certain social
relations which the elite assumed were part of the natural world and
thus not easily open to change. The sexes, most significantly, were each
thought not only to possess specific forms of language, but also to be

incapable of moving beyond the aptitudes for thinking and feeling that these forms signified.[3]

In addition to being constraints, however, forms of expression and their implications for social order created an equally characteristic sense of possibility. Language was a shared resource, the very stuff of a person's "representativeness," which permitted members of the group "to see [each other] as sources of shared knowledge and insight." A young woman in love, for example, drew upon the language of love and thus became a *lover* in her eyes and others', not just a confused individual. The planters were so few in number, and sufficiently self-conscious, that their various forms of discourse echoed one another. The imagery of novels entered into the prose of moral advice, which in turn shaped the rhetoric of family letters and the reflections of diarists. These permutations and combinations made the social order visible and unified in daily affairs, permitting individuals the satisfaction, as Henry Canby remarked of the belief in honor, of living in "two dimensions, the present and [one's] breeding."[4]

Along with a relation to the social order through ritual, language and its forms figure another way in Part One. Language shapes how individuals perceive events and relationships and how they feel about themselves and the world. A close look at the way the planters spoke about themselves, and at what they said to one another in the reaches of their intimate life, or did not say, yields a sense of their emotional experience and psychological bent. It is language that allows a person to adapt to the push and tug of desire and duty, self-esteem and fear. As the ethnographer Edward Sapir observed, "It is quite an illusion to imagine that one adjusts to reality essentially without the use of language and that language is merely an incidental means of solving specific problems of communication or reflection. The fact of the matter is that the real world is to a large extent unconsciously built up on the language habits of the group."[5] Words mediate the world and in a sense invent it. Rhetorical structures have been seen as "mere rhetoric" or "empty words" only because we have become mistakenly accustomed to seeing words and action as two separate realms. Rather, language is a kind of activity, a kind of work, the historical understanding of which is essential to the meaning that any other kind of activity could be said to have had.

The planters' reliance on letters to inspire, comfort, and control is the chief example of the way in which a certain form of language is a window on both the social order and an individual's perceptions. Personal correspondence, first mastered as a sign of family feeling in the planter class and taught as a part of formal study, may have been less self-consciously intellectual than other forms of discourse, but for the historian it has the critical advantage of being both about and of a person's experience of culture. As this study will argue, letters often were the very substance of relationships otherwise strained by distance, gender differences, or emotion. Such letters existed as a bond and a commentary on the bond. And though most letters were scarcely innovative, the conventions themselves, leavened with afterthought and aside, provide an irreplaceable insight into the intellectual life of these people. Indeed, we can read a collection of family letters as a sort of literary production that, though repetitive and often clumsy and unfocused, became a transcript of a family's life. Southern planters wrote revealingly about certain family events which provide a key to the substance of family relationships. This counterpoint of events and relationships is characteristic of letters as a genre. The planters understood typical family events—marriage, schooling, childbirth—to be the essence of family life, thick with signs of the family's worldly purpose. Such events, passing through ritual, elicited from the planters their most sustained reflections about identity and social values. The marriage of a daughter, for example, was the occasion for the family to characterize their hopes and reveal their assumptions about femininity, sexuality, and binding ties. A son's going away to school gave the family a chance to say something about the prospects of manhood or the measurement of honor. The planters stressed these events as the substance of a traditional family decorum, and, unlike the northern middle and upper classes, were not so easily attracted to the rising romanticism that pulled individuals into a modern search for inner truths at the heart of relationships. The planters' epistolary rhetoric most fully grasped events, not relationships; it was the pleasure of narrating one's own family story, rather than its final "plot," that drew the planters into writing of their relationships. Nonetheless, events and relationships ultimately were indivisible, the first leading the planters to see some of the deep ties between their society and their loved kin, and the second leading them to attend to their society, defend it, and try to be content.[6]

CHAPTER I

THE AFFAIR OF HONOR:
CHARACTER AND ESTEEM

Few images are more compelling in the mythic view of the antebellum South than that of two men, fifteen paces apart, leveling pistols at each other. Perhaps the staying power of this image derives from its sheer theatricality: the dramatic mingling of decorum and death. It harbors an intense range of emotions. Elevated values, actual risk of life, and, not least, comedy all are compressed into this peculiarly southern mode of dispute. Perhaps, too, the lasting image of the duel stems from the lure of anachronism; dueling has vanished, and images of it hold a sense of the strangeness of a past time.

However this may be, efforts to understand the duel as a cultural ritual—a way of generating collective meaning—have lagged behind the appreciation of its image-making power. Until recently, historians have tended to summon the duel for its drama and for its sense of a world now lost, making of it a colorful window-dressing for more central considerations of politics or law. But the duel was not so peripheral to the planter class, nor was it sufficient to itself. It was only the most visible part of the affair of honor, a masculine ritual that went deeply into the reaches of authority and manhood in the planter elite. Like all rituals the affair of honor expressed cultural tensions that did not disappear but instead became lodged in the moral life of the community, affecting people other than the protagonists. And like other rituals, the affair infused daily life with a "heightened appreciation of symbolic action" in ethical matters and matters of self-esteem. It made the ordinary extraordinary, lifting up routine relationships to the general view and revealing their essential force and meaning.[1]

This chapter looks at the social relationships and cultural forms that made up the affair of honor and its centerpiece, the duel. The first part of the chapter discusses the moral ideals and social thought in the published codes of honor and suggests how these changed in the antebellum years. The second part examines certain actual affairs to discover what they reveal about the participants and their sense of the social world. Throughout, the language of affairs merits special consideration not only because affairs of honor were carefully built of words and their usage, but also because the language of honor was linked to fundamental beliefs and habits which formed a sustaining cultural ideology in planter society.

The Ideal of Honor

The origins of the duel and the affair of honor as they existed in the antebellum South have been variously traced to Scotch-Irish clan warfare and to certain European, particularly Prussian, means for settling disputes between military officers. It seems fairly clear that American colonial officers and soldiers adopted some aspects of the code of honor from visiting French naval officers during the American Revolution, and that the duel served to keep military regulations free of civilian controls. Moreover, the formal duel seems to have been used by powerful Irish (or Prussian, depending on who is telling the story) families as a means of keeping kinship feuds from spilling over into general social chaos. Nineteenth-century codes published in the South often referred to the 1777 Code of Clonmel, an agreement among powerful Irish families, as the immediate, and somewhat more harsh, predecessor of the American guidelines. Whatever the exact origins, what was at first a form of military self-regulation became by the second decade of the nineteenth century a pervasive presence in the daily civil intercourse of planter-class men, even though every state in the Union had proscribed dueling by the 1830s, several since the previous century. After 1800 dueling rather swiftly came to be perceived as a southern phenomenon by southerners and northerners alike. Observing the disgrace in which Aaron Burr was held in the North after fatally wounding Alexander Hamilton, Dickson D. Bruce, Jr., notes that from that time forward this form of violence and self-control became distinctive of the planter-class South. The planter elite alone upheld the claim that the affair fostered a moral vision of social life that neither civil nor criminal law was expected to protect.[2]

The Code: Honor as Self-Control

John Lyde Wilson's *The Code of Honor; or, Rules for the Government of Principals and Seconds in Duelling*, a much-circulated manual often mentioned but not analyzed in discussions of dueling, contains an early set of rules for the affair of honor. Wilson, a former governor of South Carolina, the last state to outlaw dueling, takes the high ground even in his introductory remarks. "Those who do not know me have no right to impute a wrong motive" to the book, he writes with the personal aggressiveness typical of honor. It is regrettable, he continues, that gentlemen sometimes run afoul of each other. But it is this crisis between honorable men, not a love of blood or combat, that makes some sort of code necessary for the settlement of disputes. Turning the other cheek might well be "highly recommended and enjoined by many very good men." But in human society where conflict is inevitable (indeed, even "the angels of heaven have met in fierce encounter"), selfless behavior only invites one blow after another. Christian forbearance itself and "all that is honorable in the community" would be driven out of society if meekness became the standard of social relations.[3]

Thus, in Wilson's view, the affair of honor properly acknowledged the trials of character and social life. The code of honor and the duel itself were a bulwark against social chaos rather than a form of violence. He seems somewhat uncertain only once on this point, when he likens dueling to, first, a "determined resistance to encroachments" and, second, a "natural" part of "a continual warfare for supremacy." These seem somewhat at odds. Was dueling a resistance to aggression or a kind of aggression itself? Wilson slides over this question. He is certain, however, that the duel supported a man's most cherished possession: his character. Character, with personal honor as its badge, was not an individual's own creation. It was grounded in family, established when a youth was educated to the protective web of social relations, and then rooted in his own family. If a man lost his honor, character eroded with it, and he found himself alone, "avoided in society, his friends shunning his approach, his substance wasting, his wife and children in want around him." This catastrophe might come about as a result of his own moral lapse. But it might occur also through the work of "the slanderous tongue of the calumniator" who might appear anywhere anytime with just the artfulness required to pierce the honor of even the most vigilant man. The code of honor, useless to a man without character, was indispensable to an honorable man; yet honor, a bright shield, was curiously thin skinned.[4]

Although many of Wilson's introductory remarks are pessimistic about social relationships, even about the trustworthiness of gentlemen, he has hopes for an ideal social order which reveal what the code of honor (and if necessary, the duel) is supposed to accomplish. Dueling may eventually cease to exist, Wilson says, but not because of its opponents. It will cease because the values of honor's advocates—the gentlemen to whom he addresses himself—will become the values of society at large. These values mostly concern feeling, and wounded feelings could be destructive of much good. In light of this, Wilson would have parents teach the essentials of honorable behavior to the young.

I would have them taught that nothing was more derogatory to the honor of a gentleman than to wound the feelings of anyone, however humble. That if wrong be done to another, it was more an act of heroism and bravery to repair the injury, than to persist in error, and enter into mortal combat with the injured party. That this would be an aggravation of that which was already odious, and would put him without the pale of all decent society and honorable men. I would strongly inculcate the propriety of being tender of the feelings as well as the failings of those around him. I would teach immutable integrity, and uniform urbanity of manners. Scrupulously to guard individual honor, by a high personal self-respect, and the practice of every commendable virtue.[5]

The first and most bitter damage a man could suffer was damage to his own feelings; but he suffered a like damage if he trampled on the feelings of others. Uncorrected, hurt feelings might become a general harm to honor and finally poison the social order. Though these considerations might seem the stuff of farce, there is no mistaking the seriousness of Wilson's voice or the expansiveness of his claims. It was precisely this kind of elite self-importance that triggered the class hatreds of yeoman farmers even as it united planter-class men. The planter who stepped up to the line that Wilson drew found himself in a paradox of leadership defined by male honor. In order to lead, a man was obliged to make the intricate determinations of feeling and form that marked him as one able to see the fine detail as well as the full sweep of social necessity. But in so doing, he not only risked alienating his white allies among the "poorer sort" but also risked appearing ridiculous in the eyes of his immediate dependents, white and black. Women, children, and slaves could not be expected to attend so closely to the society their masters directed, but they were the key audience. If the balance of form and sentiment, individual temperament and social order, required a fine touch as well as a powerful will, might not a planter go too far in the spiral of moral casuistry and mistake his sensibilities for root-and-branch social order? Indeed, how did feelings become wounded in the first place and when, exactly, would the private wound become a public injury? If a man's honor demanded that he display it as a public trust, at what point did display become the posturing of an upper-class poppinjay, a "cotton snob" of the most ludicrous stripe?[6]

The eight chapters of Wilson's code have little specific to say about these matters. In contrast to the elevated moral tone of the introduction, the rules of conduct themselves are plain, even flat. But they reveal how, precisely, an affair is to be carried to its conclusion; how the ritual, once it becomes imperative, is supposed to draw conflict into itself and express it. Following the code, a man need not "submit in silence" to insult, but could become vigorous with words and actions on his own behalf—and on behalf of honor itself. Moving through the affair, he and his opponent both could be "satisfied."[7]

The fifty-six rules of the code outline an ideal and typical affair and are worth looking at in detail. They trace the route an affair should take, from the initial offense through armed confrontation, though the word "duel" is never mentioned. The rules mark out the complex boundaries of behavior and expectation that made the affair an effective measure of manly honor. In the eyes of the affair's opponents, the rules seemed ridiculously complex. But their complexity was an appropriate guide to the intricate heart of the planters' sense of their own authority. Authority resided in self-control. If one man was struck by another, for example, there was little doubt that he must challenge his attacker. But in social relations, insults rarely were so clear. A threat to a man's honor derived from words more often than from blows. If a man felt insulted by another's words, he was not to respond immediately, but was supposed to wait a day or so, stay close to his family and home, and consult with friends. If together they decided that true offense was given, the man chose a friend to deliver a note of inquiry—not a challenge—respectfully asking clarification of the remarks from the man who made them. This man, upon receiving the note and judging that it was not itself insulting, consulted with his own friends, one of whom was chosen to retrace all of the steps of the dispute in hopes of discovering a misunderstanding. The recipient of the inquiry then either gave a satisfactory explanation of his words, refused to give one, or failed trying. In the last two cases, earnest written negotiations at once began between the two men's chief friends.

If an accommodation was not worked out in writing, the insulted man sent a challenge through his second to the second of the challengee, who had no honorable alternative but to accept it. The seconds then met to work out terms of the encounter. Wilson recommends only the "usual" weapons, time, and distance and states that the man challenged should no longer have sole choice of these. Each second must be satisfied that the terms insured his man complete equality with his opponent; if one man insisted on extreme or brutal conditions, the other could post him, that is, publicly charge him with cowardice.[8]

Once the terms were agreed upon, the round of meetings and letters ended and the two men met at the prearranged site. Seconds were to have absolute control of who was present, the condition of the weapons, and such matters as medical care and transportation to and from the grounds. The right to position the principals was given to one second by lot; the other had the right to give the word to fire—actually an interval of time marked out by the words "Fire . . . one . . . two . . . three . . . stop." If the first shot scored no hit, the chief friend of the man challenged could approach his counterpart and say, "Our friends have exchanged shots, are you satisfied, or is there any cause why the contest should be continued?" The second of the challenger might either agree and suggest that the two principals "meet on middle ground, shake hands, and be friends," or he might decide that the offense was too serious to be settled by a single shot and demand either another shot or an apology. If, however, the challengee was hit by a shot, the challenger's duty was to express satisfaction and leave the ground. If the challenger was hit, the challengee must ask permission to leave the ground, "which should be assented to."⁹

In Wilson's code the duel itself was sufficient to resolve a dispute between men, but not necessary. An affair of honor began at the moment when two men could not agree in writing to a satisfactory explanation of their conflict. It was the result, that is, of a failure to agree upon meaning, and it could be settled quickly by such an agreement at any time. A confrontation or quarrel did not become an affair until this failure was explicitly stated in writing and acknowledged by both men and their friends; an affair did not lead to a duel unless words failed.

None of this process was particularly dramatic in Wilson's calm prose. His rule-book style, in fact, seems aimed at making an affair resemble a kind of litigation in which passion was beside the point. But just beneath the code's surface, two intense, interrelated themes emerge—themes that move us closer to understanding the nature of the social standards and expectations clustered at the heart of this ritual. The first is the risk of death. No matter how much the specific rules seem to bury violence under a mass of restrictions and requirements, the chance for violent death was real. Indeed, controlled, passionless prose served to counterpoint rather than conceal this fact. Moreover, the ritual isolated men from the everyday social world. Even though honor was a man's most prized possession, deeply lodged in his family, as an affair progressed his family had little to do with its care. The duel drew men apart from women and children as it pulled them away from the routine masculine places of meeting—courthouse, statehouse, dockside—and gave them a sense of time calibrated by the exchange of correspondence and perhaps by gunfire. There were practical reasons for this removal, of course, but the need for open space or secrecy does not fully account for how the duel, like all rituals, created its own time and was complete for its own purposes. The intensity of the affair compressed ordinary dealings among men into an essential aloneness, setting aside not just the tangled uncertainties of politics and planting, but finally even the center of a man's moral duty: his family. It came down to only men, those left standing and those who fell. Women and children, especially, had no words that would help. Their mute, distant dependence perhaps better served to show what was at stake: men's place atop the social hierarchy.

It is possible to break down the affair's major themes, the risk of death and the loneliness of men, into finer themes—motifs—that recur throughout Wilson's code of honor. These motifs can be seen as bridges, both conceptual and behavioral, that joined the two main themes at key points in the affair. That is, they concern both manhood and risk in different combinations, shaping the activities and the rationale of the affair into a cultural whole.

The first of these motifs concerned self-control. Wilson's code so emphasized controlled behavior that thirty-nine of the fifty-six rules pertained to events before the combatants took to the field. Self-control, first in the face of offense and finally in the face of death, became the mark of manliness throughout the confrontation. And it was self-control in the eyes of others that counted most. "Whenever you believe you are insulted," Wilson said in his first rule, "if the insult be in public, and by words or behavior, never resent it there, if you have self-command enough to avoid noticing it." Silence, in fact, was presumed to be a sign of courage and manliness, at least in the first stages of a dispute. "When you believe yourself aggrieved, be silent on the subject, speak to no one about the matter" except to close friends. If the silence had to be broken, then it should be done through written correspondence which could be closely watched for the "language of a gentleman" and for suitable caution and fairness. A sure sign of an impending dispute was a man's wordlessness and controlled withdrawal from his usual company.[10]

The opposite could always happen, however, and a man's rage might burst out. In this case, his self-control came immediately under the care of friends. "You are supposed to be cool and collected," Wilson instructed the challenger's second. "Your friend's feelings are more or less irritated." Wilson understood the opportunities that anger gave to self-indulgence. The friend was to use "every effort to soothe and tranquilize your principal" and "not see things in the same aggravated light in which he views them. . . . Endeavor to persuade him that there must have been some misunderstanding in the matter. Check him if he uses opprobrious epithets towards his adversary, and never permit improper or insulting words in the note you carry." If abusive language did reach the other principal Wilson told this man to "object to its reception and return it for that reason."[11]

This exchange of letters and words became in effect a contest in which the all-important moral advantage lay in the display of controlled resentment. If the insulted man was the most self-controlled, it was a sign of the insult's probable falseness. If the aggressor was, it could be a sign of the seriousness of his charge. Thus, in order for a dispute to ripen into a true affair, it almost paradoxically had to become more and more controlled. Ideally, by the time the principals reached the dueling ground they were self-contained almost to the point of seeming uninvolved in the proceedings. At the ground, as Wilson expressed it, "The principals are to be respectful in meeting, and neither by look or expression irritate each other. They are to be wholly passive, being entirely under the guidance of their seconds."[12] The ritual made them into pure emblems of manhood in conflict.

Here the motif of self-control intersects with a second bridging theme: the crucial role of friends. The extent to which friends could either ignite or smother a dispute cannot be overstated. In practical terms, their competence and experience in affairs could be crucially important. From the couching of the first letter to the loading of the pistol, a man's friend had enormous responsibility. As Wilson notes, "I believe that nine duels out of ten, if not ninety-nine out of a hundred, originate in the want of experience in the seconds." But their importance extended beyond their instrumental role. The principal was advised that his friend had "the custody of your honor, and by obeying him you cannot be compromised." The resolving power of a man's self-control thus depended in large part on the judgment of his second, who was instructed to "state distinctly to your principal that you will be governed only by your own judgment, that *he* will not be consulted after you are in full possession of the facts, unless it becomes necessary to make or accept the *amende honorable*, or send a challenge." In this, the friend's power was beyond even Wilson's description: "Can every insult be compromised? is a mooted and vexed question," he confessed at the conclusion of his code. "What those cases are, must depend on the seconds."[13]

The seconds, through their power to define moral conditions and practical requirements, were liaisons between an individual's honor and the status of honor among all elite men. Seconds thus performed a kind of moral casuistry of honor. They extracted self-esteem from the thicket of self-interest, passion, and misstatement. Throughout, a friend had to balance the particular offense at hand with any general "indignity to the company" of gentlemen that might result from an improper turn in the ritual. Although personal at its core, the affair was not to become a messy blood feud. Once again, the family remained in the background. Each second was specifically instructed, for example, to keep the principal's male relatives from the dispute "on the ground of consanguinity."[14]

In other ways, however, the seconds were enjoined with seeing that the dispute did spread to other gentlemen. If, for example, a second had his principal's letter repeatedly refused by the challengee, "you must make yourself the actor" and also challenge him if he continued to refuse the letter without good reason. This instruction insured that the refusal did not impute to the second "the like inequality which is charged upon your friend." Thus an affair did not disappear because one man refused to participate; a man making such a refusal might find himself facing a succession of challenges from an outraged community of gentlemen.

Similarly, each second carried a loaded pistol onto the dueling ground. If one principal fired early or otherwise grossly broke the rules, the other's second had the duty to shoot him down. If both principals refused to accept a settlement drawn up by both seconds, the latter were jointly to resign and leave the field. Moreover, should a principal refuse to fight, his second was to say to the other principal: " 'I have come upon the ground with a coward, and have to tender you my apology for an ignorance of his character; you are at liberty to post him.' " In this way, honor was supposed to pass through groups of elite men as through a circuitry. The role of friends, at once practical and symbolic, reveals a wish for a community of gentlemen who would be bound by a single code animating a single purpose. If any individual did not maintain—and display—his place in the community by word and action, his peers could seek his disgrace and even his death; by Wilson's rules, they were obligated to do so.[15]

A final motif that runs throughout Wilson's code, overlapping the crucial role of friends and the importance of self-control, is one that stressed the reciprocity between the combatants, established by an attention to timing and equality. Indeed, the proper tempo of the ritual signified the elite standing of all involved. "Let the time of demand upon your adversary after the insult be as short as possible, for he has the right to double that time in replying to you," is a typical Wilson rule.[16] Taking too much time opened a man to charges of cowardice; but taking too little made him appear impassioned and out of control. In either case, timing was related not only to the idea of honor properly served, but also to the status of a man as a gentleman as evidenced by his grasp of proper social rhythm. If attention to timing was therefore a public, almost tangible, display of character, so was a man's power not to "notice" a challenge from anyone not obviously his social equal. Wilson included a list of people who could be safely ignored: "You may refuse a note from a minor, if you have not made an associate of him, one that has been posted, one that has been publicly disgraced without resenting it, one whose occupation is unlawful, a man in his dotage and a lunatic." If a challenge came from a stranger, the first step was to verify the man's social standing.[17]

Equality had to exist beforehand; an affair did not claim to create honor but to restore it. Thus the duel can be seen as repairing authority among an elite by translating muddy issues of self-esteem into comparatively clean confrontations in which each man risked death equally in the name of his honor and the common good. Equality, made difficult in the complicated and wordy intercourse of gentlemen, was so crucial that it was condensed into a ritual that changed a moral confrontation into a physical one. A concern for equality was evident at several points in the ritual: as the value disrupted by insult, as the principle governing the ritual's timing, and as the measure of social order. A "satisfied" man was one assured of his equal standing, an assurance that came from other gentlemen whose respect for him mirrored his for them. This assurance, at least, might be secured in an otherwise glaringly unequal society. The close scrutiny of timing could not be frivolous among a class of men who set themselves up as masters over others. Slaves, women, youth, all denied access to social and political power, were kept in their place only by constant vigilance and attention to the pace of events. The code's attention to equality among elite men would not have been necessary except in a society that depended on deep inequalities of mobility, wealth, and aspiration firmly rooted by the 1820s.

For all of John Lyde Wilson's procedural inclusiveness, however, large gaps remain in his version of the affair of honor. In his desire to portray the ideal, Wilson leaches the rage from combat. His rules omit most of the driving emotions that men felt. Moreover, Wilson never spells out what a "personal indignity" actually was, either in content or style. Thus it is difficult to determine from his code the sorts of provocations that tested a gentleman's self-control. Wilson does not define "gentleman" and "character" either. The nearest he comes to describing the qualities of a gentleman is to say (without conscious irony) that "gentlemen seldom insult each other, unless they labor under some misapprehension." The uneasy implication is that the men who needed his code either had become embroiled in something most gentlemen avoided, or that misapprehension was common. In either case, the image of the gentleman is problematic. As to character, Wilson suggests only its irreducible reality; and he adds that "individuals may well differ in their estimate of an individual's character and standing in society."[18]

The last is a puzzling aside. If men "may well" differ about these things, then what was the point of an affair? Apparently, Wilson meant that two gentlemen might honestly differ about a third man's status. The social hierarchy need not be threatened by sincere differences. But even this view makes character far more subjective than the rules admit and something less than firm ground for a deadly encounter. Perhaps most strikingly in this respect, Wilson is silent about precisely how men of character might be reconciled before they were forced to take up arms. Though he hopes that dueling will become unnecessary and that affairs will not turn into duels, Wilson has almost nothing to say about the particulars of negotiated accord. Probably the best explanation of these omissions is the one that invites a look at the affair of honor on other than this formal level; that is, Wilson simply did not need to be explicit about the status, behavior, and feelings that his audience took for granted. It was assumed that gentlemen knew what an insult was and did not need to be told how they could get into a quarrel. What they needed was a map of the honorable way out. What is missing in the code are the routine conventions and common-sense assumptions that delineated disputes among men in the first place. Missing, too, is a sense of the emotional freight carried by these conventions. In his effort to equate men's personal conflicts with a wider social stability, Wilson sidesteps the heart of conflict itself.[19]

The Code: Honor as Self-Esteem

Not so the 1847 code compiled by "A Southron." Although this author covers much of the same moral territory as Wilson, the content, style, and emphasis are substantially different and suggest changes in expectations of what a code must include. From the first, Southron is notably more passionate; his voice, compared to Wilson's, conveys the injury of being insulted and the urgency of the man who sees his character slipping away in full view. "The duel is a sharp but a salutary remedy for rude and offensive conduct," he states. "Dueling, like war, is the necessary consequence of offense; and when the cause shall have ceased, the effect will no longer have existence." Southron catalogs the "poisoned shafts" that a man of reputation could not afford to overlook:

> ". . . the whips and scorns" of the times, "the oppressor's wrongs, the
> proud man's contumely," "the insolence of office," the sneers and
> scoffs and taunts, the burly, bullying look, the loud and arrogant
> tone, the thraldom so often coveted to be exercised by the physically
> strong over the physically feeble, the thousand bitter, burning
> wrongs, nameless, it may be, in detail, but not the less galling, oppressive, and intolerable from their intent and motive; wrongs which
> make us "walk without our peace," which sear our brain and turn
> our blood to fire![20]

The literary tropes scarcely mask Southron's desire to set down everything that might disrupt the harmony among gentlemen; indeed, they give force to it. But the sheer number of wrongs and their un-erring aim defy his ability to list all of them. Looks, tones, motives, sneers seem to build on one another in this passage, as they doubtless did in the experience of many elite men, until they crowd all moral horizons, allowing for little but the shove of insult. All of the wrongs are wrongs for which others are responsible, and the harm done is mea-sured by feelings of intense anger. These feelings give rise to highly subjective, but searching, discriminations; there are looks, and then there are the "burly, bullying" looks. Southron suggests an aesthetics of aggrieved manhood, and the implied circumstances of offense are as significant as their causes. The circumstances involved male "office," "thraldom," and physical domination, the very context of slaveowning political life. As an image of social reality, Southron's view is the polar opposite of Wilson's hope for a gentle, almost wordless community of men. For Southron, words and looks shoulder in where they are not wanted, and, significantly, are on the same continuum as physical enslavement.

In other ways, too, the style of Southron's thirty-nine articles reveals the texture of male social life. Like Wilson's, his task was to instruct in the ideal, and to assign credit and purpose to single combat. But the ritual encounters that emerge from his code are more clearly *examples.* His rules are akin to an itinerary whereas Wilson's are more like a road map. Southron describes particular moves instead of representing an overall plan. He tells the principal on the dueling ground, for example, that "After taking your place, you will salute your antagonist with a distant but not discourteous inclination of the head."[21] His language shows a feeling for image, a sense of memorable gesture. Southron's ritual has everything to do with appearance, and with the real social context that appearances created.

He also gives a sense of the many levels of effort and reward that the affair embodied. Several of Southron's articles not only denote the proper way of doing things, but also suggest that propriety was not the only thing to be wished for in an affair. In his first article he writes:

Affairs of honor must be conducted coolly, courteously and steadily, as a contrary course serves but to aggravate difficulties, and lead [sic] to results harsh, passionate, and discreditable to gentlemen of true and deliberate courage. Remember that deliberate conduct only can reap whatever eclat is derivable from the duel, and that a cool head produces a steady mind.[22]

The first sentence recalls the recommendation of self-control in Wil-son. But Southron goes on to suggest that coolness had the additional advantage of improving one's chances of triumphing over one's opponent, and that something more than the restoration of honor was at stake. Victory, too, permeated this ritual; a polish to the badge of honor, an "éclat," he hints, might be discovered in the course of deliberate conduct.

Along with the chance for glory, Southron acknowledges the absurd or comic postures into which duelists could fall. He finds it amusing, for example,

> to read much of the correspondence which passes on such occasions, where the original offensiveness of a phrase, or epithet, actually *exhales* under a load of verbiage and the perplexities of language in the context, whereby the offended party and the community generally are mystified into an impression that "the affair has been very satisfactorily adjusted!"[23]

Opponents of dueling noted much the same thing in order to discredit the practice. Southron's intent, of course, is to warn about how the ritual might be diverted from its purposes. Still, unlike Wilson, he is able to see humor in the fact that language could become a screen for deferring an encounter instead of a means of defining honor.

What proves to be a key issue for Southron throughout is the importance of language. Evident in his own style, his attention to language is a good way to characterize the significance of his code for the affair of honor at midcentury. In addition to his thirty-nine articles, Southron includes an appendix of thirty "hints," another sign that by 1850 the affair was more than a plain matter of rules. Fully thirty-four of the thirty-nine articles and twenty-two of the thirty hints have to do with conventions of language and behavior prior to the duel. And fourteen of the thirty-four articles (nine of the hints) specifically concern matters of language alone. If Southron's code is more complete because it includes more of the emotional texture of a dispute, then his heavy emphasis on preliminaries and language suggests that these were the actual substance of an affair. The duel itself was merely a cap on an elaborate structure built of men's most cherished values and beliefs. Questions of language—of expression, form, motif—were at the center of what the duel meant as ritual. The man with a command of the expressive conventions of dispute was already a long way toward mastering his antagonist.

Commanding language meant, first, mastering the conventions of correspondence that regulated a dispute. Southron makes it clear from the beginning that not only timing but also expressive style were crucial to controlling the rhythms of offense and satisfaction. Language was both the way in and the way out of a conflict, and it exactly reflected the character of a man. "Apologies and explanations must be promptly required," he instructs his readers. "A badly or semi-rendered apology is an unmanly proceeding, and if admitted, is more dangerous than none, as it implies on the part of an acceptor, timidity of character under a guise of courage." Improper language hurt only the man who uttered it—unless it was accepted; then both men suffered an injury. Even language intended to heal a quarrel, if not watched carefully, could do further damage. Language was a difficult tool perilously used.[24]

A written explanation or apology, therefore, should be directly expressed and deliberately worded. A careful explanation, employing conventions of respectful language, could make up for careless remarks made in political meetings or over brandy, and it was a sign of courage to know when and how to apologize. "[A] brave man, on discovering himself to be in error, will ever be as prompt to redress as to resent an injury." Timing was significant, of course: "Should the apology be rendered voluntarily, and as soon after the offense is given, as is consistent with a proper time for reflection on the part of the person offending, it will look more graceful, and will be more satisfactory to all the parties." Deliberation and balance were crucial; even a hasty comment should not be too hastily explained. Satisfaction was the chief aim, but gracefulness was more than mere timing. As in so much of Southron's view of language and conflict, the emphasis here is on the sheer force of the right words uttered at the right time in a setting worthy of gentlemen.[25]

The man receiving the correspondence, too, needed to scrutinize the style of the letter. "A gentleman must yield nothing to the *tone* of a demand . . . ," Southron notes. "Particularly if the tone or manner of such demand be *menacing.* Remember to spurn every appeal which is made to your fears." The power of language made the letters exchanged by two men fully equal in their effect. A man who chose to accept certain words was the moral equivalent of the man who chose to say them. Thus, language might be a weapon best used when skillfully put into the hands of one's opponent who might make a mistake with it. He might, for example, wish to be properly insulting but fall prey instead to overly abusive language. "As the offensive vocabulary, indeed, abounds with epithets temptingly expressive, a gentleman should be very cautious how he yields to the seduction, lest by any *profusion* of applewoman rhetoric, he render himself *unworthy of notice.*" Intending to give offense, a man who thus indulged himself might pass clean through an affair and out the other side into disgrace. The timing and tone of letters described exactly the social boundaries of legitimate conflict. Observing these boundaries, a man might master attacks on his character and even enhance his reputation solely by speaking and writing well. But failing to know the boundaries, he risked literally talking himself out of his position of mastery.[26]

Similarly, Southron finds it necessary to spell out in several articles the limits of responsibility in the handling of the actual letters themselves. So important were the physical letters that if a man desired someone other than his second to deliver one he could do so properly only if he so informed his opponent. The point of such explicit care seems to have been to make sure that the emotional charge of the correspondence was not transmitted to either unwitting or unworthy third parties. Again, Southron defines the heart of an affair by telling how to express and contain the power of language.[27]

In contrast, the truth or falsity of an accusation hardly concerns him at all and seems secondary except in one respect. If a man made a specific charge against another that he knew to be incontrovertibly true, he must fight if he is challenged because the accuser would not be able to reflect calmly upon his language and say that he had been in error: "Such retraction would involve a deliberate falsehood" and thus could not be honorably made. Southron has to admit difficulty in this case, however, because the kinds of issues at stake in a conflict were not easily verified as either true or false. This difficulty is particularly obvious in the only specific charge that Southron considers at length, that of accusing a man of cowardice. The accuser may genuinely believe that his adversary is a coward, just as the accused may truly resent it. Thus the former cannot honorably retract what he believes to be true, and the latter cannot suffer the charge to stand. Only an exchange of shots can settle the matter. And then, the accuser must also retract his charge in words if the accused courageously withstands the fire.[28]

Southron seems to get into deep water at this point, becoming uncomfortable with trying to distinguish what a man "knows" as true from what his opinion is, calling the first a truth (because it is sincerely held) and the latter a simple impression (because it may have been formed in haste and passion). Southron's concern with language thus leads him to the brink of what the ritual of the affair deeply signified—a clash between elite men wholly accustomed to investing their subjective assessments with the force of objective truths. The duel was supposed to display and resolve the "real" nature of honor and reputation, but by midcentury its necessary concern for language drew the ritual further into the shifting grounds of temperament and perception. Language, even as it seemed to provide an index to conflict and resolution, also threatened to uncover the subjective wishes and fears that lay beneath the rules.[29]

Southron is much more sure of himself when he compares words to physical blows, which he sees as the other major cause of dispute.

When two men traded blows, it was most important to move the conflict into language; gentlemen should neither let a blow go unanswered
nor leap to a brawl. At first glance, this rule seems straightfoward; but
even blows had a grammar. "No apology can be received for a blow,"
Southron states at first. However, if a blow is inflicted by mistake, the
aggressor can expect his apology to be accepted if he offers himself "to
be struck in the same manner." As with words, the reciprocity of blows
suffices—signifies—only if the two men are gentlemen: "A gentleman
cannot be degraded by a blow from an inferior," but he can reply with a
horsewhipping or a lawsuit if he chooses. A blow given intentionally,
gentleman-to-gentleman, with no reservation, obviates words altogether. A man could not honorably resort to "sending insulting notes"
after he had been struck.[30]

Even with this discussion of physical violence, and perhaps because
of his close attention to the details of insult and reconciliation, Southron's code seems somewhat removed from the somber risk of death
that looms behind Wilson's more matter-of-fact rules. What makes
Southron particularly revealing, however, is his own passionate language and his appreciation for the force of words. In his attempt to
consider passion and nuance, he establishes the emotional points of
leverage in deadly serious quarrels. He suggests that men otherwise
separated by rural distance invested their routine exercise of power in
the disruptive or restorative emotional power of language, and that the
first threat to social order arose from the relationships of planter-class
men themselves. Southron discovers a fundamental tension, problematically built into the social order, between the planters' need to dominate others (and the opportunity to do so) and the ideal of a calm, egalitarian order of gentlemen. There were a few extreme offenses, of
course, for which no apology could be accepted; but these did not
threaten equality or social stability. Being spat upon, for instance, or
having a lady grossly insulted, were so far beyond the pale that the
offending party could be dealt with by a caning. The real threat to society stemmed from unresolved, highly emotional conflict among
equally masterful men. Southron's task was to find the words and
other behavior that would restore equality, taking for granted that the
equal standing of master-class men was the prerequisite for the well-
being of society as a whole. Indeed, Southron goes even further to assume an identity between personal "satisfaction" and at least the appearance of collective justice. Personal and social worth had the same
horizon, in this view, if a man merely adhered to the code of honor.
Personally, equal standing gave a man "that . . . freedom of action so
necessary" in a dispute and, by implication, in his social leadership. Socially, the code helped to establish a community of gentlemen unified

in their aspirations because all were equally open to challenge. The code formally recognized the otherwise unspoken standards of class self-regulation; elite men adjusted their mutual standing just as they patrolled the roads for loose slaves, in fact much more carefully.[31]

If an affair was to proceed, therefore, it had to represent the ideal of male equality at all stages. To this end the community of elite men was prepared to step in to clear away any inequality that might bottle up honor. Although the virtues of family relations were invoked, and Southron acknowledged that a man's "friends" might well be kin, men alone remained at the center of the crisis. Mention of the family was essential but oblique. As in Wilson, the detailed reality addressed by the code was masculine, and intricate ranking of worth and style was re-served for elite men alone. A man need not accept a challenge by another man not known to him without first checking into the stranger's social standing. A man should not accept a challenge from another who had previously refused combat without first obtaining a "certificate of honorable acquittal" from the previous opponent. In these and related ways the code depicts an ideal society of upper-class males who band together to reinforce the most important linchpin of their power: their freedom to act unilaterally because of their unques-tioned unity.[32]

Even so, Southron's efforts to find a rule for every contingency can-not obscure the deep, tense rivalry among men that his code reveals. The presumed need for a code suggests that the social relationships of men were so volatile and uneasy that the social order itself constantly swayed. Behind the wall of rules built by Southron was a collision of temperaments that he acknowledges but does not confront. Some of his "hints" to duelists reveal, in fact, that equality was threatened by the very social circumstances that were supposed to insure it. The political life of men caused them to court the offenses that disrupted it. Noting the extreme touchiness of many men, Southron warns, "Be not *prone* to get into difficulties without a cause," and urges his readers to "cor-rect, if possible, all morbidness in your temper; else will you be daily harrassed [*sic*] by 'airy nothings,'—the butt of designing and irrespon-sible buffoons, knaves and tricksters of society, and hourly embroiled in petty hostilities." This instruction seems plain enough. But at the same time, he gives advice to "resist in a dignified, but *significant* manner, the *first efforts* of mortal man to acquire over you an arrogant ascendency." Relationships were a slippery slope and a man might slide into subservience before he could act to prevent it. Every social en-counter, every aspect of the way a man presented himself to the view of others, became part of his authority: "Be in your deportment uniformly steady, dignified and respectful. . . . Remember that *true courage* is quiet and dignified rather than *brusque* and blustering. . . . A steady look and a firm voice are good armor against impertinence."[33]

It was not inner worth that mattered, but an obvious, fully displayed awareness of self and others quite in concert with the vigilance required of a master of slaves and a paterfamilias. A master, quite different from his northern counterpart in business, had to watch everyone in this way, projecting his gaze from the salience of his own character onto society as a whole. But how was such a man to attend to this exhausting task without falling into the morbidity that Southron warned against? What actually distinguished an "airy nothing" from the impertinences that had to be resented? How could a man be sure that his social vision itself was not inappropriately distorted by vanity? In not resolving these difficulties, Southron's hints thus reveal how a man might find himself sinking into a crisis instead of staying out of it. A man was obliged to attend to others' actions and motives so closely that departures from the ideal were bound to be discovered. To be a true man, he had to stay "well upon [his] centre" while at the same time searching the conduct of others for a sign that the center might not hold.[34]

These complications in Southron's code significantly modify the three main motifs in Wilson's rules: self-control, the importance of friends, and the pivotal question of equality. Self-control, in Southron's richer and more problematic ideal, is deepened into a concern for self-esteem. Self-control was not a goal of manhood, but a means to ensure that an expansive sense of self-esteem remained intact. The key role of friends was broadened here to suggest that the emotional harmony of elite men was perceived to be a major support of class authority. If men acted and felt warmly respectful toward each other they would be obeyed by their slaves and loved by their families. Helping each other maintain equality, men were ever at work shoring up the social order, checking it, tightening it, bringing its ideals out on display through the definition and mastery of its intricate maneuvers. Mastery, in this ideal, aspired to an image of male brotherhood realized only when fully shown to all others. Elite position came to rest on shared emotions rather than on a set of interests; volatile authority as well as established position was the mark of a man.

In this way, Southron clearly departs from Wilson, suggesting by the 1850s an important shift in the image of manhood and its claims. Though still in circulation, Wilson's code clearly reflected an earlier, even eighteenth-century, concern for behavior in which appearances were largely uncomplicated by the significance of a man's feelings. Wilson's rhetoric has a military spareness completely foreign to Southron's rich language of emotion and wish. Like the political discourse of which it was a part, Southron's code bloomed into expressions of personal power and personal hurt altogether different from the sere language of order. The significance of a man's feelings in Southron can thus be seen as evidence that this male ritual had by the late 1840s uncovered a new dimension of manhood, one that gave attention to feeling as *explanation* rather than merely impulse. The difficulties that the labyrinth of emotion presented to men were offset by the obvious relish that Southron expresses for the emotional nuances of honorable conduct. By the late antebellum years, honor had a sensibility as well as an order, and the affair embodied its own kind of almost literary pleasure, its own seductive depth somewhere between public utterance and private morality.

The Making of Honor

If all else failed in an affair between two men, the duel was there to secure the honor of both men and thereby protect the honor of all. But just as all affairs of honor did not result in duels, so all disputes among elite men did not lead to affairs. A look at the various ways men actually behaved in matters of honor and character reveals the extent to which a duel was only a last resort in a field of many possible actions. It also reveals that common-sense, routine relationships among upper-class men, shaped by conventional words and actions that defined both expected and worthy behavior, strikingly reflect the mandates of the written codes. Letters between men reveal the mixture of discord and harmony seated in the code, suggesting the code's reliability as evidence of how men searched for ways to expand their authority and contain its excesses. Moreover, a look at actual affairs shows that the transition from the world of everyday political and social relations into the elevated realm of the affair did not involve a contradiction in masculine temperament. In fact, these apparent extremes of cooperation and challenge were part of a single temperament in which the ordinary and the ritualistic were joined just beneath the surface of daily routine.[35]

Looking at these aspects of actual male relationships involves examining, first, certain routine correspondence between men to discover how honor was acknowledged and, second, actual affairs of honor. I have chosen to consider three representative affairs in close detail rather than list as many as possible. One is a case of written settlement, the second an instance of an outright victory, and the third a duel to the death. An affair might proceed other ways, of course, but these three are a useful combination illuminating the range of actual experience. It is not surprising that the actual behavior of men shows more complexity than the formal code suggests; the flexibilities and confusions of experience outran predictions from the ideal. But even the ordinary dealings of men showed a marked degree of formality and controlled expression. Their common, almost reflexive relationships with one another were anything but inattentive to the ritual of class and character.

Extending Honor and Averting Affairs

The form and language of letters remain the point of entry into routines of honor. Everyday business letters between southern planters contained expressions of elaborate regard so typical that they clearly served important conventional purposes. A respectful—and therefore respectable—letter could not be without such usages. Most men doubtless did not give conventional respects and good wishes much thought, but their absence was instantly noticed. Their first purpose was to make sure that no distractions or silences occurred in the hum of communication, for ambiguities could grow into abridgments of respect requiring drastic repair. Letters between men show that the most important tasks at hand were the search for and control of public, especially political, authority. In almost any random series of letters between men of this class, the political ones would far outnumber all others. Men wrote often, and with no other major means of communication over distance available to them, they wrote with care and exactness. They kept drafts of letters and cross-references. Then they rewrote and reworded. They wrote asking the most basic questions and spent hours making the simplest arrangements because letters were their only means to do so. They wrote with care because letters truly *represented* them in a way that has faded since the late nineteenth century.

At first glance, the self-conscious style of these letters is most obviously a blend of pleasant sentiment and studied personal compliment. Such letters were warm yet distant, claiming notice but not imploring it. One such letter, typical of many, will serve as an example of the genre. Written by William Henry Trescot, an influential South Carolina lawyer, to Thomas Butler King, a Georgia congressman, it began: "Dear Sir, I can scarcely hope that you recollect as I do the introduction with which I was favored when in Washington some three winters ago. Should you have forgotten it you must allow your public character to apologize for this liberty." Graceful, conventional, yet at the same time forceful, these two sentences lightly crossed the charged threshold between two elite men. Trescot wrote to request a copy of one of King's speeches, a common and flattering transaction between political men. Yet even here, Trescot could not take too much care with King's honor.

A careless letter could all too easily become the "liberty" Trescot disarmingly allowed his to be. Letters, especially unsolicited ones, were intrusive; a direct man-to-man address implied equal standing but potentially infringed upon it. Although he had met King before, Trescot referred to the occasion only obliquely ("the introduction with which I was favored") in a way that mirrored King's reputation. This reference reinforced an equally deferential self-effacement ("I can scarcely hope that you recollect as I do") that nevertheless reflected on the soundness of Trescot's memory. In one sense, such deference defused the tense even though commonplace meeting between two men; elevated language floated above personal tensions. But just as surely, it called attention to the possible difficulty in such a meeting.[36]

Similarly, when James Robertson wrote to William Gaston to request a copy of a speech, he began: "As I have no claims on your attention, I ought to apologize to you for taking this liberty, or giving you any trouble; but the impressions I received of your character . . . encourages [sic] me to believe that you will excuse me for making this application."[37] Again, the attentive deference stands out, as does the mention of the "liberty" of the letter and the preventive apology. Clearly, much of what was at issue in a full-blown affair was budding in men's routine discourse. Exchanging letters put two men into a situation that might lead to their speaking hasty words, inadvertently jostling, and, finally, deliberately striking. The code of honor did not suddenly intrude its morality; it simply extended relationships that had outgrown more mundane conventions of behavior.

Deferential letters did not imply the writer's passivity. After all, both Trescot and Robertson went on to take the liberties they wanted to take. Holding up the recipient's reputation and apologizing for the "claim" allowed a man to go ahead in full expectation that he would not be denied. Thus the recipient was deferred to and given a burden at the same time; compliment mixed with challenge. What one man risked losing through self-effacement was compensated for by the other man's attention and compliance. If the balance was struck, the rhetoric of deference witnessed the equal standing of both men and served to reinforce the sense of legitimate leadership by all planter-class men. Because they shared these conventions—and used them with ease and certainty—the planters took them as a sign that their political power as a class was morally legitimate. This assumption lent social import to self-important talk. If any individual man at any given time was not fully the equal of any other in terms of wealth or personal charisma, this disparity need not raise questions about the leadership of the class as a whole. Both men had the right to expect equal treatment in terms of personal esteem.[38]

Yet because deferential rhetoric was a way for men to touch upon each other's honor, considerable tension marked the outwardly smooth expressions of regard. A man who engaged in conventional deference was not only displaying his own honor but taking another's into his care. Deferential rhetoric allowed men to make claims on each other through an exchange of the proper words, and the commonness of such rhetoric was exactly what made relationships between men so highly charged: no transaction was without significant meaning. It followed that men's discourse was a direct form of behavior, as men themselves acknowledged. No words were truly casual, no utterance without some possibility for perilous overflow. If he was to keep his honor unstained, a man was obliged to exercise each day an ordinary measure of that watchfulness which marked an affair. It was a watchfulness that mirrored the scrutiny, never far below the surface, that a master of slaves maintained even in the most routine management of his workers. Being responsible for one's words was joined to one's claim to mastery; being aware, exact, and above all visible, mattered whether one was on horseback in the fields or writing words as if the world listened.[39]

Honor was so expansive, therefore, that it could hardly miss being stepped upon, and the ways that affairs were averted are as revealing as the ways in which they were carried through. It is useful to look at a few instances in which disputes were avoided. The formal code of honor is visible in these cases, but so is an element of choice that escaped the written codes. Men felt their honor in danger when they *chose* to notice the absence of deference or some other normative expectation, not because the code was violated chapter and verse.

Men often found good reason not to notice a possible adversary. James H. Hammond, for example, embroiled in a bitter personal dispute with Wade Hampton, chanced to meet a friend of Hampton on the street in New York City. The meeting impressed Hammond enough that he later wrote himself a memorandum about it, but he was not sufficiently engaged at the time to become caught in the web of honor. In Hammond's view, the makings for an affair were certainly present. The quarrel with Hampton involved a charge of sexual misconduct against Hammond and thus was so personal that even an allusion to it could not be permitted. The man Hammond chanced to meet, A. J. Johnston, was undeniably a gentleman and therefore could not be dismissed. Hammond recalled pausing briefly as he and Johnston exchanged looks, then walking on:

> I had proceeded but a few steps when he called to me and said he wished to say a few words. I returned and he said he "wished it un-

derstood that this was the last conversation we were to have." He seemed dreadfully agitated from head to foot and perhaps expected that I would knock him down. . . . It was perfectly ridiculous for him to assume the championship of the Hampton set. . . . I might with propriety have taken offense and knocked him down. Under some circumstances perhaps I would have done it. But from his whole manner I felt nothing but pity and contempt, and both in my words and manner gave him to understand that such a thing coming from him could not ruffle me. I parted from him as I would have done from a stranger who accidentally rubbed against me and offered an apology which I accepted, of course.[40]

In short, Hammond decided not to "notice" Johnston. Or, rather, he decided to notice Johnston's manner and ignore the implications of his words. Johnston's deliberate breaking off of future contact was not a trivial move. But Hammond was able to decide that Johnston's support of Hampton was "ridiculous" and, more important, tell himself that Johnston had shown fear. Hammond could safely choose to ignore being cut dead by a coward, and here he was careful to characterize his own actions as entirely befitting a gentleman. Most striking, however, is the last sentence, in which he likened his encounter to one in which an apology is made. From this account, Johnston did not even come close to apologizing; but Hammond, rationalizing his own conduct in this brush with insult, found an analogy in the code of honor that suited him: Johnston, an estranged acquaintance, was like a stranger who had touched him without damage. Johnston's manifest fear had made him a stranger and thus someone who could not do truly personal harm.

This "personal" content of words or actions was crucial when a man decided whether or not to take offense. It is just the ingredient that the written codes failed to explicate because everyone took it for granted. Particularly in the rough-edged competition of political life, heated words could have double meanings, or no substantial meaning at all. It was useful therefore to have friends bear witness to verbal incidents and suggest interpretations that would put everyone on an equal footing, if possible. James Wyche, for example, wrote a lengthy letter to his friend William Gaston which detailed a recent legislative debate between Gaston and a Mr. Spaight. Wyche wrote, he explained, " . . . due to the kindness which I have experienced from you" and in hopes that he might prevent "mischief . . . if indeed any is brewing."[41] He detailed the debate between Gaston and Spaight, speaking of both men equally in the third person, and came to the conclusion that, though Gaston may have questioned Spaight's impartiality, he did not question his veracity—that is, he did not become personal. Partisanship was to be expected in political life; but a man's truthfulness was a question of character and therefore not to be brought into the heated discourse of debate.

Another way to avert an affair was for a man to make a quick, satisfactory response to a letter of inquiry. Again, men who declared that they had no intention to offend emphasized the lack of personal weight in their words and motives. One planter typically wrote:

> I did not entertain on that occasion, or any other, a sentiment unkind or offensive to you, nor mean, nor intend to offer the least violence to your feelings, nor impute any improper motive to your actions. If I have used language that has wounded your feelings, I beg you to accept the only atonement in my power—the acknowledgments of my profound regret and sorrow.[42]

The recipient found this a fully satisfying letter touching all of the code's essentials: damaged feelings, personal motives, and the power of words to wound. The writer, though, had his own request that he felt would dispense with any remaining inequality that might cling to the apology itself: "I hope you can put it in my power to say to my relatives and friends that I have not been 'very personal and offensive' to you; and that if I was, you believe it was not intended and that on the first intimation of it I voluntarily made a suitable atonement to your feelings."

In such instances, everyone of course understood that further confrontation was being avoided, just as everyone understood that a question about the personal content of language was heavy with emotion. Indeed, careful words concealed a reservoir of emotion that often overflowed. One recipient of a letter of apology reembraced his estranged friend:

> Your letter is lying open before me—the liberal outpourings of a generous heart. You do not know how *sad* it has made me, Cumming. And yet what a pleasure in the very sadness! I could almost wish you could have spared yourself the pain of writing it, yet I prize it more than anything. . . . Cumming, my love for you is so great that your simple request for forgiveness seems, in the granting, but a poor return for the pleasure of having you still the same noble friend.[43]

Other times, a potential affair simply faded away. It is difficult to tell what goes on behind the screen of language in many of these cases, but details may not matter. It is more important to appreciate how the form and timing of written exchanges could diffuse anger despite the passion they carried. In one such case in South Carolina in 1831 between Henry Townes and Benjamin F. Perry, Townes was reluctant to challenge after an insult, though protesting his readiness in the face of heated urgings from his brothers. Henry Townes and Perry avoided writing direct letters to each other, trading charges in newspapers instead. These exchanges, however passionate, did not carry the forward momentum of letters and the affair was never joined.

The quarrel began in mid-September with a political attack by Perry against Henry Townes in the press. Immediately, Townes's brothers joined in the fray. Letters exchanged by the three brothers show that the eldest, Samuel, reacted almost as though he were the one offended. In a letter to one of his brothers, he called Perry a "damned puppy," a term sure to elicit a challenge, and added, "I regret the necessity but I have written to Henry to *challenge* the scoundrel *immediately* [.] He must and shall do this or I shall disown him as a brother." Samuel Townes apparently expected his brother to give a preemptory challenge, an extreme action by the code. Significantly, no such letter was sent. Nearly three weeks later, Henry remarked upon his "determination to post P—— at once and in that way make him fight if possible, by challenging me" but added that his friends had advised him "to wait a decent time say about four weeks" and then call Perry a coward. This timing began to look like foot-dragging to the worked-up Samuel. A month later the dispute was still only in the press, and Henry was commenting on the "absurdity of P's positions" rather than on their offensiveness. Although Henry could still say he would "very much like to shoot" Perry if "my friends would let me," the initial passion had given way to newspaper insults and detailed advice passed among the three Townes brothers. Regarding the newspaper campaign, Samuel advised fine distinctions: "You should by all means keep your hands off Perry unless he should have the impudence to speak of it (designedly) in an unbecoming manner in your presence."[44]

Seeing such nuances was, of course, at the heart of this and most conflicts. One can imagine Henry Townes quite seriously sifting Perry's words not only for impudence, but for designed and unbecoming impudence. Samuel, too, grasped at the convolutions of feeling and behavior underlying the words, advising Henry, "You should not . . . permit this matter to ruffle your mind or depress your spirits, and in your conversations in public be cautious how you look. . . . I speak of it with calmness and moderation, though with a becoming feeling and spirit." A full two months after the initial quarrel it appears that Perry had himself medically disqualified from single combat, an unusual move but not one outside the code. Samuel was able to write about brother Henry that "he is . . . on safe or at all events *honorable* grounds." He did speculate that Henry might want to challenge the medical doctors who certified Perry, however, and there is no reason to suspect the strength of Samuel's conviction when he wrote, "I had rather see [Henry], as much as you know I love him, a helpless corpse than to have this matter settled in any way which is not perfectly honorable to himself." Yet clearly Samuel Townes felt that it was time to put the best face on things, for the wrangle was going nowhere and soon everybody stood to lose. In effect he simply declared that honor had been won and ignored the fact that the affair had not been joined. Many words had been published, tactics had been sifted, but the quarrel sank into a mire of threats and intentions without taking the final leap of language. The Townes-Perry conflict never crossed the threshold into ritual because the necessary words were never spoken.[45]

Bonham-Brooks: Establishing Honor

An affair was joined, it will be recalled, when satisfactory explanation of an incident or remark was not forthcoming, and two men entered into a controlled correspondence. The correspondence was the signal that the ritual was underway, that an affair and not merely a quarrel was at issue. Both men brought their expectations into line with the conventions of written expression and achieved a symbolic reciprocity in place of the disputed personal relationship which awaited repair. The swift confrontation between Milledge Luke Bonham and Preston Brooks in 1849 precipitated an affair of classic dimensions. It is an excellent example of how an affair gathered and then released its intensity in a way that established honor short of armed encounter and bloodshed. This affair also reveals the central importance of men's personal equality in disputes, and the importance of sensing imputation in language.

Events began when Preston Brooks publicly alluded to an incident that had occurred during the Mexican War in which Bonham had shot himself in the foot while cleaning his pistol. Bonham had been relieved of his regimental command in the infantry, and a board of inquiry later cleared him of any charge of cowardice. Nevertheless, the incident cast a shadow over Bonham's honor for a while. Brooks's remark was made at a Fourth of July celebration at which Bonham was given a military recognition. Brooks commented that he felt neglected; after all, *he* had not suffered the kind of talk Bonham had.[46]

Bonham heard of the remark a few days later and wrote Brooks asking for an explanation. No elite man could have mistaken the tone of Bonham's letter, and Brooks replied carefully in kind, saying that "nothing was further from my purposes or desire than to injure you." But he suggested that Bonham himself had been somewhat aggressive in writing, and that "had you *spoken* to me . . . I would have removed even a shadow of displeasure" on July 4. Brooks concluded by pointing out that he had not said that the past charges against Bonham were true, only that they had been made.[47]

Possibly Brooks meant his letter to be an apology. But an apology and an explanation were not the same thing. Bonham replied two days later that, despite the "friendly tone of the concluding paragraph," Brooks's letter was "unsatisfactory." Bonham spelled out his position clearly: he objected to Brooks's mention of the war incident in public regardless of his intent.[48] Loose conversation, as Brooks well knew, could seriously injure a man's reputation. Brooks responded the following day with a longer letter indicating his growing appreciation of the import of the correspondence. In this pivotal letter, Brooks acknowledged that a man's reputation was priceless and easily injured, but added that past injuries were facts of life not necessarily beyond public notice. Brooks drew the line as he saw it:

> I meant this *and nothing* more, viz., "that a soldier's honor is as delicate as a woman's" and that any imputation upon it, however false or malicious, was an injury—that this injury you had sustained, though . . . wrongfully and undeservedly, and that I had been more fortunate than yourself, having sustained no such injury and therefore objected [in my July 4 remarks] to being placed on the same footing [with you].[49]

This letter explicitly said what both men had only skirted in earlier letters: the issue between them was their present equal standing, not Bonham's past injury or reputation. Brooks was no stranger to issues of honor, and he certainly knew the difference between the simple existence of a past charge and the free mention of it in public. The "fact" of a past charge was hardly an excuse in a matter of honor.

Bonham seized upon this letter with a new urgency, writing that if Brooks did not clearly state that the two men were equals then Bonham would consider "my standing as a man of honor and courage" to be under attack. Brooks held to his view in a reply written the same day that his opinion about past damage to Bonham's reputation was not an insult. He added that "I already have disavowed impinging your standing as a man of honor or courage" but stopped short—and the omission was as plain as words—of saying that Bonham was his equal. At this point, both men must have known that they were locked into language that would surely pull them into a duel. What we cannot know is how much each man felt he could maneuver in the situation. Nor is it clear whether or not the affair was fueled by long-time ill feeling between the two men. An affair made such concerns secondary, however, by setting men into a ritual that inexorably made rhetoric the main action.[50]

On July 19 Bonham wrote that he would still accept an explanation if only Brooks would say that they were presently equals in all respects. Friends of both men now became closely involved shuttling letters, although Brooks and Bonham continued to write to each other directly instead of through seconds. Brooks, also on July 19, restated his argument that an opinion was not an imputation, and that his remark was "undesigned and is sincerely regretted." But this was as far as he was willing to go, despite Bonham's demand. Bonham wanted equality, not Brooks's regret and a nice distinction between opinion and imputation.[51]

So Bonham wrote on July 20: "I desire your presence in Augusta Georgia or at some convenient place on that side of the Savannah River, tomorrow at 12 o'clock . . . for the purpose of continuing our correspondence." With this euphemism, Bonham underscored the easy transition from letters to pistols. In a figure of speech, words became bullets. At this point mutual friends intervened decisively, and this letter remained undelivered for a day when a friend of Brooks reported to Bonham's second that Brooks had been bundled off on a "fishing trip." Brooks received the letter on July 21 and replied that he would meet Bonham anywhere for any reason, to which Bonham issued a formal challenge to a "hostile meeting" on July 25, adding that he would write no more letters.[52]

The efficiency of friends persisted, however. In becoming silent, Bonham became as passive as the code permitted, and he did not (or could not) prevent James H. Hammond from drafting a letter over his name and even drafting a proposed reply from Brooks. Bonham was then persuaded to append a brief note saying that "a mutual friend," presumably Hammond, had encouraged his "mature reflection" and the letter was sent away to Brooks. It asked simply whether Brooks was in fact prepared finally to deny their equal standing as gentlemen. Brooks, also under pressure from friends, responded the next day with a brief note of his own, stating, "I regard you as a man of honor and courage and of course equal to myself." Bonham was pleased to find this a satisfactory reply.[53]

The full involvement of friends, and the controlled exchange of letters, made the Brooks-Bonham encounter a true affair compared to the inchoate meeting between Townes and Perry. Moreover, Bonham's insistence that Brooks utter words verifying their equality made their dispute typical of what affairs of honor were importantly about: one upper-class man confronting another over a precise, substantive issue of manhood and social leadership. The affair reveals how the possibility of an armed confrontation maintained certain standards of social intercourse. It was an imperative exercise in class consciousness that invoked a social setting, a social time, and a moral force. What might have been just a comment in the crowd on July 4, to be picked up by anyone, or else forgotten for a while and recalled later with some arbitrary effect, became instead a public display of elite male esteem. And esteem, enlarged to social proportions by ritual language, easily spanned the gulf between injured feelings and social order.

Bonham and other elite men could not suffer ambiguity of any sort in matters of character because their authority resided there, and a failure to "resent" an innuendo might reveal a self-doubt greatly to be feared. If Brooks was being offhand, he must be made careful; if he was being deliberately offensive, he must answer to all who ultimately rested their influence on shared standards of character. As for Brooks, his manner of refusing to say the words Bonham desired was itself effective of honor. Brooks, who may have spoken too hastily, or just too loudly, was nevertheless able in the affair to bolster his own esteem and display his own mastery by withholding the necessary words until the affair had reached an intensity befitting the authority at stake (yet stopping just short of destructive grandiosity). Then both men allowed friends to adjust language and secure a resolution.

Fisher-Caldwell: Asserting Honor

The Brooks-Bonham affair was solved cleanly, and was indeed a confrontation of equals in that both men agreed about what was at stake and were adept at the argument of it. Other affairs, however, opened up ways of conflict only glimpsed in the efficient flow of letters between Bonham and Brooks. In many cases, the initial action of correspondence and choosing of seconds was followed by the publication of "facts" and letters by both sides in the form of so-called circular letters. As another literary form typical of affairs, these public notices show something more about the social order men sought to define while defending their personal honor.

"To prevent misrepresentation from going abroad, as regards the affair recently pending between D. F. Caldwell and myself, I think it proper to lay before the public, the following facts, and correspondence."[54] So began a circular letter published by North Carolina politician Charles Fisher in 1833. Consisting of twelve pages of close type, plainly headed "To the Public," this pamphlet was as much a genre of the affair as man-to-man correspondence, but represented another dimension, a complication, in conflicts of honor. Such publications had the immediate practical purpose, of course, of winning support and delaying armed confrontation. They were partisan and construed self-esteem in terms of self-interest. But reading circular letters in this light reveals only part of their meaning. As the published codes of honor did not mention circular letters at all, they may be supposed to have been an extension of values as well as tactics. At some point the teeming affair itself required a man to tie self-interest even more firmly to the general morality. Whether a pamphlet was widely circulated, or, more commonly, only passed among previously concerned persons, the general feeling of a public claim indicates that the collective stake in an affair's outcome deepened as it continued unresolved. In believing such statements necessary, men yoked their rationales to a stable set of standards and expectations which gave personal honor additional social weight.

Thus Fisher's account can be read on three levels. First, it was a part of his particular struggle for advantage over Caldwell, a struggle that Fisher eventually won by dominating the terms of the code. Second, it tapped a public ideology that invested personal concerns with social meaning. Third, it was a record, sometimes unintentional, of Fisher's self-image.

The form of the statement shaped all three levels. Fisher's pamphlet was a kind of narrative-through-letters. He related the story of his dispute by chronologically presenting, with exegesis, the letters between Caldwell and himself. Fisher began with an account of the origins of the dispute (in an election), moved into an annotated publication of selected letters, and concluded with a letter from his second that served as a kind of critical interpretation of the entire exchange. Displayed in this way, the ritual correspondence took on a new weightiness by becoming part of a published record. Although a man would likely print the letters that best served his own case, each man's equal access to "the public" acted as a check on the other's accuracy and completeness. In some ways, the circular letter was akin to a legal argument. But it also had a dramatic energy to it, the anticipation of a storyteller chasing his story.

Fisher's account typically wove personal passion into social observation. Like a courtship, each affair was like all others in some ways, but each generated its own flash points and accents. His quarrel began, Fisher related, during a contest for the state legislature in which Fisher was attacked as a dangerous secessionist by David F. Caldwell. This attack in itself was not so bad, but Fisher believed himself portrayed as a lowly tool of certain South Carolinians who were cleverly using lesser men to form a new southern confederacy. Fisher objected in print to this demeaning characterization of himself, and Caldwell in turn felt belittled and challenged him.[55]

The immediate reason behind Fisher's decision to publish his pamphlet was that Caldwell had recently published his own version. Fisher set out to correct it. His strategy, typical of many men's, was to accuse

Caldwell of a series of omissions which would imply that Fisher had been the more honorable man throughout. First, he pointed out that Caldwell's first choice as second was a man by the name of Pearson who had been previously posted as a coward and had not resented it. Fisher refused to accept correspondence from the hand of such a man. Second, Fisher claimed that Caldwell, the challenger, refused to fight with the weapons chosen properly by Fisher, as the challenged party.[56]

Fisher used these "facts" at the outset to expose Caldwell as being either careless or ignorant of the code. Fisher then went on to narrate the events leading up to the publication of his own "just understanding" of the pending affair. Everything he related reflected his own adherence to the code. As reprinted, Caldwell's first letter was not a proper request for an explanation, but a preemptory challenge:

> SIR: In pursuance of an intimation given on the 6th of the instant, I demand of you immediate satisfaction, for having used language derogatory to me in your speeches in different parts of the country. My friend, Mr. Pearson, is authorized to make the necessary arrangements.
>
> > Yours &
> > D. F. CALDWELL.

Fisher, armed with the rules, replied as though he knew in advance of Pearson's questionable status. Fisher wrote, in part, expressing surprise at a preemptory challenge that included neither a specific charge nor a request for an explanation "as is usual in such cases." Objecting next to Pearson's standing, Fisher wrote: "I have the right to require that you proceed strictly according to the rules to be observed in such cases, and that you should make the demand through unexceptionable hands."[57]

Apparently, Caldwell had indeed slipped up, for he made no attempt to keep Pearson as his second. Instead, he met with Fisher in person, in the presence of Fisher's second Burton Craige, and surprised Fisher with a challenge from Pearson. When Fisher refused it, too, again objecting to Pearson's clouded reputation, Caldwell went into the next room and penned a second, even more brief demand for satisfaction on his own behalf. Immediately, Fisher accepted the challenge in writing. At this point in the encounter, Fisher had not denied Caldwell as a worthy opponent but had placed him at a tactical and moral disadvantage by rejecting his choice of second and criticizing the form of his challenge.[58]

Caldwell's problems did not end there. His next choice as second "will not be here for several days," he wrote Fisher on August 12; in the meantime he would send another friend to make arrangements as to weapons. Fisher again took the high ground of the code to object: he would not arrange piecemeal the weapons, time, and place. He assumed an exasperated tone in recounting it:

Here the *challenging* party required a week, to *name* his second in the affair, and in the main time [*sic*] sends a third person, (not his second) to do what?—Not to adjust *all* the preliminaries; but to have the *weapons* named;—a fourth man, may have come to have *time* named; and a fifth one, to have the *place* named—and all this while, the *second* was not named.[59]

Caldwell was a bungler of his own affair of honor; not dishonorable exactly, but a buffoon. Fisher was able to hold up his adversary's behavior to a "public" that, he knew, would appreciate the import of a man unable to master the code's most obvious requirements. Fisher stopped just short of ridicule (there is no evidence that he wanted further to inflame the encounter with Caldwell) and gained momentum not only by asserting his rights, but by knowing the ritual.

On August 19, Fisher's second, Burton Craige, received a Mr. Samuel Carson who presented him with a letter of introduction as Caldwell's long-awaited second. The two men spoke briefly, then Craige presented Fisher's terms: "The weapons which he makes choice of, are sabres, usually called broad swords, the blade not exceeding thirty three inches in length, of common hilt and guard: the time, is Wednesday, the 21st inst. at 12 o'clock (noon;) and the place, is Mason's Ferry, S. C."[60]

It is easy to picture Carson's eyes widening at this information; sabers were scarcely the usual civilian weapon. He objected to the choice, respectfully enough, by noting that Caldwell was "totally unskilled in the use of the sword" and hoped that Fisher would change the weapon. As Caldwell's friend he could not consent to swords, he said, because "in affairs of this kind, perfect *equality* should be observed, or the purposes of honor are not met."[61]

Again, Fisher seized the advantage through his second, who wrote, still on August 19:

The rules of honor do not *countenance* a *conditional* challenge: the very character of the affair implies that the challenger is *always* ready to fight, *at any time, at any place,* and *with any weapons,* admissible in combat of this kind, while it is universally admitted, that the party called out has the right of naming *time, place,* and *weapons.*[62]

The letter also noted that swords would be more likely to ensure equality than pistols as "Mr. Caldwell has been practicing the use of pistols for some time" and reminded the Caldwell party that he, Fisher, had already granted his opponent a courtesy in waiting so long for him to name a second, particularly in the teeth of a preemptory challenge. In short, Fisher clearly rode atop the affair, using the code to undercut his opponent while at the same time taking the satisfaction of instructing him in the code's requirements.

Craige closed the above letter by asking that Caldwell's next letter say only whether or not he was going to fight, shrewdly gaining further advantage over Caldwell by actually telling him what to say. Carson, on behalf of Caldwell, replied the same day that his principal would "not meet Mr. Fisher with the weapons proposed," possibly thinking that the weapons still were being negotiated. Nevertheless, Carson's letter was yet another mistake because he went on to say that this decision was his alone and not Caldwell's. This move was contrary to the code that permitted everyone to rely on the premise that the second acted in all matters for his principal. Carson closed abruptly: "Our correspondence, and this affair must end here." Fisher's reply seized upon the gap between Carson's decision and Caldwell's desires by demanding to know if Caldwell, as the principal, "sanctioned this refusal to fight." This reply forced Carson to write yet again stating that his principal had indeed "terminated the correspondence and the affair."[63]

The Fisher-Caldwell affair was typical of most confrontations in that the opponents never leveled their pistols (or in this case, crossed swords) but instead engaged in a duel for the mastery of the ritual itself. They were not equals in this particular contest. Fisher won the encounter because Caldwell ultimately refused to fight with sabers. But it might not have been his victory had Fisher been unable to give a persuasive account of his own conduct and Caldwell's. He was able to do so by using Caldwell's own behavior in the ritual against him. Fisher never called Caldwell a coward, and did not speculate openly about why he had refused to fight. Indeed, Fisher's choice of sabers was risky in that it could have been viewed by other men as deliberately outrageous. By the end of the story, however, Caldwell has been portrayed as a man who, whatever his motives, was unable to command his own affair. Even given the bias to be expected in Fisher's account, Caldwell seems to have made a series of subtle but crucial errors that Fisher was subsequently able to state as facts. These errors did not really demean Caldwell's motives, but they did reflect negatively on his strength of character: Caldwell named a man under the ban as his second; he issued a preemptory challenge without asking explanation; he sent someone else to do a second's duty; he engaged in an unseemly negotiation of the weapon; he seems not to have been fully directing his second's actions. Fisher could simply cite these events and imply that his adversary probably would have obtained the wrong kind of sword or forgotten to bring a physician if the affair had continued.

The self-image displayed by Fisher, in contrast, was that of a man who behaved honorably by being ready to act and by knowing *how* to act. His strength of character, manifested in his command of the ultimate masculine ritual, drove his opponent into a refusal to fight. What this outcome suggests is a crucial link between male authority and the reliance on the aggressive use of language as a sign of moral legitimacy. Fisher was able to oppose Caldwell while at the same time claiming to know Caldwell's best interests better than he did himself. Fisher won by instructing Caldwell in something Caldwell ought to have known. Moreover, Fisher played both antagonist and arbiter, personally triumphing over Caldwell yet also bolstering the general social order by publishing his circular letter. These events were central to the elite's style of paternalism: the ability to coerce while asserting (and receiving) the moral standing to persuade. Domination was construed as advice; self-interest was at the heart of fundamental social rules, binding this kind of personal behavior to the essence of social stability.

Cilley-Graves: Serving Honor

The Brooks-Bonham affair suggests how a dispute could fully involve men in a many-layered struggle at the heart of which was a contest for the control of the language describing their relationship; this affair emptied out into calm waters. The Fisher-Caldwell affair shows how the rules of the code joined to an assertive self-justification could give one man a clear victory over another without a formal meeting. In contrast, the 1838 duel between Jonathan Cilley and William J. Graves reveals how an affair could gather a different kind of energy, sweeping language and the best efforts of men before it. It shows how the dialectic of demand and explanation could lead into the darkest reaches of male self-esteem, pulling two men into a fatal duel over a point of honor.

Of course this was not the worst outcome in the view of planter-class men; it was tragic but not disgraceful. A man may die, but the duel allowed friends and enemies alike to bear witness to the continuity of personal honor. Even so, a fatal duel threw into relief the entire range of possibilities for conflict and accord. The affair between Cilley and Graves was no exception. Indeed, the contrast between the mere nudge of events at the beginning and the catastrophe at the end struck both proponents of the duel and their critics as being the essence of the ritual itself. An advocate saw honor implicated everywhere and did not find it amiss that a word spoken or withheld might rightly kill a man. To the code's opponents, however, the missed opportunities for settlement were signs of a monstrous conceit, if not simply a cover for murder. Exploring the Cilley-Graves duel for these dynamics and what they were taken to mean calls for a look, first, at the setting and the participants; second, at the events of the affair itself, and finally at the attempts made by men to explain why everything happened as it did and why Jonathan Cilley lay dead near the Anacostia Bridge.[64]

Both duelists were United States congressmen, Cilley from Maine and Graves, the challenger, from Kentucky. Indeed, Congress formally investigated the duel shortly after it had occurred by appointing a special committee on House privileges. That Cilley was a northerner was much remarked upon. The duel was so identified with the South that commentators looked for something "southern" in Cilley's background and temperament, such as the fact that his grandfather had been a military man or that Cilley was unusually conscious of family pride. The first incident in the affair took place on the floor of the House, a setting bound to attract the most intense interest on the part of planter-class men because it was a setting for so many of their ambitions. The display of glory and shame was analogous to that in comparatively private disputes, but in this case the arena was stunningly public and filled with men who were among the most well versed in questions of honor. Congressmen not only possessed an admired status among planter-class men, but also served terms of office that made frequent political contests necessary. Most planters therefore assumed that a congressman would have many brushes with affairs; he was compelled to put personal honor at risk perhaps more often than any other kind of national political leader. Not only were Cilley and Graves both congressmen, but so were their friends. They were men who could be expected to know why one ought to proceed in an affair or how to avert one. So it was all the more impressive when eight of them rode outside Washington, D.C., on a February day to turn words into blood.[65]

The ritual power of the affair of honor was fully displayed in the Cilley-Graves duel because, everyone agreed, the duel stemmed from a point of honor, not a personal animosity. Graves felt his own honor questioned, as will be seen, when Cilley refused to accept another man's letter that Graves attempted to deliver as a second. Graves felt that this refusal meant that he had carried the letter of an unworthy man and therefore was himself less than equal to Cilley. Cilley, however, felt justified in refusing to accept either the letter or Graves's assertions. As one of Cilley's southern colleagues said of him after his death, he was the sort of man who "accepted the call, because the act was *indispensable*, to avoid disgrace to himself, to his family, and to his constituents." Cilley responded by tying his self-esteem to his duty to dependents, in this case a fatal decision.[66]

The affair germinated in a routine debate over one of the most vexing issues of the day, the Bank of the United States and its influence on the morality of public life. Representative Henry A. Wise of Virginia proposed to his colleagues on February 12, 1838, that they investigate charges of congressional corruption made in the pages of the New York *Courier and Enquirer* by its editor James Watson Webb. Wise made it clear that he was not supporting Webb's attack on unnamed congressmen, only asking Congress to "defend its honor and dignity" by inquiring into the charges. Jonathan Cilley of Maine opposed Wise's stance, noting that the House could well afford to ignore a charge from a man (Webb) who had been known to change his position on the bank after that institution had favored him with a loan. Charges by such a man were not "entitled to much credit" in Congress, Cilley said.[67]

Editor Webb, who was to play only a supporting role in the drama between Cilley and Graves, decided to notice Cilley's words after they were published in the *Globe*. Webb wrote to him on February 21 from a Washington hotel, quoting the congressman's words and concluding:

> I deem it my duty to apprise you, sir, that I am the editor of the paper in which the letter [charging corruption] was first published; and the object of this communication is, to inquire of you whether I am the editor to whom you alluded, and, if so, to ask the explanation which the character of your remarks renders necessary.[68]

It was a classic demand for an explanation, the seriousness of which could not be missed. Webb pictures himself acting from duty and nothing less; his letter was a particular act with a particular objective made "necessary" by Cilley's words. It placed the burden where Webb felt it belonged, on the character of the other man's language. Its personal nature was clear to Webb; now it was up to Cilley to interpret it differently if he could.

Webb's letter was delivered by William J. Graves the same day. Graves later said that he had read the note and had formally agreed to deliver it, indicating that he intended to act as Webb's second. Cilley was on the House floor when Graves presented the letter, and he declined to receive it there or elsewhere. The first written account of the reason for his refusal came not from Cilley, but from Graves. He wrote to Cilley later the same day, in a note dense with precision:

> In the interview which I had with you this morning, when you declined receiving from me the note of Colonel J. W. Webb, asking whether you were correctly reported in the Globe, in what you are there represented to have said of him in this House, on the 12th instant, you will please say whether you did not remark, in substance, that, in declining to receive the note, you hoped I would not consider it in any respect disrespectful to me; and that the ground on which you rested your declining to receive the note was distinctly this: that

you could not consent to get yourself into personal difficulties with conductors of public journals, for what you might think to say in debate upon this floor, in discharge of your duties as a representative of the people; and that you did not rest your objection in our interview upon any personal objections to Colonel Webb as a gentleman.[69]

In thus characterizing his conversation with Cilley, Graves phrased the response that would have satisfied him. If Cilley had accepted the words that Graves offered, he would have affirmed three crucial points of honor. First, his refusal to accept Webb's letter was not meant as an affront to Webb; the editor was his equal. Moreover, in declining to accept the letter, he intended no insult to Graves as the bearer of it. Third, an appropriate reason for refusing the letter was that Cilley claimed the privilege of House debate. Even if what he had said about Webb otherwise touched personal honor, the floor of the House was supposed to have no exit to the dueling ground.[70]

Like Webb's letter, Graves's note was proper though tense, having none of the elaborate deference characteristic of more routine correspondence between men. It was typical of follow-up inquiries in its tone of polite menace; it would not bend to include a false step or a careless reply. The recipient was in a position of having words put into his mouth, almost of being instructed. It was an assertive act, bordering on the kind of linguistic aggressiveness of the Fisher-Caldwell affair. Yet, perhaps equally significant in view of the way the Cilley-Graves encounter turned out, Graves began his letter by characterizing Webb's note in a curious way, calling it a letter "asking whether you [that is, Cilley] were correctly reported in the Globe." Webb's letter did not ask this. Webb passed over this gentler phrasing and jumped to a demand for explanation, simply assuming that Cilley had been accurately quoted. Graves thus made Webb seem more conciliatory than he had been. But Cilley, unlike Fisher in his dispute with Caldwell, did not seize upon the gap between the principal's letter and the second's characterization of it, and thus the nature of Webb's language and his abilities as a man did not become the issue. The slippage of language that moved one affair might be overlooked in another; instead, Cilley tried to get leverage by shifting to another position.

Cilley's reply, dated February 21, is also worth quoting whole because it shows that he appreciated the seriousness of his situation, and because this letter became the basis for the continuing dispute:

The note which you just placed in my hands has been received. In reply, I have to state that in your interview with me this morning, when you proposed to deliver a communication from Colonel Webb, of the New York Courier and Enquirer, I declined to receive it because I chose to be drawn into no controversy with him. I neither affirmed nor denied anything in regard to his character; but when you remarked that this course on my part might place you in an unpleasant situation, I stated to you, and now repeat, that I intended by the refusal no disrespect to you.[71]

Cilley thus carefully accepted Graves as an equal in two ways, by formally receiving the letter "placed in my hands" and by expressly disclaiming disrespect. Cilley's letter, with good reason, made his exchange with Graves seem less concerned with Webb than with Graves himself. And, strikingly, Cilley was silent about the privileges of House debate. Instead he rested his action on personal choice; he preferred not to be in a dispute with Webb. But in neither affirming nor denying his feelings about Webb, Cilley joined the issue. In the realm of honor, choosing *not* to have an opinion about another man was a risky course, as Cilley must have known. Political relationships, especially, translated men's opinions of each other into testimonials to character, and a man's every action reflected on his and others' reputation, becoming the cement of new relationships. To not express an opinion when asked for one was perilously close to denying equal standing.

Graves saw it just this way and sent a note the following day, February 22, expressing the personal significance that he was beginning to assign to events. This note was blunt, calling Cilley's reply "inexplicit, unsatisfactory, and insufficient" because it "does not *disclaim* any exception to [Webb] personally as a gentleman." Graves concluded with unmistakable emphasis, "I have therefore, to inquire *whether you declined to receive his communication on the ground of any personal exception to him as a gentleman or a man of honor?* A categorical answer is expected." No longer phrasing possible explanations, Graves demanded a particular one. This letter channeled the language of their correspondence into the narrowest category of honor in which mere personal preference was swept aside by dictates of duty.[72]

Cilley objected to this new tone and replied with the briefest letter of the entire correspondence, saying that, though he regretted that his previous letter had not satisfied Graves, "I cannot admit the right on your part to propound the question to which you ask a categorical answer and therefore decline any further response to it." The second who delivered Graves's letter—a sure sign that it was *Graves*, not Webb, who was the principal now—told Cilley that Graves's honor was under stress and only Cilley could relieve it. Cilley's reply hardly did that, and by the code's standards it was a clear statement that Cilley *would* not. Possibly Cilley felt he had to try to stop the spreading contagion of honor passed from Webb to Graves and perhaps he hoped that ending the correspondence would be the quarantine he sought. But for Graves, Cilley's reply was as irrelevant as Cilley's mere preferences regarding Webb. Graves had the right to ask his questions, he felt, because honor itself had been imperiled. Ending the correspondence would only make the imputation grow; only certain words would now satisfy.[73]

The next day, February 23, Graves challenged Cilley to "that satisfaction which is recognized among gentlemen." He did not cite Cilley's refusal to accept Webb's letter, but rather his refusal to decline to accept it on "grounds which would exonerate me from all responsibility growing out of the affair," a significant way of saying that Cilley must remove doubt that he and Graves were equals. Cilley was prepared for the challenge, sending Tennessee Congressman George W. Jones as his second with a proper letter stating his terms: the duel would be the next day; the weapons were to be rifles at eighty yards, with the position and word to be decided by lot. In all respects the terms were conventional, except the choice of rifles, which Graves's second Henry Wise thought "unusual and objectionable" but accepted anyway. After some difficulty in finding Graves a suitable rifle (at one point, Cilley's surgeon offered to lend Graves his weapon, but another was found) the parties met near the Anacostia Bridge outside of the capital at about 2:30 P.M. The combatants were positioned at right angles to the sun. Graves won by lot the choice of position, which he took about ninety yards upwind of Cilley. Cilley's second, Jones, gave the word to fire with no attempt by anyone to talk. Cilley fired first, and both men missed.[74]

Wise, acting for Graves, then asked if Cilley would not give some reason for declining to receive the Webb letter, for Cilley and Graves "have come here without animosity toward each other; they are fighting merely upon a point of honor." Cilley, as his second recalled it, responded exactly as he had before: he chose not to become involved in a controversy with Webb but he respected Graves, indeed felt toward him "the highest respect and the most kind feelings." Wise recalled Cilley as also stating that he would not voice any opinion about Webb. Wise told Jones that this statement did nothing to extract Graves from the circumstances that had brought him to the ground. Cilley's friends could not convince him to change his words, however, and the two men readied themselves for a second shot.[75]

This time Graves fired just before Cilley and again both men missed their marks. At this point something strange occurred, noted but not explained in the testimony given to the congressional committee after the duel. Nearly everyone present thought that Graves had been hit on this shot from his "motions and appearance," and several heard him say, "I must have another shot." Wise testified, "He positively, preemptorily, and repeatedly insisted upon another shot." Nobody, including the committee, risked interpreting this, and Graves himself did not elaborate, but it seems that the emotional intensity of the encounter may have taken hold of him, moving him through some blend of fear and rage to shoot his opponent and he finished with all words.[76]

Even so, the effort to adjust language continued after this second fire despite Graves's determination. It is possible to picture these six or eight men in the February cold, attempting, as their principals stood by, to put into words what all this meant, or could be construed to mean, safely within the orbit of honor. Wise, for Graves, seems to have become somewhat uncertain about just what his man felt was the final issue. While asserting that Graves did not need Cilley to certify Webb as an honorable man under any circumstances, Wise continued to demand that Cilley say something directly to affirm that Graves "has not borne the note of a man who is not a man of honor." This formulation still makes it seem that Graves did in fact need Cilley's certification of both himself and Webb. Wise had difficulty keeping these distinctions linguistically clear. Jones, on behalf of Cilley, was more imaginative in trying to shift the terms; he argued that his man had proven himself a man of honor by withstanding not one, but two shots from the man who had challenged him. Cilley obviously was not afraid of controversy, Jones said, and the exchange of fire alone should be more than enough to satisfy Graves.[77]

It was not, however, and as the rifles were being loaded once again, Wise and Jones separated from the others in a last attempt to work some agreement. Would Cilley say that he had refused the Webb letter because of the privilege of debate? No, Jones replied, because Cilley did not wish to express an opinion about the privileges of debate or his use of them. Would Cilley say that he meant no indirect offense to Graves (by refusing the Webb note)? Yes, Cilley would say that, had said that already, but would not be drawn into any controversy with or about Webb. There was other conversation, about what it is not clear, and Wise briefly consulted with other friends of Graves, most of whom recommended going ahead with the third fire. The two sides then inexplicably agreed to shorten the distance between the antagonists as well, and when the two men fired simultaneously, Cilley was wounded through the body. He dropped his rifle, beckoned to his friends, and said, "I am shot." Graves asked if he could speak to his opponent and was told that Cilley was dead.[78]

The duel was finished, but its conclusion did not end attempts to surround the affair with words that would adequately contain its emotional and political impact. Instead, new characterizations of the event immediately were forthcoming. Following convention, the two seconds wrote a joint narrative detailing the events leading up to the duel, the duel itself, and the necessity for an end to the controversy. In their "naked statement" Jones and Wise declared that the code of honor had been followed scrupulously and that the behavior of everyone had been fair and controlled. They wanted to contain whatever destructive potential that remained in the dispute; the time had come for all gentlemen to embrace the ritual itself: "We respectfully desire our respective friends to make no publication on the subject."[79]

But even as they hoped to bury the last of the dispute along with Jonathan Cilley, their own statement kept the language of it alive. Even in their joint declaration, Jones and Wise continued to differ over what Cilley had said after each of the first two shots. It is significant that they disagreed over exactly the point at issue all along: Cilley's view of Webb; or, rather, the meaning of his lack of expressed view. Jones, as Cilley's second, stated that Cilley did not say anything about Webb's character while on the dueling ground. Wise, however, remembered that Cilley positively refused twice to disclaim disrespect for Webb. "Such is the substantial difference now between the two seconds," they had to conclude. It was substantial enough to report, and its inclusion in the formal statement demonstrates once again the persistent importance attached to language. Cilley's position outlived him, becoming forever a part of his reputation.[80]

Congress was flooded with demands to do something about the outrage of Cilley's death. Memorials poured in from Cilley's home state, from antidueling societies, and from members of Congress. On March 1, 1838, five days after Cilley died, a special committee was formed to investigate the circumstances of the duel and to issue a report; it did so on April 25. The committee of seven representatives from a wide geographical area was careful to note that it was not a grand jury but rather had the specific mandate to determine whether or not any House privileges of debate had been breached in the course of events that led to Cilley's death. In order to determine this, however, the committee found it necessary to interview everyone directly involved in the affair and many others who knew the participants. At length the committee concluded that the affair and duel had in fact damaged or breached the privilege of congressional debate and recommended expelling William Graves and censuring both seconds. But for our purposes, the document further widens our perspective on the durable meaning that lay in the idea of honor and the reliance that even opponents of the duel placed on language as a measure of social relations. Although it referred to the code of honor as a "relic of unenlightened and barbarous ages," the committee nevertheless stated that Cilley had been "slain in accordance with the code" and that this finding properly bore upon the events under consideration.[81]

In fact, the committee went further. It concluded that a close, chronological ordering of the correspondence between the two men best revealed the cause of Cilley's death. While expressing doubts about the code, the committee thus validated its most important feature: the structuring of language as a way to social order. The adherence of everyone to the code ruled out the possibility, according to the committee, that Cilley "was challenged and fell for a cause not set up in the correspondence."[82] So strong was the committee's reliance on the *act* of correspondence that it concluded that Cilley had died in an excess of honor, in "the utmost extremity of human responsibility," and that the authentic cause of his death were the words of the affair:

> The committee have, therefore, come to the conclusion, that the words spoken by Mr. Cilley in debate in the House of Representatives, the refusal of Mr. Cilley to receive a demand for explanation of those words, and his refusal to assign any other reason for it than that he chose to be drawn into no difficulty upon the subject, were the causes which led to the death of Mr. Cilley.[83]

This is close to saying that Cilley killed himself by taking a position of word and deed—of deed-in-words—that proved fatal. This conclusion is striking not only for the way it sidestepped Graves's motives, but also because it came from a body of men avowedly skeptical of the code of honor. Even here the power of what the code represented—the overriding imperatives of duty, the equality of elite men, the force of language—was verified.

Finding the cultural significance of this or any affair of honor is like assigning meaning to a rich and much reworked text. There were many levels of sense and reference, many overlapping themes. It was the profusion of personal and social layers of meaning that made the duel so compelling. Looking at all layers is doubtless impossible because so many accents and gestures have been lost, and because the affair was paradoxical even in its time and even to its actors. The rules of the affair were built of language that was both highly charged and conventionally useful. Yet rules were not everything, as this chapter has tried to demonstrate; each affair also employed the language of storytelling, brimming with drama, combining and recombining narrative images of manhood, self-esteem, and power so that certain fundamental beliefs were displayed and sustained. The cultural meaning of the affair of honor lies in the relationship of its rules and its stories. The affair was theater and ideology; it *happened* and it *explained* what happened. It bridged the distance between the ideal and the actual, linking personal life to a sense of something larger, to family name, to a social continuity that outlasted conflict. To cross this bridge, by way of conclusion, means characterizing both the rules and the drama of the affair, its relation to social order, and, finally, the deeper cultural values that it gathered together. Each gives a special place to language because, as we have seen, language was of the essence.

The ideal, rule-bound nature of the affair can be quickly characterized. Whether it resulted in death or comedy (or both), the codified affair rested on the controlled personal violence of upper-class men. It revealed precisely who and what mattered: manhood and social position. Only elite men could duel; everyone else gossiped or brawled. Therefore the affair implicated a fundamental social hierarchy topped by the political life men found so absorbing. The ability of a planter to persuade or, if necessary, coerce his slaves and other dependents rested on his being included in the exclusively male world that the affair dramatized, a world founded on sudden shifts in risk and reputation. If the equality conferred by elite position was lost, his authority as master would soon follow. Collectively, planter-class men could not allow doubt about anyone's social standing to exist lest the whole structure of mastery be shaken. The affair's purpose was to display and resolve such doubt. Thus, particular affairs inevitably developed into stories about the social meaning of a man's personal morality. In the labyrinth of honor, men, armed with conventions of self-control, friendship, and equality, pursued an ideal relationship and confirmed their authority. Ritual thus took up any slack in ordinary relations, and the affair led men to "satisfaction" which, for them, had the quality of justice. The spiral of insult and amenity was intended to lead back to the establishment of white, male power, and the language was well suited to this intention: flexible, yet certain; expressive, yet definite. It restored reciprocity between two men by placing them amid common social resources each could draw upon.

To a significant and even surprising degree, actual affairs trimmed and tucked the loose ends of men's relationships to fit the code. But actual conflicts added to the social significance of the ritual by displaying how a given set of circumstances could construe the code and, at times, reveal its silences. The exact nature of offense, for example, was little remarked upon by published codes of honor, but loomed enormous in the social life of men. Far from achieving harmony, planter-class men constantly gave and took offense. Insult or the risk of it was a kind of social currency for the exchange of power. When was a man too thin skinned and when was he cowardly? It was not easy to say, and the possibilities for interpretation both fascinated and alarmed. The social significance of personal offense demanded that men guard their honor as if it were a public monument. Self-esteem was not grounded in self-control, no matter what the code implied. Self-esteem was found in a dialectic of risking one's own enlarged character, taking advantage of the risks of others, and periodically mending the damage by way of the affair.

Similarly, "satisfaction" was a quality saturated with difficult meaning. It seemed self-evident in the ideal, but in practice it was muddied with crude conceit and tender emotion. William J. Graves was satisfied when Jonathan Cilley fell, but this was not the satisfaction that obtained when Bonham had the pleasure of accepting Brooks's explanation. The core of the difficulty seems to lie in the premise that satisfaction was tied to a calm and free reciprocity, when in fact it was also linked to opportunities for self-aggrandizement and rage. Actual affairs revealed a problematic connection between men's morality and their self-indulgence; the worthy man also glowed with ambition. This difficulty in turn suggests that the dominance of upper-class men did not rest only on keeping such obvious dependents as women and slaves in tow. Men had to take on each other as well, for they, after all, were the ones who made honor matter.

The role of a man's friends in an affair also became complicated in actual encounters. As with the definitions of offense and satisfaction, the role of friends was shaped by masculine routines and by the emotional reality of male camaraderie. In actual affairs, the principals were not nearly so passive as the ideal implied. Friends might indeed help transform a conflict of pride into a bloodless triumph for their social mastery. But, as the Cilley-Graves duel shows, the opposite also could happen. When individual injury or passion outbalanced the social interest in reciprocity, bloodshed between two men could force others to declare that the commonweal had been served by tragic dispute. Rallying to create a public resolution of a quarrel, men succeeded in elevating a quarrel to the level of a public interest.

These were the key features of the affair in its social dimension. The ritual sustained the planters' position atop the social hierarchy even as it expressed tensions within that position. It shaped conflict into a story that interpreted the elite to itself. What, finally, can be said about the chief themes of this interpretation? The affair expressed, I think, three major themes, in the way that a story leaves the feelings and circumstances of the characters in its wake. First, the affair enacted and explained the equivalence between upper-class manhood and *legitimate* social authority. The affair revealed morality in all matters of authority as belonging to elite men alone. Others—the underclass, the slaves, or the remote family—were excluded. That elite men possessed inordinate political power is well known. What the affair explains was their sense of the profound moral exclusiveness of their sex and class. Even a man's family had no unique agency in an affair. To share or subvert men's power would necessitate undercutting this sense of sole legitimacy.

Second, the affair of honor marked the close tie men perceived between personal character and social reality. The affair showed men that social order was joined directly to a sense of personal esteem and well-being. They felt that the rhythm of a man's temperament exactly paralleled the dynamics of social stability, and personality became a way to measure social harmony. Thus paternalism, as expressed by the affair, was not simply an extension of a man's familial role to his other social relationships. It was a deep conviction of equivalence between his good character and the general orientation of his society. Slavery, family, and economic organization, too, were seen as properly and inextricably a part of an extensive manhood. The planter class, at least in the interpretation offered by the affair, was a society of men, not institutions. Or, rather, the honor of men overrode institutional structures like the law and subsumed them.

Finally, the affair interpreted a man's private sense of himself as tightly bound up with public display. The affair revealed to elite men the importance attached to the outer show of inner worth—so much so that at times of crisis the two realms merged. The display of self-esteem through letters, speech, and silence became in this ritual the essence of one's self. The affair impressed men with the sheer power joined to the display of self in a public setting of controlled violence which ultimately invented a story. In the most fulfilling of these stories, selfhood, honor, and power were one. Telling these stories about themselves, planter-class men renewed their belief in themselves, their explanations, and the institutional forms that served them so well.

CHAPTER II

COURTSHIP:
SEXUALITY AND FEELING

Courtship has had a strange career and a dubious standing in the study of family history. It has been submerged in the historical study of marriage, and has seemed a mere passage instead of its own social event. Courtship has seemed elusive in another way, too: as a stage for misadventure, it frequently has slipped into histories by way of comic relief. The excesses of lovers have been the stuff of entertainment. A more serious view of courtship, borrowed from social anthropology, sees it as a kind of marketplace, a social means for ranking and rating nubile youth. From this perspective, courtship is best understood as a means of controlling supply, regulating demand, and protecting estates, family lines, and sexual virtue. But this functionalist view has problems too, especially when the feelings of lovers are taken into account. To look at courtship as a market transaction misses what is most important to lovers themselves—emotion, choice, intimacy.[1]

Indeed, changes in the significance of emotion in courtship and marriage are a key to courtship's pivotal role in the making of new families. By the early nineteenth century, some recent histories have shown, the desires of courting couples began to take precedence over parental judgment. As marriage was increasingly seen as a field for personal happiness, the argument goes, courtship became a mirror for youth's sexual expression and ideals. Romantic love appeared in place of the ribaldry and blunt, material calculation of the eighteenth century, casting both into relative disuse. Simultaneously, the means for distributng property between the generations in the planter class became more regular (partible inheritance among sons, and for daughters a trend toward giving slaves as dowry). Courtship itself thus had less to do with opportunities for windfall gains in wealth. In this view, nineteenth-century courtship ritual became more "modern" and more superfluous at the same time. That is, as the transference of property became differently rationalized, and as the provenance of marriage became more tied to youthful sentiment, courtship became decorative and relatively removed from the seat of elite power.[2]

The tack taken in this chapter is quite different, though it generally confirms the change in parental decision making, the more orderly means for transferring property, and the rise of personal happiness as a reason for marriage. But courtship did not therefore become less significant. In fact, the shift in courtship's social importance is not best described in quantitative terms at all, but in terms of the *kind* of social expectations it embodied. In the early nineteenth century, the ritual of courtship in the planter class became flooded with a vocabulary of personal wish, romantic choice, profound contrast between the sexes, emotional crisis, and transcendent pleasure which reveals what women and men hoped to experience in relation to each other. Far from becoming superficial to class and society, and scarcely peculiar only to youth, the change in the ritual reveals a profound shift in the culture of family and sexuality. This chapter explores this changed context and clarifies how courtship impressed men and women not only with the power of personal affinities but also with love's reach into the social order.[3]

As with the affair of honor, courtship ritual involved a dialectic of prescribed values and actual social encounter. Volumes of advice and imagery instructing youths in how to conquer, abide, and love the other sex gave texture to actual courtships which, in turn, gradually transformed the language of novels and advice. In looking at this dialectic, we see the creation over time of a distinct social event. The ritual became part of the ideological joinery, so to say, that linked the routines of private life to a larger sense of social meaning. In this way, elevated courtship ideals were not at odds with either the actual playfulness of lovers or considerations of self-interest. It was the compelling nature of the ritual to be simultaneously elevated, playful, and interested. Courtship as both ideal and experience, as both a formal apology for gender values and as a phenomenology of intimate life, is a key to understanding planter-class culture and family life. An examination of various texts relied upon by courting men and women for an ideal sense of love precedes a look at certain actual courtships to discover the limitations and revelations in the making of love.[4]

The Ideal of Love

What might a young woman or man read that would explain love? And what sorts of reading might parents offer that would neither extinguish youths' questioning nor fully ventilate it? Courtship was touched upon in three major kinds of published literature, each undergoing change in the antebellum years and each intertwined with the others in both form and content. Each permits a glimpse of courtship's formal structure; each genre counterpointed the others and all three marked out the limits and thresholds that enabled women and men to see how to fashion love. Like most popular literature printed in the United States during this period, most of these sources were published in the North. But they were widely circulated in the South, found their way into libraries and periodicals, and therefore must be seen as a part of the southern culture of courtship.[5]

The first of these literary genres is also the one with the longest history: the treatise on morality, manners, and the proper conduct of life aimed especially at women. Descendant of sermon, the book of moral advice had become by the early nineteenth century a popular source of conventional wisdom, published in delicately leafed volumes of closely packed type. The second source of the expectations and code of courtship were the practical guides to correct forms of expression that first appeared in North American editions in the early eighteenth century. The early editions had few love scenes but later ones enlarged the number until the late-antebellum "letter-writers" included more examples of love's language than any other kind, including the language of commerce and family relations. Finally, sentimental novels, seductive like the waltz in the early nineteenth-century South, were a literary form with certain truths about courtship. Unlike the other two forms, novels were both prized and feared for their social (and emotional) simulacra of love, although all three forms increasingly moved closer together in style and content as courtship itself seemed to promise more.

The Moral Boundaries

Advice to young, unmarried women in the form of popular books on manners and education proliferated throughout the United States after 1820. Such books were widely given as gifts and became part of academy curricula. Historians have interpreted much of this literature, quite rightly, as the nineteenth-century's unique effort to surround the woman's sphere with a firm band of words. Although a few eighteenth-century works, Hannah More's for example, had a long life and remained especially popular in the South, the classical rigor of the earlier books gave way in the early nineteenth century to a more emotional, exclusive femininity. As a result, antebellum advice was less generally intellectual and more inclined to offer specific rationales for certain social relationships and behavior. Moralists took on a personal tone, often speaking in the voice of an aunt, a figure of benign kinship. Or they spoke as teachers, mature women who had wide experience in the development of girls and their institutions. The books themselves changed, too, in ways that further marked a new engagement of morality with personality after 1820. Small volumes meant for pockets replaced large ones meant for library shelves. Chapters came to be called "letters," and frontispiece engravings of young women substituted for matriarchal portraits of the authors. These books were meant to be attractive and useful to young women themselves, and students of antebellum culture have plumbed their detailed prescriptions concerning religious sentiment, dress, personal habits, and health. The unusually circumspect advice regarding courtship, however, has not been much noted. Approaching men and courtship, the moral advisers became strikingly vague in both literary style and intellectual content. Their obliqueness reveals not only particular ideological difficulties they encountered, but also the broader tensions in the culture that produced notably obscure sexual advice.[6]

In terms of style, most moral advisers were capable of writing straightforward, even lively prose. But when men came under consideration, the focus shifted off center and words became hushed and labored. Margaret Coxe, for example, pauses in her otherwise crisp discussion of social conversation to observe: "There is a point of vital importance connected with our present subject, which I dare not omit to mention, since a slight or transient failure in its practical application, may throw a shade over your whole future life; I refer to the propriety of your intercourse with gentlemen." Elevated, almost forboding, language abruptly intruded only to disappear without clarification. In the midst of her chapter on "politeness and accomplishments" Hester Chapone suddenly remarks, "In a young lady's behavior towards gentlemen, great delicacy is certainly required," but moves on without elaboration. None of the most popular authors devoted an entire chapter to courtship or even a sustained discussion.[7]

This cautious rhetoric was matched by the obscure content of the moralists' advice about men in general, even before they got around to suggesting how men were to be met. Young women were portrayed as ignorant of men yet preoccupied with them—possessed, as Chapone put it, by "too great a consciousness of the supposed views of men." On the one hand, the moralists saw ignorance as part of woman's natural innocence which would simply grow into the "sense and dignity of riper years." On the other hand, ignorance and innocence were traps for the unwary, and a woman had to scrutinize every encounter with men; even a gentleman was not what he seemed. A woman's safety was in her ability to make complicated distinctions of attitude—her own and men's. "I hope . . . that you will be able to distinguish the effects of real esteem and love from idle gallantry and unmeaning fine speeches," Chapone continues. "The slighter notice you take of these last, the better; and that, rather with good-humored contempt than with affected gravity: but, the first must be treated with seriousness and well-bred sincerity; not giving the least encouragement, which you do not mean, nor assuming airs of contempt, where it is not deserved."[8] Coxe, too, begins by recommending "dignified modesty and simplicity," but soon becomes entangled in the web of attitude and appearance:

> If a gentleman approaches you with words of flattery, and profuse attentions, especially after a short acquaintance . . . be on your guard, and extend no encouraging smile or word; for a flatterer can never be otherwise than an unprofitable companion. It is better by a dignified composure, to appear not to notice, than with smiles and blushes to disclaim flattery; since these are frequently considered as encouragements for further effusions of these "painted words."[9]

If taken as seriously as they were meant to be, these instructions were extraordinarily painstaking compared to the moralists' other kinds of advice. Every word, smile, and gesture was loaded with new meaning when men appeared on the scene. And like most advisers, Coxe gave general assurances instead of exact information. How was one to act modestly? A modest woman would know. She "need not fear that she may unwittingly converse on improper subjects, because from principle she abstains from *thinking of such.*"[10] It was all rather circular.

The latent power of female passion, as well as the untrustworthiness of men, underlay the moralists' caution. Though muted, their discussion of the power in woman's sexuality is compelling. In fact, passion was difficult to write about without evoking it, and some of the moralists' rhetoric seems more than a little taken with emotional extremity. Hester Chapone, for instance, spoke of the unique time in a woman's life when "passion has got possession of the heart, and silenced both reason and principle." Margaret Coxe wrote of a young woman's "yielding herself passively to the indulgence of precipitate or inordinate affection" which came "sweetly, brightly, imperceptibly" and not at all unappealingly. This passion could not be mistaken for the love a woman felt for her female friends. Whatever the rewards or dangers of female friendship, they could not compare to the "stronger kind of attachment" to men that waited beyond the woman's sphere. Indeed, affection between women made them more susceptible to the other passion. Young women, Hannah More thought, "get in a habit of saying, and especially writing, such ever-obliging and flattering things to each other" that they begin to look for such gratification from everyone, including men. A woman's imagination released the full force of her passion. Coxe warned that a woman built an entire world of her dreams, and when attracted to a man became involved in "engrossing emotion" and captive "not so much . . . to your heart, as to your imagination." The consequences, in More's words, were that "a tender heart and a warm imagination conspire to throw a sort of radiance round the object of [women's] love, till they are dazzled by a brightness of their own creating." Despite many warnings against headlong falling into love, More wrote, women plunged on "little alarmed at the danger of *exceeding*, though terrified at the suspicion of *coming short*, of what they take to be the extreme point of feeling." Advice of this kind doubtless reflects the moralists' attempts to make their point in language a young woman could appreciate. But in doing so, the moralists inevitably suggested the appeal of the passion they deplored. The effect of their advice is a near paradox. Unlike any other focus of moral concern in this era of clear dichotomies, sexual passion had implications that were summoned by their very denial. Relationships with men were to be desired, yet were singularly dangerous; love was risky, yet undeniably fascinating. Trying to trace an intellectual route through this moral fog, the advisers ended up not discussing courtship in any detail at all.[11]

By way of comparison, a somewhat different tension appears in the literature for men and further underscores the problem of fitting passion into a ritual. Advice for men scarcely addressed masculine passion in any sense, and it conjured up situations implying things feminine without discussing women. Charles Butler's *The American Gentleman*, for example, has a sentence or two recommending marriage as an institution and includes one chapter advocating chastity in the most abstract terms. Women are simply assumed. He discusses the "Happiness of Domestic Life" as a man's opportunity for periodic repose, without mention of women or wives, or of how to span the gap between a bachelor's chaste life and a husband's domestic one. He sees a man's romantic passion as a problem for his self-control, but not much of a problem. The real dangers, indicated by the chapters Butler devoted to them, are in business, politics, and competitions that test character and honor. Compared with this spare discussion, women's advice literature at least attempted to address the complexities of a sexual relation that, it was obvious, would loom larger in her life than in his. Passion, risk, and the need to make fine distinctions continued as feminine themes, marking out courtship as woman's moral terrain.[12]

If one assumes that many women turned to advice books at least with curiosity, if not with an urgent desire to be guided, what might they find out about men beyond the general warnings? How was one likely to meet an unattached man? What could one expect when that happened? The moral advisers reflected on questions like these in two ways, each suggesting a social context for courtship. The first had to do with novel-reading as a source of ideas about men. Moral advisers did not condemn the sentimental novel with a single voice, and once again their discussion combined stern warning with rich evocation. Novels, admitted one writer, were a major source of women's shared knowledge of "a passion the most powerful of all." The novel's "animated description [and] lively dialogue" were deeply rooted in young women's lives but must be indulged with care. Hannah More, however, compared novel-reading with drunkenness and the novel-reader to a reveler, losing herself in wishfulness and invention. Moreover, novels set high standards, and many a foolish reader, in Margaret Coxe's view, rejected a worthy lover simply because his overtures were "not made in the impassioned accents of a hero of fiction." Beneath these warnings, familiar to students of the sentimental novel, is a clear picture of a social setting for courtship, a world of reading women inventing love apart from men. Moralists wrote of the seductiveness of novels in terms of warm beds, deep comfortable chairs, rainy afternoons, and female companionship. They conjured heroes and beating hearts in the course of belittling them. The clear picture is of young women together sharing an image of men through stories of love.[13]

A second social setting for courtship—the ball or party—was quite different. In effect, it tested all that a young woman had learned or imagined. If advice literature were the only guide to courtship, elite women and men would be seen together only in brightly lit rooms amid company animated by competing designs and strategies that, even in formal advice, suggest fictional plots. Aside from the fact that men and women actually did meet each other in this way, moralists seem to have found ballroom scenes compelling because their advice was concerned with outward behavior, and the ball was a theater of behaviors. Moreover, advice literature was not without its own dramatic devices and the ball provided authors a vivid *scene* which, like courtship as a whole, elevated the ordinary.

Through these settings moralists attempted to work their moral casuistry. Margaret Coxe suggested that a young woman met men at balls in order to prove her ability to keep them at a distance and "effectually check on their part, any attempt at familiarity." A ball was relatively safe territory because men in groups would check each other's "familiarity" as well. Familiarity, in fact, was an inclusive danger. Never defined (described by Coxe only as "unpleasant"), familiarity could leak through any number of oversights: calling a man by his Christian name too soon, or in public; extending one's hand to take a man's arm before he offered it; standing alone near the dance floor for too long a time; conversing for too long with one man, and so forth. The examples multiplied, hedging a woman in while at the same time giving her a scope for extraordinary watchfulness. She might further test her femininity by alternating watchfulness and display. But this behavior, too, had its risks. Charles Butler told of women who worked to "delude a young man by encouraging his attentions for the pleasure of exhibiting him as a conquest, [or] for the purpose of exciting the assiduities of another person." Virginia Cary condemned both male and female flirts at parties, adding that they differed only in strategy. The man "*must begin* to pay attention," she wrote. Coquetry in a woman, on the other hand, "implies *artifice*." The man will openly attack her heart "for the purpose of bruising or breaking it" whereas a flirting woman's weapon was her "*seeming* pleased with lover-like attentions." Deception, conquest, and power are constant themes in such depictions. Courtship was a public, risk-filled game, and the sexes seem drawn to the very social situations that were most dangerous.[14]

Many moralists got caught in the tensions of their own advice. While telling women to "never study manners," Virginia Cary admitted that women had to defend themselves in social encounters by establishing an unassailable facade. Similarly, while recommending marriage to most of their readers, the advisers were forced by their own grim view of sexual encounters to admit that marriage was not for every woman. Margaret Coxe included an entire chapter on single life in her 1839 book, depicting it as a worthy choice for a woman. The ever-calm Hester Chapone noted that a modest and careful single woman "can never be slighted or disesteemed . . . for preferring the single state to an union [*sic*] unworthy of her. The calamities of a marriage are so much greater than can befall a *single* person." In this way the moralists turned only with difficulty from their discussion of the strangeness and struggle between the sexes to a consideration of marriage. A courtship, by its very nature, seemed to be at odds with a harmonious, reciprocal marriage. "How many miserable marriages may be traced to the inevitable falling off from fair seeming," Cary asked rhetorically. Men in particular, she thought, "judge from exterior deportment" and are easily taken in by surfaces, something that should not have puzzled Cary in view of her advice about the facade of manners. Hannah More depicted a man, "infatuated by appearances only," choosing a wife as though she were a painting at an exhibition. Once married, he will find that he is "not *matched but joined*" for life. Marriage was forever, and, as Chapone put it, "the faculties that please for an evening may not please for life."[15]

But if a woman desired marriage, what might she look forward to? Here the moralists' sharp division between the dangerous game of courtship and the holy state of matrimony seems most awkward, for they had difficulty expressing how a proper society (not to mention a rational one) could foster both. The authors agreed, however, that emotion must be pruned back. A young woman might cool her feelings by sharing them with her parents in "perfect openness," as Butler proposed. Beyond this, the advisers suggested talking to men "as one rational creature with another" whenever possible. Though it may be difficult, Coxe wrote, "endeavor to think of [men] as human beings, and to forget other distinctions." The emotions raised by courtship had to be synchronized to the rhythms of marriage, and so marriage itself was depicted as compensatingly bland. Marriage, after all, was "only one modification of human life," as Hannah More said. And though she referred to a "mystic union of marriage," Cary, too, advised her readers "to curb even your amiable feelings." It was not so much passionlessness that they recommended, but the timing and organization of passion.[16]

Just how a courtship arrived at such a point remained less than clear. In a sense, the moralists seem almost to want to sidestep courtship. But they could not because it was truly a crisis in the lives of the young. So in treating it obliquely, the moralists revealed significant conflicts in the ritual, especially for women. There was, first, the tension between elevated language—of euphemism, allusion, and double negative—and the practical distinctions that had to be made. The link between grand abstraction and close discrimination was never addressed. There was also considerable tension between the need for elaborate care and the need to appear calmly "natural." At times it seems impossible to distinguish desirable circumspection from unwanted coyness. Meeting the other sex became a complex matter of posing as oneself. Passion had its conflicts, too. It was not recommended, but neither was it proscribed, and in warning of its excesses the moralists flaunted its power. Finally a tension was implicit in the social settings of courtship. For southerners, especially, the image of young women dreaming afternoons away with fictional images of ideal love probably had particular meaning in isolated, rural life; a lover was first of all one's own creation. Yet a safe play of imagination contrasts uneasily with the swift ritual of display and conquest in crowded ballrooms. The only certainty seems to have been that women could trust other women to be moral and caring and that men were alien. Courtship thus became crucial in dividing the social world into sexual spheres in which unpredictable encounters became tied to predictable strategies. But how was the adversary in courtship transformed into the helpmate of marriage? How could a woman map a lover's progress from heated romance to the banked but lasting fires of home?[17]

A Matter of Style

Related to moralist literature were the increasingly popular manuals of epistolary style called "letter-writer" guides. Dating from the eighteenth century, these guides typically offered a mix of information about pens and paper, rules for a "good" letter, and pages of model letters for shy or stumped correspondents. The guides were, for the most part, authored anonymously and designed as both useful reference works and cues for proper behavior. Like the moralists, the letter-writer guides took up questions of right and wrong, but in a far more utilitarian way. Thorny issues in family affairs and business were treated as problems to be solved by an appropriate correspondence; interest and desire were not so powerful that they could not be channeled by the right sequence of letters. Considered collectively as a second cultural text of courtship, the letter-writer guides reveal the important ways correspondence was supposed to imagine and characterize the meeting of the sexes.[18]

Unlike the moralists, the guides did not divide their potential readership by sex. Also in contrast to moral literature, the guides acknowledged courtship openly. By the 1830s, model letters having to do with courtship and love outnumbered those in any other category, including business, family relationships, and "miscellany." The major change in form and content occurred in the first two decades of the nineteenth century, reflecting the rise of literacy, sentiment, and middle-class order in America. Prior to that time, even so-called letter- writer guides, like Goodman's 1730 volume, often included as many riddles, word definitions, and folk maxims as they did letters. Although claiming to offer epistles for "Familiarity, Friendship, and on all Occasions," Goodman included only one letter of courtship, a "plain country letter" poking fun at two rustic lovers. Instead of letters, eighteenth-century guides contained "curious dialogues relating to courtship" that promised "the most modish management of love intrigues." These were included in a grab bag of astrology, ways to carve meat, and "a Collection of the NEWEST SONGS." By the 1830s, however, guides typically offered a score or more model courtship letters organized in a separate section clearly meant for copying. In this way the guides reflected love's increasing emotional and social significance in the antebellum years. Instead of love being "something strangely hanging on my mind," as the 1730 guide expressed it, love became a realm of its own. Lovers might explore it using letters as their map.[19]

One such map is a sequence of letters, dating from the later eighteenth-century editions, which portrayed courtship as a swift and respectful ritual uniting family and feeling. The man's letter appears first (dated so that the user of the guide will be advised of proper timing) and is worth quoting at length as it sets the tone of the exchange:

My dearest Harriet—Ever since the fatal or auspicious evening that I was introduced to your endearing presence, my heart has been riveted to the lovely image of her, who must become the arbitress of my future happiness or misery; that the latter will be the case will not endure a moment of reflection, for independent of my own feelings, it would be cruel to suppose that a bosom formed of virtues most sensitive and tender, could ever consign a heart touched with those very virtues to become the victim of aspiring delusion. No, my dear Harriet, you will never overwhelm me with such a fatal reply, and thus annihilate all those endearing prospects of future felicity, which I have so ardently cherished; as an alleviation, then, to those fond feelings, which are at present severely agitated by suspense, permit me, my dear girl, to address your respected parents, for a formal recognition of my visits and attentions to you: such a concession from my Harriet, will relieve me from a state of inexpressible anxiety, and in part secure to me a glowing tranquility, which is only in the power of you, my love, to bestow.[20]

This thicket of passion and wish is followed by a model letter of rejection. Dated three days later, the woman acknowledges the letter "you have done me the honour of writing" but requests his "permission to decline your addresses in the most decided manner." His choice of her "so highly distinguished me" that she will always "bear a proper remembrance of it," but now he must conquer his "passion which can never meet a due return from me." The model letter of acceptance is scarcely warmer, though here she allows that "in giving you the permission of addressing my beloved parents upon the subject of your attachment to me, such permission must be understood as implying a reciprocity of feeling." Picking up a figure from his letter, she adds, "that I may not incur the charge of cruelty from one whom, I must acknowledge, I at present value with no ordinary esteem, I shall, with the permission of my parents, feel much pleasure in a continuation of your society." As for marriage, "time and circumstances alone must determine" whether it will follow.[21]

The man is eager to move time and circumstances along, however, and his next letter is addressed to Harriet's father and characterizes his suit as "an application to your beloved daughter for her hand." He requests the parents' sanction, adding,

> This, I flatter myself, you will do, my circumstances, family, and character, being well known to you both. I shall add only, that my happiness or misery through life depends upon your reply; and that I will make any settlement upon your dear daughter which you may judge necessary. My happiness will be founded upon the promoting of hers, with the possession of your esteem and approbation.

To which the model father replies:

My dear Sir—In reply to the letter you did me the honour of writing, I must remark, that neither my wife nor myself have ever interfered with the wishes of our excellent daughter; her whole conduct being governed with such prudence and propriety, that no room was left for advice. Your affection being mutual, we have only to observe, that we shall be highly gratified in giving our girl to you, and we doubt not but that you will enjoy as much happiness in the married state as this life will admit of.

He concludes by naming a date when the young man may visit Harriet, and the brisk sequence of five letters closes with the young man sending Harriet her own father's letter along with one of his own in which he observes that even though she still is "temporizing with my feelings" he is confident that her esteem for him will grow to equal his attachment to her. He will send her a present and look forward to their meeting.[22]

The exchange seems meant to be only a final episode in a longer relationship which the guide simply leaves to imagination or mute experience. Even so, users of the guide could learn certain conventions of timing and style as well as find phrases that made strong themes out of diffuse emotion. A man might see how to manipulate the flow of correspondence without becoming buried in the disarray of his own suit. For a woman, satisfaction and danger both revolved about her singular power of acceptance or rejection. The man organized this letter or begged for that letter; but she could create the decisive moment.

Certain themes in this sequence mirror the observations of advice manuals but impart greater detail. Immediately apparent, especially in the man's opening letter, is a rhetoric of strife and duality. Their first meeting was either "fatal or auspicious," and "happiness or misery" will be his part. Passion is linked to conflict as he speaks of annihilation, fatality, and being overwhelmed. A second theme concerns the honor, reputation, and self-esteem of all the primary actors. Seen through this motif, courtship's ritual was one of deference distributed throughout the family. A young man could not properly appeal to a woman's parents against her wishes, a young woman had to seek her parents' approval, and they in turn should respond to her dutiful act by returning to her the power she gave them. Ideally, everyone's esteem is enhanced. A third theme uses attributions of the sexual spheres to establish the bonds of courtship. The man, for example, declares that as a woman Harriet "must become" the judge of his happiness; that she might cause him misery is dismissed by attributing to her the virtues of true womanhood. He several times states as fact what he desires to have happen; it is a rhetoric that *asserts*. Though there is an intimate purpose to all of this, the effect is to put distance between the couple. She is less her person than an index of femininity. And she holds him at bay by explicit direction, stating with great care just how her letter should be read. To be any less careful of her prerogatives would cause her to be engulfed by the man's tributes to her character.

A second sequence of letters further illuminates the ritual and suggests something more about changes in it during the antebellum years. This sequence was the one multi-edition guides featured first and most frequently after 1840. Though it is difficult to date the origin of any sequence with precision, this one does not appear in eighteenth-century guides and seems to have been developed later than the one just examined. Conclusions about change must be drawn carefully, however, as some volumes printed both sequences in the same edition. This method underscores the eclectic character of the guides and suggests that antebellum courtship ritual was resistant to sudden mutation and could be shaped in part by forms developed over a century earlier.

The second sequence as it appeared in the popular *Universal* guide featured a series of eight model letters mostly between the lovers themselves. Like the first sequence, this one begins with a letter from the man and presupposes some prior relationship. In this case, the man begins even more formally:

Madam,
I have three times attempted to give you a verbal relation of the contents of this letter; but my heart has as often failed me. I know not in what light it may be considered, only if I can form any notion of my own heart, from the impression made on it by your many amiable accomplishments, my happiness in this world will in a great measure depend on your answer.[23]

The woman is given no model letter of rejection in this sequence. Her reply begins with an expression of suprise at his proposal. Although it might in part be seen as attractive modesty, she goes on to say clearly that their relation is not yet so well established. She has merely "seen you at different times" in company, she reminds him. Then she gives him directions. She refers him to her guardian "Mr. Melville." Because of his paternal care, "I don't choose to take one step in an affair of such importance without his consent and approbation." She then tells her admirer that his mother must be told of the correspondence before it can go further. As a daughter, she "would not disoblige my own relations, so neither would I . . . admit of any addresses contrary to the inclination of yours."[24]

As in the first sequence, the woman's written reply, whatever its conditions, is a sign that the courtship may continue, though here the father has been replaced by a more distant guardian. And this sequence gives the young woman much more to say, reflecting a newer, more verbal, femininity. After expressing her surprise, and before giving her instructions, she tells her suitor:

Those of your sex have often asserted, that we are fond of flattery, and like mightily to be pleased: I shall therefore suppose it true, and excuse you for those econiums bestowed on me in your letter; but am afraid, were I to comply with your proposals, you would soon be convinced that the charms you mention, and seem to value so much, are merely exterior appearances, which, like the summer's flower, will very soon fade, and all those mighty professions of love will end at last either in indifference, or, which is worse, disgust.

Like the concern for family duties, this sentiment fully echoes moralists' advice about carefulness. But appearing in a sequence of letters such words permit the woman to be more than silently cautious. She is able to articulate and therefore use the authority of the sexual spheres which a man could not safely ignore. She neither passes over nor accepts his tributes to her "amiable accomplishments" but rather aggressively categorizes them, even verges on dismissing them: he is acting only as one would expect a man to act. In giving the woman this letter, the guide in effect called attention to its own epistolary conventions, permitting a woman to judge and instruct even as she allowed the suit to continue. After she directs him to obtain his mother's approval she tells him, "If you can clear up this to my satisfaction, I shall send you a more explicit answer." Unlike the man's hedged and deferential language, hers is assured and direct, speaking both to moral universals and the specifics of her own situation.[25]

The guide pushes the courtship on. The man replies with "a thousand thanks" for her letter, and tells her that he has found the courage to approach his mother and that she fully approves. He encloses a letter from her addressed to the young woman and concludes, "If you will give me leave to wait on you, I shall then be able to explain things more particularly." The mother's letter appears next in the sequence, and nowhere in the entire model correspondence is there more open feeling than in the letters exchanged between the two women. Admitting to a mother's fondness for "an only, beloved, and dutiful son," the older woman nevertheless clearly implies that she may be trusted as only another woman could be. She describes her son as a paragon of the female vision of manhood: he is religious, tender, and persevering. Her truthfulness is sealed when she confesses that she is dying. The young woman, in her response, is as passionate in her admiration for the mother's tender feeling and "unaffected piety." In fact, marriage would give the two women a kinship bond as well, and "I do assure you, Madam, that I would prefer an alliance with you even before nobility itself, and I think it must be my own fault if ever I repent calling you mother." After this emotional peak, the younger woman simply writes her lover that she must seek her guardian's approval. In her next letter to Charles (we learn his name from his mother), she quotes her guardian verbatim (he has made inquiries and assents, wishing the both of them happiness) and lets his words be her acceptance. Here, again, it is not the woman's aloofness and modesty that are striking, but the way in which she lodges these qualities in straightforward statements about her view of the sexes. She once again summons the language of wariness and conflict, and states her own expectations. "And now, Sir, have I not told you enough? Some might think too much; but I am determined to begin with as much sincerity as I could wish to practice if standing in the presence of my Maker. To expect the same from you is reasonable; I look for it, and shall be very unhappy if disappointed." She calls an end to the ritual by instructing him to "lay aside the tedious formality of courtship, and write to me as one with whom you mean to spend your time in the world."[26]

The writers of the *Universal* guide ring down the curtain here as well, ending the sequence with a literary flourish which reveals the emerging narrative power of courtship ritual by the mid-nineteenth century. A letter from the young man (now addressed to "My Dear Angel") tells of his mother's death even as he received his lover's acceptance of him; new bonds of feeling are tied as old ones slip away. Though there is little practical reason for a letter-guide to end the sequence this way, antebellum courtship clearly had become a *story*, and even an instrumental guide could not resist seeing this one out. The same story, interestingly, ends with quite different emotion in another well-circulated guide, but reaches the same intellectual point. In this version, the guardian's approval and the happiness of the couple cause the mother to recover her health. The young man, now sending his letters to "My beloved Jane," tells her that he is "elevated to the extreme of happiness, for I may now hope the remainder of my life will be one continued scene of bliss" and that his "heart melts at the idea, and language fails." His passion is matched in Jane's final letter in which she clothes modesty with love and tells him to "hasten then with your mother, to meet us . . . and be assured that you will be received in a most welcome manner by my guardian, as well as (need I say it) by Your affectionate and faithful [Jane]." Not stopping even here, Turner's guide has the man reply that he will "fly on the wings of love, my adored Jane. . . . A few short hours, and you will be my own forever. Believe me, my life will be but too short for me to prove my gratitude. Adieu!— for a few short hours, adieu!—then we shall meet never more to separate."[27]

The point reached in both versions concerns the central role of women and the place of passion in courtship. Whether against the mother's death or with it, romantic passion took on an expressive power not apparent in the older sequence of letters. Thus it is only a beginning to say that courtship became "more" emotional in the nineteenth century or that romance overpowered family and property calculations as the basis for marriage. Romantic love did not simply displace other kinds of considerations. Instead all considerations became enveloped by an expressive passion. The man still performs and the woman still chooses in the mid-nineteenth century, but their letters pull them into a final family story so compelling that careful negotiation is secondary to a fictional narrative. It seems that letters could not resolve courtship without some recourse to a story and to the way narrative located values in a passionate drama.

Why this was so is suggested in part by a second difference between the earlier and later sequences. Although men retained their formal responsibilities and their considerable power to initiate and press correspondence, the ritual became much more part of the woman's sphere. Her sphere as an intellectual realm is far more distinct. In the earlier sequence the woman gave signs and permissions; but later she made statements and drew conclusions. To be sure, the female model in no way challenged conventional sexual morality. But the ideological shift toward women was by no means insignificant, revealing a new domain of feeling as well as thought. Woman appealed to woman, woman promised to woman; fathers were absent in this sequence of letters. Keeping aloof from men was now more than mere caution. It was a strategy for sighting false appearances, exposing insincere words, and avoiding the self-delusions that marked courtship. Of course there were new difficulties at the heart of this change. Not only was there the tension of a heterosexual ritual becoming more the province of one sex, there also was a conflict between the ritual's moral gravity and its expressive possibilities. Looking at the typical midcentury sequence of letters, a user of the guide might truly wonder whether matchmaking took place in the refinement of values or in the extension of feeling. Were love and happiness found in the proper succession of letters or in their passionate themes?

Though letter-guides gave no direct answers to questions like these, they did provide more than ideal exchanges between lovers. The main sequence of letters was followed by a number of other letters which reveal more about the social context of courtship and the ways in which the ritual could go awry. Most were to be written by women or on a woman's behalf, once again suggesting that courtship was especially a female crisis, and most responded to one or another mishap. Some letters seem rather farfetched and part of the guides' relish for narrative. The letter "from a young Lady after the small pox to her lover" seems only marginally useful for antebellum sweethearts, and the one from a "young Gentleman, in expectations of an estate from an penurious Uncle, to a young Lady of small fortune, desiring her to elope with him" seems almost a plot summary for a novel and strangely at odds with good family order. But most of the letters can be grouped into two broad categories: those that concern the failure of a courtship and those that reveal the active participation of family and friends. Conflict is prominent in both types, particularly in early nineteenth-century guides when the total number of courtship letters was smaller; eight of the eleven model letters in one guide had to do with strife between lovers or between lovers and kin. By the 1830s, the ratio of conflict letters to other kinds diminished as the total number of letters increased, perhaps indicating that the earlier guides were meant to solve difficulties whereas the later ones intended to be primers in how to court. In any event, however much conflict was to be avoided, the guides seem to say that avoiding strife was impossible given the many personal and social knots courtship was supposed to tie.[28]

The prime conflict was between lovers who quarreled. The model letters almost always concerned instances of "inconstancy" or "indifference" and imply that courtships most often failed because of deception. Love is present and then suddenly it is revealed as a sham. Such instances almost invariably involve one lover seeing the other walking or talking with another man or woman, or even simply hearing reports of walking and talking. To the modern temperament the harm seems slight. But the appearance of these letters in all the guides suggests they be taken seriously as evidence of fears hidden in the game of flirtation (and perhaps as evidence of a sure means of ending a relationship whatever the "real" reason). The tone of the letters is an arch sarcasm, aloof and cool. The letters make personal injury into a moral lesson and attribute motives to observed behavior, characterizing another's actions as a display quite easily interpreted. Promise and betrayal, appearance and deception, seeing and believing are constant themes.[29]

Conflict also appeared in letters that revealed the intense involvement of family and friends in a courtship. Like the intricacy of courtship rhetoric, the extensive participation of others in a couple's romance underscores its essence as a ritual; it was a display of everyone's hopes and fears, turning private designs into public occasions. Friends were so important to the progress of love that one letter has a woman refusing to be courted further until the man introduces her to his friends; otherwise she would be "looked upon with contempt." That friends should share delight and unhappiness is not surprising, but the guides show that friends were expected to make an office of such feelings. They became formal participants in the ritual, tying a couple to the social order. "It is always the duty of friendship to administer consolation to the unhappy," begins one letter from "a young Lady to a Friend whose Lover was false." Just as friends consoled in loss, so they rallied to conflicts. According to the guides, it was the obligation of a woman to address her friend's "disagreeable suitor" if the friend's letters became ineffectual and any further correspondence would mean continued recognition of the man. Assuming the stern voice of a "sincere friend," the woman attacks the "intruding impertinence and nonsensical jargon" of the man's letters as "both contemptible and disgusting" and insists that he stop. Further letters would be seen as signs of "consummate ignorance" on his part or perhaps as harassment which might "provoke my friend to apply to some male relative for protection." Less dramatic but in some ways more complicated is the letter in which a woman implores a man to stop his suit in which her friends and family have taken his part. The man had "obtained all her friends' consent," the guide noted, but still she did not love him. She was not free, however. "Cease . . . this hopeless, this cruel pursuit!" she writes. "By this means you will restore me to the condition you found me in, the love of my parents, and the esteem of my friends." Without friends she is reduced to her own preferences in love; preferences alone, it seems, were not reason enough for refusing an otherwise eligible man. She needs the social world he has captured.[30]

Fictive Encounters

Popular women's fiction was a third formal text of courtship, providing readers with another intellectual context for gender and giving them an immediate, dramatic sense of sexual difference. Where moral advisers sought to separate right from wrong in romance, and the letter-guides attempted to solve love's tactical problems, novels made love into a narrative of feeling. And though some planter-class men became familiar with sentimental fiction, by the 1830s it was clearly a new discourse shaped by women for women. In this sense, to look at courtship scenes in novels is to come nearer to the sensibility of a young woman's life than to read the moralists or the letter-guides. Yet critical difficulties arise regarding the historical meaning that can be pulled from these texts. What can be made, for example, of the frequent disparity in these novels between an author's explicit statements applauding dependent womanhood and scenes that show a quite different, autonomous femininity (not unlike that of the successful, competent authors themselves)? What was the relationship between literary conventions (the wicked belle, the heroine's choice between two lovers) and actual social life? And, finally, did women's fiction with its elaborate celebration of sentiment undercut the social order as many moralists charged, or did it bolster the status quo by inviting women to be self-indulgent as feminist critics maintained?[31]

None of these difficulties will be settled here, but the issues of form and perception that they raise are crucial to understanding the place of fiction in women's intellectual sphere. And these issues suggest dichotomies which are perhaps unnecessary. For instance, the disparity between statement and scene, between *telling* and *showing* on the author's part, seems less a sign of the author's confusion or hypocrisy than a key literary device—irony—central to the meaning of these stories. Saying one thing but showing something else, the authors explored the irony in women's difficult balancing of ladyhood and personhood. Even when not self-consciously crafted, the irony reveals that sometimes "the novel speaks more truly than its author," as Anne Jones remarks of southerner Augusta Evans. Similarly, the relationship between literary convention and social reality seems not so much a matter of whether convention "came true" in the lives of readers or not, but how these conventions helped to shape women's expectations of men and their very perception of love and womanhood. The powerful, recurring conventions in this fiction also bear upon the question of whether the novels can be said to either undercut or bolster the social order and woman's sphere. This may not be the most important question to ask about the conventions, however, since clearly they might do either or both depending on the bond between author and reader. Instead it is the power of convention to condense and signify tensions in the social order that becomes most important here. Conventions of this fiction were handholds, so to say, permitting readers and authors to grasp meaning in their stories and in their lives.[32]

In fiction's courtship scenes certain conventions recur, though the literary style of the scenes changed sharply between the 1820s and 1860s. Courtship scenes in the earlier years, for example, were almost never occasions for dialogue or elaborate description; a heroine's courtship was merely noted, sometimes as a lesson or more ominously as a "vortex," a dangerous passage from girlhood into womanhood. By the late antebellum period, however, courtship scenes were thickened with stories of triumph and loss; social passage had become personal narrative, paralleling shifts in moral advice and letter-guides which also emphasized emotion as an important locus of meaning. Yet amid these important changes in style, courtship scenes continued to include three conventional stages in a ritual of love. For most authors—and readers—courtship was recognized by these conventions, and romance embraced. First, the woman and the man gaze upon each other, a visual encounter deeply impressing them both. This sighting is followed by their meeting, usually in company, which sets up the separations, misunderstandings, rivals, false lovers, and other complications that move the plot. Finally, there is a crisis of feeling, sentimental and often erotic, which resolves the courtship. A close look at all three reveals fiction's map of love.

The appearance of lovers in a story is almost always accompanied by a visual moment which gives them pause and permits the author and reader the enjoyment of close, physical scrutiny. This initial sighting, a moment given over to a lover's singular gaze, displayed character and prefigured the courtship to come. In earlier antebellum novels, much of the description of women centered on their appearance from a distance, as if from across a room. Caroline Gilman's vision of "the airy-decorated figures" of beautiful women typically reflects the conventional lightness yet vagueness of feminine beauty. But by the 1840s authors were relishing much sharper imagery. Alice Graves observes her hero's "finely formed figure, the noble contour of his Roman features, and the high expanded forehead, with the rich masses of dark hair that gracefully curved around it." Mary Schoolcraft's hero was "straight as a North American Indian; admirably proportioned, with just muscle enough to be neither wiry, lean, or unromantically fat." And Emma Southworth's young women usually possessed a "slender frame, yet full formed, with rounded and tapering limbs" dear to romantic sensibility.[33]

At times the author's—and lover's—gaze suggests something of how vision fed sensuality. Susan Petigru King's hapless hero Ernest fell for the coquette Emilia ("He liked to look at her") in a way that moved swiftly from looking to desiring: "She was so fresh, so enticing; her mouth was so beautifully pink, with little milky teeth." And although King disapproved of her rake Barclay, her view lingers on the physical: "he was very handsome—what is called 'a splendid-looking man'— large and powerfully made, with well-proportioned hands and feet; his eyes were dark and expressive." Women who loved him "considered the eyes irresistible, and would allow them no rival but his mouth, which was of a beautiful but voluptuous cut. His teeth were not of a dead white, but had that slight, unbroken sallow tinge, which, like certain skins and colors, lights up at night to a dazzling whiteness." King, no stranger to nights in Charleston society, was well acquainted with the shades of white and the effect of light on skin; Barclay is so intensely seen that his physical features rival each other. Sometimes this sort of fierce description verged on the clinical. Writers frequently gave the impersonal article to personal features, noting "the beautiful bust" or "the lively eye" when describing someone. The gaze goes beyond gesture and clothing, past physical attributes to the bone. "His joints turned in their sockets with the suppleness of childhood," Schoolcraft says of a hero, and she observes her heroine's "strikingly-intellectual, large black eye, enclosed in a proportionally-ample socket (which is a rare perfection)."[34]

Aside from their sensuousness, such visualizations are important in the moral observations that accompany them. Some authors, like Caroline Gilman and Louisa Tuthill, expanded upon the moral risks in a lover's image. Others like Emma Southworth and Susan King were perfunctory and often ironic about the moral danger in beauty, especially female beauty. But none ignored the tension between true womanly beauty and female vanity. Lovers tried to distinguish the difference between the two at the outset of courtship, their gaze deepening the ritual. Beauty *seen* was only the beginning, for both heroine and coquette appeared beautiful. Southworth's Sybil Brotherton, though a virtuous, "natural" beauty, nevertheless knew the beauty she possessed and displayed it: "her eyes [were] large, clear, and blue; her lips full, glowing, and beautiful. . . . Her dark brown hair fell in long and shining ringlets upon her graceful neck and rounded bosom. Her pure and delicate beauty was set off to advantage by the rich dress of white satin and mechlin lace, and the bandeau of pearls contrasted well with her dark hair." This image is not so far removed from Susan King's hardened coquette Angelica Purvis, whose "beautiful figure was dressed always so as best to display its perfection; her little foot did not unkindly hide itself beneath her flowing skirts; her hand and arm often gesticulated with ensnaring grace beneath the very lips of her listener, and her wondrous eyes meltingly sought their meed of praise." The difference between them is subtle but crucial: the coquette strives more than the heroine. An active contrivance, down to her feet, gives the coquette's beauty a deceptive quality not found in the true belle. Yet both know they are being seen and both know how to appear.[35]

Though the tension between beauty and vanity most often was depicted as a rivalry between two characters, instead of a heroine's internal conflict, the tension was deep enough in the culture of women's fiction to give it a certain ambiguity. Some authors like Tuthill made their coquettes rather obviously unsympathetic, and others, like King, textured their "bad" women and men with seductive detail. And heroines were caught in the irony of putting purity on display. Caroline Hentz, for example, carefully tells her readers that a man looks for a woman "lovely to his sight, but far more lovely to his soul;—a meek, devoted, Christian wife." Nevertheless heroines in love possessed "dark and resplendent" eyes and "almost overpowering" physical beauty that was anything but meek. The heroine, less assertive than the coquette, was a more ambiguous figure in women's fiction. The coquette's beauty was her instrument to be used for selfish ends. But if the true belle, though *said* to be modest, was also shown to be riding a tide of her beauty might not she pull vanity along in her wake?[36]

The romantic intensity hinted at in the first scenes develops in the scenes in which the characters meet. An evening ball was a particularly dramatic way in which to bring lovers together, and, from a reader's perspective, a vivid portrayal of what to do and expect from oneself and men. The ball was magic, yet bounded by an obvious decorum; it was a world apart, yet included people known in everyday life. As in life, the fictional ball often was an elite young woman's first occasion to display her social accomplishments and enjoy being considered a lady. This is not to say that the ball was any less a moral risk for novelists than it was for the moral advisers. Changes in fictional party scenes during the antebellum period, however, reveal that the risks were increasingly taken and explored. Caroline Gilman's *Recollections of a Southern Matron*, the first major fictional work about southern womanhood, is representative of the way early novels gingerly immersed their planter-class heroines into the "gay season." From January to March, the season brought plantation girls and their parents to the city for a round of parties and to meet men. Gilman's heroine Cornelia, a sweetly natural belle who delights in the quiet of her rural life, accompanies her mother to Charleston for "the realization of what is *termed* pleasure" but she has been suitably warned that it is a time "which shatters the constitution and confuses the brain." As calm as a moralist, Cornelia sees parties as challenges to womanhood in which conscience is a mainstay and matrimony a solution: "I was soon drawn into the vortex; and, when once entered, nothing but the voice of conscience or the sobering tie of matrimony brings us back. It is, however, surprising to observe how soon Southern wives fall into the habits of quiet domestic life, whatever may have been their previous tastes."[37] But whereas Gilman moves her readers quickly from ballroom to domesticity (suggesting nonetheless that something quite extraordinary happens at parties), novelists by the late 1840s were likely to show readers the events of a ball as a kind of apotheosis of girlhood. Caroline Hentz's coquette Clara, for instance, was trained from age ten by her conniving mother for the time she would first appear in society. Clara is taught that her image in the ballroom is a stage on which men are easily manipulated. But her mother pushes her too far, and with the aid of a benign uncle, Clara learns painful lessons of vanity and falseness.[38]

Such risks made the ballroom scene the foremost fictional context for sexual display by the 1840s. The typical scene, guiding women to the very threshold of courtship, suggested what to see and how to reveal as well as what to avoid. In a King story a young man suddenly truly sees a girl he had only casually noticed prior to the ball; what he sees is what a woman might hope to be and what a man expected to discover: "He watched her as she waltzed: her style was more languid and luxurious, than light and elastic. She was graceful, but very quiet, and soon stopped, as calm and unruffled in breathing and complexion as when she started. Not a tinge more of color, and with her flounces just as perfect in their symmetrical carelessness."[39] But just as the reader is pulled into the pleasures of detail, the whole ballroom comes rushing back, as it does in a scene from Hentz, with a vision far removed from the grim "vortex" image of earlier fiction. Now the woman is not swept away, but moves through a world singularly hers:

> The Hall was brilliantly lighted, the music was the most animating kind, airy forms floated on the gaze, most elaborately and elegantly adorned, and in the midst of these Ellen shone transcendent. . . . conscious of being admired, she glided through the dance, gracefully holding her flowing drapery, smiling, blushing, coquetting, and flirting. Compliments were breathed continually into her ears.[40]

Beyond these images of risk and pleasure, ballroom scenes developed dramas of sexual encounter given an intensity by the brief duration of a party. A party uncovered realities obscured by the drag of daily routine, and despite the moral risks a heroine might assert her natural attractions to sudden good effect. In Louisa Tuthill's *Reality*, for example, Irene Hazlehill, heiress and belle, ignores "half-a-dozen elbows . . . simultaneously pointed towards her" as she moves through her party to greet the impoverished but honorable George Raymond. George feels out of place not only because of the display of wealth but also because of being a man in a woman's realm. Irene offers to introduce him "to some young lady, if you dance," and he, "thus challenged," asks Irene to be his first partner. She agrees, and "gracefully guided him through the intricate mazes" of the quadrille. A heroine became the center of a small world; she dominated by a look, a song. In a story by Caroline Hentz, the heroine Nora and the aloof hero St. Leger are attracted to one another at a party but it is she who brings them together. Singing "with great sweetness and taste," she looks up at him and others seeing her gaze urge St. Leger to join her. "I firmly believe," says the story's narrator, "that one glance thawed the ice of reserve that had imparted such coldness. . . . His fine dark eyes responded." Coquettes, too, control events, but lack deep feeling and motives beyond self-interest. Susan King wasted no euphemisms on Angelica Purvis, and her words have the sting of experience: "She liked to keep a train of 'adorers' always on hand, and at the same point; to make them whirl for her pleasure as a juggler spins his plates; with one touch to set them off, match their revolutions, give a twirl of her finger to bring up an expiring waltzer, retire a step or two to admire the effect, and then again apply the slight impetus where it was needed." For the coquette, however, there was neither love nor relationship beyond the ballroom, and her considerable powers were directed to making the party her life. In doing this, King writes, "her flirtations, strange as it may seem, were strictly *proper*. She was too clever by far to permit a familiarity, which, however much it may momentarily increase the admiration of the other sex, eventually leads to their indifference—perchance disgust." Fear of "familiarity" also blocked any chance for intimacy, and relations with men became locked into conflict and were spoken of as such. A coquette in a Caroline Hentz story is typical in her desire not to love, but to "captivate" a man: "I will win Alston, if I die . . . and it will be such a triumph."[41]

The best women's novelists, of course, were not so simpleminded as to suggest that all women were either "true" or coquettes, or that for a man it was always unattractive to be flirted with. Indeed, female characters often move from empty liaisons to a discovery of true love, and some men learn to cease being wary of all women. But the ballroom scenes established conflict and play, drama, and contrasting images of femininity as basic to courtship. Entertaining as narrative, such scenes also held lessons for young women readers. Beauty and character must go together; an attentive woman might become mistress of her own courtship. Insofar as men were strange creatures, they were puzzled by this female realm. Direction lay in woman's touch, as powerful as it was light.[42]

After the ballroom, lovers were brought together in courtship in a variety of scenes—outings, rides in the country, after church meetings, in drawing rooms. Perhaps drawing-room scenes develop most richly the sightings and parties that preceded them. Like the ballroom, the drawing room was an interior space controlled by women; the difference lay in the drawing room's proximity to routine domestic life. A man who is more than a flirt must seek out a true woman here, and female authors delighted in showing men obviously out of place, "on the tenter-hooks of awkwardness," in Mary Schoolcraft's words, "for their legs are so obtrusive, that they cannot contrive what to do with them." Worthy men fumbled with skeins of yarn and worried over the distance between chairs. Here a man of honor had to master *talk* with a lady, to show that "in conversation, he was fluent and graceful, and he could pass from the lightest to the gravest subjects without any appearance of effort." Drawing-room scenes added words to the ritual of courtship, and used conversation to get past love's fascinations.[43]

These scenes thus set standards for young women whose actual drawing-room experience had not yet caught up with their reading. Even in the literary tastes of experienced writers and readers, the drawing-room scene was essential to the progress of a courtship. Again, sexual conflict often was the theme, ever present and potentially destructive. Here King's Emilia Forrester, a coquette, fences with Harry Newton:

> "Are you amiably disposed this evening, Miss Forrester?"
> "Are you so dull at divining?"
> "Your smile promises well—but in spite of your charming air and the frank sweetness about your lips, there is indeed, loveliest lady, a certain—a certain—I dare not say it—"
> "A certain what, certainly where? Speak out: you have, sir, our right gracious and royal permission"; she extended her arm with a playful gesture of regal state.
> "A certain 'lurking devil' in your soft bright eyes. You are, in spite of the outward gentleness, the innocent calmness which pervades your style tonight—, you are 'not to put too fine a point upon it,' eminently and wickedly dangerous. Now order up the executioner, take off my head—but, I have said it." "And suppose I am dangerous, what is that to you? Who's afraid? Mr. Harry Newton?"[44]

Such repartee was meant to sound contrived (though not ridiculous) and has the feel of a not entirely playful athletic contest, of flying arrows or serve-and-volley. The man plays a conventional game of "guessing" the woman's temper of an evening, and it is not surprising that he relies on describing her physical features to her at considerable length. He attempts to take charge by telling her what she is feeling, a fictional character using the devices of fiction. But the coquette parries him by being combative ("Are you so dull . . . ?") in a way that tested a gentleman's drawing-room mettle. Such a woman knew that parries were thrusts, and thrived on superficial encounter. What Harry finally manages to utter, in a half-sly, half-timid way, is that she is "dangerous," a conventional compliment well suited to courtship's risk-and-warfare theme. Yet at the end of this exchange, he is still not out of the verbal woods. He remains on the defensive, forced to extend her regal ploy by playing the next victim of her ax and compelled to face the fear that lurks beneath his own playfulness.

A drawing-room coquette might change her style to fit her suitors or her moods, and deft writers like King and Southworth relished scenes that captured the rhythms of these shifts. The same King coquette has another naive suitor who, though fascinated, has been unable to do more than talk generally of love. Emilia Forrester once again takes charge:

"I never saw a man really in love."
"What sort of man have you seen? If Miss Forrester has never met a man in love, it must be because she willfully closes her eyes when they approach her."
"Oh, pardon me! I have seen *love-making*—plenty of it . . . but the thing does not last; it has no stamina, no root, no foundation. It is a pretty pastime, a convenient way of amusing oneself; but it is not love. You would not call such ephemeral fancies, love? Women are fickle enough, but men! angels preserve us! . . . Here I stand waiting for the 'divine fire' to strike me. If it ever comes, I shall bare my heart to receive it. Till then," and her large eyes dreamily and softly met Ernest's admiring look, "I shall wait, and—doubt. Do you like violets? The recent rains have made them so sweet!"[45]

King's are among the best of these scenes, and this one is a minor masterpiece of conversational tactics. Emilia knows exactly what she is doing; Ernest does not. He thinks they are conversing about love and men, and attempts to use the topic as a foil for paying her a compliment. She, on the other hand, moves quite competently through a flirtation: her criticism of men as a sex becomes a statement about her own worldliness; but before it can seem too callous, she balances it by letting him glimpse what he wishes for: she really is awaiting true love. Before he can recover from this blend of toughness and vulnerable admission, Emilia once again sweeps up the conversation and now they must speak of violets.

For a true woman, in contrast, the drawing room was the stage for a true courtship. The room could be a place where the appearances of the ballroom were thrown off, where face-to-face talk challenged romantic fascination. Often, a woman is portrayed in the drawing room with two men, each of whom, in the literary convention, represents different male temperaments she might desire (or her readers might encounter). Hentz's heroine Nora finds herself one afternoon with Elmwood, a man who quietly loves her, and St. Leger, who has just begun to pursue her aggressively. After Elmwood praises her generosity, Nora says, "I value your praises, because I do not deem them compliments," that is, a flirtation. St. Leger sees the challenge, and bluntly responds, "And you should value mine, because they *are compliments* . . . a gentleman never takes the trouble to compliment a lady whom he does not wish to please." But Nora will not cross wits with him. She is no coquette, and the point she makes is one meant to extract them from repartee. "As he believes compliment the only passport to her favor, it is natural he should make use of it," she observes, implying that St. Leger would do well to drop such a notion. Similarly, a true man might transform a coquette once genuine conversation replaced display and wit. Clifton, in Hentz's story "The Beauty Transformed," so moves the superficial Catherine that "she found it impossible to preserve with Clifton those artificial manners for which she had been so much applauded. His graceful gravity checked the affected laugh, which so often rang without merriment. Whenever she met his mild, serious, yet deeply penetrating eye, she forgot to add a languishing softness, or sparkling brilliance to her own." Eye and voice, in the coquette a false front, are the first to alter under the influence of a true man. Drawing-room scenes, when they portrayed the taming of an aggressive suitor or the sobering of a showy belle, permitted authors to show closeness between lovers and allowed readers to glimpse how emotional intimacy might begin.[46]

This ideal was complicated, however, by a third way women's fiction represented courtship: scenes that showed the power of romantic passion. It was an essential part of writers' style, and doubtless of their readers' expectations, that passion come suddenly and succinctly, on a tangent to ordinary routine and the wordy byplay of courtship. The terseness of these scenes was the key to their power; not descriptive detail but timing made passion what it was. Thus scenes that seem to the modern temperament to be too oblique to be erotic were quite otherwise for antebellum readers. And though writers and their audience expected passion to occur in courtship, passion existed in tension with women's control of the ritual. Thus Emma Southworth typically has a strong, articulate woman tease her friend for having fallen in love by reminding her that they once "divided the present generation of men into two classes—monsters and imbeciles; to which does your fiancé belong?" Yet Southworth, no sentimentalist, has many other passages like the one in which a woman tells her female friend, "In this soul of mine there exists a vast capacity for, and propensity to, *inordinate affection.* . . . My affections are hoarded up only to be lavished on the one who shall seek and call them out. . . . You are my *friend,* . . . but ah! dear girl, there is still a *great void* unfilled—a *vast want* unsatisfied."[47]

Passion broke through formal structure, and when it entered into a courtship it swept away everything that the ritual had built; passion was "inordinate." Caroline Hentz says of her heroine Linda, "The moment that woman has an *assurance* of the love [of her lover] . . . must be the happiest of her existence . Linda had reached the crisis of her being. . . . She had touched one bright, luminous point—one dazzling focus of bliss—where her spirit fainted from the excess of joy and light." Hentz distances the moment (it "must be" happy) but sheer eroticism takes over anyway. True men, too, were staggered by passion, and the rhetoric of spirituality heightened rather than decreased the feelings of a man who "forgot all the strong resolutions with which he had armed himself, and suffered his soul to gush forth in one full, deep stream of long repressed passion. . . . He did not know that he knelt; he was borne down by the tide of his overpowering emotions."[48]

The difference between passion and everything else that went before is perhaps best shown by the inability of lovers to put passion into words. The first sign of passion in many of these scenes is the sudden absence of the smooth river of language that has carried lover and novel alike. Ernest tries to find the words but can only stammer phrases to Emilia: "You have been so kind to me—you are so very, very attractive—there is about you such an atmosphere of charm and loveliness—I find you—in short, I do not understand myself. This fortnight passed almost constantly with you—" and so on. In a passionate scene of parting from her lover, Hentz's Linda finds herself "bankrupt . . . in words." Another Hentz heroine, Nora, can only say, "My heart is so full . . . I have no language to express my boundless contentment." Though words—the words used quite literally to *make* love—fail once love is created, the authors use wordlessness to underscore the elements of passion, sight and sound. Recalling the initial moment of sighting between lovers, scenes of passion are built of the imagery of eye and voice. "What mysterious power there is in the human voice!" says Tuthill. "The tone of [his] voice thrilled through every nerve of the trembling Irene." A tone, a look could either fix or destroy all that the ritual had established. Susan King's hapless heroine Lily misreads a passionate look: "It was the crisis of her life. Had she not misunderstood her cousin at that moment, probably this story would never have been written." Inordinate and yet subtle, passion was the decisive moment in courtship. The ritual was brought to a single point and then either moved beyond it or fell apart.[49]

Another way in which authors combined passion and courtship, however, counterpointed this theme of crisis. Women felt passion by remembering and desiring it, by imagination. Though less consciously drawn, these scenes had special significance for young, rural women for whom courtship or the presence of a lover was often an occasional thing. Many such scenes hinge upon letters received or lost. Alice Graves's heroine is handed a letter from her lover and "what a tide of emotions swelled in her heart, and she hastened to the solitude of her own room, that she might read it unseen by another. She glanced her eye rapidly over its pages as if she wished to take the whole contents at once, and then read it again and again." Also deeply felt are scenes in which women, with "imagination . . . so extravagant in its boundless fertility," celebrate passion in memory. One heroine "would steal away to some favorite haunt, and sitting down on a grassy bank overshadowed by embowering elms, she would recall the beautiful scene through which she had journeyed and treasure up every expression that had fallen from the lips of Mr. Harcourt." Women frequently knew that they created passion as much as they "surrendered" to it. Reading such scenes, taking them in as real in the realm of love and as expectations worth holding dear, women might learn the powerful ways of passion that the moralists feared: it came from within not from without.[50]

In a sense, the vision of passion as imagination brings courtship in fiction full circle. For not only might a woman remember her absent lover, she might prefigure one she wanted. Even the most moral of the authors, Alice Graves for example, while warning of the overheated imagination nevertheless created characters who can say with certainty of a man they have not yet met: "I have seen him often in my mind's eye." For women, imagining passion was to confirm it, and they compensated for the scarcity of men and the limited knowledge of their sphere by taking the least part for the whole. A man scarcely appeared in a novel before heroines' imaginations began their work. Hearing a man's voice, one young woman finds it "the exponent of character, to which her vivid imagination furnished a history." Another, told of a man's reputation, became caught up "in picturing him as the living prototype of her fancy's sketch." In countless such scenes, a passionate imagination is passion itself, stringing together all the moments in the ritual from first sighting to final union.[51]

The Making of Love

The three formal texts of courtship ritual obviously did not combine to make as clear a code as the one governing an affair of honor. The ideal certainty among men promised by the code of honor had no place between the sexes. But courtship texts did share recurring themes which became guides for sexual experience: the intricate fascination with the deep differences between the sexes and their implied alienation; the conflict between the artifice necessary to sexual attraction and the desire for a "true" mate; the tension between personal preference in love and the social armature of marriage. These themes appear in actual courtships in the planter class. The maps of feeling and perception provided by the formal ritual are quite evident in these encounters, not only as a set of general bearings, but also as rather precise directions centered around the power of language to create a satisfying texture of decorum and desire. Southerners seem to have relied upon these maps to a much greater extent than northerners even though, as we have seen, explicitly southern advice and imagery appeared only infrequently in courtship's formal texts. The antebellum northern lovers who populate Ellen K. Rothman's study of courtship were notably less bound by form and convention, perhaps because marriage in the free states had none of the overt social display of racial authority and class continuity so important to the planter class. It follows that the ambiguities in the formal ritual, in particular the tension between feeling and form, essence and appearance, that clouded the route from courtship to marriage, were more brightly illuminated by southern lovemaking.[52]

Imagining the Other

How men and women speculated about the other sex and about courtship in general reveals expectations of love which followed rather closely many of the fictional images and moral ideals just examined. Planter youth truly expected to find beauty, accomplishment, and character in a lover just as they grew anxious about not finding such a paragon, or, perhaps worse, actually meeting one. They often expressed their speculations in conventional ways which served to abstract the opposite sex from everyday life, and, to the degree that such speculations were stereotypes, served to stereotype self-knowledge as well. Wondering about marriage, a young Georgia preacher typically praised the power of the ideal woman as a "sweet and all but despotic sway" to which he would lovingly submit. The ideal woman moved with grace in the domestic circle, "and there wields (sweet enchantress) the mystic sceptre, love."[53] Equally caught up in the ideal, a young South Carolinian, fresh from a tour of Europe, wrote feelingly of the Spanish woman:

> She is possessed of a strong character that can sacrifice all for the object of love. But to crown all she is gifted with manners such as none other than herself can boast for she has proscribed *Art* from her boudoir and will receive instructions only from the simple voice of Nature. . . . Would that some of the unnatural and affected belles of Newport and Saratoga could see with what ease she accomplishes the most difficult conquests and with what generosity treats those who are not numbered among her favorites.[54]

In this man's wish, the woman who sacrifices for love becomes powerful as only a woman could. Her power was nature itself, and she was kind.

The dichotomy between contrived attractions and natural ones was a constant worry for planter youth who wished for love. Though drawn to "the Carolina Mocking bird, alias Ellen Brenan," and praising her to his diary as a "gay, lively girl," in every gesture feminine and exciting, Samuel Leland was forced to admit that she had long ago lost "that quality which so highly adorns a woman, viz., modesty." Marion Singleton also defined the moral dimension of sexual attraction by drawing a line between vanity and modesty when, only half in jest, she told her younger sister, "*you* are in as fair a way to be attacked and destroyed by a disease called *vanity* as any young lady of my acquaintance." Their aunt's " 'airy nothings' in the form of compliments will unfit you for the sober realities of home." Women searched for ways to praise the manly ideal while balancing appearance and reality. Inner virtues were important, but men were praised as well for their outward display of manliness. Most planter women would have agreed with a young North Carolinian who complimented a recent house guest as "a most excellent man, so pure, so warm-hearted, so pious," but considered as an ideal, he fell short. " 'Tis a pity that his manners are not prepossessing to strangers," she continued, "and that his voice is defective; for he really is a man of some talents."[55]

Other dichotomies fill the pages of advice that planters wrote to each other in anticipation of courting. As Jane Censer and others have pointed out, the planters often easily mixed material calculation and romantic passion in their general thoughts about love. Henry Townes, for example, advised his brother George, "Matrimony is always a serious affair but becomes incalculably more so in proportion to the smallness of the *capital* . . . which each of the parties are able to produce." Thinking he might be misunderstood, Henry added, "(I mean and use the word in its everyday and business signification—Money, and not in the poetical sense—love)." But only calculation of both, he continued, would safeguard what marriage was devised to protect: "Your character, happiness and *comfort.*" Considerations of love and interest led in turn to speculation about what types of women there were, and how to approach them. Young men discussed it constantly. H. A. Jones decided that "there are two classes of Ladies, or rather Ladies act upon two distinct principles in their *bearing* towards young men—some women have to be *wooed*—others only wish to know how much, or what, a man has." He concluded that more love had to be made to wealthier women. But he was tentative about this observation. Women knew far more than he about female character, and when a decision had to be made, "an intimate female [has] more influence with a Lady in these matters" than any man.[56] Whatever it was that women needed or wanted, it was best to proceed with caution masked by lighthearted gallantry. Joseph Cumming wrote his younger brother Harford advice that combined a moralist's care for detail with a fictive spirit:

> Cultivate a deferential bearing towards the fair sex generally, but never be at all particular in your attentions. Never at a party dance more than three successive cotillions with the same lady: in the same

evening don't give more than two locks of your hair to different ladies; and, by no means have at the same time more than six daguerratypes [*sic*]. In a word, avoid the appearance as well as the reality of flirting . . . [and] you will have a clear conscience, few bristling tags at the top of your head, and no packages of returned letters.[57]

Deference to ladies gave them due respect and at the same time protected a man from courtship's flood of tokens and signs. Keep afloat, the elder brother advised, on the tide of women's favor by seeing them all together on the ballroom floor, and give none the chance to cause pain.

Self-confident plans for mastery, however, were counterpointed by wishes for pleasure. Though a few men, like one North Carolina minister, chided themselves for the "weakness" of sexual feelings, most expressed their erotic delight with the creature woman. "By the by talking of Atlanta," Louis Wigfall wrote to his friend John Manning, "I saw there and became acquainted with 'the *prettiest* creature—fresh from Milan.' 'Who gave me some sensations' &c." A less worldly South Carolinian wrote his former classmate of his admiration for a "*Miss Davis*," confessing that though he had no plans to court her, "I should, I confess however, envy most cursedly the celestial bliss of any fellow who should have the great good fortune to hornswoggle her. I should envy him in every step of the progress." (Interestingly, he allowed that he admired her for "*such boldness of intellect*" as well as for her beauty.) Another Carolina youth, at school in College Point, Long Island, wrote to his friend Augustin Taveau in Charleston about "looking at some French pictures of the Fair sect [*sic*] and it would have done you good if you had seen them they were superb showing women in the naked state. . . . I suppose you have fine times at Night with the Girls down Home. I long to get home as I have not Ground one girl since I left— don't you think I must be ready to burst as a ripe watermelon being kept so long from it." Just who were these sexually available "Girls down Home" is not clear, though references to parties and picnics make it seem that they were not slave women. In another letter the same youth linked open sexuality to undesirable women by contrasting "the sweet South Carolina girls" to the "ugly, fat blustering *Yankee* girls, who are good for only one thing and I need not mention what that is." It is not possible to know the blend of wish and reportage in this and other accounts, but the most powerful female objects of sexual wishes were ones a planter could love as well as "ground." In mock despair, a young man wrote his friend, "I am most sadly in love and likely to be for *ten months* at least. What shall I do? I love to——heart reeling and a stiff prick . . . it has given me the "love cholic.' "[58]

All of this reeling and grounding seems so far out of line with the deference and caution due to ladies that it is difficult to say for certain what it reveals about the sexual lives of young men. Whatever the sexual involvement of planter-class women, however, men shared a language of sexuality only among themselves, a fact that distanced women as surely as deference. Even if all such tales were fantasies, an idiom of ready, uncontrollable sexuality was for male satisfaction only. Thomas Jefferson Withers, for example, imagined his friend James Hammond "charging over the pinebarrens of your locality, braying like an ass, at every she-male you can discover," certain that "your *elongated protuberance*—your *fleshen pole*—has acquired complete mastery over you." It was a ridiculous image, but also a tribute to an exclusive masculinity. Such language could exclude women altogether. Withers liked to recall nights when he and Hammond had shared a bed, remembering the latter "poking and punching a writhing bed-fellow with your long fleshen pole—the exquisite touches of which I have often had the honor of feeling. Let me say unto thee, that unless thou changest former habits in this particular, thou wilt be represented by every future chum as a nuisance. . . . Sir, you roughen the downey slumbers of your bed-fellow by such hostile furious lunges as you are in the habit of making at him when his is least prepared for defense." The comic warmth, accented by the parody of romantic love rhetoric, nevertheless suggests an exclusive power associated with male sexuality. Women did not appear in such episodes except as hidden in the pine barrens of young men's lives. For their part, women did not write at all about physical sexuality. But men had a way of similarly disappearing from their letters as well. What remained were wishes for heterosexual love written by women to women in which men appeared only as part of the imagery of sighs, whispers, night.[59]

Distance between men and women, a hedge against loss, sometimes yielded to hostility. Some women, like Mary Townes, felt beseiged by unreliable men. She never referred to her suitors by name, and once asked her brother to tell her "how to dispose of the troublesome cattle for the better kind."[60] For some men, like James H. Hammond, a lifetime taught a bitter misogyny, and so he advised his eldest son:

> Women were made to breed—men to do the work of this world. As a toy for recreation, and we soon tire of any given one for this, or as bringing wealth or position, men are tempted to marry them and thus the world is kept peopled. One woman in ten thousand—not one more—has mind enough to be a true "*help-meet*" to a man of mind. *Every* young man thinks he finds one—one in ten thousand does. A man on the other hand—a *real* man is worth to a woman the purchase of all her charms, her wealth, her rank, however poor and ob-

scure he is. . . . Somehow—God forgive me—I never could bear poor *girls.* When pretty and pure I pitied but nevertheless avoided them. Even the sweetest pill of that kind should be gilded.[61]

Though extraordinarily hateful, Hammond's summary points to social and emotional truths buried in the planters' speculation about the sexes and love. He was cruelly incisive about the dynamics of romantic wishfulness: at its core was an awkward dichotomy of woman as transcendent lover and honest helper, an uneasy union of passion and utility. Beneath Hammond's misogyny was untold loss felt as betrayal and expressed as common sense to his son. Woman, the "sweetest pill," remained as alien and anonymous as she was merely useful.

In southerners' ruminations about falling in love, women could thus be toys as well as visions of beauty; strong, prepossessing men could be turned into "cattle." In part, these extremes were possible because even the most apparently confident generalizations were formed early and in the absence of much experience. Far removed from the mature Hammond's bitter certainty, but a necessary intellectual balance to it, is the voice of his friend Withers twenty-five years before. It was then, in the 1830s, that both young men were ambitious teachers isolated in the upcountry, anxious to become something more. Withers wrote in a rare moment of plain style: "I shall assuredly put myself to no trouble to marry; for although I believe that a happy accomplishment of that important object would do much to advance my honorable progress in the world . . . I know of no woman I would be willing to marry."[62] Louis Wigfall, who, like Hammond and Withers would figure prominently in the South's move toward secession, wrote a friend similarly, saying he would marry if only he could find "*not* a mistress; but a *companion* and a *friend."* Wigfall cut a bit closer to why it was so difficult:

> I am not intimately enough acquainted with *any* woman to judge with any degree of accuracy her character and the truth is it is impossible to become sufficiently well acquainted with any lady unless you have been raised in the same house. I hold it to be absolute folly for a man to agree to spend his life with an individual upon a Ball room acquaintance.[63]

Apart from mothers and sisters most women were unknown, whatever the incitements of ballroom, conversation, and wish. Although Hammond claimed to know all about womanhood and Wigfall lamented not knowing any women well, the two men's views fed similar meanings in the world of separate sexual spheres: the sexes were very different, indeed dangerous, in their mutual desire. Love was laced with folly and disappointment as well as with pleasure and glory. Stripped of its effusions, romantic wishfulness was a profound ignorance. It could slip quickly into fear and hatred, or into homosexual as well as homosocial ties.

Meeting the Other

Yet for most men and women, most of the time, speculation about the other sex gave way to the first opportunities for courtship. Unattached men and women met in church, at holiday parties held in the country, at spas, during the "gay season" in cities, and increasingly in the antebellum years at academy social events. A church social, of course, was quite different from a gay season ball, and a formal academy soiree contrasted with a casual spring afternoon drive. But certain broad characteristics linked all of these settings together. All required careful arrangement and were not particularly open to spontaneity. All settings brought women and men together in groups. Large, generally attended events were the standard occasions for first introduction and subsequent acquaintance. In the later antebellum years it seems that certain diversions encouraged the group to break into couples—the waltz, for example, supplanted the cotillion—but in spite of some pairing off the gatherings retained a collective style. Moreover, men and women were usually already acquainted with each other in some way, if slightly, either through kinship connections or by general reputation. Even at regional academies or resorts, women and men infrequently met total strangers. Most academies were supported by sets of families who knew of each other, and spas, too, tended to draw the same people year after year. At the least, a pervasive sense of class identity gave a familiar pattern to the circumstances of meeting. In these ways, certainly not fully open to conscious appraisal, elite women and men met only their "own kind," shut off from other classes and even regions by an abiding tradition of circumscribed social occasions. As these events were relatively infrequent, often seasonal, the experience of meeting the other sex was concentrated and likely to be intense. Gatherings were typically described as a whirl of people who congregated in an exceptional place for what might be an extraordinary event.[64]

When they wrote about such settings, planter-class women and men drew upon imagery that mirrored fiction and paralleled the circumstances implied by moralists. Oscar Lieber, usually not one to let fly his rhetoric, wrote feelingly of a bittersweet party just before the war, of the lamp-lit evening and the "cool night breeze and a perfect ocean of crinoline." A North Carolina planter wrote his friend of a resort's "pleasures of moonlight walks and water parties, the sipping of juleps and sherry cobblers, the daily indulgence of the afternoon siesta, the evening conversations, the quiet Tableau, the mazy waltz etc. etc." Mary Moragne, a young upcountry girl, found classical and romantic figures in a gathering in 1837, recalling to her journal "the stately, storming vivacious Burt, or the pretty, rogueish, cross-eyed Meeky:—there was that pretty smiling Adonis—Wardlow and that saucy Endymion of a Bowie." The day was without hyprocrisy, "like the gurgling of a fountain. . . . Oh such a day of romping, rioting, uproarious mirth!" she wrote. "Such dancing, singing, card playing, and *such laughing:*—it beggars all description."[65]

Passages in Ella Thomas's diary also reveal the intensely social nature of men and women meeting, the press of people, the conversation and appearance, and the naming of who was there:

> I then came up and prepared for Church wearing a white embroidered Swiss dress . . . *Mike* and *Reab Nisbet* sat directly before me. *Mr. Poe* quite a gentleman from Washington City sat just behind them. George Jones, Bill Roberts, Ike Wilcox, *Dick Nisbet* and some others were there. *Bessie* and *Emmie Hines* sat just behind us. *Emmie* as usual looked quite pretty. We had a most delightful walk back to college. The moon was shining most beautifully and in fact as *Dr. Ellison* remarked—" the nights have been very *sweet* for the last week."[66]

In a similar way, the letters of Egbert Ross name a number of young women whom he met while at Hillsborough Military Academy in 1860. As so many others did, he often recorded how he knew them and where they fit into family groups or educational institutions. "They have quite a number of pretty young ladies here," Ross wrote his sister. " I have seen Pat Murphy's sister several times. . . . She is connected with the female school here. . . . I have also seen Miss Maggie [McLeston?] formerly of Miss Burwell's school." The institutions that shaped expectations of duty and love also brought young elites together to realize them.[67]

Parties, visits, and other gatherings became the scenes for memorable flirtations not unlike such scenes in novels and moral advice. And these scenes burned brightest when flirtation shaded into love. Samuel Leland wrote of "Miss Mary" in his diary one evening after their brief acquaintance was transformed by a walk together that afternoon. Leland tried to parse it out, to find in the ritual the key to feeling:

> I am not vain; but she showed in every action such as leaning toward me, so happy when I was near her; taking pains to sing all my favourite songs. Letting me wear a *ring* she had promised never to allow to be taken off her finger, and wearing mine in turn; always sitting near

me—during the walk we last took, taking my proffered arm, and when I commenced to talk of my feelings and coming near to me, almost ceasing to walk for fear we would get to the house before I declared myself—and then after all that dashing my hopes to the ground, in such a way as made me only begin to love her in earnest. The world would say you were dealing with a *coquette.* She has not one particle of it about her.[68]

He sees the ritual of it, the meaning of "a walk" in a rarified atmosphere of love. He even knows what "the world" would say: that he has been taken in; that her leaning close, the slowing pace, the wearing of rings and taking of arms all add up to false love. Yet here the moves of a coquette do not add up to coquetry. Leland even admitted that he had begun the walk intending "just a little flirtation." But "before I was aware of it, I found that she was almost necessary to my happiness."[69]

This was the language of falling in love: a woman or man, at first one of many, became indispensable. The planters rarely analyzed particular reasons for falling in love because love was not particular to individuals. Love was destined to be; it was in the world, and the planters possessed few words for the scrutiny of their motives in discovering it. Once abstract speculation about the other sex was replaced by meetings at parties and resorts, most lovers made the decisions and were swayed by the emotions that courtship promised to resolve. It gave a rhetoric to the fluctuations of love and character. Many suitors, like Samuel Leland, admitted that in meeting the opposite sex "my motives [are] entirely selfish." He set out to meet women but sometimes found it "difficult for me to explain my object in visiting them." Courtship ritual provided the explanation. In the gestures and implications of his walk with Miss Mary, Leland found a mystery and a promise equal to his loneliness. Yet these initial terms of meeting soon changed. Another man, finding himself moving beyond flirtation, wondered aloud to his lady, "How we should meet . . . where, when, and in whose presence is what troubles me." Such concerns signaled the end to casual, collective gatherings and the beginning of formal courtship. Crossing that threshold—or not crossing it—meant embracing the full ritual that, it was hoped, would pose the questions and give the answers to one's purposes.[70]

Sometimes the threshold was not crossed, but even failed courtships reveal something important about the ritual. In some instances, a break was steeped in the romance of loss. One woman wrote of her younger sister as "quite in the doleful, pitiful dumps" over an "adoration" of hers who had returned to his academy. Trying to brighten her sister's " 'endarkened soul' " the woman walks with her and the two sing sentimental songs. Though rather wry at the beginning of her description, the older woman ends her account absorbed in the idiom of novels: "We sat on the bend between the pine trees . . . , she leaning against one . . . and I against the other and as she sat there, with the shadows playing on her face, and her eyes uplifted, and dewy with emotion, she really looked very pretty." Even when a flirtation was more lightly ended, it was not without certain proprieties. A young man, discovering that his newly awakened love for a woman had diminished, was told by his father that " 'twas an unlucky case, but the only way was to state it clearly to the young lady, return her letters, and be off."[71]

If one or the other lover attempted further to press a dying courtship, the matter became difficult. Though most suitors hoped to give or receive rejections like the one a young man termed "*polite*, and *kind* and *ladylike*," often other measures were used. One woman met a man at Saratoga Springs who so repelled her with his vanity that she directly "declined all particular civilities to myself,"—refusing to be singled out by his gaze, letters, or company— "and attached myself constantly to Brother." The suitor understood exactly what she intended, complaining that he "had never been so pointedly kept at a distance by any lady in his life." Similarly, another woman believed that a man had successfully ended rumors of their courtship because he had "*often* I think decidedly *cut* me and shown me little acts of coldness, which etiquette would have forbidden toward others." Though running the risk of open insult, a person who wished not to be involved in a courtship relied on "little acts" flouting the other's esteem. In the charged atmosphere of courtship, these acts loomed large and significant, making self-esteem the currency of lovers.[72]

At its most involved and extreme, the failure of courtship to take hold once again brought to the surface much of the distance and doubt inherent in the sexual spheres. One woman wrote of her brother's snarled affair in which he thought he was acting honorably by not demanding of the woman her company exclusive of other men. His sweetheart interpreted this as a lack of faith in her own honorable ability to help the relation ripen into courtship. Honor clashed with honor, and the relationship ended. Maria Bryan, the much-courted and highly critical daughter of a well-to-do Augusta planter and politician, rejected suitors for asserting certain male prerogatives. Her letters mix disappointment with caricatures of manly show and bluster. She wrote her sister Julia Cumming of receiving a letter from a Colonel Foster "which has really vexed me." He had continued to court her (here she quoted him) by "making a reavowal of his own regard" rather than playing heed to her wishes, which he termed her "peculiar and romantic notions." Maria thought him blinded by his own self-love and took the telling step: "I shall write that our correspondence may now cease, since the terms of it are so little understood. When he wrote of fashion and politics I was content to read his epistles." Annoyed by another suitor's presuming to define both her reservations to marriage and their insignificance, Maria was further irked when he accused her of preventing him "from devoting his life to the business of making me happy." His was a self-love, Maria declared, born of romantic wishes. He persisted in seeing her as an ingénue waiting to meet, as he put it, "some perfect character drawn by your imagination." Yet he himself struck Maria as ludicrously fictive. "You have read in novels of those men who gaze and look as though they are going to take one in bodily," she wrote her sister after seeing the man one afternoon. "Well, instead of taking a chair, he just looked at me as if he could think of nothing else but the lovely vision before him." Standing apart from the conventions, not entering into the ritual, Maria Bryan saw her suitor as a type, a figure of masculine pretension perhaps entertaining in a novel but appalling in one's parlor.[73]

Finding Love's Language

Why an acquaintance or a flirtation developed into a courtship is not, of course, easily answered. But the private reflections of individuals reveal them using the ritual and the power of its conventions to make meaning out of love. Samuel Leland, for example, decided that ballroom games had become senseless and that he must visit a certain young woman at her father's house. There he discovered that "she was more attractive . . . than she was at the party." The drawing room had worked its domestic magic. Some six months after meeting the "very pleasant lady" who was to become his wife, Leland noted in his diary: "*she improves*," attributing to her the change in his own perceptions. Shortly thereafter he rode the tide of romantic convention and "took the liberty of pressing upon her lips the *First Kiss*." Though he clearly used courtship ritual to feel his way toward love, Leland's private reflections, like those of many lovers, were laconic. Lovers' letters to each other are the best trail through the thicket of feeling and convention. In style, appearance, and fully expressed values, letters articulated a pattern of need and fulfillment that mirrored social expectations as well as personal feeling. As such, they are a locus of historical understanding of class and gender; they reveal individuals bending cultural meanings to their own purposes. Even though these purposes rarely strayed from the standards and expectations central to planter-class culture, the letters of lovers are evidence of the ways in which individuals recognized, claimed, and partly recast those standards and expectations. In the antebellum years, the tug-of-war between cultural values and individual wishes was given new shape by the ascendance of romantic love as a widely shared value for personal relationships. Mirroring this development, courtship letters changed by the nineteenth century from brief notes which resembled guarded legal documents to longer, effusive expositions of narration and introspection. Indeed, it was only after the turn of the nineteenth century that letters assumed their primary place in courtship as the essential link between lovers. To be sure, letters did not do everything that was important in this regard. But they did a great deal. Separated by distance, social proprieties, delayed communication, and having no other recourse, planters made their letters carry the burden of face-to-face meetings. Correspondence, therefore, was a fundamental activity of courtship, and loomed much larger in a relationship than might first be expected. Courtship letters not only gave an account of a love affair, they wove the very fabric of courtship itself. They were the single most visible sign of a love relation, as letter-writer guides and the moralists implied.[74]

A certain kind of correspondence signaled the beginning of a formal courtship, just as a certain kind of letter initiated an affair of honor. And, like the language of honor, words of love were at once highly conventional and yet thick with personal meaning; the first is the route to understand the texture of the second. The planters held on to the conventions of courtship letters long after the propertied classes in the North began to cast them aside. As Ellen K. Rothman has shown, northern lovers by the mid-nineteenth century expressed themselves rather straightforwardly, valuing candor and emotional likeness in one another's letters. By contrast, the planters continued to adhere to the older forms, however modified by romantic or sentimental idiom, which gave a formal superstructure to their desires. In courtship, as in the gentleman's duel, conventional language carried an individual's intentions while at the same time controlling and clarifying a broader, social range of meaning. Meanings were far more numerous and diffuse, however, in courtship than in the duel. Whereas the affair of honor attempted to discharge conflict by affirming the equality of men, courtship had the less precise aim of bringing the sexes and their social spheres into a ritual encounter characterized by mystery, passion, propriety, and a risk-filled pass at intimacy almost certain to raise conflict. Though a stable marriage was the apparent goal, and through it a reinforced social order serving planter-class interests, the emotional and moral extremities belonging to gender made courtship a ritual of far-reaching and possibly dangerous potential.[75]

In antebellum courtships the usages governing the exchange of letters (their proper sequence and their frequency) had a longer history than the romantic conventions governing their rhetoric. Indeed, most suitors observed and remarked upon the conventions regarding the number, frequency, and physical appearance of letters first. Traditionally, as the letter-guides indicated, eighteenth-century love letters had been marked by an emphasis on timing and formal compliment rather than on personal turns of phrase. Such letters were "favors" not because they invited intimacy, but because they displayed an understanding of the rules. Moreover, the eighteenth-century letter took its persuasive power from a relatively sparse set of usages which did nothing to display personal inventiveness; rather, youths took refuge in the *position* of lover, in expressing themselves like one another.

That these conventions were still much in use in the South after 1820, despite the emergence of romantic love, can be seen in the care writers took with the physical appearance of their letters. In any given collection of family correspondence, courtship letters possess a singular heft and density. Women and men alike wrote second and often third drafts of their love letters. They used the heaviest, often embossed paper, the finest nibs and ink. Handwriting conformed to the best academy style; the effect, especially in women's letters, is curiously anonymous in its formality—a message from the woman's sphere. Though an occasional hasty letter with crossed-out words or ink blots was permissible between family members, courtship letters had to be without blemish. Letters made unacceptable by the slightest smudge or variation in handwriting were relegated to the copybook. Frequently courtship letters were not fastened by the wax seal commonly used prior to the late 1850s but were enclosed in envelopes, giving them added weight and mystery.

Writers themselves called attention to the formal weightiness of letters and the significance of appearance. It is impossible to read many courtship letters without finding a constant subtext on the physical act of writing. Though it was rare by 1820 to have a writer "take pen in hand," correspondents made many similar commenting-while-doing references which called attention to the act of exchange. Once a correspondence was established, lovers frequently noted how much pleasure they felt in sitting down to write a letter. References to the act of writing also could be a playful way of setting the terms for a correspondence, as when one young man wrote to his sweetheart, in part to apologize for his brevity, "I have only written a note . . . a *note* so evidently in *tune* that I shall expect to be paid in *kind* by my Mary; at least I'll *let-her*." Paper and writing instruments took on a life of their own, with writers constantly tracing figures of speech in which they are "admonished" by the end of the sheet of paper, "told" by the pen to start or to stop, and "enticed" by a blank page. In writing about writing, lovers thus underscored the link between letters, language, and true feeling. Letters became part of their reputation. Elizabeth McCall did not exaggerate the feelings of most correspondents when she was shocked to hear that her letters had reached her suitor crumpled and soiled. She was genuinely "mortified to hear what an appearance my letters have exhibited," and was certain that her sweetheart "could hardly have received much pleasure from the letters; when their outward appearance was such." She wondered whether her slave who posted the letters (yet another extension of her reputation) could be at fault or whether the postmaster at Greenville might be negligent.[76]

Beyond appearance and the act of writing, the number and timing of letters preoccupied lovers. How frequently letters should be written, and who owed what to whom, became an index to other, less tangible obligations. Mary Jones wrote her fiancé Robert Q. Mallard, "I shall expect a letter on Friday, and it would be very pleasant to receive one on Tuesday; that might provoke me to write on Thursday." Discussing the terms of exchange thus permitted lovers, however playfully, to sort out questions of dominance and duty and to segment time and feeling into letters written and received. Elizabeth McCall was only slightly more explicit than most lovers when she wrote Benjamin F. Perry in 1837: "I will perform my promise of answering all of your letters; but cannot promise that they shall be *three* pages *each. Two* pages *certainly* ought to satisfy you; sometimes a page and a half; and *even* one page. I expect however at *least three* pages from you; and I am not unreasonable; for it takes you as short a time to write a *long* letter as I do to write a *short* one." Convinced by this logic—or persuaded by Elizabeth's energy—Perry agreed, pleased that the terms had been spelled out so exactly. In most courtships these matters of epistolary exchange were worked out in the earliest stages and thereafter remained a regular, if largely unspoken, pattern in the relationship. Some courtships, however, never quite got past the issues of mutual obligation that these conventions embodied. Lovers frequently separated by distance sometimes became obsessed with the matter of quantity and timing. The letters of Tristrim Skinner and Eliza Harwood, for example, almost invariably opened with some comment on the state of their correspondence. Chided by Eliza for a late letter, Tristrim wrote in early November 1848 that because of the press of plantation work he was forced "to give you a selfish reason for not being prompt" with his letter. A week later he again found it necessary to apologize, this time for writing her too *soon* after her most recent letter. Eliza replied by telling him not to worry, but nevertheless took note of his cool reception of her "too-short" letter. Throughout this long, on-again, off-again relation, their letters were strung together by such themes. They expressed their most ready approval or disappointment as judgments about their correspondence. Clearly, like many other couples, they were working out through their letters some rather complicated needs involving assertions of control and fear of loss which doubtless were more deep-seated than their courtship. After their marriage in August 1849 it is especially poignant to hear Eliza immediately take up the familiar theme of exchange: [Today] I got what I most highly prize . . . a letter from *my own dear husband*." Her new, confident voice did not wholly mask her old concern for what he owed her.[77]

After the first years of the nineteenth century, the older, formal conventions of letter-exchange were counterpointed by an emerging romantic vernacular. The old framework of appropriate timing and number shuddered under the surge of sentiment. By the 1820s, letters as an expressive genre were seized as an especially meaningful instrument of love. As Janet Altman has observed, the letter as a literary mediator is interestingly poised between being a bridge over distance and a barrier to a more direct encounter; it calls attention to the gap between lovers even as it pours words into it. Thus, in one way or another, the subject matter of these letters inevitably becomes the giving and taking of confidences. Trust or its absence was the game and the prize.[78] Women's letters, in particular, played with this theme in enormously inventive ways, especially when a flirtation was at the threshold of something more serious.

A South Carolina woman, for example, wrote to a man who had paid her some attention:

> Charleston, 4th Nov. 1829
> A lady, not unacquainted with Mr. Hammond's poetical attainments, takes the liberty of requesting anonymously, a few verses or a bunch of flowers. She is aware of trespassing upon time that may be more usefully and profitably employed and therefore throws herself upon Mr. H's generosity and gallantry. Should Mr. H. feel warranted to reply to her request, a letter addressed to S. H. Stanhope, Chston, So Ca will be received.[79]

This brief masterpiece of convention and desire deserves some explication. Well-chosen understatement and the overall tone of exquisite qualification displays the writer's self-confidence. The absence of a salutation and a signature not only protects her anonymity but also quickly draws the reader into the letter, giving her voice an intimate, close-to-the-ear effect. Her use of the third person form of address protects her privacy and keeps him at a certain distance even while promising an intimate reward equal to the self-conscious formality. The letter plays with contradiction. It is a love letter that easily (or so it seems) grants love's superfluity but at the same time asserts its prerogatives. Her bold request for a token of his love alluringly counterpoints her self-effacing words. In complimenting him, she displays more than flattery in her ironic and doubtless seductive echo of male language: she shows her knowledge of his sphere and its vocabulary of trespass, profit, and warranted conduct. What seems on first look to be stilted, even rigid language must be understood as attractively flexible—neither too aloof nor too demanding, an idiom that signaled passion by screening it with irony and apparent anonymity. The recipient could be expected to at once admire her poise, honor her open request, and thereby test himself against the challenge concealed within.

Other letters typical of early courtship were playful, making puns, tossing about literary allusions, and making much of guessing games laced with mock anger or woe. One young man began a letter to his lady, "Does it bode well or ill to the preservation of our future 'peace relations' that . . . I shall have to ask pardon for offenses committed? Miss Mary, do you know you have put confidence in one who is—shall I say it—a thief?" There follows a story of how he "stole" her picture from the parlor and took it to his bedroom and now has to admit his "crime." "I know that yours is a gentle nature," he concluded, "and will therefore take it for granted that I am forgiven."[80] Such devices agreeably startled the recipient, made her eyes widen in mock or real wonder, and then attributed to her the "feminine" response. Invention was to be answered by invention; allusion and pun, the devices of academy youth, now turned to love. There were letters, too, that expressed passion in full fictive extension. As Emmie Roberts wrote her new sweetheart: "You cannot imagine how delightful the thought that I am your *first* love. . . . How inexpressibly pleasing to know that those pure and holy feelings have never been stirred by another . . . how happy, how truly grateful am I that it was my fate to make such a conquest. . . . It is my daily prayer and earnest desire to become all that you believe and wish me to be."[81] She was immersed in the romantic ideal, treasuring its singularity, purity, and victory, and hoping to complete him by becoming his image of her.

All of these expressions early in courtship share certain qualities. All attribute and prescribe the ideals of manhood and womanhood in quite obvious ways; all play with trust, and delight in the artful display of feeling, whether in irony, humor, or passion. All flourish in the absence of the lover: they suggest how men and women experimented with their image of themselves as lovers. They revealed fears as well—fears as central to the ritual as its aspirations—of falseness, alienation, and conflict. As courtship was joined, a lover was caught up in a ritual almost like a paradox: one had to risk the game, guide it, cherish it, all the while searching for the single player who would free one from it.

These early devices were limited, however, as lovers soon discovered. After the first acrobatics, women and men were faced with what to say next. Moralists were completely silent about the choices and, as we have seen, letter-writer guides did not concern themselves with a sustained correspondence, implying that courtships were somehow completed quickly. Lovers' letters reveal them testing the bounds of epistolary style, valuing beauty and interest in their letters but also worrying that their mutual work might fall short of the ideal. As young Emmie Roberts confessed to her new lover, "After reading your letter I am almost ashamed to send mine, for yours is written so sweetly, so beautifully." Though addressed to one person alone, letters could not escape being measured against the genre. Elizabeth McCall, unusually plain-spoken for a woman just out of her teens, asked her fiancé to read her letters only once. Not just vanity, but a literary sense was behind her request. "You know," she wrote, "there are some things that glanced over slightly appear tolerably well; but which on a more minute inspection appears [sic] to disadvantage; therefore, view mine in the best light you can; read them once; and be satisfied." His letters, however, met the test of public standards. They were "Love Letters such as I like; for they *could* be read with *interest* by others."[82]

Pursuing beauty and interest, lovers struggled to determine what could be said and how to say it, and in this sense they attempted to move beyond the conventions that had been so useful in establishing the relationship. To do this was often not easy. Like many lovers, Robert Mallard strove to express both his sense of ceremony and his particular pleasure, but found himself lapsing into the rhetoric of fiction: "Now I am to commence a correspondence with one . . . whom I feel the mysterious tide of my affections gushing forth with a sweetness and power never before experienced," adding the question: "And is it true that my Mary has honored me with this mark of her confidence?" Campbell R. Bryce praised his fiancée Sarah M. Henry as the one who inspired him to go beyond convention and to seek intimacy through his letters; yet he continued to refer to her in the third person, reestablishing a ritual distance. He valued their correspondence, he wrote, for the "opportunity it affords me of holding with her a sweet though distant converse of dwelling (as I must do while my mind is more particularly occupied with thoughts of her as I write) upon those charms which held me with so strong a fascination and of assuring her of the continued warmth and sincerity of the feelings which this fascination kindled in my bosom." To see Bryce struggling to say something else besides does not deny the sincerity of these elevated sentiments. He looked forward to their correspondence as being "warm and affectionate," but worried that he had not practiced "those thousand little conceits" that made up formal love letters. He was anxious about the conceits of fiction, too: "I have sometimes feared that, in this first affair of the heart in which your feelings are engaged (I hope warmly and deeply) you may have been disappointed in finding my language in its ardour of expression fall so far short of what you may have read in the heated pages of romance or what you may have conceived in the warmth of your own generous feelings." Though he thought her finally too intelligent for that, he nevertheless voiced a fear common to many men: how would they measure up to the female imagination? Bryce frequently expressed his satisfaction with Sarah's regular letters and praised (in a rather schoolmasterish way) the young woman's prose. In so doing, he found himself analyzing the whole matter of courtship correspondence and thus their relationship itself. He told her not to be concerned about the style of her letters, adding, "The surest way of learning to write gracefully is not to labour too much in attempting to write faultlessly. An easy style can only be attained by ease and freedom of thought."[83] He suggested that they should no longer think of their letters as formal (though it seems that Bryce himself was writing two drafts of his letters to her at this point—so much for ease of expression) and begged her not to worry about what to say. His reasoning reveals much about the restrictions on intimacy in such loving-by-letter:

> You need be at no trouble for a subject when anything respecting yourself or anything in which you take an interest, will certainly interest me. . . . If you do [worry] I shall be obliged in my turn to lament my inability to afford you any pleasure either with what I write or the manner in which it is written. Let each of us bear in mind we are writing confidentially to the other, and without any considerations of the inspection of third persons.[84]

Clearly, Bryce was trying to break out of the letter-guide idiom and free their correspondence to reflect something beyond the early stages of a courtship—he wanted to move them from writing Love Letters to writing of themselves and their doings, but the transition was not an easy one. They first had to think of themselves as less exhalted than they had taken pleasure in being; they were not, he reminded her, always under scrutiny and "we may ease ourselves on this score with the safe, although not very flattering consolation, that our humble correspondence will not, like the distinguished loves of Abelard and Eloise, be transmitted to a sympathizing posterity." But he could not altogether resist playing the visible lover anyway, adding, "If we ever have the good fortune to be so immortalized, may it be by a second Pope, who will say that for us which we have neither the genius nor the skill to say for ourselves."[85]

Similarly, Robert Mallard wrote Mary Jones that, at first, lovers had to "be guarded in their epistolary intercourse; that what is said may be forgotten, but what is written is thrown into durable form; and that in the event of the engagement ceasing . . . these 'love letters,' or *duplicates*, might prove inconvenient." But they were beyond that point, he decided, and he would not "put ever a rein on feeling and say 'Miss' when I *feel 'Dear.'* " Two months later, Mallard still took note of the prudent course, but went on building a bridge of intimacy with his words. Though he had sometimes wondered if he violated decorum ("when I sit down to write you, my heart warms, and straightway words find their way to the sheet"), he now resolved that "no phantom fear with finger on his lip shall warn me into silence when I would pour into my Mary's ear the sweet soft words of love." Caught up in romantic imagery, yet cautioned by the ritual's formality, Mallard nonetheless began to use both in order to establish something else. Like Campbell Bryce and Sarah Henry, Mallard and Mary Jones slowly began to sight what lay beyond the pleasures and limits of early courtship discourse and to see that they would have to cut some of the ritual's bonds that had brought them together. This is not to say that they would cease thinking of their correspondence as a literary work, but that the narrative would have to change in ways not yet fully seen. As the cycle of courtship turned, lovers hoped to reread their story, "from that first piece of poetry which made its appearance without a name, to the letter given me by yourself a few nights before" and know what love and sexuality were. They would save the letters, protect them, travel with them, sleep with them under their pillows, and say many times over, "Your letters will be my only source of pleasure."[86]

Reaching into the Lives of Others

As a courtship deepened with new opportunities for intimacy, thriving upon but changing the formal ritual of romantic love, it also extended into the lives of friends and family. Just as lovers' experimentation with the conventions of love revealed new meanings in emotion and introspection, so the involvement of others helped to underscore courtship's social and class character. The culture of romantic love exalted the individual, but the ritual of courtship served to set the individual more firmly in his or her social place. When that place was atop the social order, the role of family and friends became a powerful one. Far from making the decisions or testing the pleasures of love in isolation, planter youth relied upon (and sometimes chafed under) the constant appraisal of others who felt themselves entitled by the bonds of affection and the ties of kin and class to judge the growth of a new union. Like the reliance on the intricacies of formal ritual, the close involvement of others in a courtship was distinctively southern. In the North, well-to-do youth increasingly used romantic sentiment to shield themselves from public prying. But for the planters, love and the significance it lent to feelings seem to have drawn family and friends into an even tighter bond with the lovers; romance was no bar to other relations of life or to the requirements of mastery. The knowledge and support that lovers expected from their kin and confidants went hand in hand with the inner discovery of meaning in love's pattern.[87]

Although moralists warned that friends, however trustworthy in most respects, often disappointed in matters of the heart; southerners wrote each other frequently under the spur of their romances. A North Carolina woman wrote to her friend, typically, "Don't forget to tell me all you can . . . about Wm. Hill—give him a long space in your letters, and be sure to mention what he says and does when you put my *queries* to him. I am *singularly* interested in him, tho he does not know it." A young man wrote: "If you see Minor Sadler tell him to write to me, and tell him send that message that he wished delivered to a certain young lady. Tell him if he will write I can give him some news in regard to her that will deeply interest him." Of great interest was the sort of news Rebecca Haigh sent to her friend Kate DeRosset: "What I said about Col. Meares, is indeed Kate *sober truth*—I speak *confidentially* and *authoritatively*—he is interested most deeply in you, and were he to receive the slightest encouragement, would press his suit without delay. Kate I know he is anything but indifferent to you; . . . I know *you* have a decided particularity for him; am I not right? I speak plainly and earnestly . . . he is a '*noble*' fellow and I have set my heart upon the accomplishment of this affair." In letters of this kind, flushed with an urgency that mixed information with prediction, "interest" was a key word. A singular attention, an almost studious scrutiny, was the most telling way to define the quality of love. Deep interest became the forerunner of passion; as in a novel, the lover's gaze isolated the object of affection. Friends helped with information, inspired courage and excitement; but also, as these letters show, made it inevitable that information and desire became public.[88]

Like Rebecca Haigh, many friends repeatedly proclaimed their sincerity. But others, taking a high rhetorical ground, displayed a rather complicated web of emotion and judgment. One woman, writing on her female friend's behalf, wrought a bantering, chivalric prose, asking the man, "Can it be so, that you have, like a brave 'hero' determined to *come*, and like a second Lochinvar, bear the 'bride' away on your swift courser amid the applause of your friends? Or are you *so cold* and calculating, as to resist the tender and heartfelt avowel of your lady-love[?]. . . . If the latter, I can only say that you are not the gallant knight I supposed you to be. You should be willing to break a dozen lances in her favor." Her language was playful hyperbole but put a claim on a gentleman's honor. It could not be altogether ignored even if a man chose to laugh at the elevated tone. Similarly, one man exhorted his friend that it was time that he "left the shores of celibacy and launched your bark upon a tide of matrimony." He raised the stakes higher by referring to marriage as "a *duty you owe yourself*—your *family* and *Society* at large," and then plunged to the specifics: "[I] desire that you visit us purposely to see *Emma Anthony* as we already see your way clear and guaranty [*sic*] to your full success. You have seen the Filly and need no description. . . . Emma is a Methodist of fine family—pretty face and figure as you know and is worth morally 100000000 and pecuniarily 7 or 8 thousand." Like chivalric rhetoric, this sort of language summoned a sense of manly duty to social class and kin even as it moved swiftly into more practical calculations. But even useful information might not allay a person's feeling pressured to court and marry. Many lovers felt as one young woman who found herself "much teazed [*sic*]" by her friends over a man's suit. Her friends, "particularly desirous of it, so it seemed, were constantly pressing it upon me and construing the merest act of kindness on his part into particular attention." Friends sometimes had specific interests to further, while other times they simply enjoyed helping those on the shelf "tumble off into the matrimonial field," as one woman phrased it. In a sense, the moralists were right: courtship seeped into all the relations of friends, initially as a matter for rumor and exaggeration. But it also became a way of gauging social standards of womanhood and manhood, and a way to bring soaring wishes for beauty and transcendence into everyone's lives. Social courtship bluntly matched fortunes and compared religious faiths, but it also gave way easily to narratives of true love and character. It became the thickest texture of social relations.[89]

The letters of family as well as friends shaped courtship, showing a ritual valued for its insights into human nature as well as for its clear passage to marriage; courtship was an occasion for the exercise of family prerogatives and an occasion for generalizations about triumphant womanhood or manhood and happy family fortune. Regarding favorably his niece's engagement, a planter spoke in the language of male success. The prospective nephew "is everything I could wish. . . . He has already distinguished himself at the bar and is getting a most extensive practice. He is a member of the Legislature now and will be in Congress in less than five years. He is only 25 years old and good looking. He is *rich*, worth 10 or 15 thousand dollars, a man of excellent kind feelings bold able bodied and independent." Henry Townes furthered his brother's courtship because, once married, "his wife and his pride will operate powerfully and beneficially upon him. . . . As soon as a young man marries he ought to be made to feel that his own and his wife's salvation in this world depends on his own exertions alone." He complimented his brother's fiancée as a woman who "has pride, and ambition and *excellent* sense and will stimulate S. to 'deeds of noble daring.' " Though careful in their material calculations, the planters, like their moralists, perceived courtship as furthering extensive goals of character and honor. A successful courtship revealed harmony in the sexual spheres and order in society even as it secured worldly independence.[90]

It was not at all unusual for family members to think collectively about who did or did not join the family. Though his brother seemed disinclined to marry Carrie Teague, Henry Townes wrote, "I am more and more pleased with Miss Carrie and think we must have her in the family in some way." Planter-class youth confided in aunts and uncles, brothers and sisters, about the happy news of their courtship, of "the good Fortune which has befallen himself and myself," as Rebecca Cameron wrote her aunt. Whether approving or not, family always was present, evoking the priority of family ties. A Georgia planter, wondering whether his sister had been "a little taken" with a certain young man, noted that "I somehow feel as if she ought not to think of anybody that we don't know; but tell her that I will give him a hearty fraternal greeting if she is so determined." Maria Bryan, responding to her older brother's failure to obtain the approval of his sweetheart's family, admitted that she, Maria, might have been responsible by acting in disapproving ways which were "considered as the expression of the feelings of [our] family." The easy approval from a lover's kin, as the letter-guides implied, was far less certain if younger sisters as well as parents could effectively chill a romance. Family influence in courtship thus was not simply a hierarchal one of parents over children, but a collective one that required a lover to solicit aid or approval from many different quarters, making himself vulnerable first to this one, then to that one. Yet, at the same time, the many-sided, "public" courtship meant that it was unlikely that all doors would be closed at once to his suit. If younger sisters could register family disapproval they could also advocate a brother's cause.[91]

The open, social character of courtship at times weighed heavily on lovers. Neither fear of moral risks nor snarled communications could so thoroughly crush a courtship as could family strife. One troubled couple, plagued by family disapproval, "*have determined,*" as the woman's brother put it, "that as far as the public is concerned, their engagement is at an end." When Samuel Townes met family resistance to his engagement to Joanna Hall he responded to their "feelings of mortification and regret" with more "perfect and *unmixed misery* than

[I] have experienced during the whole course of my life." And a North Carolina woman believed that her daughter was unwisely influenced by her fiancé's family, and expressed herself "completely disgusted with these public engagements" and the overblown expectations they raised. Other parents, particularly fathers, acted in a traditional way simply to declare a courtship at an end when they had not been asked for approval. Augustin Taveau's sweetheart, for instance, haplessly opened a letter from him in the presence of her family, was compelled to read it, and thereby exposed their secret relationship. Her father returned all of Taveau's letters and pronounced the correspondence at an end. Joseph Bryan's Saratoga Springs suit was interrupted when the young woman's father was informed of it and forbade it, despite his daughter's feeling "shocked at the indelicate position in which she was placed" by the sudden ending. Other fathers relied on their moral and personal leadership in the family to persuade offspring, a gentler but scarcely less paternalistic tactic. "She knows my opinions and apprehensions on this subject," Thomas Lenoir wrote to his wife of their daughter Laura's courtship. "And will no doubt give them their due weight in coming to a final conclusion on the matter." To be certain, Lenoir spelled it out; Laura "should come to the conclusion that it would be best for [her] to defer this matter for awhile or forever, to endeavor to exercise as much Generalship as she possibly can, in making a safe and justifiable retreat from so hazardous an engagement." If she agreed, continued this strategist of marital campaigns, he himself would take responsibility for the suitor's "*perhaps reasonable*" disappointment. In contrast to his writing to his wife, Lenoir confessed to his brother that he had "some reason to suppose" that the lovers "expect to occupy one bed . . . on the night of the 5th January, and set out the next day" for a new home in Alabama.[92]

Elopement was perhaps the greatest trespass against courtship's social character, and the deep outrage felt by family and friends upon hearing of one is ample evidence of the extent of their emotional involvement. Not only was personal esteem at stake, but the planter community's honor as a whole was implicated. Even premarital pregnancy, which might be concealed for a time and then publicly ignored if the community chose, was not the open affront to social order that elopement was felt to be. When "Kate" ran away and married her music teacher, her uncle H. A. Elbert was amazed at such behavior "against the wishes of all her friends and without our knowledge." He tried to put a good face on matters by observing that the new husband was esteemed by other gentlemen, even though he was forced to earn a living by his teaching. Kate's father, however, was "exceedingly angry and grieved." Seven months later Elbert reported him "still inveterate in his wrath towards poor Kate and her husband" despite friends' counsel of forgiveness and the duty to promote family harmony. It is clear that the older man had had his honor severely wounded and that the injury precluded paternal indulgence. In another instance, sixteen-year-old Sally Cantey, at school in Philadelphia, was secretly married in the early spring of 1830. Horrified at Sally's "unaccountable and truely criminal conduct," the mother of one of her friends told her own daughter that, were Sally hers, "I should feel that she had severed the tie forever that had bound her to me as a Mother and henceforth I would never receive her as my child." This woman, Rebecca Singleton, was so at a loss to explain such a destructive act in the Cantey's family life that she thought Sally must have been deranged by the slaves who had cared for her as a child. Even later, Singleton ordered her daughters to "withdraw entirely from the acquaintance [with Sally] . . . as you must be in greater or less degree contaminated by such an association." Contamination, anger, grief, all bespeak the intensity of courtship's social ritual and its extension to the very boundaries of family image and personal honor. Even among the more forgiving, no one suggested that choosing a mate was a matter of simple personal preference, as it increasingly was among the propertied classes of the North. Nor did the planters suggest that elopement was anything less than a serious trespass against family obligation as well as good sense, as it had been in the South for as long as most people could recall.[93]

Southerners became eloquent about family life and its obligations in a quite different way when a courtship became properly channeled into a proposal of marriage. With the cycle of courtship about to close, planters frequently returned to the formal idiom of moralist and letter-guide, to the conventions that let them say "what it is impossible to express." An engagement prompted everyone involved to reflect on the meaning of family life in as full a mythic sense as their command of ritual allowed. Sometimes soothing in its familiarity, sometimes inspiring in its immutability, this phase of the ritual did not enlighten so much as it approved, in the name of everyone. Timeless values rose to the surface of letters. One young woman's former seminary principal wrote her that "if you make as docile, as affectionate, in one word, as *good* a wife, as you were a pupil of St. Mary's, you will be to him an inestimable treasure."[94] She was also gently but firmly lectured by her aunt, a much-loved relative whose rhetoric on this occasion probably lent as much authority to the moralists as it quite obviously borrowed:

[Marriage] binds you for time and for eternity to him on whom your first affections are placed: and who holds the happiness of your future life in his keeping. What a sacred trust it is that you have committed to him, and how equally great are your own responsibilities as a *wife!* . . . Col. Meares will accept my affectionate regards. I shall learn to love him for your sake, and for his *own,* if he fulfills his promise "to love and to cherish" my darling Kate.[95]

In this tribute to womanhood and family, the writer's adherence to convention gave substance to her good wishes. The female motifs—the eternity of the marriage relation, the dependence of a woman on her husband, the reciprocal obligations, and, not least, the conditional affection here offered to the groom—established the exact balance of reassurance and caution.

Parents performed the final measure of duty and character to help complete the ritual. Again, the extent to which the planters relied on formal expressions reveals the importance of the social and personal pass to which courtship had brought them. Nothing less than family unity and social order paralleled the path cut by the exalted self-esteem of lovers, and southerners responded appropriately. In 1836 Robina Norwood wrote to her son's future mother-in-law from the moral position of "*Mother*" writing to a *Mother*" to recommend her son's character in a way that drew upon the power of the masculine ideal. His "friends will never have cause to blush for his conduct," she wrote. "I can only say he has never discovered the slightest tendency to dissipation of any kind . . . nor can I recollect having, ever since his infancy, had the occassion [*sic*] *seriously* to reprove him. He has always appeared determined to exert himself in any way that was in his power to become independent." At the heart of this love affair, echoing the moralists' generalizations and letter-writer prose, was male character. The effort, autonomy, and sobriety essential to mastery is prefaced by the distinctively southern evocation of honor in the male sphere.[96]

A man's formal proposal to the woman's father brought about a man-to-man confrontation that frequently mirrored such scenes in the letter-guides. Waddy Thompson's ratification of his daughter's engagement to John Jones is typically brief yet thick with the formal armor of double negatives:

> Dear Sir   I have received your letter of the 10 Instant and in reply have to say that my entire confidence in the discretion and good feelings of my daughter does not permit me to doubt that she would not have engaged herself to any gentleman upon whom her affections were not firmly fixed and I therefore very freely ratify the engagement which she has made. You will be received into my family with all the cordial affection which you are aware has been shown to your sister.[97]

Here brevity is balanced by phrasing that even a lawyer would have pronounced slowly. Thompson defers to his daughter and in so doing lifts the affair into the realm of principle: she could not have engaged herself "to any gentleman" wrongly and so her engagement to Jones was almost a matter of marital casuistry. A South Carolinian nearly quoted letter-guide prose when he wrote to his prospective son-in-law Franklin H. Elmore, "My dear Sir, I declare to you I have written and torn up three letters [written?] in reply to yours . . . , so difficult is it to give up [a] child always dutiful and affectionate and whom more and more day by day has become necessary to my comfort."[98]

Elmore received this letter a week later and the same day wrote two letters of his own. Familiar themes of manly obligation and satisfaction resound differently in each. To his prospective father-in-law he wrote of his inability "to give expression to the feeling your kindness and confidence has excited in giving me the most precious evidence of your good opinion." Buoyed by this confidence in his character, Elmore formulated themes of loss and duty in which neither the young woman nor his love for her was directly mentioned:

> You have increased my obligations beyond measure, by the manner in which the gift has been made. I can only, in return, tender you my heartfelt thanks, which are equally due to Mrs. Taylor. While at the same time I do not forgo the hope, that the future may reconcile many of the regrets you both feel, in giving away a daughter deservedly dear to your hearts. It shall be my constant care to remember how much of the happiness of both of you is confided in me and so to act as not to make you regret the trust.[99]

To Harriet he wrote:

> My Dearest Harriet,
> I hope you will indulge the ready promptitude with which my adventurous pen has responded to my feelings in the above address—it has indeed spoken the unalterable language of truth; and unfolds, what is to me, equally the source of happiness and pride. The last mail brought me the long and anxiously desired answer of your Parents, which puts the welcome seal of approbation on my hopes. . . . The relief that has given to my anxiety and suspense, is greatly inhanced [*sic*], by the happy anticipation of the future so that I, who have so little in common with the children of fancy, have even caught myself under its magic, picturing many a sunny scene of felicity in the future . . . , [of] a house of happiness, a refuge from the troubles and a resting place from the toils of life. . . . how shall I repay all this?[100]

Such letters deftly catch hold of the themes everyone expected to hear from a young man. Self-esteem and social obligation are firmly joined, with parental approval as the seal. The ritual itself, to which Elmore closely adhered in these two letters, first heightened then relieved the anxious hopes raised by courtship by tracing a line between self-indulgence and self-control. In the voice of a son, he acknowledged his responsibility for the parents' loss, tying his filial duty to his new family. But in the voice of a lover soon to be a husband, he delighted in his beloved and found, too, the image of his manliness. His pen leading him on, he glimpsed the dream of domesticity and the debt at the center of his new achievement. He embraced the effort and repose, loss and possession in his fortune as a man, and he used the pleasure of the letter-writing moment to witness courtship receding before the new "unalterable language of truth."

At the completion of courtship, consummation and loss appeared inseparable. The making of a new family and the duties of the male and female spheres cast sudden light on both future and past. The language of superlatives must be seen as accurately reflecting the raised expectations and fears of gender, self, and society inherent in an impending marriage. If marriage was for lovers the "end of all your doubts and fears and . . . the consummation of all your cherished hopes and fond anticipations," it was also a hushed withdrawal from a former life, and feelings of loss balanced the gain. It was common for otherwise happy young women and men to darken their last courtship letters with formalities as they saw the time approaching when "I am called upon to fill a station the highest and holiest in which women can engage," as Eliza Rivers told her brother. She deliberately chose to be formal with him, to drop the lightness that usually filled her letters, and thank him for his "kind and paternal protection" in her now vanished girlhood. Perhaps women especially felt the loss of childhood home and the separation from parents with particular sharpness, and as a legitimate reason for delay in setting the wedding date. Though obviously impatient to marry, for instance, Robert Mallard acceded to his fiancée's wish for an indefinite postponement on account of "your attachment to your parents." In reply to Emmie Roberts, who had written to say that the wedding date must be set soon because her fiancé desired it, her mother asked, "Can he miss you, can he be more lonely without you than I?" And a young woman lamented only half-jokingly to her mother, "Oh mother I can't bear the idea of losing another sister! how can I do without her dear society?" It was common talk. A sister or daughter marrying was "lost," and one of the promises men usually made was that they would neither forbid long visits nor, if possible, live far removed from the bride's family.[101]

Before concluding with a look at the more personal meanings the planters might fashion from courtship, we must take stock of the ritual's social dimension. Planter-class courtship was collective and open, even public, across a wide range of settings and expressions. Its distinctively southern character has important implications for our view of love and marriage in the antebellum South. From the first group meetings and displays of compliment and favor, through the formal exchange of correspondence leading either to an engagement or a break, southerners sought love and its meaning with constant reference to a set of consciously shared values involving class and family. At every stage of the cycle they felt themselves to be on display, and at no stage was it either easy or fitting to exclude others from involving themselves in love's progress. Despite conflict, family members could not appropriately be excluded for "meddling" or otherwise being interested. Courtship made love a matter that reached beyond the lovers, and the ritual taught youth to see a close relationship between personal desires and a general well-being as defined by their class. It was a relationship that inevitably lent broad, social proportions to the plans and wishes of individuals, reinforcing their sense of legitimate mastery.

At every stage, lovers show again and again in correspondence a common understanding of courtship as an emotional experience tied to considerations of social class. Indeed, correspondence itself represented a social as well as personal commitment. Though "affectionate" has been used to describe the style of nineteenth-century courtship and marriage, "affective" seems a better (if rather bloodless) term; for as we have seen, feelings of all sorts were significant, not just warm and caring ones. Shaped by ritual, feelings *explained* things. Lovers learned to prize each other emotionally for qualities that referred back to their distinct social world: fidelity when tempted by the many master-class opportunities for the indulgence of vanity or deception; singularity amid a hierarchy of others; and suitability when measured by the social duties of a sex's sphere. By the same token, love failed or was betrayed by the falseness, ordinariness, and idiosyncrasy in tension with these ideal qualities. Thus the pivotal experience of courtship, and the nature of sexuality itself, were joined to specific class values associated with the display of mastery. And not unlike the excesses of the affair of honor, the extremities of courtship could lead youth into confusion over just how substantial all of the gestures and words actually were. Was the point of it all to appear, or to be? And if mere appearance won the mate and the applause of family and friends, was there any harm done to the general order of things?

These southern patterns qualify the view that nineteenth-century American courtship was increasingly marked by autonomous couples choosing to marry for love. The emphasis on autonomy seems misplaced in a ritual that owed so much to family, friends, and obvious social values. The southern elite safeguarded its peculiar interests by making romantic love inextricable from social order. Love could not become an individual's quest for a separate haven, as it was becoming in the North, if the planters' sense of society was to be well served. Moreover, as we have seen, the planters' courtship combined romantic love with the traditional concern for wealth and kinship. In this regard, too, the view of antebellum courtship as based on feeling should not lead us to conclude that other considerations had lapsed, particularly for the southern elite. If anything, the new emphasis on emotion served to deepen and extend the importance southerners placed on all of the social aspects of courtship, including calculations of family interests. Fathers and especially mothers were part of the shift toward feeling, adapting their demands of their offspring to romantic forms; parental authority proved flexible enough to reason from feeling as well as from interest. The emphasis on feeling permitted the web of family relations to draw more closely around two youths as they moved toward making a new family of their own.

Love and Biography: Three Courtships

Each couple had to sort out the ritual's feelings and consequences in their own lives, and it is the personal texture of obligation and desire fashioned from courtship that deepens our understanding of the unique importance accorded gender in the planter class. This chapter concludes, therefore, with three courtships shaped by the questions of identity and intimacy raised by the ritual. In the first, a young man claims his sphere; in the second a young woman encounters hers; and in the last, a South Carolina couple moves beyond theirs.

On its surface, the Georgia courtship of Henry Harford Cumming in 1823–24 appears uncomplicated and quite successful. It resulted in a marriage that lasted for forty years, producing eight living children and a helpmeet relationship. But a closer look at Cumming's courtship letters reveals him discovering some unexpected things. Working to win his lady, Cumming found himself learning about being a man. Intending to write courtship letters for his sweetheart, he found himself writing about himself. Neither outcome was necessary to the success of his suit, perhaps, but both taught him indelible lessons about the strategies of the heart.

In his letters to Julia A. Bryan, Henry Cumming displayed his accomplishments in fine style. He made puns and presented elegant compliments in the best oblique, powerful manner. He addressed her in the third person, and made certain to ornament feeling with general observation and literary allusion. He bent his every effort to "occupy an important place in her esteem." And although Julia responded (sometimes, however, permitting a line or two to do the work of a letter), Henry began to feel thwarted. Julia avoided setting a wedding date even after they had declared their love for each other and secured family approval. She was nineteen years old, he twenty-four; what reason was there to hurry? Marrying too hastily, she said, would be "consenting to make [my] self miserable." She even referred to the wedding day as the "day that is to bring evil" upon her. Henry was first puzzled, then annoyed; it seemed, he told her, "that while you are increasing my happiness, you seem to *yourself* . . . to be in danger of diminishing your own."[102] He kept up the pressure of his campaign, determined to create love out of opposition. His letters to Julia began to repeat conversations they had had, going back over ground that he refused to concede. As a wedding day, he recalled suggesting " 'some day in the last week of January [and] to this you replied 'No.' 'The first week in February?' 'No.' 'The Second?' 'I don't know.' 'The fifteenth of February?' 'No.' 'The sixteenth?' 'No.' 'The seventeenth?' 'Oh, I don't know.' 'Shall it take place between the 15th and the 18th?' To this you replied 'Yes'—'Well'—'If you please.' "[103]

Along with attempts to lock Julia into her own words, Henry continued to persuade her by writing eagerly of the love they would share. Although his letters were within proper bounds, Henry encountered resistance here as well. As the months passed, he perceived Julia shrinking from an intimacy that was not only a "necessary" part of his happiness but of hers as well. She, however, continued to remind him of her worry over "some things that must *necessarily* occur in the untried situation" of marriage. At times Henry tried to make light of sexual fears by joking, for example, that "we might occupy adjoining houses arranged so that we might just *see* each other all the livelong day and then *sigh* away the night. . . . For tho' young Leander did nightly cross the raging Hellespont to reach his dear Hero . . . 'twas surely only that he might *see* her." At other times, however, Henry was greatly distressed over what he felt was her lack of interest in his feeling and all that it implied. She was altogether wrapped up in her own world with its own images, he complained, scorning "such a '*milk and honey*' thing as a *love-letter*" though continuing to accept his. "I will not, for a moment, allow myself to believe that it will not give you *pleasure* to [write]," he told her. To believe otherwise would leave him "on a sea of anxieties and doubts."[104]

Neither Julia nor Henry considered these exchanges as a prelude to ending their courtship. Letters continued to be exchanged, occasional meetings brought them together, and friends and family went on supporting the match. But the struggle between them, however much a part of their love affair, began to influence the way Henry wrote to her and perceived himself. The more he fell into love, and the more he encountered the strangeness of her likes and aversions, the more Henry felt himself drifting apart from his accustomed life. She made him feel, he told her, "the necessity of appearing in a borrowed character." He was sure neither what this character represented nor, indeed, what it had to do with the man he thought himself to be. His "extravagant protestations of affection" to her began to frighten himself as well, and he resolved to control his "unmanly bursts of feeling." He believed that this behavior is what she wished and promised, "I will not again play the Baby as it seems I did." He placed the whole affair into her care, asking her to give him the "means for making me more like the ideal personage you prefer. . . . I am still young and flexible." But at the same time, Henry wrote of his manliness in a surer way, telling her that perhaps she already had an ideal lover: "a venerable but still vivacious old gentleman" who would be sexually unthreatening and content "to permit you to rule." Gradually Henry's letters shifted to a discourse on manhood, especially his own. Did she think him too sensitive? Well, perhaps he was. On the other hand, "Perhaps you are afraid of *touching* a *heart* already too tender. If this be the case you mistake me much—I have far more of the 'sterner stuff' in my nature than you are inclined to think." Pursuing an ideal Julia, Henry ran up against the real one and encountered, to his surprise, vexed questions about his own nature. What ought a man to want, and what sort of heart ought he to have? [105]

In the fashion of most courtships, clear answers were not forthcoming. Nevertheless, Julia Bryan and Henry Cumming were married February 24, 1824, at Rotherwood plantation near Mount Zion, Georgia. What did Henry Cumming believe his new wife had shown him? What did his courtship finally contribute to what he once called the "love-policy" behind his desires? It had to do with power and its uses in love—the mythic power of romance and the quite worldly powers of the sexes. In looking at the quality of his manliness Henry Cumming claimed a married man's sphere. It was a territory of compromise but also of sure identity. He wished to please Julia and "I submit myself to your guidance," he wrote her; but only "so far as a *man can submit.*" Their contest had not drained away affection and sexuality (he still warmed to "a 'sidelong glance' from an eye like Yours"), but Henry came to perceive that their love was in fact founded in a "singular union of opposing feelings" which mystified him as it drew him on. Though sometimes he regretted the conflict of their temperaments, when one or the other of them had to play the "base strings of Humility," he also confessed to a "thrilling sense of delight" in those differences. He was describing the male sphere from within, defining it by its collision with the female. As he adjusted his own needs to fit the new "untried situation," Henry created a new self-image as well. Opposites and oppositions of all kinds which clarified his manhood would not have happened without her. "It must be admitted," he told Julia, "that you have managed me admirably well." He became dependent on her "mingling the moral sweets and acids" in their relation "as to produce by their union a very 'delectable" kind of beverage." Henry Cumming drank deeply, and friends agreed on his wedding day that the young man, soon to become a successful lawyer, planter, and politician in Augusta, had chosen wisely and courted well.[106]

The courtship of Penelope Skinner shows how personal meanings agitated by the ritual lay beneath the calm, social surface of a companionate marriage. When Penelope wrote her older brother Tristrim in the early spring of 1840 to tell him that she was to be married and that her fiancé "is devotedly attached to me and I to him so we can get along," she seems to have been about to embark on a mature, sensible union.[107] Yet a closer look at her courtship suggests much more about the emotional underpinnings of such marriages at a particular point in a woman's life. Penelope's romantic alternatives were channeled by both Tristrim and their father Joseph Blount Skinner, and her situation as a recently "finished," nineteen-year-old woman isolated in her father's house contributed to the meaning marriage came to have for her. In courtship, Penelope like many women first gazed upon the limits of feminine influence.

Joseph Skinner had established himself as an important planter near Edenton, North Carolina, before the birth of his only son Tristrim Lowther in 1820. Skinner emerges from his letters as a blunt, outspoken paterfamilias of the old style, and in the older fashion he sent Tristrim to school in Philadelphia at age fourteen. Penelope was not sent North to be "finished" but was enrolled in a much-admired female seminary in Hillsboro, North Carolina. She returned from her schooling to the plantation where she became mistress of her father's house. Indeed, it was a household, not a family, that she had a sense of mastering; her father was often absent on planting business, as was Tristrim. In some ways, Penelope was satisfied to return home, relieved that she no longer had to write her brother in academic French or stare at the Hillsboro countryside. In other ways, however, she longed for her seminary friends. She missed the female intimacy punctuated by the excitement of shared activities and hopes. Romance and love were frequent topics in her letters to Tristrim. Even before leaving Hillsboro, she wrote to him about marriage and about the courtships of her friends. She was straightforward and not shy. She was looking for a lover, and she felt she could choose. "I cannot see anyone to suit my fancy and beaux are not *very* scarce with me," she wrote Tristrim. "Do not tell if I tell you something. I refused three or four a week before last. So you see your little sister is not forgotten in the crowd." Success for Penelope was success in love, obvious social success "in the crowd," and her last weeks in the academy were keyed to a high pitch of romantic anticipation. She and her friends were preparing to leave the world of school, and marriage and men were thick in the air. "A lady told me the other day she expected I had had more offers than any other Lady in the state," Penelope told Tristrim. "I said nothing but thought it very probable."[108]

Once home in Edenton, however, Penelope could write of little else than pacing around the empty house and of happy times recalled and wished for. She made sly, sometimes cutting remarks about her father who had become a surprisingly watchful gatekeeper despite his frequent absences. The young woman was wistful in her letters to her brother, and maternal. She advised him on his social contacts, told him to study diligently, and remember her to his male friends "when you go to see the girls." When a former beau turned up in Williamsburg, Penelope urged Tristrim to meet him: "I know you would like him he is such a favorite of mine. Notice if you see him if he has my ring on. I fear he has forgotten me by this time."[109] By the autumn of 1838, now nine months home, Penelope spent entire days in melancholy dreaming, broken only, it seemed, by letters from women friends engaged to be married. Her discontent peaked in the winter of 1838 when, alone in the house for hours, she wrote Tristrim:

> I really feel so wretched that I know not what to do. Father is so strict and particular that the young men will I fear soon begin not to come here at all. I do my best to make them spend their time pleasantly but he is as cross and crabbist [sic] as it is possible for anyone to be and insists on my being so—but no, the crosser he is the more agreeable I shall be. He even says that they ought to entertain me and that I must sit still and listen to them but it has ever been customary in my day for persons to entertain their visitors and I shall do it to the best of my abilities in spite of all he can say or do—for at times he is unreasonable and that everyone knows. But I suppose I must not complain— the next eligible offer I have I am gone, for anything would be better than this dull gloomy place.[110]

Quite unlike her father, and stifled by him, Penelope believed that courtship was a matter for her own abilities and feelings. Courtship "in my day" should offer more than an opportunity to sit by passively and hope for the best.

Penelope's struggle to control her own affairs was joined in the winter of 1838 when she allowed James French to ask her father for permission to court her. She probably saw the contest ahead; in any event, she knew enough to try to enlist Tristrim's support. She wrote him in confidence that "I am partially engaged to James French—papa seems quite pleased with the match—he is a fine fellow [and] you would like him." She cautiously added, "If we are married at all I think it will be in February, provided Pa is willing." And, ever the excited purveyor of family romance, she asked her brother to "find out from Cousin Barbara how she would like to have me marry Mr. F." The engagement was "partial," of course, because Joseph Skinner's approval had not been obtained, and had Penelope known of her father's letter to Tristrim four days earlier she would not have been so sanguine. Writing "in strictest confidence," the elder Skinner observed that French ("whom you saw at the Springs") had "paid a visit to your sister, and had mentioned to me his intention to propose himself to her." Joseph wished to keep a short rein on the affair, and asked his son to make inquiries into French's reputation. His instructions were model lessons in male duty, combining paternal watchfulness with a delicacy always present when one man probed the character of another. "[Y]ou can inquire . . . by merely observing that your have *heard* he had been at my house and there would be no impropriety in asking about him," Skinner wrote his son. "Maybe some of your young acquaintances in college may have heard or know something about him. . . . [N]obody shall know what you write to me, not even your sister. I must make up my mind, and you must be *free*, frank, and *full* in all you know or can hear."[111]

Penelope challenged her father for Tristrim's support in the ensuing investigation of James French's character. The men spared no effort to obtain estimates of French's morals and prospects. A few face-to-face meetings between the suitor and the father evidently produced more tension than clear air, however, and by late January 1839, Penelope no longer supposed her father pleased by French. "Poor man," she wrote of her suitor, "if he ever gets me he will be worthy of me for he has suffered enough for my sake." Sometimes Penelope seemed on the verge of resigning herself to her father's control, as when she told Tristrim to "not let my wishes prevent you from saying all you know [to father], I know there is nothing but disappointment in this world." Forced to await the outcome of the men's negotiations, she nevertheless tried to ease some of the pressure on Tristrim and assured him, "You are a good fellow Brother." But Penelope also fought for French, faulting her father for caring too much for "what the world has to say about me or my affairs. I cannot please the world, nor do I care to do so." Her courtship, she insisted, should be ruled not by opinion but by her personal happiness. She told her father as much, and took every chance she could to counter his opinions. When Joseph wrote Tristrim that French seemed "too much pleased with himself, to please others," for example, adding that the suitor "has given a very flattering account of himself," Penelope caught her father's letter before it was posted and wrote in the margin: "[French] has also told his faults—which he has of course as well as others."[112]

But despite Penelope's efforts, and despite French's own marshaling of friends and references, Joseph Skinner stayed against the courtship. It is not clear why. Nothing that Tristrim discovered yielded any sure reason to reject the man. In fact, several friends touted French's "*integrity* and *honor*," and even Tristrim ventured once that Penelope "loves him very much." It seems that Joseph, and ultimately Tristrim as well, were put off by what they took to be French's vanity and his "not . . . having more than his share" of intellect. In any case, when Penelope wrote her brother dejectedly in March, "Well, I have discarded Mr. French," both Tristrim and their father approved. "Pa is delighted at the news." she confirmed bitterly. For his part, Tristrim wrote Joseph that he was "very glad to hear" of Penelope's rejection and that "all her friends here expressed their satisfaction as soon as they heard it." Penelope herself had to act to end the suit, but it is clear that she was hustled toward her decision by family and friends.[113]

From here on, Penelope's courtship story was shaped by her disappointment in the French affair, her nearly frantic efforts to be rid of her father's house, and her increasingly critical observations about men in general. Together these mapped the remainder of Penelope's life as a single woman. Even as she mourned the loss of French she cast about for someone else, and her conflation of romantic love and a desire for freedom from her father remained at the center of courtship's meaning for her. Even though Tristrim had come out against her wishes in the French affair, Penelope continued to enlist her brother's help. "Who is Judge Christian attentive to at present[?]" she asked him. "Do you think I stand any chance?" At this point, the spring of 1839, Thomas Warren, a medical doctor in Edenton, entered the picture. Warren was one of the men to whom James French had appealed as a character reference. Now Warren made his own case, cautiously at first, by spending more and more time in Joseph Skinner's house. In the midst of lamenting her isolation, Penelope observed in April that "Dr. Warren is almost my only *constant* visitor. He enables me to spend many an hour agreeably which would otherwise hang very heavily upon my mind." The hours spent with Warren helped her to keep her promise to her father not to see French, though the latter attempted to call on her. "He could not believe it possible," Penelope remarked after one of French's letters, "that I should turn him off." Her resolve was as strong as her discontent, however, the struggle giving her a new strength of will. "Mr. French has been here again," she wrote Tristrim, "But I sent him sailing and hope never to see him again."[114]

Throughout the summer and fall of 1839 Penelope continued to receive Warren but at some point also became interested in a Mr. S., a man met at a resort and popular with her friends, who soon dominated her reveries. There were new difficulties, however. Penelope was kept waiting on more than one occasion for his letters. Joseph Skinner was skeptical of Mr. S., and Penelope once again faced a courtship transformed into a test of wills and a possible break with her father. Disappointment layered disappointment, and by January 1840 Penelope was writing in a different tone of her love life: "I think it is time for me to take it in hand." When she once again did not receive an expected letter from Mr. S., she reacted with wounded pride ("To think that *I* should have been disappointed") and a growing skepticism of men in general. Men probably were untrustworthy and love quite likely a chimera; yet perhaps marriage would put both in their place. Ending her uncertainty as an unmarried daughter became her first goal. "I declare I am pretty miserable and have a strong notion of marrying Dr. T. W.," she told her brother. "What do you think of it[?] If I marry him I will go away from here to live and never come back again." Penelope wondered if her father would approve of Warren and believed that if she married against his wishes he might even cut her off from her inheritance. She kept her lines open with Tristrim, telling him that "I know you would help me when you become Master of Ceremonies here."[115]

By late January the "rascally" behavior of the silent Mr. S. led Penelope to write him off and reflect on how in the past year Thomas Warren had "behaved so handsomely even when I had injured him so deeply." Looking back on her courtships over the past eighteen months, the young woman began to see her situation more clearly and pare down her romantic expectations until they became a quite manageable cluster of companionate qualities. "Indeed I love him more than ever," she wrote of Warren. "And if Father would give his consent I do not know what might happen." Warren, she continued,

is not rich, nor of great birth, but he is my equal and my *superior* in some respects. Everybody loves him. I have been anxious to marry a great man, one who would be distinguished in the world, more to please my Father than myself. So I gave up on one whom I loved devotedly [i.e., French] for one whom I admired and who I knew would please my friends [i.e., Mr. S.] and now see what it has all come to. The most distinguished men do not make the happiest husbands by a great deal, neither does wealth for I have that and am not happy.[116]

Penelope began to understand her story. Her quest for a lover had become a fruitless search for a great man, whether in her father's terms or love's. And however much she remained bound by the feelings of family and friends she strengthened her own critical perspective as well; Warren, after all, was her superior only in some respects. This constellation of impulse and intention was integral to her marriage to Warren in March 1840. Writing Tristrim that she had decided "to become Mrs. Dr. Warren," Penelope repeated that she was "heartily sick and tired of the life I lead, it is too dull and melancholy. Therefore I have come to the conclusion to be married and that speedily. Pa also seems quite up to it." The ambivalence of marriage and "greatness" was strong in this letter, too, as was her sense of being a lover on display. In her marriage, she admitted to Tristrim,

> I know I am going to do nothing brilliant or in any way calculated to make a show, but I hope to be happy and that is all I ask. . . . Dr. Warren is thought a very fine young man by everyone. . . . He is also one whom I know will put up with Pa's queer ways and that is a great matter. Everyone knows I have had greater offers as it regards wealth and distinction, but that is not all in this world. He is devotedly attached to me and I to him so we can get along. I will leave you to make all the show that is required to keep up the *family greatness.*[117]

It turned out that love was *not* all. Her fiancé was a fine man with whom she could get along, but neither Penelope nor anyone else felt that love had triumphed. Her courtship had pushed love from the foreground of her life. Yet, if not bliss, did not Penelope achieve a "good" match? She seems filled, in the letters just quoted, with the wisdom of a sensible, companionate marriage. Attentive to family, cognizant of her social place, and aware that a man's social agreeableness outweighed intimate charm or greatness, Penelope doubtless would have had the approval of moralists Hester Chapone or Virginia Cary. But such approval misses entirely the personal meaning of this sensible marriage. It misses the effort involved in carving a niche in the woman's sphere. Amid the push and pull of romantic love, the demands of father and brother, and the sense of being isolated on display before men and "everyone," she made a decision that held all at bay while she changed the most pressing circumstance of her life. She was ready to give up girlhood and be a married woman not because she loved, but because the time had come to mark out the first circle in the woman's sphere.

This chapter has argued that courtship, in bringing the sexes together, traced a distinctive, lasting pattern of attraction and alienation between them. Passing simultaneously, and with tension, through the social cycle of courtship and through an inward search for meaning, elite southerners built their personal sense of the sexual spheres. But it should not be concluded that intimate companionship—a trusting fa-

miliarity and delight in personal qualities—never happened in courtship. Some lovers (relatively few, it seems) shaped the conventions of
love and gender to permit intimacy. Rothman, in her study of northern
courtship, found that lovers greatly valued candor for "the counter-
weight it provided to the idealization inherent in romantic love. Openness would ensure that a lover was loved for himself or herself."[118] But
among southerners openness not only threatened the shared sense of
certainty found in the sexual spheres, it threatened the social order
founded on gender division. Candor in this society was far more problematic. It might pass too swiftly into confessions which would sweep
away the social orderliness protected by ritual along with love's personal illusions. Courtships that took this risk, however, reveal something more about the personal course love might take. The 1859 courtship of James H. (Harry) Hammond, Jr., and Emily H. Cumming was
one such courtship.

Although their families had been acquainted for many years, Harry
and Emily did not begin their romance until the early spring of 1859
when Emily was twenty-four and Harry twenty-six. Emily was living
with her parents in Augusta, Georgia, and Harry was about one hundred
miles away in Athens, where he was a professor at Franklin College.
Harry's early letters to Emily were careful second drafts, written in an
unusually fine, spidery hand for a man, full of the suppressed emotion
typical of a new courtship. But Harry possessed a literary sense which
soon went beyond convention to an earthier, plainer style. A single example of an early letter manifests his romantic yet personal voice:

> Ever since coming back from Augusta, I have been taking all the hol-
> iday I could to think over and congratulate myself upon the pleasant
> hours which your charity allowed me to spend in your company
> while I was there. I have been eating your candy. And I have been
> reading the novel (Kingsley's) you lent me. . . . You will pardon me
> . . . for expressing the overflowingness of my gratitude to you. In-
> deed so much has this feeling taken possession of me that I more than
> once had a mind to turn down this page of my heart keeping there
> what was already written on it and filling the other side with alto-
> gether new characters.[119]

Alluding to "this feeling" is enough to announce his love, yet his indirec-
tion is not coy. He mixes the tropes of love (the "pleasant hours," the
"pages of my heart," her "charity") with solid, direct images ("I have
been eating your candy") in a way quite unusual in a budding courtship. He closed this letter by wondering whether Emily, like himself,
had noticed two sorts of people in the world: the sort who busily "improve" everything and the sort who have a "buoyancy and cheerfulness" that make "your blood warmer, and your eye brighter." His

wondering aloud, of course, is a variation on courtship's indirect form of address, for clearly he means to say that she is the second sort, buoyant and warm. Yet in this letter, the distance such rhetoric creates serves to sharpen the closeness he wishes her to feel rather than to alienate feeling altogether, as so often happened. Without being too familiar, his early letters prefigured intimacy by not confusing the rhetoric of love with whatever else love might promise.

This is not to say that Emily and Harry were not often caught up in conventional expressions and swept away by the possession-and-loss language of romance. Just before their formal engagement in July 1859 Harry in particular strayed from his plain style into florid pleas for her to command his life through love. The "fate of our love," he wrote, "is, happen what may, *wholly in your hands* and at your disposal alone." Sometimes he appointed her his queen, after the fashion, so he might tease her about the "severity you are pleased to treat your humble and much enduring subject." At times Emily answered in kind, flirting with him by describing belles of her acquaintance who might interest him and asking him whether he did not rather prefer a woman "so 'coquettish' and so graceful, and witty, too." And even his proposal of marriage can be seen as entirely, if movingly, conventional, "Emmy . . . let me give not only the next afternoon, but all the afternoons and days of my life to add what I could to your pleasure." Nor is it to say that the two of them did not find themselves in conflict over many of the same issues as other lovers. For a time, religion was a difficulty between them. Harry doubted that she found him religious enough and yet pressed her to join the Episcopal church, saying only half-jokingly that "it would cause me more pain than you can imagine to hear of your being Baptized or anything like that." More frequently, they fell out over letters. The usually patient Harry, who began most of his letters with a scene or a story, opened one October 1859 letter with a slap: "Your excuse for not finishing the last page of your letter astonishes me. I have written you every day until yesterday and then failing to hear from you I restrained myself." Emily became angry with him in turn, and did not write or else told him very little of what she was doing. Distance between them, and the words to span it, were central. He once despaired, for both of them, "Shall I ever learn to give myself such expression as will translate my feelings justly?"[120]

In this way they were, as much as any young couple in love, exploring courtship for its limits and bonds. But they achieved more. In style and in content, their letters consistently cleared new terrain, allowed them to keep what they had and to discover even more. It is finally impossible to say why they were able to do so, but certain conditions of their lives hold part of the answer. Unlike many elite southerners,

Harry and Emily shared something of work. Both were teachers, and although her home tutoring of Augusta students was different from his academic career, their letters show that they had much in common by way of anecdote and observation. She could understand his accounts of student tricks and muddled lectures and he could appreciate her desire to turn her teaching into work as an "authoress." Both were offspring of harsh, self-made planter-class men. Long settled into his paternal sphere, Henry H. Cumming was a force in Augusta politics. Harry's father, James H. Hammond, was a formidable figure in South Carolina politics and planting, and a daunting figure at home. Perhaps Emily and Harry shared a sense of filial oppression that helped bridge the gap between the sexes. Harry was a quiet young man who walked with a slight limp and who considered himself a failure in planting (as his father did) and a nonentity in politics. Emily thought herself less than beautiful, physically frail, and constantly felt the strain of satisfying a stentorian father and a close, anxious mother. Raised to grasp greatness, both of them desired it very little.[121]

But their letters are the best evidence of their route to intimacy. Both used their letters to recall, in great detail, times spent together. Instead of waxing poetic or playing word games, they wrote of their walks, the Sunday visits, the evenings on the piazza of Emily's Augusta home where they watched the moon rise and talked about the deep heavens and the (perhaps) pointless strivings of mankind. They read the same things and read them to each other, and then they wrote both critically and personally about it. More than passing the time, their courtship reading became a threshold for their intellects and mutual tastes. "Read Paradise Lost if you have nothing to do," Harry wrote Emily in the summer of 1859, "and mark the best passages. I will get them by heart for you." She wrote back, "Aunt Sophia offered to lend me, Mrs. King's new book 'Sylvia's World.' But I would not take it." She did not approve of Susan Petigru King's "morale, as you put it," and decided that Harry would be better off to read "all the Carolina literature W. G. Simms and all." Harry was delighted to have her choose readings, and praised her for leading him back to Shakespeare.[122] Reading not only fueled their letters and kept a mutual project before them, it also reached deeper. Harry recalled Emily's "low sweet tones" as she read the Bible to him, and combined conventional images of love with personal memories to stitch past and future together:

> Do you recollect laying your hand on my hand as you [read?], as that touch thrilled through me it carried me back through years of my life to when I used to sit by mother during the long Sunday afternoons, and listen for the first time to those old, an[d] never to be forgotten

stories in the Bible, and when I would be lost in the pathos or the interest of the narrative . . . she would sometimes lay her hand upon my hand, I know not whether it was to give her authority to what she was reading, or an instinctive desire on her part, that I should realize that she under God was the source of those first impressions to me.[123]

Each wrote, too, about the emotional satisfactions of love letters. They wrote not to register letters sent and received, but of the tactile pleasure of correspondence. Emily wrote that her "letters have two meanings to me and I can connect no other with them, first I write them because it is delightful to feel that the words which I am one day scratching away here, are the next to bring to you, if not much meaning, and interest, at least a faint idea of how constantly I think of you, and love you, but most of all they mean that you will with this idea fresh in your mind, after reading them, sit down and with a few touches of that magic pen of yours, make me the most elated of little women." In the same way, Harry enjoyed thinking that his letter "is mine now, in my hands, but day after tomorrow it will be yours, and will tremble and bend in those little fingers. . . . It is a friend passive, mute, but infinitely obliging, it carries the woof . . . that binds the warp of our thoughts and feelings to the texture of our lives."[124]

Nearly all of Harry's letters, and most of Emily's, rely on physical description as the heart of emotional expression. They rarely let stylized rhetoric inflate their solid imagery. After an evening spent with her, he would immediately write to her: "As I stand here with my pen in my hand," about the time just passed, about the "night, and those dark eyes, and that soft silken hair, and the white dress, and all that there is of such mysterious and thrilling pleasure." He brought these images to the sharp focus of the present, imagining her in her world. "And you Emmy," he wrote in a typical passage, "have you too slept well? and are you now walking in this bright fresh morning?" He imagined her by her window, "your elbow on your knee, your left hand supporting your cheek." He wanted, and often received, what he called her "I and me" letters strong with images from her life that anchored his own view of her. Her letters permitted him to see, and he took what he could from all of them. "I can just catch a glimpse of you standing by Maria," he wrote of one letter, "and opening that yellow envelope, then a moment more at your writing desk, and even there the representation becomes dim, for I have never seen that desk, and then a curtain a hundred miles thick falls between us."[125]

This kind of reflective detail saturates their correspondence. Though not consciously thematic, it nevertheless gave their relationship its intellectual shape. The early sympathy between them ripened into intimacy by the summer of 1859 as they both sought a personal closeness belied by courtship games and display. They used typical courtship rhetoric only so they might move beyond it. Both lovers, for example, tempered flights of romantic wishfulness with clear, even critical appreciations of its dangers. Harry knew how imagination and the distance between them could easily lead him to an all-absorbing desire for the magical feminine. But he assured Emily that no matter how much he desired the femininity she represented, "I do not look upon you at all . . . as a mystery or as a myth." He would struggle with all his might, he told her on another occasion, against a time "when the object of our love proves other than we thought it."[126]

Along with precautions of this sort, Emily and Harry were often able to write lightly about the responsibility of being a man or a woman. They were able to put into words the ways in which their sex-bound obligations became misconstrued or ridiculous. Harry lightly diffused Emily's anxiety early in their courtship, for example, regarding the frequency of their letters. He wrote, "I never made a request that you would write to me once a week, did I? It seems to me the most improbable thing. I remember talking about it and saying something paradoxical. I don't believe I knew what [I meant] then, and I am sure I do not now. . . . Write to me whenever you can and will—let them not only be free gifts but gifts willingly and heartily bestowed."[127] As to the social duties that each met in their respective sphere, they could be wry and sympathetic—and learned to expect each other to be. She wrote of making the feminine rounds of visiting with her mother in a humorous vein many women would not have risked in a letter to a lover. "Pity me! Pity me!" she wrote,

> I am just starting out on a visiting tour, with my inexorable parent, who will hear of no delay, no reprieve, but moves sternly on. I have exhausted every argument that occurred to a distressed heart, suggested that every one would be at home [*sic*], that it was very warm, and very dusty, and finally entreated her at least to wait for one of my pretty days, but this she considered would be an indefinite postponement, and so it remains that I go.[128]

Returning that afternoon from her "martyrdom" of five visits, she knew that Harry "would have been proud of me, could you have witnessed my social achievements . . . , so happy, and successful was I in all my '*efforts*' to be pleasing and amiable." And looking forward to being his wife, she told him, "you know I can't talk and do not expect much from me, in that line." Harry, too, wrote of the "sacrifice" he made by attending gay season parties, forced to respond to the invitations of women of his acquaintance in Athens. The ladies took their daughters to some decorated home where "young men in black coats droop into the small hot rooms after them. It is a piteous spectacle. . . . Fruit cake and roast pig . . . feed the fire of life and love and wit that sparkles in the young ladies eyes, and comes sighing like a furnace from the young men's lips. I decline as often as it is prudent."[129]

Along with sharing an ironic sense of their duties, Emily and Harry also spoke of their felt deficiencies of character in strikingly open ways. Instead of appearing always in control, Harry more than once wrote of burning a letter to her after he became fouled in literary attempts "which spoiled the good sense of my letter, just as effectually as it would have been obliterated by turning my inkstand over on it." They revealed to each other the times when they were exhausted or inept with family and friends, and frequently were candid about their self-doubts. Emily wondered, for example, if he did "not wish that I was better tempered, and slightly more equable? That I had the lovely angelic temperament and disposition with which it is polite and orthodox to suppose women gifted? Well—I heartily echo the wish."[130]

More seriously, they resolved their conflicts by seeing their own expectations relatively; that is, not as absolute demands they had a right to make in a courtship, but as matters of temperament they would work to understand or change. They conversed. After Harry expressed his astonishment at her silence on one occasion, she was able, near the end of her long letter, to reply, "You were *right cross* to me, Harry . . . and you know I am not prepared to make any sort of allowance for any such weakness from *you*." Harry responded with an apology and an admission of having lived "selfishly drawn up into myself for years" so that his fear of losing her caused him to strike out at her. As a man, he explained, he had been self-important and guarded, "a stone, a block, and now that you have told this stone to live" he still did not quite know how. Emily's reply also centered on the content and conditions of their quarrel, rather than simply blaming or absolving, as many women felt entitled to do. Like Harry, she saw the dimension of gender and found herself also implicated. If he was a block or a stone, "You know . . . in the abstract how frail, and weak in mind, and purpose, women are, for the most part." She hoped he would be able, once married to her, to tolerate "the inconveniences of a particular daily exhibition" of feminine weakness. The theme of gender and temperament ran throughout their letters, moving past self-pity into conversation about their deepest doubts regarding the future. Emily, "so happy that I can venture to tell you what I have just written," confided her frequent "vexation" with her own life as a woman and admitted that on the "verge of a changed untried existence" of married life she was afraid. And Harry put into words his dislike of planting and indifference to politics, confessing in an extraordinary admission for a planter-class male, that "I look forward to no grand career. . . . In a word, neither my abilities, nor my taste, induce me to hope for anything but the most ordinary of lives."[131]

Harry Hammond and Emily Cumming achieved a rare view of themselves as embedded in their culture. Seeing the irony, humor, and struggle in the spheres of men and women, they arrived at an uncommon pass in courtship. They used the ritual to go beyond its divisiveness and alienation. He did not picture Emily apart in her sphere, but felt her within him as he taught his students, "looking at them," giving his own look a new authority. No epiphany, such times became part of his routine and his self-image. "I'm not over busy," he wrote one Tuesday morning, "and I feel solid, smooth and angular. I hope the boys will find me well defined." As marriage approached, they weighed the joint project of their life together, rare in courtship letters. They traded views "on the 'more prosaic side' of our lives" in matters of money, household, and obligations to family. They must demand equality from each other, Harry wrote her, and then backed away: "demand is not the word, I request it." They delighted in imagining life after marriage, in concrete images not abstract duties. Harry took note of her "complaint of the cold mornings; this is a point where we do not sympathize—they are new life to me." Their differences worked to mutual advantage, however: she would get all of the blankets and "I shall have the pleasure of wrapping you up." The fires of romantic love were banked into the more tangible warmth of winter evenings when "I will have my studies, you will darn stockings, and correct french exercises, and read the newspapers and the reviews, and wind your watch up."[132]

Though idealized in its own way, Harry Hammond's vision of domestic happiness must be seen as rather subversive in its southern context. It is a vision from inside the woman's sphere. Embracing it, Harry tucked himself away from the gaze of kin, competitor, and slave. What he wanted—and here he was an exception that underscored the rule— was to have his personal tie to Emily cut across the usual way the planters divided up the social order. He described their relationship as blurring the essential line between the sexes, a division on which rested every level of the social hierarchy. And in freeing his personal wishes from the usual masculine effort to keep up appearances, he challenged a key expectation that his society held for young men: the expectation that they would move out into the world and shape it by shaping their honor. In seeking intimacy with his wife, Harry Hammond necessarily turned his back on this dominant vision of reality. Instead, his courtship helped him to decide that reality was at home, and that even though this meant facing domestic risks to his happiness, married life's unmet needs and unmade beds, at least they would be risks of his own choosing.

CHAPTER III

COMING OF AGE:
DUTY AND SATISFACTION

In the affair of honor, the planters implicated the family in a man's good character, and in courtship they based new families on gender division and social unity. The aim of this chapter is to explore another ritual of worth, aspiration, and intellectual style, one that sustained the established planter family as both a field for personal meaning and an indispensable social instrument. At no point in the cycle of family life, not even in the face of death, were the planters more likely to reflect eloquently on family and culture than when children came of age. At no other point did family talk become so laden with expectations and directions, and the mails so thick with letters. Of course, youth's coming of age was not so prescriptive a ritual as either the affair of honor or courtship. But even though its events were more diffuse and its timing less strict, coming of age involved a heightened consciousness of ultimate values and a powerful language that importantly shaped the planters' sense of self, family, and society.[1]

Offspring leaving the home for school usually signaled the beginning of this ritual, and it was tightly joined to the onset of adolescence and its changes. Planter-class parents saw the combined challenges of schooling and adolescence as education in its broadest sense: leading youth into moral adulthood. This chapter focuses on education in this sense, as the structure of learning and growing up, as the proof and crisis of a family's worth. Coming of age summoned a discourse on family life rich with the terms of intimacy and authority. At the center of this change, of course, was the changing relation between parents and children. Generational satisfactions and conflicts became sharper and sometimes clarified in the coming of age. The emerging shift in relations between parents and children shaped academy curricula and routine which in turn helped to structure family relations in ways reflecting a common sense of growing up.

A necessary preface is a characterization of elite marriage relationships, in part because certain relations between the sexes in the relatively broad field of marriage were significantly different from those just examined in the narrow pass of courtship, and in part because the relation of husband to wife had much to do with the ways they advised their children and conceived of maturity. After looking at the personal texture of marriage, we will turn to the important values the planters discovered in family life and furthered through educating their children. Finally, we will consider schooling itself as the pivotal experience shaping one generation's link to the next, the rules and routines of academies and the nature of the discourse between parents and children. In a less precise but more spacious way, this discourse echoed the language of class, gender, and rural life heard in the rituals of honor and love.

Marriage and the Place of Love and Work

Even though marriage eased somewhat the intense ritual of courtship it did not foreclose sweeping characterizations of the marital relation. John Grimball, like many men, took regular note in his diary of his wedding anniversary and the "wife to whom I am devotedly attached." And, rather differently, many planters would have agreed with the wry worldliness of what one man intended as a compliment: "The riches and happiness of every married man depend on his Wife. She can wear out, ride out, and eat out more than any profession can bring in." An ironic misogyny was the occasion for jokes about the married man. As Louis Wigfall told John Manning in 1840, "John, my dear fellow, I fear you have ruined yourself by marrying. . . . Women are dangerous things to fool with—Woman ruined the first man—the wisest man the best man—the strongest man—(Adam, Solomon, David, Sampson) & I expect she will ruin the last man." Though women were less likely to make inclusive pronouncements of any sort in their letters, the literature—moral, fictional, popular—read by both sexes mirrored a range of sentiment about marriage, from the exalted to the wary. Moral advisers, of course, advocated the correctness of marrying and often its satisfactions. Novelists like Mary Schoolcraft fashioned stories in which marital happiness and respect were the touchstone of all human relationships. However, other advisers betrayed serious misgivings about marriage. The litigious style of works like Jasper Adams's text on moral philosophy tended to suggest that marriage was really like any other contract that regulated a conflict of interest. Many women's novelists, too, told stories in which there scarcely appears a good man or a union without turmoil. The breadth of the spectrum invites interpretation; general views of antebellum marriage reached all the way from holiness to farce and beyond to the most embittered sexual strife.[2]

Recent scholarship touching on southern marriage in the antebellum years, though not focusing as such on the surprising variety of attitudes, has begun to examine the changing nature of the marital relation. Bertram Wyatt-Brown and Anne Scott, among others, see a widening fissure between the increasing importance accorded to mutual affection and the tenacious claims of southern men on marital dominance. Jane Censer, on the other hand, has suggested that genuine harmony and respect characterized most planter unions. No one disputes that many planter marriages seem to have had ample room for affection, though Scott and Catherine Clinton have rightly emphasized the disorienting gap between romance and the "practical" compromises of marriage faced by women. But neither do most historians dispute that distinct patterns of conflict between wives and husbands existed as well, though some observers place the blame on a suffocating male dominance and others focus on the tendency of men to abandon the home, neglecting wife and children. Whatever the mixture of perceptions and motives, there is general agreement that whatever the opportunities for affection, southern marriage nevertheless was marked by a unique potential for an "emotional chasm between husband and wife," in Bertram Wyatt-Brown's words. It was a gap derived from the planters' double vision of marriage as both a unique opportunity for personal intimacy (whether desired or feared) and a reflection of a larger social hierarchy.[3]

The letters wife and husband wrote to each other about marital correspondence itself convey his view. One lasting sign of courtship's otherwise swift passage was the formal importance of letters, and themes of intimacy and authority jointly shaped epistolary practice in marriage. Many elite couples at first simply extended courtship conventions into their married life as witness to their mutual regard. Campbell Bryce typically praised his wife for "your uniform punctuality in writing" which, in his absence, evoked his domain "of home & family & friends." Another man, searching his own letters for signs of his authority, told his spouse that he discovered "much more uneasiness in writing to my wife than I used to feel in corresponding with my intended. . . . I mean anxiety that there should be nothing in my letter that might tend to lessen your regard for me." More frequently, however, separated couples wrote of how the act of writing invited intimacy. Elizabeth Perry told her husband Benjamin that regular letters were "essential" to their happiness and took their correspondence as proof that "our love *increases*, instead of diminishing." Writing about writing was a unique communion; letters themselves became the bond of love, whereas their absence instilled anxiety and misgiving. An expected letter that did not arrive, as one worried husband said, "assumes all the force and character of stubborn reality," a vacant field for the projection of his fears. Newly married couples were criticized for breaking off correspondence with friends and family, reflecting a fear that the intimacies of marriage might counter other obligations. "It seems," one woman wrote her friend now married some months, "that amidst the accumulation of *new duties* you have entirely forgotten *old duties*. . . . You cannot *now* expect . . . the privileges of a *Bride* from your correspondents." Not hearing from his sister since her marriage, Hugh Ball remarked with some annoyance, "I suppose she does not care a fig for me now."[4]

Linking marriage to the loss of other desirable relationships was a particularly strong theme in women's letters, especially early in a marriage. Margaret Manigault's picture of her daughter apart from family, "secluded from all her female friends" in a house with her new husband, is a typical image of the isolated wife. Though not more dependent than men on ties to family, women more often expressed their loss, perhaps because the sudden absence of family after marriage impressed women anew with the loneliness of rural life and the necessity of coming to terms with the duties of managing a household. Men could and did travel, often immediately after the wedding, and consequently had many more topics to write about. Though intense feelings of loss doubtless were not solely a southern phenomenon, the isolation of the plantation gave them a particular emphasis. In letter after letter, southern women wrote with great feeling about the irremedial loss of "society" that marriage brought about. As Maria Bryan wrote her sister Julia, "[W]e are most truly, *truly* sorry to give you up, and there was a day or two since delivered of a little dead-born wish that you might never have married but that we two have been nice, snug old maids living together." A few weeks later Maria's loss still pulled at her, "when I think . . . that you are now never to be with me, that you will by degrees become far more attached to other objects, and estranged from *me*." When she herself was married nine years later, Maria wrote bitterly of her husband's absence and her days spent "alone among total strangers."[5]

Recalling the anxiety of courtship, such expressions of loss were frequently counterpointed by no less deeply felt expressions of love. For some couples, the reserved and formal words of courtship, its elevated passion and emotional strain, became slowly transformed by marriage into a familiar affection. Often the change was not without hesitation, and one young man told his wife (after "reading and kissing over and over again" her letter), "I believe you can now allow me to say *I love you* without its introducing any of those unaccountable feelings." Earlier he had written, in a curious tangle of emotion, that he had to learn how to move from being a lover to being a husband, a difficult thing to do because "in spite of your being my wife I *can't help* loving you." Yet many men and women became as comfortable, if laconic, as the man who described an anniversary of his engagement as "the best day's work I ever did." A few couples wrote of needing one another sexually, of missing "the *pleasures* of natural and ardent love." Two months after their marriage, Kate DeRosset Meares wrote to her husband Gaston that she had "appropriated the *outside*, and *cooler* portion of the bed" in his absence, but "how willingly would I have jumped into a hot sea for one goodnight kiss from you." When Julia Cumming was away to the upcountry visiting her parents, Henry longed to "pillow my head on my Julia's bosom." At once conventional and intense, a South Carolina bride wrote to her absent husband, "I have no one to *caress* and be *caressed by*. . . . Is it not delightful to have a husband whose *presence* you *sigh* for, & whose absence you regret; whose *bosom* is your *pillow* at *night*, & whose arms are *ever ready* to protect you, who loves you *devotedly. It is delightful.*"[6]

Such unmixed professions of love were relatively scarce in letters, however. It was more common for declarations of affection to be mingled with expressions of longing and loss. Together the two themes formed the texture of marital correspondence. Elizabeth Perry, an unusually outspoken woman on all matters, told her husband Benjamin that "I *regret* your absences *now* much more than when we were *engaged*" and added: "I take no pains to keep my love within proper bounds; & have no scruples as to loving you too *much.*" Frequent separations meant that love was discovered by looking at oneself: "you can only imagine my feelings by your own" was a way to declare love reminiscent of courtship's distances. Love was a matter of imagination; it was constantly reinvented by partners in marriage. At home in Wilmington, North Carolina, Eliza DeRosset wrote to her husband of fifteen years, "How much I dearly love you is not easy to put on paper but how deeply engraven in the depths of my heart you only can know, by a corresponding feeling in your own bosom for the wife who adores you." And for many couples, long separations, with slow letters as the only lifeline, uneasily prefigured death. On the reverse of his wife's letter to him, Thomas Warren wrote to himself passionately, "This letter afforded much relief to my distressed mind . . . sustain her health Oh! lord for to me she is dearer than all things besides." Death might end a marriage, but the image of love endured. "And now she is gone," Samuel Leland wrote in his diary a few hours after the death of his wife.

"Hope of her living is at an end. . . . There she is, but Death reigns triumphant. . . . I cannot realize that *my wife* is *dead,* that her soul is in Heaven, but it is so."[7]

Expressions of loss and love flowed into the planters' more social views on marriage, too, especially when work was discussed. That plantation mistresses *worked,* and that political ambition inspired most elite men far more than planting, is generally well known but needs emphasis here as central to their vision of marriage. Women frequently were the daily managers of plantation affairs, and men handled the long-range business aspects and traveled about becoming politically effective. Women's work was exact and instrumental, hidden away from public life in a personal, rural timelessness; men's was volatile and formal, constructed from timed calculations and public words. Thus, as love in spite of loss was the substance of personal marital discourse, so the separation between spouses was seen as reflecting the basic social circumstances of marital responsibility. A distance between husband and wife became, quite problematically, a sign of a flourishing relationship.[8]

Therefore a couple often wrote about their work in ways that proclaimed it a joint effort yet emphasized its striking dissimilarities. For women there was no need to prove the importance of what they were doing, yet most wrote in ways that underscored their husband's absence. Recounting her dealings with recalcitrant slaves, Anne Middleton told her husband forcefully, "I am obliged to act promptly and on my own judgment now that you are not here." It was just as common for wives to write longingly, as did Eliza DeRosset, "I am lonely, lonely, only hard at work trying to work away time until you return." A man was apt to see such work as part of a mutual effort that he directed from afar, making the major decisions. One North Carolina woman was shocked when her husband suddenly sold their property because another profitable arrangement had come through while he was traveling about. Less dramatically, women often were simply puzzled by men's work. Able to write concretely about her own daily routine, Maria Bryan Harford could only tell her sister that she had "little, very little of Mr. Harford's society for he is entirely engrossed in the most perplexing business" that occupied his time with her, took him away from her, but that she could scarcely describe.[9]

Men themselves often had great difficulty putting into words what it was they did. Though some husbands obviously did not wish to take the time to explain the intricate business deals or politics in which they were engaged, many men attempted to explain only to write sentences knotted together by literary figures of speech. They wrote of their work as "imperative duty," as sacrifice, independence, and fatigue amid the "tumultuous uproar of the senseless multitude." Sometimes becoming particular about parties and politics, and occasionally expressing his worries and self-doubts, James H. Hammond was more inclined to write his wife in the voice of the ironic master yearning for his haven. "Notwithstanding the exciting business in which it is my misfortune to be engaged," he began one letter in 1834, "you are seldom absent from my thoughts, and many a sleepless hour I have spent thinking of you and my dear little boys. Kiss them a thousand times for me . . . and tell them I shall soon be home."[10]

Such utterances from one sphere to the other had their exceptions, of course. There were domestic men and a few political women. Doubtless some women would have agreed with Julia Cumming, who, apparently wishing to be alone, admonished her husband to go out and do his manly work in the world more often. And Elizabeth Perry, far from complaining of her husband's absence, drove him on into politics. She pushed him to be the entrepreneur of his own character, to "acquire reputation." She taunted him for being satisfied as "a *plodding Greenville Attorney*," and consistently defined his career interests as her own. "I can *never consent* to your leaving the legislature," she wrote. "The two reasons you give for wishing to leave, namely, love of home, & finding legislation hard, I cannot admit of, the first is effeminate, the second selfish." But even these women, in welcoming their husbands' absence, ended up furthering the profound separation between the sexes which lay at the heart of the working elite marriage.[11]

Education and the Hope for Family Unity

Tensions between the sexes ran so deeply in both the private values and public duties of marriage that typical moralist warnings like Virginia Cary's ("Conjugal love is too delicate in its texture, not to undergo a thousand violences") seem none too exaggerated. The intellectual acrobatics required of the planters to see separation as a sign of intimacy and hierarchy as the seal on mutual effort led most planters to search tirelessly for evidence that these things were so. Neither work nor the inner sense of love, but the family, was the chief evidence. And thus children, their growth into goodness and achievement through the care of parents, became the primary focus of the planters' attempts to join social order to personal happiness. It was not only a public ideal; the hum of hundreds of private voices combined to chorus praise of the family.[12]

Everyone had explicit family ideology to draw upon, in addition to inchoate experience. Jasper Adams's text on moral philosophy, widely circulated in southern homes and schools, was one such source. For

Adams, a family was founded on a "union of feeling and sentiment" which created a necessary calm at the center of domestic life. It was a calm not unlike an individual's clear conscience, without which everything else slipped away. Adams, however, was unable to say much about how to attain guiltless intimacy in the family. Instead, he discussed the organization of familial authority, and it is not surprising to find the father directing the harmonious group. In a formulation familiar to students of the American family, Adams portrayed domestic relations as a structure of reciprocal duties which implied that legitimate demands might come from all points in the family circle. He detailed parents' duties toward their children (to assure health; to teach manners, discipline, and scholastic study; to guide in matters of work and marriage, and materially to "outfit" them for a start in life) and children's toward their parents (to honor, obey, and to realize as far as possible parental expectations for their adult life).[13]

Although harmony was most obvious in this exposition of family life, the chances for discord were never far beneath. The value placed on reciprocal duties suggests the need for an independent check on paternal power, but Adams offered only a heavenly one. Thus the father's decisions essentially were arbitrary. The "quietness" Adams saw at the core of family life seems more than a little precarious in view of the constant tug and pull between family reciprocity and paternal authority. Relationships esteemed by society as "the most natural, the most permanent, and the most effective of good" were curiously subject to disorder. Indeed, Adams suggests at times that family life was beyond anyone's ability to control, including a father's, as bewildering domestic obligations "occur every day, and almost every hour of every day." The subtle and pressing arrangements of family life, Adams observed, were probably best understood not in secular, moral terms at all, but in a religious framework. His many quotations from the Bible were also present in the everyday expressions of parents intent on raising children, not on making moral philosophy. At the center of the ideological family was a kind of religious faith, one refracted by human affairs. As one planter put it, "To be religious you must be good, in all the relations of life, & do your duty [assigned?] you on this earth. We must controll the evil impulses & passions of our nature, & be kind to all. . . . We must learn patience & indurance & long forbearance, & be content with our lot on this earth."[14]

If such meaning and social purpose were to be understood in terms of family life, and family life itself understood in terms of relations between parents and children, then the most critical point in this equation was reached when children entered adolescence. This observation is not to imply that planters had nothing to say about the rearing of infants and young children. Planter wives and husbands pronounced on the merits of male or female children, discussed nursing and health, and frequently reported or inquired about the sayings and doings of their small offspring. But by far the most important words were uttered when children reached the age when they not only still depended on parents but also began to represent them in the world, and when they themselves could enter into a written correspondence with their elders, that is, with the decision of many parents to send their daughters and sons away for further schooling in the values and activities (including the writing of letters) that infused parental advice. Educational institutions, rather than a rigorous concept of adolescence, embodied the importance accorded this phase in a family's cycle, although some of the tensions associated with modern adolescence appear in antebellum southern opinion. One influential educator, for example, was expressing common knowledge when he called ages thirteen to nineteen "the rapids," and D. R. Hundley among other observers of southern society noted that teen-age boys (who, he noted, preferred to be called "youths") were often "impertinent [in] speech and coxcombical [in] behavior." Female moral advisers, as already noted, described moodiness and melancholy among teen-age girls. Even so, elite parents were more articulate about children going to school than about "adolescence" and, as Joseph F. Kett has suggested, thought more in terms of a child's approach to mature "independence" than his or her "stage of life."[15]

Youth leaving home, becoming schooled, and attaining adulthood thus became inextricable themes in the planters' most sustained reflections about the family. Of course the value of education was also seen as an *individual's* particular achievements in "training the body to healthful exercises, and elegant accomplishments, in cultivating and developing the mental powers, in regulating the passions." But these were firmly tied to the perceived rhythms of *collective* life, especially in terms of family. Francis Lieber typically described a teacher as one "called [upon] to bind and interlock one generation with the other by the transmission of truth and wisdom, and to evoke noble, pure, patriotic, righteous and benevolent feelings in the breasts of the young." Many parents were likewise moved to speak in the most portentous way about the cycle of the generations when their children moved out into the world. Paul Cameron wrote to his seventeen-year-old son Duncan in a style that numerous other fathers echoed: "My life is drawing to a close. . . . I hope my dear boy that you will do all you can to fit yourself to become the chief support of the family when I shall leave it." The advent of schooling signaled ties between family and the outside world, and not least youths' accession to elite power and position, and many a parent hoped to be able to reflect, as Thomas Ruffin did in

1865, that "enjoyment of the aged consists in the respect, reverence &
love of children & children's children. This is my joy; and, thank God! I
have it to the full!"[16]

Along with generational duties, the social obligations of the sexes
made up a salient theme in the planters' pronouncements on education. Southern women, of course, heard many of the same exhortations
as their northern sisters, exhortations pushed by a rhetoric at once
modest and highly charged. Women, as one popular educator wrote
with regard to marriage, "may be fitted to fulfil [*sic*] with honour to
themselves, and with happiness to others, the duties of a station for
which God created woman, and to which so large a proportion of our
sex is called." Like her northern counterpart, the young southern
woman was told that all eyes were upon her, and that her gentle firmness gave a tone to the people and events she encountered. But an elite
southern woman also heard words addressed to her alone. Slavery,
more precisely the daily presence of black slaves in a lady's domain,
displayed her accomplishments in a uniquely dangerous way. It was
woman's task to temper the worst effects of slavery on black people,
while at the same time preventing its "deleterious influence" from
spreading to the white family. It was a task at once urgent and disturb-
ingly abstract. Equally demanding yet elevated was the advice given to
young men. Though expected to be sober, courageous, and hard working like any American, the young southern man received advice that
subtly stressed his unique opportunities for self-ruin. Fathers impressed their sons with the combined power of their sex and race by
warning them against the social consequences of its abuse. Alone
among males, young southern elites had to beware the many opportunities to "spend your time in idleness . . . to spend your money in extravagance and dissipation," which would critically weaken society as
well as character. Gentlemen were exhorted in language that implied
they always were under the gaze of dependents and that a misstep
could mean more than mere personal failure. A man's full social authority was at stake. As one brother urged his younger sibling: "Keep it
habitually & always in mind that the foundation of all your present and
prospective happiness as well as usefulness & standing in society will
depend on the steady maintenance of a deportment regulated by principles of honor, of virtue, truth. . . . Never-never be seduced by any
alurements [*sic*] that the world can give to swerve [you] from duty as a
good man."[17]

Moreover, the particular duties of southern women and men, and
therefore their particular educational advantages and limits, were situ-
ated in a rural life praised by those who formulated education's deepest value. The ways of rural life presented difficulties never fully re-

solved, however, or even fully confronted. Caroline Gilman, for example, at times extolled the educational advantages of country life where "breathing space is given for the young pulsations of the opening feelings." But she also worried about the "danger of the aristocracy of solitude" which plantation life inevitably carried with it, and she at least once advocated an end to isolated home tutoring in spite of her scorn for the "paltry rivalry of schools." Similarly, D. R. Hundley's almost caricatured dichtomy of the Southern Gentlemen and the Cotton Snob oddly depicts the gentleman (who "almost invariably lives in the country") as a distant, colorless model of abstract virtue, whereas the snob is seen close up, powerful amid the activity of his busy social world. Though protecting morality, rural life might somehow sap the vitality of those who led society. Indeed, social influence was a problematic quality in a rural world in which the self-conscious social "events" of spas, visiting, and the hunt substituted for true social intercourse.[18]

As early as the end of the eighteenth century the broad values ascribed to the generations, gender, and rural society had begun to take a distinctly new institutional shape in the rise of regional academies. These schools, most of which boarded students in addition to taking on a few "day scholars," had their origins in boys' Latin grammar schools and in the itinerant, semi-institutionalized tutoring by successful individual teachers. Increasingly concerned that home education was not intellectually sufficient, many elite parents also supported institutions as a clear sign of class cohesion. Academies, especially after 1820, were organized by groups of local planters, financed by tuition and by the sale of shares or subscriptions, and sometimes chartered by the state. Planter trustees hired headmasters, approved curricula, established operating procedures and size of student body, and thus demonstrated a "public" commitment to formally educating their children. Though essentially ecumenical, some of the more successful academies were founded as arms of evangelical Protestant churches. Incorporated and unincorporated academies and boarding schools numbered in the thousands nationally by the 1850s and, particularly in the South, were evidence of elite position and power despite the fact that they developed unevenly, varied widely in quality, and frequently failed.[19]

Home education did not disappear, of course, especially for young children. One reason for the academies' uneven development was the lingering commitment to home schooling among many families. Even by the 1840s, a surprising number of the moral advisers read by the elite were warning against superficial "fashion" and lack of religious discipline in academies. Many parents would have agreed with the South Carolina woman who wrote of the comfort of having "your children educated under your own eyes, and to have them with you always." Parents also wrote of enjoying the companionship of a personable tutor as well as valuing his or her learning, and a few parents like Edmund Ruffin were challenged to experiment with pedagogy and curriculum. But the energy (and anxiety) of a Ruffin was relatively rare, and the glimpses we have of home schooling reveals it to have been indeed a slow business directed by family routine rather than intellectual goals. When Maria Bryan, for example, undertook the lessons of her niece and nephews over a period of two years, the letters of ten-year-old Alfred show a rather broad course of study which he seems to have found pleasant and not too taxing. "I study Ancient History and arritmetic [*sic*] and Latin and Geography and Music," one letter home began. "And Aunt Maria says that as soon as I get along in my other studies she will begin to teach me how to pronounce French. . . . Uncle has been reading *Nicholas Nickelby* [*sic*] to me and I like it very much." However, his lessons often were quite brief—an hour or two a day—relegated to the evening, disturbed by slaves, and interrupted by the preparation of meals. Once Maria discovered that her niece had been reading a novel for days instead of studying the Saxon kings of England.[20]

The haphazard nature of home schooling, coupled with the planters' desire for formal, visible institutions, served to persuade more and more parents to support academy education. By the later 1830s, academies' circular literature was making claims exactly suited to allaying parents' fears and tempting them with the organized expertise of institutions. For girls, academies would "distribute in their just proportions, the *useful* and the *ornamental*" through an experienced attentiveness few parents could achieve at home. For boys, academies offered tested, competitive programs "exciting to industry" and securing an all-important "improvement." Academy circulars echoed and re-echoed the point: no matter how good the southern home, it could not provide the academy's "constant supervision, salutary restraint, competent guidance and instruction, and affectionate intercourse." Youth was, in the words of one prominent headmaster, "the most critical period of human existence." It was the "great moral climacteric" few parents were prepared to meet. Moreover, academies increasingly traded on their function as college preparatory schools once university education took on new importance by the 1830s. It was in this decade that the elite began to stress "Southern education for Southrons," a home-grown schooling protecting a cherished way of life. As academies became more established and widespread, other reasons emerged for sending youth away, reasons that once again reflected unfavorably on the home. One postbellum student of women's education noted that the plantation's "occasions for despondency, discouragement, and all the temptations that beseige the home of a more favored class" were common reasons for boarding girls at school. Manipulative or erratic tutors, sometimes depicted as intruders in the home, were avoided by making use of an institution. Finally, there were reasons which had little to do with book learning. Some parents were relieved to send away a wild son or a morose daughter. And J. B. Grimball recorded in his diary that "my principal motive for sending Lewis from home is that the change of climate may make him grow, for he is exceedingly small for his age."[21]

Most academies drew students from local families, although a few took students from throughout the South. St. Mary's Episcopal school at Raleigh, North Carolina, the Salem Academy, also at Raleigh, the Montpelier Institute, Savannah, Georgia, and Madame Talvande's at Charleston, South Carolina, were renowned for women's education. For men, academies at Hillsborough, North Carolina, Barnwell, South Carolina, and Moses Waddel's at Willington, North Carolina, were popular. Outside the South, Madame Greland's school for girls in Philadelphia, and Madame Chegaray's in New York City, the Round Hill school for boys in Northampton, Massachusetts, and the male Flushing Institute on Long Island drew up to one-third southerners in the 1830s and served as models for smaller academies south of the Mason-Dixon line. Most students ranged in age from thirteen to eighteen and most academies enrolled from twenty-five to fifty students each year. Generally, academies held two five-month terms each year for an annual tuition fee ranging from 100 to 250 dollars. The fee covered room, board, and the basic courses: mathematics, history, rhetoric and composition, geography, moral philosophy, English literature, and modern languages, usually French and Italian. By the 1840s, Latin was optional in many boys' schools though still available in many girls'. Music and dancing were usually offered to both sexes for an additional fee, and girls might also pay extra for courses in embroidery, drawing, and painting. Some schools added surcharges for linen and bedding, and even for bed space, and others included these in the general fee. Parents were billed for paper, ink, supplies, and for damage to academy property. In short, even though they varied considerably in terms of the size, fees, and reputation throughout the antebellum years, academies increasingly assumed the responsibility for schooling and socializing elite youth and fought to hold it. The records of the Williamston Academy near Williamston, North Carolina, for example, reveal its struggle from the 1820s against the overconfidence of flush times and against periodic collapses at the hands of unwilling subscribers, drunken teachers, and violent students. Classes continued through 1866 in spite of "the advance of the Yankees . . . both by land and water." Schoolmasters and institutions that survived the war, often subsisting on payment-by-barter for food and shelter, were testimony to their social and intellectual durability.[22]

Almost everyone agreed that a teacher was the linchpin of an academy, though very little is known about the great majority of the women and men who did the work. Teaching, North and South, tended to be a temporary employment for young women before marriage and for young men before their bar exams. Although during this era increasing numbers of women were trained as teachers at such institutions as Emma Willard's academy in Troy, New York, they could find employment only in girls' academies in the South. Boys remained in the care of men. When a trustee of the Newbern, North Carolina, academy advertised nationally for a principal teacher, he received replies from most southern states and from Ohio and Connecticut. A wide variety of men offered themselves for the job: a veteran of sixteen years' teaching, a former principal, and a translator of Greek literature. But most were recent college graduates. Many applicants supplied letters of recommendation touting their academic attainments and character, one as "a *Southern* man." In general, a few young people clearly intended to teach as a career, but most employers and prospective teachers would have agreed with one young man in Oxford, Mississippi, who characterized teaching, "This sort of life may do for a year, but it won't do longer." For 300 to 500 dollars per year, the teacher kept order, taught eight to nine hours of lessons and individual recitations a day, answered parents' letters, and then moved on.[23]

This skeletal image of academy teachers is filled out by fiction and memoir in which the teacher, particularly a principal, emerges as a strong character in the lives of southern youth. Teachers, far more than ministers or governesses, appear frequently in recollections and stories as the most memorable adults apart from kin. Though many characterizations are stylized, the style itself is significant of what teachers imparted in the way of adult values and behavior. Two clear themes recur: the teacher as ruler and the teacher as loving parent, both of which spun scenes of gender and authority. Even after the passage of many years, remembered teachers took on the substance of values personified. The teacher as ruler often was recalled as being fair if not altogether wise. As one woman remembered a Miss Everston, "She was tall and slender; cold, quiet, severe, austere, and caustic are adjectives which the girls used in describing her, but they generally agreed she was strictly just, inspiring respect if not affection." Novelist Caroline Hentz portrayed a headmistress typical of many: "No Queen, surrounded by her court, ever bore a loftier presence or carried herself more royally, than [Miss Manly]. Certainly no Queen ever felt more proud of her subjects, or reigned with a more absolute dominion over them." Teachers themselves, however, emphasized their role as affectionate parent, and this theme, too, shaped the memoirs of their students. Joseph Cogswell was recalled as the emotional center of his schools. One alumnus remembered him as "the organizer, manager, and father of the community. His department especially was that of moral and affectionate influence, besides which he was head farmer, builder, gardener and treasurer of the place." Of another principal, a former student recalled, "How we loved and reverenced him! A young and very handsome man . . . [he] gauged the worth and extent of his scholars with a glance, and beneath the breadth of brow shone and sparkled his bright blue eyes with kind appreciation of our efforts to please him." Such descriptions combine the rhetoric of love with an image of a kind and wise parent; or, in a novelist's phrase, "the guardianship of a mother, and the tenderness of a friend." Uniting justice and love, teachers played an intense formative role in the lives of young southerners, many of whom for the first time transferred their feelings to an adult outside of family. Headmaster William Muhlenberg, for instance, queried his boys in Latin, rapping knuckles calmly, and yet walked about the corridors in creaking boots "that he might not appear to steal upon boys unawares."[24] And Mary Chesnut remembered Madame Talvande: she "had the faculty of inspiring terror," yet her authority permitted—even invited—a certain intimacy:

> We had opportunities of regarding her from various points of view. Different rooms in the house looked down upon her dressing room. So in warm weather, when open windows were a necessity, we saw her in absolute dishabille—her head tied up in a red bandana, and her torn and soiled dressing gown flying in the breeze. Slippers down at the heel, or kicked off.
>
> At ten every day she descended upon us in the school room. She advanced with airy grace and rapid pace; smiling, bowing, curtsying, flirting a gossamer handkerchief redolent of cologne.[25]

Such memories are more than colorful vignettes. They evoke the compelling personal relationships that made the academies effective. The view of Madame Talvande the airy lady, contrasted with Talvande the down-at-the-heels woman, only begins to suggest the many small ways in which academies gave elite youth a sense of appearance and reality, and how the general outline of their tuition, size, and history merely touches upon the ways in which they served elite imperatives of gender and class. Behind the walls in the daily routine was lodged the actual pattern of the coming of age. Academy routine, which became the core of a student's daily assumptions and habits, was the ritual of the institution. And in the written sources that reveal it, an anomaly appears. As might be expected, academic study took up most of each day; yet students, teachers, and the official literature of the institutions have less to say about classroom time than they do about other activities. It was the full social range of the sealed-in academy world that shaped youth to the most important obligations and gratifications of adulthood. Parents and teachers prized a familylike balance of authority and intimacy which gave isolated rural youth a sense of the *social order* and their place at its head.[26]

"My Dear Child," begins a letter addressed to new students at a North Carolina female academy. "You have left your home, your brothers and sisters, and your parents." But she should not despair, for the academy would be her world and she would learn to take pleasure in "this large family of which you have become a sister." Family rhetoric abounded in academy literature, and in daily practice as well. Like many other principals and teachers, Madame Talvande took a close, maternal interest in all of her girls, even the "Cynthias of the Minute"— those youths sent for only a few months' finishing. The colonels of boys' military academies likewise spoke paternally to their students, but rhetoric was not the only tool. New students were first impressed with the separateness of the academy world; like powerful parents, academy principals restricted students' movement, controlled their money, and dictated their dress. Walls, sometimes topped by cut glass or sharp stone, fenced in students and fenced out the world. Especially at girls' schools, visitors were restricted to one or two afternoons a week, and the permission of day scholars' slaves to bring them lunch only served to impress the boarders with their dependence on the institution. Packages, sometimes even mail, were inspected by headmasters, who also had the duty of periodically checking students' material possessions. Regarding *"Pocket Money,"* declared one 1840 circular, "there is very little use for this at the school." Parents were asked to send no more than twenty dollars' cash for each year. Uniforms were common, military dress or dark suits for boys, and some distinctive combination of color, hat, and ribbon for girls. In short, the material boundaries and accouterments of academy routine not only served to impress students with their being under supervision, but also established a set of common conditions and thus the basis of a common identity. On the student side of the line drawn between student and teacher was a consciously shaped equality unlike anything youths had known at home. The academy walls and grounds became their horizon, and when they moved beyond them on outings or drills, they moved together as a single body.[27]

Academies and a World Apart

According to academy circulars and descriptions, daily routine was structured by a regular course of classes and activities, and the memoirs of teachers and students testify that this was usually the case. For both sexes, the day typically began at 6 or 6:30 A.M. with prayers and sometimes a class. Breakfast followed an hour or so later, and then academic work filled the hours until noon when dinner was served. In some schools, an hour of rest followed and then two to three more hours of classes (and military drill for boys). Early evenings were given over to "exercise and amusement," followed by the evening meal at 7 P.M., and then individual study until 9 or 9:30. Bells or bugle signaled the activities, in the company of junior teachers or preceptors at the larger schools, often themselves recent graduates.[28]

For youths accustomed to roam at will on their parents' plantation, the full, structured days at the academy were a sharp change. Yet many students such as Egbert Ross at North Carolina's Hillsborough Academy seem to have liked the routine, finding it predictable, fair, and "very conducive to health." Of course it could be drudgery as well, and even some teachers complained about the long days, drill, and difficult students. Teacher Frank Schaller, also of Hillsborough, contemplated standing in the cold March rain with his young troops and wrote, "I wish it was Saturday again and the month of May had come." But academy routine seems to have been enjoyed most for its standards of decorum and personal appearance. William Muhlenberg was the model for many antebellum headmasters in constantly monitoring his boys' language and their table manners. Young women seem to have had their posture and gait forever under critical review. The fictional Miss Manly delivered a set of real orders to her charges, instructing them, "heads up—chins down—shoulders back—backs in—elbows close—and toes out. . . . In moving your elbows, avoid making a sharp angle, but form the curved line of grace in every motion." Such scrutiny was at once loving and demanding, and became part of girls' movement from class to dining room and then to bed. Most difficult was learning not to overdo it. Former teacher Louisa Tuthill wrote of the ridiculous girl who "looks in the glass forty times a day . . . and tumbles over on her face almost as often, trying to stand with her toes turned straight out." Almost no aspect of a youth's habits or person seems to have been beyond comment and instruction. Young Harriott Rutledge wrote of a teacher who told her students to trim their fingernails "round and not square." Apparently there was nothing cold or authoritarian about how such measures were usually given; but even in a kind atmosphere, the link between appearance and authority could not be mistaken. Coming of age meant learning how to display oneself with the right emphasis. Young Egbert Ross had learned his lesson: he wrote to his sister proudly, "The professors all appear to like me. . . . I have paid them a great deal of deference and the consequence is that they respect me for so doing."[29]

The occurrence of infractions or the breaking down of discipline also shows the significance academies accorded to outward bearing. Disciplinary measures were clearly set forth in most schools and were well known among students. At the first violation a student was warned, and at the second subjected to some sort of shaming: a public reprimand for boys and a seat on the "idle bench" for girls. Loss of free time or other privileges might follow, and then solitary confinement to a room, or at one school, to a space between two buildings. Suspension and expulsion were the last resort. Some extreme cases became the talk of the academy. Youths of both sexes occasionally ran away, and at one North Carolina school in 1829, a "deliberate conspiracy was formed among the larger boys" against the headmaster; church was disrupted, pistols drawn, and parents called in before it ended quietly. Such outbreaks, though rare, were only the most obvious instances of the academy's chief tension: in relying on highly structured routine yet rewarding individual achievement, the academy risked a particular crisis in authority. When students, especially boys, carried self-assertion beyond academic competition they quite easily ran up against one or another rule and raised an issue of contention. The academy set out to make boys and girls into masters, but it also attempted to restrain and channel them; small, daily contests of authority and self-control were common and reveal difficulties of combining personal assertiveness with class responsibility. "She is antagonistic in the highest degree," it was written of one girl. "But . . . let her see that Reason or Religion demands her submission, and she yields." Walter Lenoir's principal reported, "I am pleased to add, that he is getting rid of the *opinionativeness* which used to render his manners in the academy, especially when he committed a blunder in writing, not infrequently offensive." Whatever the praises sung to individual merit, the academy clearly supported collective order, measured by outward bearing, as a prerequisite to becoming adult.[30]

The main reason that the academy did not give way to this institutional tension was that the structured habits and behaviors shaped genuine emotional closeness among students and even between students and some teachers. Contributing to this closeness were the special celebrations and events during the academy year: the evergreens, candles, and music of Christmas, the parades and oratory of the Fourth of July, the soirees and exhibition drills. At these times, the academy's inhabitants felt its authority as a bond. Women recalled being ranked in order of height or age (or sometimes beauty) and then whisked through the streets as a single body to attend a soiree, under the gaze of citizens and boys from the local male academy. Boys gave public military drills attended by young ladies, and afterward a picnic brought them together. Consciousness of class as well as sex heightened these occasions. Mary Chesnut remembered balls at which the planter elite danced upon a stage and the others below. "How each . . . found its proper level I never could guess," she wrote. "I suppose we were hustled up on stage."[31]

Yet the way in which an academy was a world apart, and the often intense emotional warmth and shared identity it fostered, is best seen in the round of ordinary daily life. Of course there were cliques and jealousies which even young students recognized as colored by the assumptions of social class; but the strongest theme running through letters and recollections is one of safeness and delight. Caroline Hentz described her school's "blooming girls, . . . buoyant as skylarks, frolicsome as young colts," and young Mary Ferrand told her grandmother happily, "we have a great many little girls to play with and we all agree very well together we . . . run about and jump our rope." Mary Ann Lenoir found her companions "a right merry set," and wrote of singing songs and crowning a Queen of the May. Even class and study time often seems pleasant in young women's letters. Charlotte Daly contentedly described "the never ending routine of St. Mary's, and how hour crowds upon hour and bell echoes bell, ever compelling us to part from our own private plans." She wrote her friend of the usual " 'ding dong' of pianos [and] the customary amount of 'transposing' words" echoing through the building. Supposed to be at her lessons, another student scribbled, "Miss Everton [*sic*] . . . is at present giving out paper and pens to a crowd of eager applicants. Just imagine the scene. . . . In vain Miss Everton insists that *this one* had paper *last* week." And though it was against the rules at most academies, treats of food found their way into students' hands. "The usual quantity of Aunt Polly's hunks makes there [*sic*] appearance," one girl assured her absent friend. Mary Chesnut recalled a black woman, Maum Jute, who "nearly every night . . . slipped into our room with a contraband supper—in winter oysters, sausages—and rice. In summer ices—nugat—and candy always. Coconut candy and powder candy . . . A style of confectionary called 'Love Kisses' all egg and butter."[32]

For young women, especially, the private alcoves for sleeping, decorated with pictures and personal belongings, were favorite places. Beds in a row, curtained at night on three sides, washstands at one end, and at the other an alcove for a preceptor, was the typical arrangement in both male and female academies. Though moral advisers warned teachers against having "pets," and grimly instructed students not to overdo "confidential discourse," most academies quite explicitly fostered such closeness. The students, girls and boys, routinely slept two to a bed, often in an attic room which added to the sense of being apart and confidential. One woman recalled, "We two girls could snuggle up together in each other's arms, and sleep the sleep that only the young can ever know and enjoy." Similarly, at Madame Talvande's, "We secured a modicum of privacy by bed curtains formed of our frocks and petticoats. . . . Twelve young barbarians coupled in this room and never under one ceiling rioted a lighter hearted more joyous band."[33]

Academic lessons must be seen in this larger context of shared habit and intimate personal routine, as part of a full world rather than as an isolated scholastic existence. Of course classic texts and repetitive methods were most common, and it is difficult to generalize about what exactly was learned. Rote method, copying, public declamation (and thus public failure or success), all seem tiresome by modern standards and doubtless left many students weary and restless. But even rote learning in this world apart reinforced the sense of shared values and the existence of an objective fund of knowledge to be steadily acquired. Copying the words of Milton or Napoleon improved handwriting but also lent the cadence of the great to youth laboring away in Augusta, Raleigh, and Charleston. Some students clearly took hold of their minds and their "powers of perception, attention, memory, imagination, judgment, reasoning, and invention," whereas others may well have agreed with one man who recalled his schooling as a time "to love the girls, and to repeat the first two lines of the multiplication tables." But whether merely endured or eagerly embraced, lessons were a part of the social here-and-now inside the academy walls.[34]

Student copybooks reveal that the daily pattern of learning was sometimes humorous, sometimes melancholy, and often simply diffuse. A collection of nine books belonging to one girl ranged from the Bible and Milton to Hannah More and Lydia Sigourney. Student notebooks were filled at random, and in close order, with copied poems (from Scott, Milton, Burns), original verse (with opening lines like "Farewell! Farewell! Farewell!" and "On a Lake where drooped a willow"), ribald songs, patriotic speeches, recipes for shoe polish, ways to cut pie crust, and handwriting exercises ("Honor those who are Honest 1 2 3"). Pages are filled with doodles and experimentation with signatures. Occasionally a personal voice emerges. One might look askance at a young woman's essay "On going to school" that begins, "nothing is more pleasant than to enter and see the scholars all silently pursuing their studies." But her essay "On Arithmetic" has a genuine ring to it: "I think it is the most difficult study that I ever attempted." Girls typically wrote brief essays on "Modesty," and "Charity," though at times copied battle scenes from texts, as did boys. Still, typical gender divisions show up in choice of theme, execution, and handwriting style. Women tended toward describing moral or aesthetic qualities in an evermore spidery penmanship and men tended toward attacking debatable questions ("Was the execution of Major Andre justifiable?") in a larger hand traced with broad-nibbed pens. Most copybooks contain little concerning contemporary events, and few "I think" or "I feel" statements. British history as often as American supplied examples, and though Pliny, Tacitus, and other classics were rare in lesson books, so was the sentimental, personal voice of the "modern" nineteenth century.[35]

The World Apart and Family Realities

The sense that copybooks give of students laboring away at their lessons, confining between two covers an array of quotations and styles that somehow implied maturity, raises again the question of the academy's relation to the family. Some schools were enormously popular, others failed to sustain parents' good will. There were indifferent students and eager ones; rote penmanship exercises in dreary columns were offset by the exciting discovery of verse and argument. But despite variation, the academy flourished as an institution, and therefore, it would seem, must have supported the family life it was built upon. It is not enough to point to the order, the routine, or to the rituals of mastery and gender as though these precisely signify what parents and students took away as *learned.* However important were the values, discipline, institutional mappings, they do not in themselves tell us what is most important to know about them: how was the joinery between education and family made stronger? In what ways did young elite women and men belong more to their class and more fully express a certain vision of society when they left the academy than when they entered? Complete answers cannot be reached, of course, but a route can be found in the developing discourse of parents and children, the conscious purpose of which was to make the bridge between school and family. This discourse reveals two fundamental intellectual consequences of the academy experience, each with major implications for the culture of planter family life. In the first place, parent-child discourse increasingly derived from the formal curriculum itself. Correspondence between parents and children was the foremost proof that the school was doing what it was supposed to do. Letters were the best, and often the only, evidence that sons and daughters were growing up to be worthy persons. For students, such correspondence was a primary intellectual activity and prefaced a lifetime of appropriate self-expression and self-conscious mastery. For their parents, it was the occasion to shape that mastery. The correspondence was personal as well, and letters between children and parents uncovered, often for the first time, much of the emotional texture of their relationship. The mixed character of such discourse, at once a part of formal schooling and a part of intimate life, thus went beyond the daily reportage that crowded the surface of individual letters. It must be seen as an *act* in which a shifting combination of content and form structured the coming of age more closely than any other product of academy life. In the second place, the emerging discourse reveals a striking disparity in what parents and children each believed to be the most important meaning of the academy experience. This difference was not an open conflict, in most cases, but does suggest crucially different interpretations attached to education which help explain the key tensions in youths' coming of age—tensions that inevitably were framed anew in the values of gender, class, and family, and became part of the planters' common sense.[36]

Two aspects of language and its usage, both underlying parent-child correspondence, were particularly accepted as intellectual truths with grave social extension. Both have obvious links to the aspects of education that stressed the public display of self. The first was that written or spoken expression was the unifying aim of all knowledge and one of education's most important social adhesives. In the words of educator Almira Phelps, "the different branches of knowledge . . . are all conducive to one great end, that of enabling a person to compose with elegance and facility." Accuracy in language, as mentor Charles Butler pointed out, made knowledge a moral force. Second, language was a key to gender differences. The advice and instruction given to men and women regarding rhetoric and usage consistently evoked gender in a way that other kinds of advice (regarding piety, for example) did not. Each sex was understood to have its own linguistic terrain with its own rewards and perils, and instruction in language was thus quite openly instruction in gender ideals. Typically, women were accorded more attention in this matter than were men. Men might be advised to master certain genres, the eulogy or the political oration, for instance, or to attend to certain key words, such as "honor," but their general education made fewer specific references to their sex except when explicit differences with women were at issue. "A lady neither writes nor speaks to a gentleman as she would to one of her own sex, and a gentleman addresses a lady in a style of more courteousness and respect than he does a male correspondent," according to one popular guide to usage. Women, on the other hand, were often portrayed as being generally susceptible to language to the point of self-indulgence, and were understood as having an almost preternatural affinity for words. They were supposed to be given to exaggeration, to "voluminous correspondence" on light topics, and unduly to model their letters on fiction's overwrought prose and dramatic gesture. Women also had peculiar epistolary habits which teachers discouraged. Not only did women reserve "the most important part of a letter for the postscript," they *played* with letters, "fold[ing] their notes in a manner, that is a difficult task to open them." Certain contradictions, not to mention envy, are apparent in this attempt to control women's expression. On the one hand, female students were schooled to appreciate "good" literature as well as any male, to cultivate rhetoric, and to use proper spelling, grammar, and so forth. However, as a woman had an alarming facility for language, she might be driven toward self-expression in a way that would confound her or those who attempted to direct her. She was criticized for trivial talk, yet told not to engage in weighty political or theoretical discussion. She was praised for her singular grace in conversation, but feared for her special capacity for words.[37]

Other difficulties in the use of language emerged in the instructions to students on the duty of family correspondence. Writing to parents was a duty, of course; time was set apart for it and instruction devoted to it in all academies. But it was also supposed to be a pleasure, something a youth would *desire* to do. This mixture of desire and obligation gave a distinct tone to letter-writing instruction: it was a happy task, joyously assumed by individual sons and daughters. But at the same time it was socially significant if neglected. Much discussion, often quite confusing, centered on the qualities of a good, familiar letter. Some advisers tried to simplify the whole endeavor. "A correspondence between two persons, is simply a conversation reduced to writing," one text began confidently. There is no need for approaching the task with gravity, for "the general rules which govern other styles of composition, are, for the most part, applicable to letter-writing: ease and simplicity, an even flow of unlabored diction, and an artless arrangement of obvious sentiments." Some advisers, like Lydia Sigourney, even went so far as to suggest feeling one's way to proper form. "We learn to talk without rules," she wrote, "and letter-writing is but talk upon paper. . . . Pouring out the thoughts, in the epistolary style, has such power to confer pleasure, to kindle sympathy, to comfort affliction." Other educators, however, saw this as dangerously antinomian. Louisa Tuthill, while cautioning against the falseness of "exterior grace alone," nevertheless warned, "Letters should never be carelessly written. . . . Even the folding and superscription of a letter tell something of the character of the writer, and the deference she deems due her correspondents." Another adviser wrote, "False grammar, in good society, is not tolerated, even *en famille*, neither can it be in a letter. In the most familiar epistle, we should recollect what we owe to our language, to our correspondent, and to ourselves.[38]

The conflict between correct form and ease of expression, as between duty and affection, is shown in a well-circulated little book used to teach the art of letter writing. In it, ten-year-old Emily wishes to write her older brother Charles at college, and is gently taught by him how to do it. Her education mirrors the ideal of family correspondence as well its ambiguities. Charles leads her quickly through her first efforts, each letter becoming an occasion for another lesson: learning basic form (margins, salutation), being neither too conventionally stiff nor "vulgar," attaining a prose style without using the dictionary at every turn, and learning to arrange thoughts so interest will be sustained. In doing this, Emily finds herself learning much broader lessons of mature character: she must set aside time to write, be patient in waiting for Charles's replies, and want to please him with what she says. Her progress is marked by expressive qualities treated as absolutes which even Charles finds hard to pin down, "naturalness," for instance, "familiarity," and "ease." The best he can do is observe that letter-writing is its own work, somewhere near conversation but "a *little more* studied." In short, for all the suggestion that letters were a self-evident genre, ambiguities in the teaching of epistolary style reveal that it was quite unlike "naturally" learning to talk. It was a social form that demanded practice and display, and fed upon the active presence of others of like mind.[39]

Parents struggled with just these issues, laboring to impress their children that letters were vessels of definite capacity and form which must hold the emerging changes in family life. Often parents wrote initially about the act of writing letters, thus beginning a narrative of their family life which combined epistolary content and form into a kind of morality. John C. Calhoun, who began a satisfying correspondence with his daughter Anna when she went to school in Columbia, South Carolina, in 1831, told the fourteen-year-old girl, "I do not know a more desirable acquirement (I mean of the literary kind) in a lady, than that of writing a good letter." Boys, too, were typically informed, as was Charles Manigault, that "writing a good letter is so gentlemanly an accomplishment," and essential to maintaining elite standards. Parents paraphrased letter-writer guides in their efforts to emphasize the formal importance of correspondence. Proper form witnessed intimacy and love, not just propriety. "Letterwriting is for the purpose of replacing in a measure the communications and conversations we should enjoy if we were together," Matilda Lieber told her son Hamilton. And Thomas Ruffin called for more careful letters from his grandson Duncan Cameron by telling him, "Such letters will improve you in your education and increase your love to [your mother] and me and all your family." Faced with this advice, children soon learned to watch their writing (often composing more than one draft of their early letters home) and to make excuses when they felt a letter did not measure up. Apologizing for her bad handwriting and any errors, schoolgirl Many Ann Lenoir echoed many young students by noting the "bad pen" and the "continual racket, singing, laughing, talking &c" which accounted for her poor epistolary form. Sometime such disclaimers worked, sometimes not. Even indulgent parents became didactic over letters. In correcting her son's spelling, a South Carolina woman observed, "While we are upon this topic, I must warn you against a stile [sic] which is called Mercantile. It consists in leaving out the pronouns. One instance of it was to be found in your letter." She and many other parents mixed critiques with praise, revealing the extent to which letters were the most regular, visible evidence parents had of an academy youth's coming of age. One young man was told, "It *is* a nice letter, that would do credit to any boy your age," and many parents would have agreed with Eliza DeRosset, who wrote her daughter Kate in 1844, "Your letter was a real pleasure to us, we hope to see an improvement very often."[40]

Significantly, major parental themes changed little over a fifty-year span. "My Dear Daughter," wrote John P. Richardson to Elizabeth in the spring of 1806,

> Highly gratified by the assurance of your affection, and the mark of attention which you have paid your parent in writing to me again, without having received another letter from me; I cannot forbear to express the pleasure your conduct has given me, and in turn I shall endeavor to do you justice as a correspondent in answering your Letters punctually.[41]

The concern with timing, and the joining of affection and obligation also structured letters nearly a half-century later. Armand DeRosset wrote his daughter Kate in 1847,

> Your sweet affectionate letter of the 12th (received yesterday) again reminds me how badly I have been treating you . . . by allowing even little hindrances to prevent me from writing to you. But you will not, I am sure, think me forgetful of you—or that I do not value very highly your ever welcome letters as proofs of the affection of my precious Kate.[42]

These two letters importantly differ in certain conventions, however. Richardson, typical of the earlier period, strongly emphasizes the formal act of writing by announcing how it compels him to acknowledge his pleasure. DeRosset uses the sentimental convention of ascribing (and thus prescribing) hoped-for feelings to his daughter as a way of telling her he values her. Similarly, DeRosset's openly personal enjoyment of the sweetness of his daughter's letter contrasts with Richardson's more "positional" statement of satisfaction in which he mixes third and first person. Still, for both men, timing, reciprocity, love, and obligation join to display the essence of family feeling.

Comment on letters became the primary means for parental pronouncements on character, gender, and class, and parents often struggled to phrase exactly what it was they wanted their children to do or become. Letters to young men tended to be considerably more inflated and portentous than those to young women. From sons' complaints of homesickness or restlessness, for instance, parents consistently extracted lessons of manhood. Yet a curious abstractness colored their advice. "It is necessary that all boys should leave home & Mother & friends to get an education that will fit them for usefulness in the world," a son was told. "[Homesickness] must be overcome in a manly & christian way by determining to do what you know to be your duty." Unable to explain his advice in any other way, another planter wrote to his younger brother: *"Be decent."* Both fathers and mothers wrote their sons in such terms, though fathers assumed the burden of it. They frequently alternated between grand abstractions and instances of specific conduct, investing a single event (a school recitation, for example) with great meaning and drawing from it ties that bound sons to good public behavior. Money spent foolishly or, worse, debts contracted while at school, were certain to elicit alarmed letters from fathers. Neglecting schoolwork or failing to socialize easily with teachers and new schoolmates led fathers to shame their sons by summoning "the regret of your friends" in addition to parental disapproval. Fathers less frequently than mothers openly praised sons for their academic achievements, and then in terms that depicted exemplary young men as "highly interesting" but more important, as socially prepossessing. Social presence—clear, forceful expression, absence of shyness or awkwardness, and attention to physical appearance—brought forth a father's warmest approval.[43]

Some of the advice parents wrote to their daughters was also quite abstract, suggesting mutually accepted, unspoken assumptions but implying that parents had some difficulty being exact about what a good woman was to be. Parents asked their daughters about specific classes and achievements, but frequently labored over generalized recommendations and unexplicated directions. "I trust you are giving great diligence to the discharge of all your duties," one father wrote typically. John P. Richardson expressed his hope that "the company and Society of my dear daughters will be rendered doubly pleasing by the *refinement* of the mind and the *improvement* of the person," but either assumed that no further elaboration was needed or was unable to provide a specific one. Like young men, women were given a dual task of intellectual achievement and the attainment of social "accomplishments." Few parents refused their daughters attendance at balls or the theater, but most were quick to point out that such outings were lessons in grace and social carriage and not simple enjoyments. Parents' letters make it seem that young women were far more tractable than sons, and this probably was so. Letters of reprimand written to girls had little to do with money or lack of discipline, but with daughters' moodiness or willfulness. And daughters heard more open praise than did sons. In complimenting Kate DeRosset's achievements, in typical fashion, her parents encouraged her to write in great detail about her daily routine and urged her to keep a diary. "Yes! my Dear Girl!" wrote another father in an intimate fashion most parents did not use with boys, "these are subjects that can never become uninteresting or viewed with indifference by your tender Father." In their position as parents, they encouraged both daughters and sons by referring to what was due parents. Certainly they did not neglect writing about mundane home news or telling their children they missed them; but these softer themes invariably were shaped to a spine of obligation and love.[44]

Children's letters home, in striking contrast, were shaped by the wholly new life they encountered behind academy walls. At first, a longing for home shaped most youths' letters, as did a certain resistance to school rules and routine. Mary Ann Lenoir, like many sister students, wrote long homesick passages depicting her family in great detail: "Father, and Thomas out in the cornfield & *you* [Mother] in the garden tying up and trimming the rosebushes or putting the house to rights . . . sister Laura in her old place in the hall her basket by her, *smiling at her work* . . . Sally is up stairs making a little *bag* or pincushion. Walter of course with a book in his hand, and Rufus waiting on old Ned." The longing for familiar places and loved family combined with initial dislike for the lack of privacy and structured regimen of the academy. Mary Ann Lenoir complained that the girls were too much confined to the academy because the headmistress feared their meeting men on outings. Boys seem to have frequently tested academy government at the beginning of their schooling, complaining to parents about the lack of free movement, money, and of tyrannical headmasters or captains.[45]

Homesickness and resistance soon wore away, however, and youths' letters home reveal them to have been concerned with showing filial duty without, significantly, answering lengthy parental exhortations in kind. For the most part, the labored parental abstractions simply found no echo in the letters of their children. Some children, like one North Carolina boy, were disingenuously blunt about duty: "I have been playing a very hard game of bandy to day and don't feel in the humour of writing this evening at all; but however I will try." Others followed guidebook form with obligatory words certain to be approved by sharp-eyed parents: "I find all my studies interesting, and when I know the pleasure it will give the best and kindest of fathers for me to improve, they are doubly so" has the ring of a classroom exercise; but even so it is important because it was so common a phrasing. Less common, but also revealing of the turns children's letters could take, are letters in which youths more or less gingerly explored the possibilities of a new kind of discourse apart from home news and their dutiful compliance. At times, students talked about their study in ways that invited an intellectual or moral response by parents. One young woman, in relating how her Christmas holiday passed, ventured to her mother that she had been reading a novel with her teacher and friends, and yet "I know you will approve of the book when you hear . . . it contained more of history & less of love than Novels generally do." Louisa Lenoir wrote to her mother, "I am now reading the reign of Elizabeth. I have heard some persons say they loved Elizabeth; but I don't know how they can, for, although I may admire her talents, when ever I think of her deceitful transactions with, & her cruel treatment of Mary, queen of Scots, I never can love her." She added that though she was only a schoolgirl she felt her opinion should stand "until I am convinced of [its] falsity." Though hardly novel, such intellectual inroads indicate that for at least some students reading and study opened possibilities for mature conversation with their parents; possibilities, it should be said, that were seldom fully explored in correspondence. Even less frequently, certain youths characterized their relations with their parents directly, in recounting a conversation or recalling an event that transpired on a visit home. These direct observations counterpointed the more usual declarations of filial love and duty with a sense of difficulty and distance. One young man, for example, found the courage to tell his grandfather that the reason all the grandchildren spoke in such low tones "arose from diffidence for one thing and not knowing what was agreeable to you for another." And after a visit home, fourteen-year-old Anne Cumming was able to tell her father,

> I have never, my dear Father, doubted that my parents were my best friends and it is strange, tho' my own fault, that I have not confided in them as I ought, as it should have been my pleasure to have done. . . . I must say that I would have entered a free conversation with you . . . but there was nothing on my part to talk of but school and school affairs, and I did think when you had been troubled with law business to tire you with what must appear childish and foolish.

There is no reason to suppose that she was alone in feeling such things, though there seems to have been little room in parent-child correspondence for their expression.[46]

By far the most common motif in student letters home, however, was enjoyment of academy life and friends. This motif might be seen in part as a conventional expression of duty, as students in the early homesick weeks were urged to bear up and embrace the institution. But, as suggested earlier, the intimate student life of academies came to dominate letters home in a way that far outstripped obligation. Letters from girls, especially, recount scenes of emotional closeness and delight in a female world. After listing her studies, one young woman wrote to her parents with great enthusiasm about long, confidential early morning walks with friends, of joining a "working society" for missionaries in Greece, and "nipping about over the yard playing prisoners-baist [sic] and how many miles to milz-bright, like so many mountain Tomboys." Kate DeRosset wrote her father in 1844 of the pleasure of a formal town excursion when "we walked two and two, eight under each teacher with Mr. Smedes at the head." And another girl, happily telling her mother her new nickname, "Sprout," added how pleasureful her days had become with a schoolmate "for whom I have formed a very strong attachment." Less frequently, but no less feelingly, young men, too, wrote of their delight in academy life. A North Carolina boy told excitedly of his military school forming a company of guards in 1846 ("with wooden muskets and uniform jackets"), and a Georgia boy told of being whipped for fighting but proud to admit that his teacher "was perfectly right" in so keeping the collective peace. And a young man in school in Philadelphia boasted of his intellectual and physical change after a year away from home: "I grow very fast."[47]

The immediacy and concreteness of student letters contrast sharply with their parents' abstract pronouncements, suggesting that two very different kinds of education were taking place, indeed two very different academies were perceived. Parents summoned all-inclusive values which implied that academies oriented youth to their future mastery. Young women and men, however, spoke in the present tense, taking pleasure in the fact that the academy was a world of its own apart from whatever adulthood would demand. For the most part, this disjunction did not openly trouble family relations, and parents and children continued on their separate paths. In some families, however, the different perceptions created conflict which reveals something more of the social and personal adhesions of family life and the place of education.[48]

The experience of young Augustin L. Taveau is instructive, not because his education as such either caused or resolved his conflict with his parents, but because his going away to school, his coming of age, exposed divergent needs for authority and intimacy. Augustin Louis Taveau was a wealthy planter of the South Carolina lowcountry who considered himself a writer. Born in 1828 to Louis A. Taveau and Martha Swinton Ball Taveau, Augustin grew up amid comfortable wealth and a crowd of siblings and half-siblings. He attended the College of Charleston and read law with James L. Petigru. Augustin's father, an assertive, patriarchal master of the old school who enjoyed gaming and long absences from home, and his mother, a devout Christian who wielded her religion against her husband's tyrannies, were at loggerheads almost from their marriage in 1821 but especially by the time Augustin was eight or nine years old. Their conflict, over property and personal differences in belief and habit, shaped young Augustin's boyhood in ways that did not emerge until he entered Mt. Zion Academy in Winnsboro, North Carolina, in 1838 at the extraordinarily young age of ten. The pattern of family correspondence graphically reveals just how young Taveau's absence brought long-smoldering family conflict to flame.[49]

Before 1838, Louis Taveau's letters to his wife were as flowery as they were distant, fashioned from a kind of frozen courtship rhetoric, and she responded with sharply pointed scriptural quotations and scarcely veiled references to absent husbands. However, they also expressed affection, and the elder Taveau generally included a note to his children along with his letters to their mother. But Augustin's departure for Mt. Zion, and thus his debut as a correspondent, tore the weak fabric of family life. As the youngest child and only son, Augustin immediately became the absent focus of a bitter contest between his parents for proof of his loyalty and achievement. Martha Taveau, missing him and dreading a life to come without her children, wrote long passages to the schoolboy warning him of the vanity of the world and the sinfulness of most men. Her letters alternated sharply in tone and voice, sometimes imploring him in the third person as "Mother" and at other times making wordly deals for his salvation (she would "send you *some cash*" if he memorized scripture). She bore her son heavy burdens of wishfulness, begging him on more than one occasion "to turn out . . . a *great scholar* and also a great *Christian*; that is all my hope and all my desire." She desired him to "be a blessing both to your parents, and to the Church and State" and she did not exclude descriptions of his father "dissipating at the Races and Theatres; every day dining out." She made Augustin's father into the very image of a manhood to be avoided.[50]

Whereas Martha Taveau longed for her son and never seemed to have enough paper on which to pen her hopes, Louis Taveau resented having to write and thus acknowledge the independence of the now-absent Augustin. The elder Taveau had no genius for correspondence, but his brief letters more than ably claimed his measure of domestic disharmony. Though "painfull" to write, his missives were frequently laced with hostile references to his wife's religiosity couched (with many misspellings) as manly lessons: "*Our bread* my Son comes out of the land. Consequently it is my duty *as a Father to put my shoulder to the wheell*—it is not in praying that we may survive in this world." Louis Taveau constantly suspected the worst from his son, imagining him wasting his time, forbidding him to learn how to fence (it was "too serious"), and turning Augustin's infrequent anecdotes into personal affronts. "Your head, my son, is rather light," he wrote after Augustin told of going to the theater. "The Plays seems to absorbe all kinds of feelings towards your Parents whose happiness should be to have a Son who feels a strong love for them and appreciates the sacrifices they make for his education." For Louis Taveau, education was instruction in filial duty. He searched every letter from his son for signs that "your temper [is] rather disrespectfull to your Father" and repeatedly praised his own attempts to "do everything in my power for your welfare." Louis seems to have been impervious to other views, driving his own points home even by seizing upon Augustin's expressions of regret. "You [say] you are very sorry that I am scolding you so often for your bad spelling and writting: I am, [I] assure you, double-sorry myself."[51]

Augustin's tight and muted letters to both parents before about 1844 reflect the psychological pressure their conflicting expectations bred in him. He adopted neither his mother's religious rhetoric nor his father's almost ludicrous, stentorian tone. His letters were undeviatingly dutiful during his early Mt. Zion years; so much so that his parents' worries and projections seem almost as if they were addressed to some other son. However, the exaggerated masculine and feminine styles of his parents, rooted in their own conflict, were given a new and finally self-destructive expression when he went away to school and found his own tongue. He did so through his letters, taking up in 1840 what would become a calming, close correspondence with his sister, Caroline Rosalie, who was closest in age. Coming to see his father as "ridiculous" and a "tyrant," Augustin began to frame replies, while at the same time increasingly holding his mother's extreme religious protests at bay, by being gently noncommittal and sometimes rather flippant. Deciding that Yale University was "too much *in Yankeeland*," Louis tried to persuade his son not to concern himself further about formal education, a persuasion Augustin resisted by praising books and the literary life. The son was not above putting in the knife, sending back his father's letters with the spelling and grammar corrected, and writing letters in verse. He also tried reconciliation, but by 1845 correspondence could no longer cut through the bad feeling. Though Augustin desired to have a sense of his father's intentions and sentiments, something that would tell him "exactly in what light we stand towards each other," the elder Taveau continued to write paternal epigrams: "A well educated son ought not to go anywhere without being authorize[d] by his father." By the time of his mother's death in 1847, Augustin had staked out an emotional terrain apart from both of his parents. He found it most satisfying—and safe—to write in the voice of an aesthete, confounding his father and gaily slipping away from his mother's godly nets.[52]

Augustin Taveau doubtless was as much marked by the conflict in his family as he was able to weather it. What is important is that, timidly at first, he began to perceive that his real education in the years 1838–45 was his discovery of his cramped place as a son and escaping it. Arranging his father's letters, and looking back on his own, he came to understand that manhood and mastery were at issue ("you think I am desirous of rising up the Man," he had once told Louis) and that schooling was as much about these matters as it was about studies and friendship. His pressing conflict, opened to his view for the first time in the letters he received and wrote while in school, gave him a sure, lasting perspective on the mystery of his distant parents and his coming of age. "How unhappy is that son's position," he penciled in the margin of one of his father's tirades in 1848, "when a father is unable to *comprehend* language!—When the unburthening of a *confiding heart*, is misconstrued into offence and *disrespect!*"[53]

The Coming of "Fame" and "Tender Regrets"

Looking back in the summer of 1855 on a diary begun eighteen years earlier, James H. Hammond was moved to reflect: "My religious, political and social opinions have not been *revolutionized* since then, but they have greatly *matured*. And of course much *changed*. The *seeds* will probably be found—or some of them—here; the *fruit* I propose—if I have time and *heart*—to put in future pages."[54] Although Hammond's academy days as student and teacher had long since passed, his observation, with its concern for change and its botanic imagery, embodied the sort of self-reflection bespeaking elite education. Hammond's emphasis on change, maturity, and perhaps most revealingly *heart* recalls the planters' search for links between lasting values and an individual's emotional experience. Exploring this search here had led us, first, to look at the temper of married life as wives and husbands themselves perceived it. Marriage as an emotional bond was fundamentally based on separate realms separately inhabited, which nevertheless had to hold work and values celebrated in the name of a unified couple if the planters' mastery were to be preserved. A "good" marriage rested on formal *declarations* of mutual obligation and affection in the face of gender differences and frequent separations; to speak of devotion and duty was thus to create it. Marriage, therefore, was particularly liable to intense feelings of loss and alienation when circumstances interrupted or obscured the ritual declarations. Even in the face of ordinary circumstances—rural distances and the profound otherness of slaves— planters constantly had to tend to the most visible signs of their emotional tie, calling attention to it through their letters and creating in their families the relationships that bore witness to it. Thus, to characterize planter-class marriage as "affectionate" as Daniel Blake Smith, Jane Censer, and others have (and therefore argue for its modernity), is only partly true. All sorts of affect (and its absence) were invested with great significance in the antebellum years: marriage was not simply more loving in some absolute way than a century earlier. On the other hand, to characterize marriages as "paternalistic" and therefore traditional makes the best sense only when we realize that southern men, as well as women, were part of a family culture that ascribed great explanatory importance to the emotions, particularly those utterable in terms of loss and love. Paternalism is perhaps most apparent in the ways males dominated the economic, legal, and other instrumental functions of marriage; in terms of emotional life, both sexes struggled with the perils and enjoyments of a bond that tied intimacy to separation.

This chapter has further framed the connection between personal experience and social values by exploring the strong link between definitions of moral, responsible adulthood and generational duties—a link that served to join hopes for social continuity to the domain of an individual's family. That is, the most meaningful imperatives of social life were phrased consistently in the language of kinship obligation and reward. Moreover, because the planters characteristically joined this vision of the good society to an array of subtle distinctions between the sexes, they perceived cultural orientations as rooted in biology and thus not open to social change or political discourse. Though this sense of family and social order had its satisfactions, the planters did not entirely escape the shadow thrown by fears of isolation and intellectual rigidity. The elite's own sense of its rightful leadership invariably summoned these problematic conditions of its authority, in much the same way as its sense of marital duties created difficulties for personal intimacy.

The fundamental supports of elite social life were given unique structure in academy education at the crucial point in a family's cycle when boys and girls were to come of age. The considerable achievements of the academy as a social institution should not be underestimated. Given the needs and priorities of the elite, the academy did indeed provide a measure of scholarship, class cohesion, and social preparation for adulthood which effectively guided youths' coming of age. But ultimately more important was the way in which the academy became the site for a collision, so to say, between the social functions of education and the personal experience of adolescence. Parents and educators worked to shape the values of mature womanhood and manhood by emphasizing the explicit rules and abstract values offspring were supposed to grasp in order to master the world outside. In quite a different way, youth found themselves in a complete world inside the walls, in an absorbing routine far more satisfying than the academic and moral lessons that punctuated it. Consequently, the meaning of academy education was expressed quite differently in the discourse of parents and children. Parents consistently relied upon themes of authority, stressing the academy as means to moral ends and practical achievements. The children's themes most strikingly concerned intimacy, an enjoyment of emotional closeness in a closed society of equals. In many ways, the disparity between felt intimacy and mandated authority in these particular circumstances was the key tension in the coming of age. It arose not because hopes for intimacy were always opposed to the demands of authority; rather, the two imperatives were problematically intertwined in the social and personal lives of the planters, and would reappear throughout their lives in different situations not the least of which were courtship and the affair of honor.

By way of conclusion, and in order to suggest some of the consequences of this tension as felt by planter youth themselves, we can look at what happened as academy days ended. For young men, the completion of schooling threw open a door on a wide field of manhood, daunting in its challenge and promise. Whether teaching school while reading law, helping at the plantation, or traveling, or some combination of these, young men frequently wrote of having none of the firm, defined tasks that academy life had accustomed them to expect. A few sons openly asked their fathers to tell them what to do next, and many simply drifted into teaching or became understudy planters to their fathers or fathers' overseers. There was no slackening in paternal exhortation. If anything, the supposed prospect for glorious achievement added a new edge of urgency. But achievement in what, and in what measure? Men were driven on to fame by their parents, yet cautioned against ambition; the manly obligations that had come to be rote in the academy now seemed so far-ranging as to be more worrisome than tempting. The tension between duty and ambition drove men to try to parse manhood into a kind of formula that stressed a balance between self-control and self-indulgence. James Chesnut, Sr., for example, told his son to strive for honor among his equals but also to beware of "arrogance or superciliousness . . . , an unfortunate characteristic among some of our *Southern Lads.*" However, young planter-class men also received advice pushing them to grand achievements no matter what. Manhood was not to be found in a passive wish for harmony. "*Damn the world,*" Samuel Townes told his younger brother. "You have to shift for yourself and have a right to consult your own preferences." Elisha Hammond told his son James, "I don't despair in the least of you being in time one of the first men of the Union." That this expectation created a particular anxiety is seen in many of young Hammond's letters and diary speculations in which wishes for fame and ambition are balanced by self-reminders of controlled effort. In one sense, James believed that a worthy man simply appeared in the world and was recognized; he idolized John C. Calhoun for many years as possessing this sort of mastery. "Can't run after popularity," Hammond told himself. "It must *follow.*" But he had also been schooled to believe that fame must be sought, and that all men did so. "In whatsoever situation man is placed," he reflected, "to distinguish himself is the chief end of all his wishes[.] To become [a] little more thought of is what he toils for from morn to even.' " The manly task, forever fascinating to men of Hammond's class, was feverishly to pursue one's own interests, but in a way that let others establish one's honorable reputation.[55]

The immediate social arena for this effort could not be the isolated work of planting, but the excitement of politics—a close, male world resembling not a little the academy it superseded. "You ought to know more about politics than you do," one young man was typically advised. "It is expected of every grown & educated young man to know something of politics & be able to take a hand in conversing on such subjects." Yet politics as a domain of achievement put ambition precisely into conflict with the disinterested obligations of a good man, and thrust men into personal conflict with one another, as we have seen. Not everyone could be first among equals. "Whether you desire it or not you must win 'Rhetorical honors' when ever you come into political life," one young man explained to his friend in the language of the academy. But he himself was ambivalent about this demand for public display, and felt obliged to add that he would rather be known as "a man who never feared to peril either his person or his popularity in the conscientious discharge of his duty." Expressed almost archetypally as the planter-class contrast between appearance and inner worth, his choice was exactly between personal ambition and social obligation confronting young men as they passed from the academy into the larger world they expected to dominate. And although young men on occasion could be flippant about their yet untried powers, political and otherwise, and could say along with James Hammond, "I am in humour to be ambitious . . . Heigho!" still they worried the knot of ambition and duty, and struggled to justify to themselves how politics might be made to reflect the moral aims of academy life. Hammond's father had tried to console him in 1826 when the young man was feeling bereft and overworked teaching school in the upcountry of South Carolina. But Elisha Hammond's consolations were inevitably phrased as just the abstract urgings to mastery which so unsettled his son: "I am anxious that you should acquit yourself honorably and achieve fame." Nearly a dozen years later, James was still struggling, and would struggle all his life, with the duality of honor and ambition. "I have so accustomed myself to *avoid honours,*" he wrote in his diary at age thirty-two, "rather than to seek them, that I fear I am fast losing the spirit to *encounter* anything for them even on occasion."[56]

One deeply felt consequence of this tension was the difficulty men experienced in keeping up academy friendships. Recalling their recent days together in a South Carolina school, a young man told his friend, "With you I could speak of everything—Love, Ambition, Life and all things and all feelings of my heart were known to you." Men cherished this sense of being "*kindred souls . . .* in the honorable principles and devotion to Justice truth and patriotism." But in leaving the academy, they found it difficult to sustain such intimacy; full friendships began to seem boyish and somewhat eroded under the pressures of new, political alliances. Men expressed a strong sense of loss in their assessment of their changed situation, in their feeling that "those Elysian Fields of my boyish immagination [*sic*]" had become littered with "Thorns and Briars." Another young man echoed, "The gay and flitting shadows of ideal life are fast giving place to the sober realities of existence. . . . We are thrown upon the performance of the solemn duties of *thinking* and *acting* for ourselves. Boyish trifles are to yield to substantive materials which are to determine the character of our histories." The sense of deep loss, of parting with a loved world now less than useful, was mirrored in the wholly abstract vision of what would replace it. The academy did not anticipate these trials of manhood, and the new alignment of duty and ambition was as disorienting as it was inevitable.[57]

Young women leaving the academy, in contrast, felt themselves facing a contracting world. As we saw in chapter 2, young women, through family and peer importunities or through inclination, tended to be pushed toward courtship and marriage as a matter of course. Marriage was an uncharted territory, and one not especially hospitable to energetic, schooled minds. Thus, it is scarcely surprising that compared with the abstract and grand rhetoric of young men, women's discourse was personal and muted. Women fresh from school were advised to begin thinking immediately about their practical duties-to-be as wife and mother, and to drop the clannish remnants of academy life like the "school slang, which they have *sported* among themselves." Charles Butler wrote, "Few circumstances can be more dangerous than for a young woman, by being abruptly withdrawn from a state of pupilage, to have a large portion of vacant time suddenly thrown upon her hands, and to be left to fill the chasm with trifles and dissipation." To speak of chasms and vacancies was to reveal why young women were encouraged to take up womanly duties in their parents' house until they had their own, and to continue their reading and other improvements.[58]

Many young women did just that, but amid their new, post-academy routine they gave words to their sense of vastly changed circumstances. Like men, they sought to keep up the intimacy of school relationships while they kept to their homes. But unlike men, women had no counter pull of vast worldly fame to strain friendships. If they were strained the prospect of courtship was usually the cause; women wondered whether their friends were "so caressed by the beauxs [*sic*] that you cannot take the time to write." Yet it is clear that women's writing, to a much greater extent than men's, continued to foster deep same-sex friendships. Their words were lovers' words. "Yes Elizabeth," Louisa Lenoir wrote, "you are still dear to me as ever; but . . . is it possible that Lizzy no longer loves me? can she prove false? but no, I will not believe it." Telling her absent friend about a new acquaintance, Charlotte Daly said, "I am sure she would win all your heart away from me. . . . She would love you, I know, and I am equally certain that she would completely *enchant* you, for she is one of the loveliest beings."[59]

These hopes for intimacy savor of something held in suspension, something not quite real. Women counterpointed their figures of love with a frequent theme evoking the power of the imagination and the willingness to dream. Away from school and friends, perhaps not yet courted or wishing to be, young women felt full of the aspirations nurtured in the academy but cut adrift beyond its walls. Dreaming is a powerful motif in the writings of young, unmarried women, who, like Mary Moragne, enjoyed days in "the glad woods laughing in the sunshine,—the sweet tremulous tones of the birds—the incense of flowers" on her father's plantation. "I have been busy writing and indulging in my usual *day dreams*," wrote another young woman. Hours of walking, working the needle, reading, conversing with family, writing absent friends—all quite different from the bells and rules and clatter of the academy—left many young women with a sense of sorrow mixed with pride in the new prospect of being a grown woman. Indeed, the two were inseparable in letters. "I suppose, Kate, you are beginning to feel at home," a woman speculated to her friend who had graduated and returned to her parents' home. "And are in some measure quietly realizing that you are, *almost* a young lady. Do you not feel some tender regrets at throwing off your school-girl character even partially? With all the bright promise of the future, the 'shifting sunny mist' in which our fond, eager hope enveloped it, there is still much to chasten our burning aspirations . . . [in] the breaking up of so many very happy associations." Whereas men felt the wide open risks of mastery, women felt the "quiet" scaling down of hopes; women harbored as memory the academy days men struggled to use or escape.[60]

PART TWO

FAMILY

The Routines of Intimacy

Part One focused on ritual and the way it oriented women and men to their duties and hopes. The affair of honor, courtship, and the coming of age were in many obvious ways dissimilar. They engaged people at quite different points in their lives. They ranged in intensity and formality from the starkly defined affair to the comparatively roomy passage into adulthood. The affair stressed rules and sequence, as did courtship, but the affair's business was to return two men to the company of equals, whereas courtship established its couple. Coming of age, like courtship, brought unlikes together, age and youth, man and woman; but growing up was to gain an identity, whereas lovers in some ways lost their identities.

But these dissimilarities masked the rituals' deeper compatibility. It was a compatibility, when grasped, that exalted woman and man, lover and striver, and made habit and conviction one. The three rituals involved the same cultural themes, refracting them differently but directing them toward similar ends. All three relied upon, and helped to celebrate, gender differences which were placed beyond social change in a realm of almost biological certainty. All three elevated personal life, not by giving individuality unchallenged sway, but by knitting intimate experience to family and social well-being. All three rituals traced a boundary between appearance and substance, initially setting one against the other but finally blurring the distinction between powerful image and necessary reality. At first it was play: a youth enjoyed creating her world with other "old maid" school friends; duelists relished the contours of insult and reply; lovers delighted in the strangeness of going past themselves. But it became more than play. Inventor and invention became one, and the indulgence of their fictions held them as did nothing else. Ritual fascinated because it displayed exactly the universal mastery particular individuals of the planter class desperately needed to possess. Embodying honor, love, and knowledge was essential to their social preeminence, and in discovering these qualities, the planters borrowed substance from them. Ritual attracted an increasingly embattled elite, fearful of being shunted aside by reformist Christian morality, excluded by the driving materialism of the North, mocked by social changes that could not be outwitted with words. There were additional advantages in a slave society to one's appearing larger than life and smoothly in charge.

But focusing on the form of ritual perhaps overemphasizes the drama of circumstance; individuals appear to be living not their full lives, but only those transitions hooked by love and power. An affair of honor or a love affair, after all, was stirring because most women and men, most of the time, built their lives more gently with layers of daily routine which comforted and verified. Part Two aims to explore this routine within the context of the family. Once again, the language of the planters has a structure of restraint and entitlement to guide us. The effort here is to take everydayness as an intellectual map rather than a vacuum, to look at the routine of kin-joined lives in three planter families, and at the texture of daily reality as a field for the intrusion of ritual. Chapter 4 shows the family life of a prominent North Carolina jurist and planter in the 1820s and 1830s, focusing on the father's efforts to create love and honor among his children and on the resistance and duty he encountered. Chapter 5 concerns the family of a Presbyterian minister in the 1840s and 1850s, especially the passage of a daughter into womanhood. Chapter 6, also set in the 1840s and 1850s, looks at the conflict between family forms and emotional needs in the relationships of a Georgia planter family who struggled to order the different spheres of wife and husband, parent and child. Each chapter is a chronological slice of a family's biography, a narrative reconstructed from family letters, to suggest how the rituals of manhood and womanhood were bent by the novelties and rote preoccupations, even the silences, that make up the ordinary run of days. The biographical focus also shows how change took place in the family cycle, and how ritual eased change in family relationships, justifying the continuity of the social order. In these family stories, each different in its pitch of conflict and resolution, the key word is continuity. Not sameness or harmony, for often these people stumbled or fought their way toward what they wanted, but endurance marks their family ties.

The rituals of planter-class life explored as cultural artifacts in Part One may thus be seen in Part Two as fuel, so to say, for individuals who worked to be worthy, to love, and to know. The three family biographies establish a sense of the wholeness of family life, of the narrative energy in their letters, and of the way private talk made use of public themes. The planters' cultural experience, then, was made from patterns of ritual and routine. Again and again the planters commented on the beauty and usefulness of these patterns, examined them, relied upon them, and despaired at their absence. Rituals paraded belief in a way not unlike the doctrine of a religion, whereas daily routine found a place in the planters' words in somewhat the same understated way that the devotions of a religion counterpoint its doctrine. Central assumptions—a common sense—were plainly acted upon without analysis in ways that implied a subtle intellectual activity complementing more formal thought. Ritual and routine in the cycle of a family's life were in fact a dialectic of sorts: in ritual the planters were self-conscious, in routine they were intimate; in ritual they made themselves representative of others, in routine they established something of their own; ritual generated many obvious texts, whereas routine remained largely inchoate in the comings and goings of days, in what was repeated and therefore discovered anew.

CHAPTER IV

THE GASTONS:
THE TREASURE OF OFFSPRING

"I scarcely see a person except on business, and scarcely know what those around me are doing. Yet I am by no means unhappy. I enjoy health, have constant employment, trust that my children are enjoying themselves and believe that I am doing my duty." William Gaston wrote these words to his daughter Hannah in August 1828, a month short of his fiftieth birthday. They are rather uncharacteristic of Gaston, who rarely generalized about the pattern of his daily life. Nevertheless, this brief reflection precisely captures Gaston's temperament and what might be called his paternal style. Deliberate, spare, almost curious at his own routine, it suggests a life at once brimming with ordered activity and yet strangely isolated. He rose at sunrise as usual, he told Hannah, and then went to his bank. Afternoons found him back at his town house with his two youngest daughters Eliza and Catherine, aged eleven and nine. Hannah, who was seventeen in 1828, no doubt recognized her father's ways. That summer she was visiting her elder sister Susan, who had recently moved to New York City with her new husband. Had Hannah been at home in her father's house in Newbern, North Carolina, she, too, would have seen him in the afternoon to report on her domestic activities and on the lessons recited by Eliza and Catherine under her supervision. Like Susan before her, Hannah was mistress of her widower father's house, and though she may well have raised an eyebrow at Gaston's reference to his children enjoying themselves, she would have found her father's mention of work, offspring, and duty as familiar as the doorways and fences of home. Indeed, these values were the very substance of Gaston's view of his home and the world beyond it. They structured his life as a man, a life he himself defined, sometimes surprisingly, as rooted in his responsibilities as a father.[1]

Gaston joined the values of manhood to the demands of his own fatherhood, fashioning a coherent sense of family which shaped his children's lives to the rituals of love, honor, and social position. He took his fatherhood seriously. His struggles with his son over what a man should be, and his patient, finally ambivalent, love for his daughters must be seen as deriving from a *style* of paternalism necessarily displayed to all because Gaston was a man of his class, and matters of love and duty were not merely personal. But biography complicates the socially typical, and Gaston's style must also be seen as a way of *perceiving*, an outlook formed not only of ideas but also of wishes and fears. From his youth, Gaston strove to fit the mischances of life into the ordered pattern of manly honor and paternal love that he believed was the last bulwark against chaos. His paternalism was marked by the tension between his desire to know his children and love them, and his efforts to bend personality to family position, family routine to abstract principles, and love to obligation.

Any number of planter-class men strove in a similar way with their paternalism, but William Gaston's life possesses an instructive combination of qualities and circumstances. As a member of the elite, he had a firm social position; as slaveowner, planter, legislator, jurist, and father he had the wealth and institutional power to dominate people and the intellectual focus to explain why he should. His ample correspondence, including not only letters received but copies of the letters he wrote, are clear evidence of the rhythm of his social life and of his sense of social purpose. Other, more particular, features of Gaston's life make him well suited to reveal the personal workings of paternalism. His five children survived to maturity and came of age in the typical pattern from schooling to marriage. Thus Gaston faced the difficulties and rewards of child rearing common to most other parents. (That he was the sole parent was atypical but not unusual, and as we will see, the absence of a wife and mother in these years did not eliminate the maternal position in his household or discount the importance of the female sphere in the Gaston family. Indeed, Gaston's letters suggest that, because an actual wife did not exist, he had to invent one. This conclusion reveals as much if not more about a certain facet of paternalism's limits and character than had a wife shared his home.) Moreover, Gaston exercised an understated authority which challenges a simple explanation of paternalism's effectiveness. He was no flamboyant tyrant whose dominance is easy to explain. He was certain of his values, and jealous of his equal standing among his peers, but he was cautious in manner. In this sense he was more typical of men of his class than was a strident master. A third reason Gaston is of particular interest is also related to his place in time. He fascinates because his attitudes, expressions, and habits were on the cusp of an eighteenth-century world which stressed order, proportion, and reason in human affairs and a new world which emphasized transcendence, organicism, and feeling. The way in which one impulse tugged against the other was central to Gaston's worldview and to his struggle as man and father, and thus is especially valuable to an understanding of how paternalism balanced indulgence and control.[2]

Gaston wrote his thumbnail report to Hannah during an important year in the family's life. Eighteen hundred twenty-eight was the mid-point in the twelve-year span during which the five Gaston children came of age. Susan Gaston, long her father's mainstay, had left home, and although Gaston's calm letter to Hannah belied it, he was by no means confident that she could replace Susan. It was also a year of great anxiety for Gaston regarding his only son and eldest child Alexander, who seemed to be frittering away the time a young man needed to establish his intellectual leadership and social mastery. Then there were Catherine and Eliza, whom Gaston thought of as his second group of offspring, who soon were to be of an age when academy schooling might best replace home lessons. These events threw the Gaston household into flux, and the years 1826–30 form the core of the period considered here. It is useful to preface what William Gaston's relationship with his children reveals about the style and perceptions of his paternalism with a sketch of Gaston's background and a brief consideration of his temperament. Both give a context for the family events which so concerned him.

Gaston, born in 1778, is perhaps best known as justice of the North Carolina State Supreme Court, although his two-thousand-acre Brice Creek plantation occupied much of his interest, as did his duties as bank president in Newbern. Gaston's father, Alexander, a physician trained at the University of Edinburgh, acquired the plantation in the mid-eighteenth century. The elder Gaston was shot and killed in 1781 while crossing a river in a boat; William believed Tory troops responsible for the murder. Both of Gaston's parents were Roman Catholic, though his mother in particular was concerned for his faith. He was sent to Georgetown University, the first Catholic university in the United States, and later studied law. He was admitted to the North Carolina bar in 1798 and assumed his brother-in-law's legal practice when the latter was appointed to the bench shortly thereafter. After thus establishing himself with relative ease as an able lawyer and promising public man in Newbern, Gaston courted and married Susan Hay in 1803, the first of three wives who would die from complications of childbirth. Susan, who was sixteen when she married the quiet, even-tempered young lawyer, was a fine match, a belle not given to coquetry. When Gaston was elected to the state legislature a year later, his personal good fortune seemed to parallel the young Republic's vigorous rise. Soon after, however, Susan Hay Gaston died, sick with a high fever after childbirth. Though shaken, Gaston continued in the legislature, added to his planting interests, and married a cousin, Hannah McClure, in 1805. They had three children: Alexander (b. 1807), Susan (b. 1808), and Hannah (b. 1811). Two years after Hannah's birth, Gaston won a seat in the U.S. Congress. But in that same year his wife, returning home in haste upon news that British troops were landing on the Carolina coast, died in childbirth, as did the premature baby. Gaston remarried in 1816 to Eliza Worthington, and the couple had two daughters, Eliza (b. 1817) and Catherine (b. 1819). An infection after Catherine's birth took the mother's life, and Gaston determined not to marry again but to raise his children as best he could, first with assistance from his married sister and then from the older girls.[3]

One measure of William Gaston's temperament is the absence of written memorials to his three wives. He was capable of acknowledging deep feeling in letters to intimates, but he almost never recalled his wives to anyone. Nor did he, in the fashion of other men, remark upon the anniversaries of their deaths. That he mourned his wives would seem undeniable; yet God's will would be done in the perilous passage of life on earth. Fundamentals of Catholic belief surely strengthened his determination to accept what had been given him, but religion was less obvious than a cautious, skeptical temperament. The world had its gratifications, but to be satisfied with them was to be dangerously close to folly. Gaston inhabited a moral and emotional landscape in which the qualities of courage, honor, and (perhaps above all) duty were the natural and unalterable foundations of human life, as were folly and self-interest.[4]

In this sense, he shared in what we have come to see as a cultural pattern, rooted in the eighteenth century, in which personal wishes and emotional vitality were seen as deriving from the social and natural worlds. It was a pattern easily given to the drama of ritual. A man was measured not by his inner feelings in the face of reward or peril, but by his ability to display his stature. Neither the intricacies of feeling nor the truths of introspection were as meaningful as whether or not a man could accurately gauge what honor or duty, perceived as "out there" in the world, required of him. Gaston was no William Byrd, whose diary reveals little interest in emotional life, nor was he a Landon Carter, a man forever vexed by emotion he was not equipped to understand. But Gaston did possess a wariness of feeling and, as Jan Lewis has said of eighteenth-century Virginians, sought quietude in human relations rather than their emotional richness. For Gaston, the life worth living was one in which a man clearly saw his own limits and those of humanity at large and then had the discipline to turn those limitations into a reserve of moral authority.[5]

Gaston's courtship of Eliza Worthington was an opportunity for him to find balance in matters of the heart, to search courtship ritual for a kind of justice between the sexes. His letters to her sometimes plodded, sometimes danced with deliberate pun and story; above all they led her decorously from her father's home to his. When he asked that she accept him by placing his letter into her father's hands, love was never more in scale. Similarly, Gaston's sense of his own honor was as close as one could come to the controlled letter and spirit of John Lyde Wilson's code. Neither hot-blooded nor impervious to personal slight, Gaston apparently never dueled but was involved in at least two rather serious affairs of honor during his public career. Interestingly, one involved remarks that characterized him as unreliable on the question of harsh punishment for insurrectionary slaves. Gaston considered the remarks inappropriately personal. (It was one of the rare times in which slavery is even alluded to in Gaston's correspondence. Slaves themselves are shadowy figures in his letters. He mentioned them as individuals now and then, but they seem almost too basic to reach into Gaston's elevated prose style.) Gaston cherished his honor as well as any elite man, but in a way that prized coolness and decorum rather than the thrill of attack. He was not above narrating others' affairs, however, as a long and rather literary account of an 1831 encounter shows. But in general he kept his personal honor bright through care and quiet watchfulness in the risky arena of men in love with politics.[6]

The political world, and more broadly the world of men in public life of all sorts, illuminates Gaston's temperament perhaps better than any set of relationships outside of his family. His personal reserve in affairs of love and honor was matched by his spare, Federalist convictions. He saw the law and the judiciary in particular as bastions against the fashion and tumult of politics. Chief Justice John Marshall was his model public man, a man of selfless courage and effective intellect. Gaston saw Andrew Jackson as a "weak and violent idol." Gaston believed with great fervor in the stability of carefully wrought institutions placed in the hands of honorable men known to one another. He was therefore criticized for being part of an elitist clique, and there is no denying that a belief in a natural aristocracy was central to his conception of political process and public responsibility. Yet Gaston, as always, did not hold himself aloof from the burden of his own standards. He assumed elective office in 1831, for example, genuinely fatigued with the job of legislation but feeling obligated to do so. When he did actively campaign for public office, as in his candidacy for a position on the North Carolina Supreme Court, his concern for propriety and his worry that his Catholicism disqualified him constitutionally for the office caused him to write of his campaign as much with doubt as with desire. Many times with unmistakable sincerity Gaston told his friends that his career rested on their judgment; he gave his advisers, in the best male tradition, the responsibility for permitting him to exercise his own judgment. Public life for Gaston was in essence a life with other upper-class men "in whose integrity, knowledge of me, knowledge of what would be expected from me, and in whose frankness I can confide." In order to know "what does duty demand of me," Gaston needed friends who knew *him* apart from the authority he might assume, and who would measure the conditions for its assumption. For Gaston, party politics was often a feeble imitation of the manly, civic life he feared the American Republic was losing in the 1830s. He strove to be the kind of man he felt the time required but no longer rewarded, a man who was, in the words of a friend's praise, "truly virtuous, chaste, benevolent, and able."[7]

That most of these adjectives belonged to the female sex by the 1850s, and scarcely would have been used to characterize the world of politics, would not have surprised William Gaston had he lived to see that decade. Elevated in his principles, and restricted in his conception of political process, Gaston joined his sense of public life to his watchful, even bleak, view of human nature at large. He linked his belief in the burdensome honor of public trusteeship to a conviction of life's transient rewards. This conviction was a kind of genteel nihilism—a considered despair for the permanence and pleasure of human relationships. Even so, Gaston's sense of his civic role led him to be available to men who did not share in his understanding, to those seeking his official favors, requesting his presence at this or that meeting or town, ruined men asking his support against a tide of ill fortune or alcohol. Gaston patiently, paternally replied to them all, keeping copies of his letters which form a kind of ledger of an elite public man whose power to dispense favors was inextricably tied to his ability to articulate morality. He lectured alcoholic men on their characters, political office seekers on their duties, and constantly found signs that life was short and satisfaction thin. "Good God! what frail beings we are!" he wrote his daughter upon the death of an alcoholic acquaintance. "That such a man should fall victim to deliberate intemperance is one of the most shocking instances of human infirmity that ever came within my observation. . . . He *knew* that he was killing himself by inches, was sensible of the enormity of such conduct, was warned in the name of his children and of God to desist, and yet he continued to swallow the liquid poison." Gaston expected such men. Yet he felt sapped by the futility of the loss; he seemed unable to account completely for the waste of character and talent he warned others to expect of the world. This view drove him to a worldly detachment somewhat at odds with his immediate interests. As a social and political leader, he was of course obliged to manipulate arguments before the bench, draft the prose of legislation, manage the resources and boundaries of Brice Creek, and deal with the exhausting parade of men of all stations who served him, complimented him, required him, made demands of him. But as a man who thought of his authority as power accepted in trust rather than seized through ambition, Gaston had to keep moral as well as tactical accounts. The making of proper distinctions and fine judgments so essential to an honorable man was at the core of both his self-esteem and his power. Still, beneath the calm tone of his routine decisions was the chance that he might be unable to account for the deepest difficulty of all: why men destroy their own order. Coded in the order of things, perhaps, was their disastrous end. "I am too full of conflicting sensation to define or to communicate my feelings," Gaston wrote at the death of a friend. "The predominant one is a *deep* conviction of the nothingness of worldly joy, worldly pursuits, and worldly cares."[8]

If there was a pull away from hopelessness, it was his family. Even in the elevated style of his paternalism, William Gaston was profoundly moved by the depth of family affection and unity. He named his son after his father, and his firstborn daughter after his deceased (and childless) first wife. He named his second daughter after her mother, and his third after hers. These people were present in their names, alive in his speech. When a niece named her son William, Gaston, much moved, wrote to her mother: "Say to [Margaret] . . . that I feel sensibly the proof of regard with which they have honored me in the name conferred upon their infant." Gaston's family relations were beacons in an otherwise clouded social world. His own children, of course, were the brightest lights. Yet here, too, was a chance for loss. "All my earthly treasure is my children," he wrote in 1826. "And where our treasure there also is our anxiety." Taken together, his children's lives reflected upon his temperament, illuminating it like nothing else in his life and testing its resistance to melancholy. Gaston thought that the subject of his children singularly colored his thoughts and words. "When my children are around me I give way to the cheerfulness which their presence inspires and delight to join in their gaiety and sports," he told Hannah. "But when they are far away, the remembrance of them is connected with a melancholy or rather pensive tenderness which communicates its character to all I write." Gaston felt deeply the motherlessness of his children's lives, particularly when they came of schooling age. Home education was not suitable, he felt, for giving a girl the social experience she needed to develop a lady's poise. A woman's wider sphere demanded a style that the intimacy of family could not create on its own. He feared, too, that it would be delinquent of him to raise girls apart from female instruction, and that local North Carolina schools in the mid-1820s were simply not to be entrusted with this special task. But in thus sending first Susan and then Hannah to school in other cities, he separated himself from them and melancholy set in. He was moved to reflect generally on all of his offspring, and his letters show an unmistakable concern because of distance and the inevitable alienation. "I have abundant satisfaction in my children," he once wrote to Susan. "They have many excellent qualities and above all they love me tenderly and wish to please me. Yet I feel great solicitude about them. However, I will not trouble you with my anxieties. Ultimately I trust everything will turn out as I ought to expect." Typically Gaston was balancing anxiety over nameless dangers with pride in the way his children bore witness to his fatherhood. His last observation, variously repeated in many of his letters, perhaps reveals best of all the particular blend of authority and morality that oriented his paternalism: at a distance from his children, he had to trust that all was well and would turn out not only as he expected, but as he *ought* to expect. His children had to realize not just something plausible or likely; they must measure up also to the moral standards he constantly set for himself.[9]

This dynamic was most fully realized in Gaston's relationship with his eldest daughter, Susan, and so it is illuminating to characterize their bond before Susan was married in 1828 and then to contrast it to Gaston's ties with his next two oldest offspring. Typical paternal pride and anxiety fill Gaston's letters to his friend Joseph Hopkinson when the latter watched over Susan while she was at Madame Sigoignes's school in Philadelphia from 1822 to 1823. Susan lived with the Hopkinson family and Gaston's regular but rather vague, almost indecisive, letters show him to have been somewhat puzzled about a young lady's coming of age. Distance from Susan was Gaston's chief frame of reference. In most of his letters to Hopkinson, Gaston remarked in one way or another on the separation between himself and his daughter. He greatly appreciated Hopkinson's offer to let Susan live with his family rather than board at the school. Gaston clearly feared close association among young women, even under the most decorous of headmistresses. Gaston requested that Hopkinson "from time to time" ascertain Susan's complete situation—her lessons, books, teachers, and sister students. He begged Hopkinson to speak to him plainly if he saw anything amiss in "mind manners habits," and tempered his pride in his daughter with advice on how to manipulate her. His thoughts on care for her easily expanded into suggestions on carefulness for the womanhood she embodied. Gaston's view was almost positivist, his language most like a craftsman. "My parental partiality deceives me much if she have not the *material* out of which an amiable woman may be educed," he wrote to Hopkinson. "Skill and care in *management* are necessary—perhaps in regard to her, particularly necessary."[10]

It is not clear what he meant by the last, but it is certain that he expected Susan, guided by the love he felt for her, to return from Philadelphia a lady. Gaston was convinced that becoming a lady meant becoming schooled in manner as well as mind. But he agonized over the matter of Susan's being seen socially and, therefore, meeting men. On the one hand, to exclude Susan from male company would interfere with her full development as a lady (and might even be construed as casting doubt on the propriety of the Hopkinsons' home.) On the other, social intercourse in drawing rooms signaled adulthood, and Gaston was concerned lest Susan rush too quickly into being a woman while still occupied with becoming a lady. In his letters to Hopkinson, Gaston's paternal carefulness mingled with his desire to please his daughter:

> That she should *occasionally* and without form mingle in your family circle would afford me high gratification. But I believe it would be better that she should not frequently have this enjoyment. When a girl sees much society her mind is liable to become dissipated— serious studies are regarded as irksome—and she is too apt to fancy herself a woman. My dear daughter has years yet in which I wish her to be considered, and to consider herself, a child.[11]

He added that he "could not refuse" her permission to go to the theater at times, "but I would be quite as well pleased that she did not ask it," and worried lest such outings "give her an early fancy for deep vanity, etc., etc." Gaston's desire to indulge his eldest daughter (though "without form") was joined to a moralist's deep conviction of women's propensity for moral faults. Perhaps no other attitude better reveals Gaston's sense of Susan as both his child and a woman—precisely the point at which she found herself in 1823. Rather than whisk her through the coming of age, Gaston wished to regulate the passage to *his* sense of what womanhood required. Yet he was not completely certain about womanhood. Susan's meeting men perplexed him, and he confessed to Hopkinson, "On the subject of Susan's seeing company I have a difficulty in forming a definite opinion." Gaston was sensitive to the "many advantages" a woman could take from candle-lit evenings in a friend's drawing room, but decided that Susan at age fifteen was not yet woman enough to use them. And so, many miles away from the actual daily life of his daughter—a life he attempted to regulate but could not fully visualize—Gaston did his duty by directing his good friend Hopkinson as to her dress, books, and company.[12]

Thus William Gaston based his understanding of his daughter's coming of age neither on observing her nor on extensive correspondence with her. Her responsibilities as his daughter and as a young woman were understanding enough. By 1823 it was clear, as it probably had been for some time, that Susan would return to Newbern to be mistress of her father's home. If this expectation was ever discussed, let alone debated, between Susan and her father, the evidence does not survive. Gaston expressed his strict standards for her in such reasonable words of love and duty that their very impersonality became the mark of true paternal care. When the sixteen-year-old Susan took up her duties as mistress of her father's home in 1824, the apparent ease and obedience with which she did so bound her still more closely to Gaston, validating the precepts of her schooling and the hopes of her father. Their relationship after 1824 became the standard by which the other children were judged, with all the controlling love Gaston and Susan together could bring to bear, and became the center of family life as securely as a marriage.[13]

Of immediate concern was the early schooling of Susan's half-sisters Eliza and Catherine, the latter called Kate, who were aged eight and six in 1825. Gaston wished Susan to begin their lessons at home, and apparently worried that he might not be able financially to support his "little girls" in academies. Hannah and Alexander already were in school, and Gaston increasingly prepared Susan to assume responsibility for the youngest girls' intellectual growth. He instructed his eldest daughter to instruct them in the basics of reading and writing, and later included arithmetic and even Latin in their home curriculum. Occasionally receiving some help from her aunt, Susan thus became not only mother to her half-sisters but teacher as well. The girls' education, which Gaston took quite seriously, became the major topic of Susan's correspondence with her father. As with Susan's own schooling, Gaston emphasized control and structure; his language regarding his daughters' attainments and routines stressed precision yet remained curiously unspecific, leaving to Susan, as a woman, most of the details. "I fear they [the girls] will give you some trouble," he wrote her in 1826. "But you must render it less by establishing fixed hours and a regular system. . . . Your government in this respect cannot be too exact. Their health and comeliness render rigid discipline on this subject necessary." As Gaston relied on Susan to be a mother to the younger girls, he increasingly was able to express his profound desire for a feminine presence in their lives. Gender organized knowledge and explained behavior. He worried that Eliza and Kate might find him too anxious, for example, but "they will excuse me not only because of the motive [i.e., his love for them] but because they have no mother whose gentle counsels and mild influence may imperceptibly lead them on in the ways of excellence." Susan would supply that peculiarly feminine tone, and indeed rather early on Gaston began to rely upon Susan to counsel not only the little girls but her older brother as well. Hearing reports of Alexander's achievements at his academy, Gaston told Susan of his "delight which none but a parent can feel but of which a sister may form some conception." Because her sisterly powers came close to parental ones, however, Gaston urged, "Write to him my darling child and let him know how much his conduct cheers his fond father's heart." Gaston would similarly urge Susan to speak, from the woman's sphere, to Alexander throughout the years to come. And as Gaston relied on Susan to act as mother, he inevitably created in her a kind of wife.[14]

Susan seems to have willingly taken on her assignment without complaint. After the academy, she claimed her old home as a new household, and became quite visible in Newbern society. Her filial duty flourished in this safe arena for the display of her womanly talents, giving her experience not only in the raising of children, but also in the management of household slaves, household budget, and, increasingly by 1827, Gaston's social engagements. Susan was, in effect, learning the work and attitudes of married life, and she could scarcely escape notice by the unmarried men of the town. As in her domestic work and mothering, in courtship, too, Susan turned first to her father and to the sureness of ritual. She referred marriage proposals to Gaston, and he responded formally by applauding her dutiful behavior which he declared he would never abuse. When informed of a proposal, he invariably expressed "my approbation of the candor with which you have communicated it to me." Gaston was at the center of their life together, in his own and Susan's view, and his paternal love pushed aside even the ardor of a suitor. "You have no bosom in which to repose confidence so thoroughly devoted to your happiness as that of your Father. I will never control—if possible I will not even influence—you on subjects of that sort. But my best counsel (when asked) and my tenderest sympathy shall always be yours." In such ways was the authority of a father clothed in loving selflessness. Gaston said—he believed—that his daughter's decisions in courtship were her own, but really they could not be conceived outside of his orbit. Though advocating her autonomy, Gaston believed a daughter's heart could never be separate from a father's incomparable advice.[15]

To point out the tension between Gaston's open disclaimer of influence and his not very hidden desire that Susan rely upon him as upon no one else is not to suggest that Gaston was aware of it. He doubtless was not at all concerned that he portrayed himself as the central figure in her life because she, in a way, was the central figure in his. What both father and daughter were aware of was their deep, mutual love for each other, expressed in full when Susan did in fact become engaged. William Gaston had been well aware of the attentions paid his daughter by lawyer and commercial agent Robert Donaldson, at least since the spring of 1827. When Susan wrote her father of her desire to marry, Gaston's reply to Donaldson reveals how letter-guide convention might be infused with personal passion:

> My dear Sir
> Such is the confidence I repose in the judgment of my beloved daughter that my approbation can scarcely fail to sanction her choice. I owe it, however, to truth to add that every information that has reached me of your character induces me to acquiesce, not [illegible] but cheerfully, in the election which she has made. In consenting to your union with my child I feel that I am about to bestow a gift the value of which none can know so well as myself. She has long been the pride, the joy, the solace of my heart. God grant that she may discharge the duties which she may owe to you with the same unequalled, inimitable excellence which has characterized her in the performance of those that were due to her Father! A greater blessing than this I cannot wish you.
>
> > Very Truly and respectfully yours,
> > Wm: Gaston[16]

He again disclaims final authority in matters of Susan's heart. But this letter, with the full force of courtship ritual, in fact asserts his authority as nothing less than what was owed to truth. He has inquired into Donaldson's character as a father ought, but beyond this inquiry he claims to know the essential value of Susan as no one else ever will. Susan had done no more than that "due to her Father," but she nonetheless emerges as a deeply loved paragon of womanhood. She is a "gift" which her father may bestow and which Donaldson will have to strive to appreciate for what "she may owe" to him.

Susan's emotional attachment to her father became even more open in the months that preceded her February 1828 wedding. Whatever her anxieties at her impending marriage, none stood out more clearly or lent itself to words more eloquently than her fear of losing her father and his love. She felt intense guilt at leaving him home to himself. Though Gaston, too, had times when he dreaded losing Susan's companionship and her work, he drove himself to do what ought to be done. He admitted to being selfishly concerned for his own well-being, but wrote in response to her doubts:

> As for *you*, my Susan, to whom I am bound not only by the ties of parental love but by those of intimate association, as for you who for several years have been my dearest companion and friend, do not reproach yourself that you have consented to leave me. In this my child you violate no duty. It is indeed impossible that I should look

forward to so great a change in your condition with indifference—
without alternate emotions of hope and fear. But such is the lot of
mortality. . . . Perfect happiness on Earth! 'Tis a madman's dream.
Look not for it. Receive with pious gratitude whatever of happiness
God may bestow—enjoy it with tempered cheerfulness.[17]

Speaking to himself as much as to Susan at the close of this letter,
Gaston discovered that the loss of his daughter had the solace of once
more proving his worldview correct. Gaston's wifelessness may have
heightened Susan's guilt at leaving him, but it cannot account for it.
After all, Gaston's youngest girls were fast approaching adolescence
and the early child-rearing years were over. Rather, Susan seems to
have been dismayed at leaving a love relationship based on a safe reciprocity for one which held the promise of love but also fearful myster-
ies. Gaston found it necessary to write Susan more than once that she
need not punish herself for growing up, putting his paternal comfort in
the service of the elevated vision of social womanhood implicit in
courtship:

Blame not yourself, my dearest, for having consented to unite yourself with one who loves you with devoted affection and whom you
have every reason to believe worthy of your love. You ought not to
have rejected his addresses because their acceptance would separate
you from me. Think not that I shall remain unrewarded for my parental cares. If you but discharge the new duties to which you will be
called with fidelity and ability, adorn your station by virtue and religion, make your husband and your husband's friends happy, comfort the distressed, relieve the poor and diffuse joy around you, think
you that your Father will mourn because he hears of your excel-
lences and does not constantly witness them?[18]

The rhetorical question was not intended to leave room for more than
the solace of a negative response. Again, from a ritual height, struggling
to come to terms with what could be a domestic crisis for him as well as
for Susan, Gaston spoke as much from the realm of fatherhood as intimately to her. And in formally releasing her from his home, he did not
remove from her a woman's burden of being a luminous spirit who
deftly combined joy with duty. He had raised a daughter most difficult
to give up: a woman and a child, competent enough to direct the personalities and work of a slaveowning household, yet dutiful enough to
regret even the "naturalness" of a lady's destiny.

Apart from his sense of loss at Susan's going (she would live in New
York City, and Robert Donaldson would become Gaston's cotton
agent), Gaston also feared his family would suffer, too. Alexander, he

believed, needed the close counsel of his nearest sister. Eliza and Catherine were at the age when a decision had to be made about sending them to an academy, a decision both financial and intellectual by 1827. Gaston hoped to settle debts incurred in planting before more of his offspring came of marrying age, and feared that he could not do so while paying for academy education. He wanted to justify keeping the youngest girls at home by telling himself that home education was as good as Madame Sigoignes's academy but he could not quite do so. Everything should turn out as he ought to expect, but what if it did not? For men of Gaston's temperament and family convictions, the next oldest daughter would naturally step in to fill the tutor's place. But Hannah Gaston, twenty years old in 1828, was as much a problem as a solution.[19]

Hannah is a shadowy figure in the Gaston family history precisely because she disappointed her father: she did not—would not—write letters. Her father was at pains to coax a letter from her. Writing to Susan four months before her wedding, Gaston typically expressed his worries. Busy with plans for the shift in his household arrangements and family relationships, he praised Susan for the progress Kate and Eliza had made in Latin. "If Hannah will hear them their lessons everyday," he added, "she will not only benefit them but improve herself. Why is it that I get no letters from her?" Hannah had returned to Newbern by 1828 from Miss Marcilly's school in Baltimore. While she was away, Gaston had noted her reticence, her short letters his praise did nothing to lengthen. His overseeing her studies was more directed to Hannah personally (though she was living with relatives in Baltimore) than his concern with Susan's schooling had been three years before. Much of his direct exhortation doubtless stemmed from a surer grasp of what schooling for young women should involve. But much of it seems also to have derived from his plan to replace Susan with Hannah when the time came. Gaston warned Hannah of this plan as early as 1826, when he alluded several times to her need to prepare herself for domestic "eventualities." Many topics led him to make the same point. "I am gratified that you have an opportunity to hear chemical lectures," he wrote Hannah. "Avail yourself my daughter of every occasion to *store your mind with useful knowledge*. What duties you may be called on to perform in this world of probation and vicissitude is impossible to foresee. Qualify yourself if possible to meet *every* emergency." The emergency Gaston had in mind did not, however, relate to chemical studies: "It may be inconvenient for me to send from home my two youngest daughters. Can it be necessary if my two eldest can instruct them? The period is approaching when you may greatly contribute to the forming of their infant minds to all that is virtuous and estimable."

Despite this foreshadowing, and notwithstanding the wreathes of rhetoric adorning his letters ("How meritorious will not this be in the sight of God! What pleasure will it not give your fond father!") Hannah replied only reluctantly and often not at all. When days passed without a letter, Gaston reprimanded her for "that lethargy of soul which I so dread and abhor—which paralyzes all energies of intellect and ultimately blasts the best affections of the heart."[20]

In addition to casting Hannah's immediate future in terms of incontrovertible duty, Gaston compared her to Susan with unmistakable, if unconscious, preference for his eldest daughter. His constant references to Susan, couched in the language of filial duty and paternal approbation, amounted to a narrative of Susan's perfection. What Gaston intended as a model for Hannah, based on the common sense of a daughter's family position, took on the substance of a goad that denied Hannah her own temperament and personal wishes. Perhaps, too, Gaston's concern not to raise Susan's vanity led him to express his most fulsome praise of her to Hannah; in any event he seemed oblivious to the effect on the younger girl. "I cannot mention her name without telling you what a comfort and joy she has proved to me," Gaston typically said of Susan. "I am proud of her—she is so good—so exemplary in the performance of the weighty duties imposed on her at so early an age. May I be equally as proud of my beloved Hannah! Whatever troubles I may meet with from other quarters if my children do well I shall be contented and blest." With words like these a father's wish became identical to a family's well-being; in such terms did a father's desire become a daughter's instruction. Hannah's succession to her father's right hand would be established by his uttering it, and Gaston's rhetoric barely distinguished between wish and imperative; a father's contentment was blessed. When Hannah simply did not respond, Gaston's tone sharpened and became, if not more explicit—his talk of love and duty was explicit enough—at least more down to earth. "When you return home," he wrote Hannah at Miss Marcilly's school, "you must be fitted to aid—perhaps to succeed—Susan in training your little sisters in the paths of virture and knowledge. The expense of your education is to me a serious inconvenience. But if you can fit yourself by it to save similar expenses in the education of Eliza and Catherine, you can then return with interest what I have bestowed you." This was plain enough, even though, as usual with Hannah, Gaston was slightly reticent; she would "perhaps" succeed Susan. Yet he brushes past his doubts here. Evidence that Hannah had learned her academy lessons had to be presented in the family circle. Although she was a finished young woman, her acquirements for the moment still revolved about her family, or more precisely Gaston's paternal view of the family.[21]

Yet work in the family—a woman's work and a daughter's—was not all of Gaston's desire. Hannah must be a lady as well, and here also Gaston did not ease up on comparisons with Susan. When Hannah pleased him, he praised her in ways that coupled her with her sister in the woman's sphere, writing her slyly in 1828 that "the beaux" had let it be known that Hannah "fill[s] Susan's place with perfect ability." Established in her father's home as its lady, however much against her will, Hannah by 1828 had thus become the household's belle. But it was not just for the beaus that she bloomed. It was for her father as well. While visiting Susan in New York in the summer of 1828, Hannah took lessons on the piano, something that Gaston typically saw as bolstering an entire field of character: "[It] will strengthen your memory, refine your taste, and enrich your style." But it had other advantages. "You must learn several new songs," he told her. "And learn to sing them well, that you may be able to cheer and soothe your Father when he is vexed with care, worn with toil, or crossed in business." A young woman's accomplishments, however much aimed at personal improvement or the beaus, had the additional use of delighting her father. In this, too, Hannah stood in Susan's shadow, and Hannah's ladylike attainments, the music of her piano, assumed a competitive dimension that Susan never knew and Hannah never completely avoided. Gaston's efforts to have his daughters please him took on the rhetoric of paternal narratives in fiction. He became the very figure of fatherly need ("vexed with care, worn with toil"). He seized the power locked into conventional images of a paterfamilias whose home sheltered him, whose daughters justified his care. Whether repaying him for the expense of their schooling, or singing sweetly to him as he sought freedom from the snags of manhood, Gaston's daughters provided a vision of family unity wholly derived from *his* needs and *his* sense of them. It was a vision in which a father's affections were the end of all accomplishment and gender the measure of family relations.[22]

This intimate dynamic of the family was at the heart of elite paternalism, putting the family at the heart of the social order. It is seen in a different way in Gaston's relation to his son, Alexander. If Hannah sometimes perplexed or annoyed Gaston, Alexander alarmed him. Alexander, too, only infrequently wrote to his father, though Gaston seems not to have been so concerned as he was in Hannah's case; a girl more than a boy had to keep close with words. What distressed Gaston was his son's flightiness, of which a lack of correspondence was only a sign. From the beginning of his education at a military academy in 1823 to his establishment as Gaston's chief representative on the plantation in 1829 or 1830, Alexander Gaston was the subject of his father's most anguished letters and the chief object of his paternal anxiety. Gaston came as close as he ever did to being overwrought in his letters when Alexander's doings were at issue, and he wrote all members of his family, except the youngest girls, about his concern. Gaston's sister, Susan, and even Hannah, heard his worries about the son "who came into the world too young," a possible reference to premature birth but also an allusion to Gaston's sense of Alexander's prolonged immaturity.[23]

As a male, Alexander shared a sensibility and was much more of a known object that a father could shape to familiar ends. From the beginning of his son's education, Gaston showed none of the tentativeness he expressed with Susan (as the first daughter) or Hannah (as the relatively recalcitrant one). Quite certain of how a son should mature, Gaston strove to say something positive about Alexander, but often ended up criticizing his son's ways. Writing to a friend in 1823, Gaston faintly praised Alexander as "not inattentive to his studies," tepid words in a father's mouth. "If I can succeed in converting a passion for military glory into an ambition for forensic distinction I hope to make something of him," he concluded. The project confounded Gaston. Though sending his son to a military academy, Gaston more than once discounted Alexander's accounts of drills and maneuvers as boy's play. Praise for Alexander's "excellent heart, good principles and a devoted affection for me" was invariably linked to Gaston's calm self-centeredness rather than his son's achievements. "Alexander is not prosecuting his studies with diligence," Gaston told Hannah in 1826. "I trust that he will yet realize my fondest hopes." By this time, Alexander's desire to be a poet had replaced his military ambitions, and Gaston chafed at his son's distance from home and blamed himself for not being strict enough. His view of Alexander betrayed not only his inattention to his son's delight in academy routine, but an almost willful ignorance of its significance. What mattered most, indeed what supplanted Alexander's actual experience, was the father's image of a son *working* at manhood. "Alexander I *hope* is seriously engaged in his studies," Gaston wrote his sister. "I dare not use a stronger phrase than 'hope.' God knows what he will turn out to be finally! He has the capacity to learn whatever he will take the labor to learn—but I have permitted him to have his own way so much, and he has contracted such habits of literary trifling, that he will find a steady, persevering application a very hard task." What Gaston overlooked was that his son's "literary triflings" were the substance of what he had discovered in the company of brother students. The desire for "forensic distinction" and "persevering application" was the father's alone.[24]

Alexander's capacity—for work, for attention to his duty as a son— nevertheless remained an open question after the end of his schooling led him back to Brice Creek and his father's home. It seemed inappropriate to Gaston to have his son idle about the house writing, so he placed Alexander in charge of certain work in planting. Though letters from Alexander were rare, it seems that he was not unhappy at Brice Creek, seldom coming to town and parrying his father's attempts to interest him in the public responsibilities that inspired political ambition. In the early spring of 1828, Alexander fell in love with a young woman named Eliza Jones, giving his father new cause for concern. Gaston could scarcely bring himself to name the dreaded outcome, marriage: "My poor dear boy is always giving me anxiety," he wrote Susan three weeks after her own wedding. "I should certainly deprecate the event you allude to on *many—very many*—accounts." But what disturbed Gaston most was that Alexander had not confessed his love for Eliza to him. It was an alarming breach of father-son confidence. "Why can he not—why will he not—repose confidence in his own father?" Gaston wrote in bewilderment to Susan. "Where else is he to find a friend on whose attachment and fidelity he can so confidently rely?" By "friend" Gaston doubtless meant the older sense of a trusted patron or benefactor, and this usage may reveal the source of his perplexity. Alexander had an altogether different view of his father, one at odds with the kind of disinterested trustee Gaston believed himself to be. Though Gaston seems to have had no sense of this difference, or of how his paternal directives actually undercut his ability to be his son's friend, he clearly perceived his son's alienation from him. Once again, Gaston turned to Susan for help: "Tell him in your gentle but impressive way not to committ himself on a matter of such infinite importance without consulting his Father. It would be a contempt of his opinions, an ungrateful return for his solicitudes." Gaston lapses into the third person here as in many other instances in which his word and his view were to rule. And once again he expects behavior that will reciprocate paternal care. Now and again he may have glimpsed how his care was overbearing (he told Susan, as if seeking corroboration, "I am not a tyrant to be feared and hated"), but he persisted nonetheless, finally confronting Alexander himself. Gaston's account of their meeting again unites a narrative of paternal love with an unquestioning confidence in the rightness of paternal judgment. "Poor fellow I pity him sincerely!" he wrote. "He is much more deeply interested [in marriage] than I had imagined. I told him mildly but explicitly all that I thought and concluded with assuring him that I should not forbid his doing in the affair what he pleased but I could never sanction his choice with my approbation. He wept. I did not speak further to him." It is probable, as it would not have been a century earlier, that a father's withholding of approval did not necessarily imply a withholding of a son's patrimony. But this aside, the measure of Gaston's paternalism lay in his cool account of an emotional confrontation, indeed his apparent coolness throughout. Father denied son, and the son wept. Alexander's desires drew pity, but no other paternal emotion, nor did Gaston second-guess his certainty, even in a letter to his best-loved daughter.[25]

Intense but private, preoccupying but not crippling, the conflict between father and son over work, marriage, and manhood continued into the spring of 1828. Alexander, with no other means of support and nowhere else to go, stayed on at the plantation and a complete break was avoided. In May, Gaston determined to send his twenty-one-year-old son to visit Susan in New York City in order to remove him from love's way. Lamenting that Alexander "seems to have a total disinclination for business of any kind," Gaston implored his new son-in-law "to get him into a lawyer's office—to get him into *any business* . . . that could qualify him for usefulness and enable him to walk the world of reality instead of that fairy region of imagination in which he is wandering forever." A career for Alexander in politics and public office was no longer in Gaston's mind; he would settle for usefulness. But at last Eliza Jones herself snapped the strain by refusing Alexander's marriage proposal, a stunning blow to the young man. Gaston's relieved response typically placed Alexander's particular struggles squarely into the general realm of manliness, drawing from a son's life the lessons of gender and class which for Gaston were so thoroughly a part of common sense that pity, not anger, formed his words. "My poor boy!" he wrote Susan. "I feel for him *deeply*. I am sure that his pride is wounded. Would to God! that the wound may prove a salutary one! Would that he could see before it is too late that Genius, Fancy and personal accomplishments without steadiness and a manly application to the business of life, cannot obtain for him the respect of one sex or the favor of the other." The image of a salutary wound was so central to Gaston's view of life that his son's loss could be seen as manliness's gain. The son's romantic crisis became, in the father's view, further proof of those human affairs which cautioned but did not startle a mature man. It was all a matter of women and men, their separate natures, and the work suitable and privileged to both. His son's "personal accomplishments," from his literary interests to his courtship, could never come close to matching the attainments befitting a true man. The lessons of love and influence awaited the unwary and the learned alike; gender, far from being ignored in Gaston's cool calculus, fed the social logic of his class. "No well-regulated female mind can *love*—although it may *like*—the man who is not respected by his fellows," Gaston declared. To attain love, Alexander had to do what his father had all along told him—to go out among *men*, strive with them in the male sphere of public achievement; the women would follow.[26]

With Hannah's silences and Alexander's disappointing emotional migrations, William Gaston's family relationships by 1829 denied much of the affectionate reciprocity and unity that his paternalism had led him to expect. Only Susan, far away in Yankeeland, continued to be the sort of child Gaston could have predicted. Yet he was realistic, priding himself in his planting, business, and politics as a man whose daily moderation was only the surface of a profound ability to come to terms with whatever life dealt. Though anxious about his family life, Gaston came to accept its texture, the given circumstances that demanded a sensible response by a rational man. It is useful, then, to pause briefly here, as Gaston himself did in 1828–29, to assess his paternalism as the new decade began. Despite distance and imperfect communication by letter, in fact because of them, Gaston self-consciously asserted his fatherhood in order to shape his family to the manly values of honor, moderation, and reciprocity. Yet his paternalism, in the years between 1823 and 1830, was itself shaped by two related considerations in which manliness was not so seamless as it might appear. First, though disinclined to marry a fourth time, Gaston needed the presence of a woman to order his family life. His attachment to Susan as a helpmate shows how paternal leadership required the feminine; gender was at the heart of Gaston's most personal sense of worth and work. It is obvious that Susan's labor in child rearing and household management was crucial to Gaston's comfort. Less obviously, but more pervasively, Susan's presence gave his home and his life a necessary feminine counterpoint, a moral balance and an aesthetic one. Without it, Gaston could not measure his own worth. But with his self-esteem held intact by constant reference to Susan, Gaston oriented himself to his world and his social responsibilities. These responsibilities were shaped by the second basic consideration of his paternalism: his most important expectations of family and gender were simultaneously a psychology and a sociology. What honor displayed, what the community demanded, unalterably was joined to the psychological needs of his children. Gaston's vision of his children, from the beginning of their schooling, did not see personality as separate from social categories of gender. He worried that his daughters were moving too quickly into womanhood and that his son would not enter manhood at all. Hannah was too circumspect for a woman and Alexander too expressive for a man. Gaston was as sadly affronted by Hannah's wordlessness as he was delighted by Susan's loving words. His son's failure to take his place among men caused Gaston his deepest regret and his most strained paternal exhortation. With the coming of age, Alexander was supposed to speak as a man and Hannah was supposed to replace Susan in a natural succession not open to exception or even to full intellectual scrutiny. Offspring would gain the spiritual legacies that were their due only if they matched their lives to the responsibilities of their sex and their family position.[27]

In a sense, Gaston had failed with Alexander and Hannah by 1828: failed to stir in them the acknowledgment of the values that animated Susan. Though it is true that Alexander did not marry against his father's wishes, and subsequently seems to have taken over a greater amount of plantation management, he remained committed to pursuits that precluded a career in law and public life. For her part, Hannah did indeed return to Newbern in 1829 to be mistress of Gaston's household (and to be seen about town as the next marriageable daughter). But for reasons that no doubt in part reflected a refusal to follow Susan's path, Hannah did not fully undertake the mothering of her younger sisters. Yet more remarkable than his failure to have his children fulfill his paternal expectations was Gaston's unbending faith that those expectations were part of a natural inevitability. Burden or satisfaction, family relations forever revolved around him as a father, a man, and a social leader.

The next four years closed out Gaston's duties as rearer of his youthful offspring, and the events and relationships that characterized them are further evidence of what paternalism could mean to elite family life. Again, what makes the Gastons useful as a case study is the apparent tranquillity of their life together—no heated breaks, no bitter animosity, no elopements, disinheritings, banishments—based upon a paternalism that had limitations as clear as its insights. The years between 1829 and 1834 reveal Gaston turning once again to Susan who once again responded, even from New York, as the daughter on which he could depend; this bond between daughter and father remains the clearest angle of vision on what paternalism might accomplish and explain. And in these years Eliza, ten years younger than Susan, emerges as her successor. Eliza's own adjustment to her father's rule gave his paternalism a continuity as the personal (and ideological) force it was—in Gaston's life as well as his children's.

Faced with Hannah's unwillingness to supervise her sisters fully, Gaston began in the spring of 1829 to seek a school for Eliza and Catherine. At her father's request, Susan traveled to Washington, D.C., to inspect a school in Georgetown, the Academy of the Visitation, reputed to be intellectually sound as well as morally safe. Susan reported that "the Nunnery" looked fine and moreover was near to kin of Gaston's second wife who could be relied upon to help. Gaston sent his daughters to the school in July. Eliza and Catherine, aged twelve and ten, remained there a year; but Gaston apparently became displeased with the academy and withdrew them for a time in July 1830. There is evidence that Gaston was not satisfied with the intellectual quality of the education, though as a Catholic academy the school was certainly protective of his daughters' morals. Still, Gaston seems to have chafed even about this aspect, suspecting that the school was too isolated, too removed from the sort of social life awaiting a planter-class woman. He vacillated about reenrolling the girls. Throughout the fall of 1830, Gaston corresponded both with Susan and with kin in Georgetown, receiving good reports from the former, who touted the teachers and the curriculum. By December Catherine and Eliza were back at the school, but Gaston's desire to have them learn Latin still went unanswered, and reports from Susan and others increasingly turned up drawbacks to the institution: It *was* isolated, perhaps too comfortably Catholic, and, worst of all, seemed academically inferior in more than the absence of Latin. Again, Gaston's concern for the intellectual training of his daughters is notable, and evidence that even a traditional man could not detach a woman's intellect from manner. Because the school was convenient, and relatively inexpensive, Gaston hesitated, but by the autumn of 1831 he decided against the Nunnery, and called upon Susan to find a New York City school where the girls might board but still be under her watchful eye. Eliza and Catherine returned to North Carolina until Susan completed her canvass of New York City academies and decided upon Madame Chegaray's, the well-known, moderately expensive institute on Houston Street. The shift from a Catholic academy to one of New York's most prestigious, "French" boarding schools was a sharp one, and Gaston had new reservations. Yet Susan convinced him that the scholastic strengths of Chegaray's more than balanced the lures to vanity concealed in the city; and, most important, she was there to monitor any change in her sisters' values or style. Within a year, Susan was satisfied that Eliza and Catherine, having acquired Latin, were finished to her father's standards, and, in view of the rising cost of tuition, might safely end their formal schooling. Gaston's trust in Susan did not preclude him from writing frequent letters giving her advice and asking questions, and he also wrote regularly to Catherine and Eliza. These were busy, full years for Gaston, and so the concern in much of his correspondence for his daughters is additional evidence of the importance he attached to their intellectual and social development. During these years he made adjustments in his planting and in the slaves he rented; he gave up what he estimated to be nearly one-third of his annual income to take a seat in the state assembly in the name of civic duty; he began a serious consideration of whether to make himself a candidate for the state supreme court, worrying to himself and friends that the North Carolina constitution quite likely prohibited a Catholic from the office; both Alexander and Hannah were married, happily it seems, throwing his Newbern life into further changes. Through all of these events, Gaston's interest and attention to his youngest daughters' education never flagged, and more than any issue in his life it continued to define him as a father and bind him to the most important woman in his life, Susan.[28]

If anything, the relationship between father and eldest daughter grew more intimately expressive after Susan moved North. Though she was not present to aid Gaston in his daily routine, she took pains to remain the permanent, obedient force in his life that permitted his paternalism to flourish. Through her letters, Susan remained her father's intimate. And as her father's deputy, she continued to be somewhat alienated from Alexander and Hannah. Though professing happiness when Alexander's second offer of marriage to the elusive Eliza Jones was accepted in the spring of 1830, this time with his father's cautious approval, Susan did not conceal a superior tone when Alexander failed to inform her of his engagement. She was "not much surprised to hear of his engagement," she told her father. "I saw his attachment for her was unabated. . . . I rejoice at it now tho 2 years ago I so strenuously opposed it. I knew then she would not have him." Sounding much like Gaston himself, Susan allowed that her older brother still was too young to marry. Her image of him "engrossed with his sweet 'dream of life' " so closely paralleled Gaston's own that Alexander doubtless sensed an indentical disapproval of his less-than-manly life. The usually mild Susan did not resist the barb when writing of her brother. Though she felt "quite piqued that neither my letter of congratulation to him or the one to Eliza was deemed worthy of a reply," she channeled her annoyance into a familiar condescension. "He should be a happy man," she wrote Gaston. "His are halcyon days now. No doubt he has [happiness] in his world of his own imaginings." Gaston reaffirmed her place as his confidante by writing quite differently to her than to his other offspring, especially about this and other personal matters. When Hannah's first child was born, for example, Gaston (who well understood the perils childbirth held for family life) wrote her a letter in his best formal style, combining personal feeling with the finest conventional rhetoric, giving both the strength they did not have separately. "I can no longer, my beloved child, deny myself the gratification of expressing to you my fond congratulations on the happy result of your late severe trial," he wrote. Then in terms that must have had a certain irony for the aloof Hannah, and perhaps for her father, Gaston hoped the child would grow up with "affection, docility, piety and virtue to reward you for all you have borne for her sake." He commended his daughter for having transformed herself into a mother: "Your office is . . . one of high dignity and importance," and expressed his satisfaction at the name of the new granddaughter. It was vintage Gaston: mining convention for every trace of order and for each just measure of praise. Yet to Susan he confided his desire to see "the little stranger" in terms far more intimate than he expressed to the mother of the child. And, in what amounted almost to gossip for the restrained Gaston, he told Susan, "My curiosity is much excited to behold [Hannah] in her maternal character."[29]

Perhaps more than her position as Gaston's ally and confidante, Susan's work with the two youngest girls reveals their continuing helpmate bond. She worked for her father as a wife would have, despite distance and her own family's demands. Increasingly, Gaston heaped duties upon Susan, appealing both to the social influence of a woman and to her personal obligation to him as a father. He would give her his preferences regarding the girls, for example, but often admit, "I am at a loss to decide" the exact ordering of their subjects and necessities; "you will decide." He did not shed his own concern, but he increasingly placed the tangle of detail in Susan's hands in the most telling way: "They are *your* children," he wrote her in 1831, [and] "have been *solemnly* confided to your care, and admirably have you thus far answered to the charge. I hope and trust to live until I see them take their places in society as excellent members of it—but if it should not be, my precious Susan, be you their Mother!"[30]

Susan responded by keeping the exact account of her sisters' development that Gaston required. From the spring of 1829, when she concurred with Gaston that the girls should go to an academy, for "they both have uncommonly fine minds," and observed that other young women would soften the manners of homebound girls (a slap at Hannah's inattention), Susan forged a role in which she was guardian of her sisters' interest, protector of a father's hopes for his youngest girls, and educational observer. She filled letters with reports on Eliza's and Catherine's growth, on cost, on their school experiences, and on their temperaments. Sometimes she was intent on cheering Gaston, telling him that the separation between himself and his girls was worth it; that once educated, "They might accomplish wonders." But more often, Susan was simply precise and measured, quite like her father. "Eliza and Kate pass most of their morning in reading aloud to me," she wrote in 1832. "They have grown most astonishingly; their minds, however, most fortunately, keep pace with their figures. They understand and relish Plutarch's Lives better than many women of twenty." Her vivid accounts drew her father close to all of them, and it is easy to picture her storing incidents and, more challengingly, qualities for later description. She, not Gaston, saw the girls becoming women, but Susan wanted her father to see. Writing of fifteen-year-old Catherine, Susan told him, "[Kate], I am happy to see, attaches no importance to her personal appearance. She is said to have the most perfect face in N. York. I think a hint from you about *suavity* of *manner* would have a good effect. She has rather too much hauteur *in manner*, tho *not* in *heart* and an expression of your admiration of affability and kindness of demeanor would be beneficial." Susan became the perfect initiator into the woman's sphere, combining sisterly observation with a parent's influence to achieve the balance of manner and substance that was at the heart of a lady's world.[31]

Yet more than her place in the family and even more than her work-aday letters home, Susan's personal words to her father were testimony to an emotional bond undiminished by either distance or other ties. Her words trace a figure of love, at once needy and dutiful, and, like Gaston's paternalism, remarkably unaltered over the years. There is something finally exclusive in their correspondence; they talk about others in detail, always from a shared point of view. Susan almost never wrote intimately of her own family, for instance, apart from reporting on health and general comings and goings. Indeed, when she once wrote her father of missing her absent husband and wished that Gaston "knew him as I do. . . . He is all that you could desire for me," Gaston responded with a rare sharpness that such feelings should always be credited to God's mercy; to become "hardened or intoxicated by pleasure," even in marriage, was wrong. Susan's love for her father was most certain to be uttered when she believed herself unable to convince him of it. "I often wish you could read my whole heart, my own dear father," she wrote typically in 1831. "And thus understand my feelings for you. Let life be as chequered and long as it may, the consciousness of having pleased you and made you happy will never fail to be an inexhaustible source of happiness. I only wish I were truly worthy of you." Four years later, after trying her hand at writing for publication and being less than satisfied, she despaired that her intellectual precocity had settled to merely a "*very ordinary* capacity" for words and thought. "I should rejoice to be able to write anything worth reading," she told Gaston "and *above all* other things, a memoir of my venerated Father, if I could do justice to it." She invariably tied her most thoroughly felt expressions of love to these self-denigrations, joining some tenacious part of her girlhood to her adult life as a New York City woman, mother, and wife of a successful businessman. Girlhood hung on, and like Gaston's own paternalism, her filial expressions revealed emotions remarkable for their continuity and depth. The voice of the twenty-eight-year-old woman was not so different—indeed it was the same—as that of the fifteen-year-old who had written so lovingly of some day returning to live with her father in his home. Inter-

vening years and relations had somehow left this filial attachment unchanged; surely it was the phenomenon on which the broad and
effective paternalism of William Gaston rested.[32]

William Gaston found another source of family continuity in Eliza,
who, in 1834, willingly took over as mistress of the family home in
Newbern. It may be going too far to say that Eliza was the joint creation
of Gaston and Susan, but in a sense of course she was. As the elder of
the two "second daughters," Eliza, like Susan before her, bore the burden of her father's anxiety for her and her sister's education, heard his
exhortations to help the younger one gain her social and intellectual
bearings. While at school, Eliza read Gaston's didactic letters which reminded her, "Firmness of principle in man or woman is the basis of all
excellence" and yet she also saw the words "Eliza, my love." His advice
and affection, penned from far away Carolina, tied the intricate moral
knots for an elite, teen-age girl: "Adhere to what your conscience tells
you is right at all costs and at whatever hazard. But be gentle, kind and
gracious to everyone around you. Make no fuss or parade about your
principles, but let them quietly yet decisively give a character to all
your action." And, whether or not she knew it, Eliza read advice inspired by Susan and then uttered by Gaston to herself and Catherine:
"Be on your guard, my sweet children, against one foible to which peculiar circumstances expose you. Avoid every appearance of *hauteur*. I
am far from advising a hypocritical or fawning courtesy. But as you are
bound to regard all human beings with kindness, as children of the
same Father as yourselves, show that kindness in tone, manner and
demeanor." Closely echoing moralists such as Hannah More, Gaston
strove to see that his children, like himself, lent character to every action and judged particular circumstances (in this instance, Eliza's meeting men) with a moral remove that did not so much preclude the
warmth of life as give it the drama of ritual. His letters could be specific,
of course, as when he told Eliza not to worry too much over school
examinations or when he instructed her not to make gossip from a
duel, but for the most part his abstraction of duty from desire was
thoroughly consistent with his letters to Susan nine years before.[33]

Unlike Susan, however, Eliza did not link her obedience to her father
with so open a need for his love. Almost from her first letters home,
Eliza *conversed* with Gaston. With Susan as a mediator, Eliza probably
had more emotional room to maneuver, and in some ways she struck
Gaston as similar to Susan in her intellectuality and cheerful nature.
But whatever the similarity, Eliza's letters to her father more nearly
matched his own in conventional usages. Eager to please him, she yet
knew how formally to compliment; happy when he praised her, she
also knew what to say to draw the praise from him. Eliza had none of

Susan's early anxious carefulness, writing instead with the easy (if sometimes obvious) consciousness of a young belle. For example, she consistently presented her father with topics to which he could respond, and reminded him that his authority truly guided her learning. At age twelve, she penned, "I am reading Hamilton on Education; it is very amusing and also interesting. I think there are some of the most beautiful passages in it that I have ever seen. I am learning Swiss waltz with variations. I hope by the time you come I will know them perfect." Eliza created in words her sense of herself and her father, using Susan's hints, her own wishes, and the events and exercises of the academy. "We have lately been engaged in writing addresses to our parents," she disingenuously wrote Gaston from school in 1831. She included a poem for him (it "is not worth your attention as it is nearly my first attempt") and told of imagining him as he read it. If Gaston was a distant figure compared to her friends, teachers, and Susan, he was yet the court of final appeal, and one with whom she might safely experiment with the language of young ladyhood, finding out how the phrases worked and which ones pleased.[34]

And so Gaston read letters of her studies, of friends and outings. Sometimes they savored of schoolbook exercises, but no matter; the habit would become a lovely feminine presence. "I cannot tell, my dear Father, which is my favorite study," she wrote in response to his question, blending schoolgirl misspellings with studied epistolary style: "I am rather inclined to think Latin and Algebra; the former because it is my Father's desire that I should improve in it; the latter, I think strenthens [sic] the mind and also allows you to exercise your own ingenuity." She might well have said the same about her own letters. From her passage through schoolbook, writing exercise, and hours devoted to writing home, Eliza learned to be a Gaston as well as a lady. In closing one 1831 letter to her father she wrote, "It costs your daughter much to be separated from you, but we would not be worthy of you were we not reconciled to it." It is a sentiment more worthy of Gaston than perhaps she knew. Mirroring his spare satisfactions drawn from hopes deferred, Eliza simultaneously protested an unhappy fate and complimented them both for the character to live with it. In this way did another daughter join herself to her father's rule and praise the both of them for enjoying it.[35]

A remarkable consistency appears in William Gaston's view of his family life, despite differences in his relationships with his children. Even with the many disappointments and adjustments in the years between 1823 and 1834, Gaston's trust in his own values never wavered because he was able to believe that they were more than his own mere desires; they were the social realities of fatherhood and manhood. Certain elements of his paternalism, appearing as themes in his letters, remained unshaken and basic to Gaston's style and to his very perception of the social world. These elements intellectually combined many levels of habit, conviction, and imagination. The first was an unbreakable bond between love and duty. His expressions of love were never free from a sense of obligation, giving affection the bridle of loss and guilt. A father and a child gave and received the love *owed* them. Yet far from diminishing a sense of love, the tie between love and duty gave family affection its lasting edge and meaning. Related was Gaston's appreciation of the discipline to be found in principled moderation. In Gaston's paternalism, and in the world he tried to inhabit, there was no good, and much potential harm, in self-indulgent love or hate. Every human relation had its proportion established "out there" in the world, and the gratifications of family life for father or offspring could not exist without these limits. What he conceived of as discipline was not grim self-denial so much as the quiet satisfaction of a known horizon. The bond between love and duty, and the conviction that a moderate order was necessary in life, led Gaston unerringly to certain decisions but blinded him to a sense of various perspectives on his family's experience. His fathering was founded on the widely held principles of honor, hierarchal control, and gender division which did not allow for family affairs to be seen as matters of opinion, self-interest, and power. Much less did this paternal style permit an awareness of how wish and desire (especially his own) shaped family patterns. Consequently Gaston consistently anchored his paternalism not in personality (where opinion and wish puzzled or disconcerted him), but in family position. Whether praising Susan, admonishing Hannah, or exhorting Alexander, William Gaston exercised the power inherent in family position, not the intimacy that clouded judgment. In this sense, "son" became as real in some ways as "Alexander"; Gaston could pronounce his deep love for his son while at the same time deny completely the importance of Alexander's desires. Gaston perceived a loved inhabitant of sonhood, and he pitied or praised according to a son's position. Thus, while Gaston sought responses from his children, he craved obedience—not to his will (or so he believed) but to the evident principles and positions marked out along the treacherous path through life. He believed that it was obedience to these, and not to himself, that gave his own principles and position their weight and worth. And the events of his children's lives (a failed courtship, a desire for privacy, a taste for loss) had to be read back to them as lessons in how to be.

CHAPTER V

THE LACYS:
THE THING, NOT ITS VISION

As a man of God, the Reverend Drury Lacy relied upon many families and upon the many ties of family: his flock in Raleigh, North Carolina, whom he tended as Presbyterian minister and brother-in-Christ with the help of his wife Williana; his children, a daughter and three sons by 1844, all under fifteen years of age, with another child soon to be born. His slaves, too, he strove to treat as family, with patient instruction and measured work, in a careful way which would set him apart from glib masters whose distant workers were "our black family" in name only. Hurt by the slights of northern ministers, Lacy wrote from Cincinnati in 1845: "I do *now* most earnestly desire and pray that a Good Providence may yet open a way by which my children may be educated and reared and live in a free state. Slavery, I am convinced, is the direst calamity to the prosperity of any country." At the same time he wanted Williana and his children to know that his convictions and northern abolitionism "are no more akin than I am to the man on the moon." Slavery must be eased or avoided if not abolished. Like the rest of the too worldly world, slavery was a potential bar to grace, a bar that a good man might seize in order to lean closer to God. When he rose on Sundays to speak God's word Lacy sometimes felt his mind go blank, but faith in his own sonship to God brought him the words he needed to renew the kinship of Christian love. Thus did family and the idea of family span the gulf between the world's ways and heaven's resolution. A preacher had to embrace all sorts of men, including men whose "principal topic of conversation is horse-racing, cock-fighting, betting and abusing Methodism—Baptism—Presbeterianism [*sic*]." Some were the most powerful men in the community, men whom Lacy needed to know and to join if God's word was to have its effect. Yet in formulating religion for the planter class, Lacy trusted that he would not fall into its worst ways. Drawing close to his wife and his children,

Lacy knew that God would lift him above such temptation. Even as a young man courting Williana, he wrote of his desire for "the honey of old forms and customs" of which a man's family was the sweetest.[1]

Being in this world but prizing another, looking to God yet also cherishing the presence of wife and children, Drury Lacy sent his eldest child Bessie away to school with true misgiving and thorough appreciation for the ritual coming of age. The Lacys were an emotionally close family for the times, in part because of the bonds of evangelical Christianity and the expressiveness they encouraged. Coupled with the mid-nineteenth-century idiom of sentiment and introspection, this expressiveness characterized not only the women in the family, but the men as well. In their letters to one another, the Lacys were open to the full emotional significance of the rituals that put family events and relationships into powerful words, words that established resources of feeling and perception not so available to the Gastons twenty-five years before. Specifically, this chapter looks at a family's narrative in order to illuminate a woman's courtship and her coming of age, perhaps the most closely watched passage in planter society. The biographical focus reveals the joinery between these two rituals, how one prepared the ground for the other, and how both enabled a woman to define her sphere. Bessie did not go gently into womanhood, and her particular tensions cast light on the personal meaning of gender division, family hierarchy, and the ritual gap between how to appear and how to be.

Bessie Lacy left home for the Edgeworth Female Seminary near Greensboro, North Carolina, in early 1845, and from the very beginning her father was moved to write frequently of kinship and godliness, of his aspirations for her and his loss of her. As soon as she left home he wrote of home's unmatched goodness and of the perils she now faced. "I fear so much on your account," he told the thirteen-year-old. "I do not feel afraid of your not improving in mind nor advancing rapidly in your studies. But I fear [for] your disposition and your morals. . . . It is a dangerous step to send any girl from *home*; its sacred influence keeps them from much harm." A good part of his disquiet lay in his distress at her absence, and he was not cautious about telling her of his feelings regardless of what the homesick girl might feel. "I cannot tell you my dear how much I have missed you and how restless and unsettled I feel," he wrote soon after she left. "Some great change seems to have taken place. I walk from room to room looking for something and can find nothing. Bessie is gone and I cannot find her, or hear her, or see her." His relief was to imagine, in fond, close detail, her new life even as he told her how to live. His particular images, loving as they were, served precise aims. "Take care of your health, my dear Bess," he characteristically wrote. "Be careful to avoid night air, wet feet, hot sun;

wear your bonnet, disappoint the freckles, clean your teeth, make them look pure and white as 'monumental alabaster.' There now, a quotation from Shakespeare should make you do it." More sweepingly, again with concern for her morality, the minister urged his daughter to think hard upon her family. "Never forget that your fathers, many generations back, have been holy, pious men, the first to resist evil, the first to promote good," he instructed her. "You are descended from a stock that must not be stained. . . . You will feel very badly [i.e., homesick] when your father first leaves you, but you must take courage." Forefathers lined up behind her, ready to assist, perhaps to judge; the family myth would, the father hoped, strengthen Bessie as it had him.[2]

Strength was found in expression, in the word. During Bessie's first term Drury wrote frequently, never failing to coax replies from her. "You must write to me very soon, write just as you talk," he told her in June 1845. "And never be reserved to your Mother; you may tell me anything, for I know how to take it." He freely admitted that only because he wrote to her and heard from her was he able to brave her absence. But his conversation was not only of his feelings and his love. He wrote at considerable length about the advantages and pitfalls of academy education. He favored a formal school because he valued intellect and systematic instruction; yet at the same time he feared that no institution would be attentive enough to Bessie's other needs. He generally approved of Edgeworth seminary but, after one exchange of letters on term marks, he wrote her, "I am afraid that you . . . are advanced to classes and to studies for which you are not prepared by previous study." He worried that new academic methods did not rigorously train girls' minds. "I should have greatly preferred your being drilled at least 2 years in reading *Caesar* and Sallust from *lid to lid*," he told her after she reported on her Latin studies. He wanted his daughter truly to know Latin, to move from Sallust to Virgil in a measured way, not with the " 'hop, skip, and jump' plan" which he saw in her accounts of classes. He did not wish her to work merely for a mark and then abandon the ancients, and he took her intellectual life seriously even though it was her family and her femininity that ultimately bound everything together: "I want you to be an elegant linguist, an accomplished pianist, and of all things, a dutiful, affectionate, and pious daughter and sister."[3]

Drury Lacy found less cause for disappointment as the year wore on. Bessie's letters became longer and more shapely, and she worked at keeping family bonds tight. She worried when three-year-old Willie became ill, promised to play a duet with ten-year-old Horace as soon as he learned piano, and wrote of her studies and play. She also told of missing her parents, and at the least mention of homesickness or any other preoccupation, Drury responded with advice that combined fatherly imperatives with more personal attempts to keep himself tied to her world, to speak to a daughter who was becoming a young woman. Drury's concern for Bessie's temperament, especially, led him to draw a moral lesson from almost any circumstance at hand. The world was full of lessons well suited to a girl in school. Once when Bessie wrote of a happy outing in the winter woods with her friends, he turned the event into a warning about a young woman's "unbridled imagination" and the hazards of "supposing a thousand unreal and foolish things." Somewhat awkwardly he added, "I do not mean that you should not play. I want you to play with all your might when it's necessary." He turned daily precautions into ritual maps of character. He guided his daughter to the proper behavior by making right action seem timeless and great. When she caught cold, for example, he told her to wear flannel as had Thomas Jefferson. With a palpable shift he added, "Great women, too, as well as great men, become wise by the possession of nerves, *sour stomach*, and headaches—poor Madame deStaël had her morning gowns and Miss Hannah Moore [*sic*] spent many a day with her head bound up unable to do anything but dot her I's and cross t's." The great became ill; so when ill, recall the great. Taken together, Drury's letters were a moral commonplace book. Everything he wrote, often with keen affection and shy humor, was aimed at turning Bessie's eye upon the lessons in her life, channeling the events of her schooling to the time when she would have to live without the school. In working to place his daughter in the woman's sphere, Drury Lacy praised her feminine "accomplishments," but believed that character was her best hope. Her future happiness lay not in what her accomplishments might bring—husband, beauty, security—but in the satisfaction of pulling moral knowledge from random circumstance.[4]

Williana Lacy's interest in her daughter's schooling was no less immediate. If anything, it was more richly drawn and exact. In a gently self-effacing way, Williana wrote Bessie in January 1845 that "your father has sent you such a perfect moral lecture that I shall go to the other extreme and send you the trash that swims on the top of my mind." Yet her letters were anything but disposable, as Williana doubtless knew. Often she wrote in tandem with her husband, each spinning out pages of stories, images, and instructions with conscious literary invention. Drury wrote to Bessie in the margin of one of Williana's long messages, "I hope [you] will read, mark, and inwardly digest this letter of [your] beloved Mother—one of the best letters I ever read. Surely you ought to be one of the best daughters that ever was—having such a mother. I only wish you had such a *father*." Deferring to each other, the parents complemented each other, and although they did not overtly

divide the moral and personal territory of the correspondence, each
wrote from the distinct perspective of mother and father, woman and
man. Whereas Drury combined elevated mandates with academic allusion, Williana spoke more easily, woman to woman, with surprising
confidence in her daughter's maturity. Williana was more precise in
her answers to Bessie's questions and more anchored in the exact circumstances of Bessie's new surroundings. Williana was, for example,
far more direct about the reasons for sending Bessie away to school. "It
is a serious matter to be living in this world . . . —everything we do
lives," she wrote in the summer of 1845.

> There is a sort of immortality attached to our very frailties that is
> alarming. . . . Many of these things, these dangerous probabilities,
> made us hesitate whether to send you to school at all. I thought about
> it and talked about it and prayed about it. What should be done: let
> you stay at home learning as little as it suited our convenience? or as
> our various avocations might leave an inch or two of time to devote
> to you; this would not do for one who was growing up to young
> womanhood.

Despite drawbacks of its own, and apart from intellectual goals, the
academy would compel Bessie "to learn to sustain yourself, to learn
self-government, to subdue your temper, to become what you desire,
what you please." Williana knew the tension in a young woman's effort
to subdue herself while also learning to desire, and darkly recalled her
own coming of age. Though the social nature of the academy should
give her daughter a necessary sense of "justice, conscientious dealing
and thorough instruction," Williana was deeply anxious lest the community of young women capture Bessie's sensibilities too soon for justice. "Beware, my Bessie, of forming hasty friendships before you are
acquainted with persons," Williana wrote with an insider's knowledge.
"Sympathy is very soothing, and to find an object of love tenderly and
fondly, very gratifying." But a girl could not know how temporary this
sympathy would be; nor indeed, how girls sometimes shattered each
other's sympathies. "I can safely say that all the harm I did at school
was induced in this way—true, my own heart was evil, but it was
brought out by companions who were worse. . . . I can't unsay what I
said then, nor can I undo what I then did. I can only remember it with
deep regret." The female world of the academy invited but also snared,
and although Williana's warnings may have been couched somberly
because her daughter was absent, the mother's principal fear was that
the very academy that would fit Bessie for the world might also leave
her marked by evil and regret.[5]

Yet keeping aloof from other girls and indulging in homesickness
would not do, either. Like her husband, Williana responded to Bessie's

complaints about not having her way and missing home. But Williana summoned a woman's resources, not those of the heroes of history and literature. "You cannot feel like you were at home anywhere," she reminded Bessie. "Many inconveniences are necessary accompaniments of large boarding schools." The academy not only taught a girl her books and her Latin, but also that she "may not meet with the same tenderness you did at home. . . . Tenderness will not take you through the world or enable you to bear its trying realities. My dear it is no fairy scene that that [sic] you will have to enter when you leave school and grow up to womanhood." Seeking womanhood meant satisfying her mother as well as her father, and Williana pointedly told Bessie that she wanted a daughter whom "I will not be ashamed of, but proud of, and pleased with." Like learning to recognize true friends, learning to distinguish between showy femininity and genuine womanhood was a young woman's challenge. Williana wrote, with fictive intensity, of meeting an old schoolmate, now "a dashing widow," and finding herself attracted to the woman's conversation and physical beauty. Yet she had "too much in *bold relief*," too much open display, leaving "no sparkling gem to be found under the surface, exciting that quick, unintentional admiration that an unexpected good is sure to call forth." Femininity was in this sudden, unlooked for variation on the ordinary, this signal in an otherwise dark world. Williana did not deny that "there are pleasant exteriors . . . and very happy conversational powers—an ease of manner that is charming and a *habit* of smiling that is very attractive," only that these should not be so polished as to outshine the deeper qualities with which women invented unexpected good.[6]

While Williana Lacy sounded these depths of womanhood, touching upon the tension between natural womanliness and schooled femininity, she also evoked easier themes of home life and family pleasures. All of her serious concerns, she told Bessie, were not merely "*philosophizing to keep away the cake*," and cakes and candy were forthcoming. She also sent a dollar now and then consistent with school policy, "to buy you little knickknacks," and reported to Bessie on shopping trips, newly married friends, and the general well-being of the family. "The servants send their love, particularly yr. Mammy," she wrote, and she described brief but vivid scenes of herself and Drury at supper, in the evening by the fire, visiting in town or caring for the children ("your father . . . is such an excellent nurse"). She depicted family events that Bessie would have celebrated had she been home. "Singleton has a tooth!!," Williana wrote of the youngest boy. "We had a squealing concert over it when we found it was actually coming through the gum, and Horace took him and marched in double-quick time all over the room to the tune 'Old Dan Tucker.' Singleton looked very wise and very conscious. . . . he is very fat and large."[7]

Bessie responded to the love in her parents' letters, to the care and constancy that made love out of letters. Her first two terms at Edgeworth were difficult in the ways her parents implied, and she at least once in 1845 tried to convince Drury to let her stay at home. In this request she was homesick and a little selfish; yet by that summer she also was responding to a grave crisis at hand for the family. Williana Lacy was ill, severely so she began to suspect. The birth of Singleton in early 1845 had weakened her physical health measurably, and doubtless her lengthening periods of staying in bed must have worked on Bessie's desire to remain at home. Indeed, it is evidence of the seriousness with which the Lacys viewed Bessie's education that they did not keep her home to help Drury. The minister, his wife wrote, had curtailed his pastoral work in order to stay close to home, and in the fall they obtained a second black woman to relieve Williana of some work. Bessie was told to keep at her studies, yet Williana's worsening condition began to leak into her correspondence. "I tremble when I think what will be your situation and responsibilities," she told her daughter. "Very probably you will have no Mother to direct you very long. . . . Do not form too strong friendships. Not a girl at Edgeworth is capable of giving you good advice." Linking her own death to new warnings about the temptations of the academy sisterhood, Williana pressed her daughter to listen to her teachers and above all to her father. The mother's letters became briefer by early 1846, though no less constant and detailed. She wryly scolded Bessie for "feel[ing] about your hair— try to bear the cross of having such thick hair. That is your thorn in the flesh—and remember that is a thorn that many ladies are trying to procure at the expense of many bottles of *Bars* oil." But, increasingly, she was simply blunt about her hopes and fears, and Bessie heard her mother wishing out loud. Complications of woman's education fell away; growing up a woman was a peculiar balance of image and action. "Every smart, nice-looking girl I see makes me think . . . I wonder if Bess will look that way. I wonder if she will learn how to behave, to talk well and do well—for after all that is about the amount of education. I care very little for the accomplished Miss . . . who can neither *talk* nor *hush*." Her mother was certain enough at these times, but Bessie also heard a new despair, sometimes shockingly bared. Williana had always written of the world's deceptions, but now for the first time she wrote of her own life "frittered away and gone" in the face of worldly trials. Her last letters were not didactic, but confessional. "I have lived a useless life," she once wrote. "I have wasted it. I have done nothing. You know that fig tree Christ looked upon and found nothing but leaves? *I am that fig tree.*"[8]

Williana Lacy died in May 1846, in her fortieth year. Bessie returned home to find her father shaken by his grief and its power over him.

Oddly, he found that he could preach forcefully, with a spare grace he had not formerly achieved. He wrote poetry for the first time in years, grieving verse labored over at night. A widower with five children, including three sons under six years of age, faced a difficult challenge. Bessie felt that she should stay at home for good, but by the end of 1846 she was back at Edgeworth. Her father's letters were briefer, but he continued to press her to respect her intellect and to resist the dreaming temperament of young women. Bessie, immediately after her return, was more subdued and less inclined to complain of teasing classmates and the lack of privacy. She also began to anticipate her father's judgments, adopting his standards and taking a new perspective on her own schoolgirl self. Her letters, though dressed in academy rhetoric, revealed for the first time a fear that she might fail her father:

> My dearest Father I am truly ashamed to send such a bad looking letter for I fear 'twill grieve your heart for me to be so negligent in epistolary composition. Oh no one can tell how I miss the kind . . . letters of my dear, dear Mother. Oh I wish some kind friends would try and some degree fill her place by giving me such advice as a thoughtless schoolgirl like myself needs. What would I do without you, my dearly beloved Father[?] Who would watch over me and write to me[?][9]

Letters, love, and who might fill a mother's place were in Bessie's thoughts each time she wrote Drury in late 1846, and they appeared in new combination when she wrote brother Horace, recently enrolled in Hillsborough Military Academy. In the voice of a mother, Bessie "fear[ed] greatly for your morals. You are so fond of play and excitement, and are so easily enticed to follow bad boys." She counseled him (at age twelve, Horace was only two years younger than she) to avoid wickedness now, while he was young. "Oh my dearest brother! If I could only fill the place of our beloved Mother!" Bessie echoed her father's words to Horace, becoming the family's feminine guard of morality even as she looked to her father for her own protection. She showed some schoolgirl self-consciousness, yet at the same time she discovered a new voice and said womanly things about duty and care. Bessie was less inclined to ask for candy and soap and more apt to think aloud of home, mother, and what possible place a daughter could fill.[10]

In part because of Bessie's mothering, and in part because of Horace's beginning his own formal schooling at Hillsborough, Drury's paternal efforts were focused on Horace as 1847 began. Although Drury's married sister frequently visited him to help in the management of the minister's household, he alone wrote letters to his children. Horace heard many of the same things as Bessie, their father working moral instruction into the very heart of his correspondence. "It is Education, in its proper meaning, that I desire for you," he characteristically wrote Horace. "*E, out of, and duco, to lead*; to lead out, to lead out yr. mind—and discipline its several faculties in proper proportion—not to cram your head with ideas merely." As with Bessie, Drury worried that Horace would fall into bad company. Yet distinct differences in the way he wrote daughter and son reflected the personal depth of gender division. Whereas he gave Bessie instructions about her teeth and her freckles, he presented Horace with a broad moral map he thought proper to a male's greater province. And he expressed a sharpness Bessie never heard. "Don't you remember I told you you would have no reason to fear . . . *if* you would study hard and behave well?" Drury told his son in September 1847. "Nor need you be afraid of any reasonable man so long as you *do yr. duty*. You will never get another whipping as long as you are under the management of three such men as yr. most worthy and excellent teachers *if* you will only *do yr. duty*." The father's letters never spelled out Horace's duty, however; certainly not to the extent that Williana's informed Bessie of what a worthy woman should be. As with so many planter-class fathers, exhortation, not explanation, was the minister's plan; his son's success or shame finally resided in the eyes of other men, not in his own ability to explain manhood. Pleased with Horace's marks in the fall of 1847, Drury nevertheless quoted Horace's principal to him: " 'Horace is doing very well, but if he had more application he would succeed *admirably*.' " Drury exclaimed: "Application! Application! You would succeed *admirably*! Just think how easy [*sic*] you may not only 'do very well' but secure the *admiration* of Dr. Wilson. And is it not worth striving for?" Others stood by to judge, too, when Drury reprimanded his son, usually over Horace's "propensity to spend money without, for a moment, thinking of its value." About five dollars' credit Horace took from Hillsborough merchants, Drury wrote angrily, "[Y]ou will compel me to expose you to the public, as I certainly shall not pay any debts of your own contracting."[11]

Horace's self-indulgence and thoughtlessness, in his father's view, had consequences far more dire than anything Bessie might do. The failures of a daughter were failures of moral refinement, of a balance between "talk and hush." The failures of a son were open trespasses against the social order and the fitness to be master. This distinction was true for Drury Lacy even though he was not an altogether harsh, distant arbiter. The personal, emotional expression that marked his evangelism and shaped many of his letters to Bessie also appeared in his words to Horace. For all of his urgent warnings about duty and self-control, Drury was sometimes able to show his feelings to his son, straying beyond judgment into self-revelation. He begged Horace to think of Williana and to mourn with him the great loss they had suffered. And he was intimate enough to take offense. He was truly stung when Horace criticized one of his more hasty letters and reported that the other boys had laughed at its sloppiness. "*You know* . . . that yr. father *can* write a pretty decent hand and a pretty decent letter," Drury wrote defensively, adding that a hastily written letter was best kept in the family.[12] The minister was not above accenting his advice with examples from his own failures, a rare thing among fathers. What Drury lacked in filling out his abstract advice he sometimes made up with vivid illustration. He recognized himself in his son, and pointed out the likeness:

> *Keep cool*, don't be in a hurry. You are naturally as easily embarrassed as I am, perhaps not quite as much so. You cannot tell how very awkward it often makes me feel, and to how very great a disadvantage I appear, from this unhappy defect in my temperament. . . . *Be self-possessed.* I can give you this advice from my own painful experience. I never rise in the pulpit even to this day without being almost blind for a moment or two; although I try so hard to realize the presence of God's awful majesty! It is a great weakness and I am ashamed of it, but I can't help it. I had no one to guard me against it when young.[13]

Exposing his weakness to his son would protect as well as educate him in matters in which feeling awkward and appearing to an advantage were linked together. Alone at day's end, Drury Lacy framed such letters to his son and daughter. He made certain that the younger boys penned brief notes to Horace and Bessie, and when the black servant left to deliver the "precious billets," Drury Lacy saw the very substance of family life go with him.

At Edgeworth Bessie eagerly awaited her father's letters, sometimes watching the road for the messenger. As the spring of her mother's death turned into summer, Bessie, quite suddenly it seems, embraced Edgeworth seminary as her own. She no longer felt stifled by the closeness of the fifty other young women, but was intrigued by the different personalities, especially among the nineteen boarding students who formed a kind of inner circle. During the next eighteen months, Bessie discovered not the bad girls and moral dangers her parents had feared, but the almost self-sufficient warmth of good girls like herself. Her new-found liking for the academy spilled into long descriptions of friends and days. "It is very cold indeed, and the folks are filling the ice houses," she wrote her brother Drury, Jr., in January 1847. "There is a great big stove in the lower hall, and the stovepipe runs all the way upstairs through the recitation room, and that warms the attic where we all sleep. *Soon in the morning* we are awakened by the ringing of a great big bell that rings up and down the attic til we get up. Then we make up our beds and run down in the trunk room or rather the dressing room and wash our face and hands and comb our hair." Though study was rigorous—up to six hours a day at lectures and recitation—she told her eight-year-old brother that the "*heap* of fun" the girls had by themselves made up for the lessons. "Thus we spend our days," she wrote contentedly. She saw herself as a girl looking into womanhood, and so could joke with her father that after walking a chalkline one day (to give her the physical carriage of a lady) the next day found her bedecked as a gypsy fortune teller at a church fair. In a single afternoon she recited Virgil and skipped rope, and the alternation of decorum and play particularly pleased her. "We Edgeworth girls" was a constant refrain in her letters by late 1846. "Sarah and Mary Dewey and myself are invited to dine at the Methodist College," she wrote her father. "I will have to behave first rate over there for everybody watched Edgeworth girls and the College girls [before] to see which behaved the best, but I believe we have the majority on our side." Behaving the best, appearing to the best advantage, mentally concentrating on the beauty that, in a woman, simply revealed itself, all began to make its own sense within Edgeworth's walls. The girls competed with one another, Bessie told Drury, and class standing in beauty and grace were as established as that in composition or rhetoric. She reported matter-of-factly: "Miss Louisa Morehead is the present belle. . . . She combines the intelligence of Miss Letitia, the grace and beauty of Miss Avery, with the simplicity and artlessness of Miss Lizzie. 'Edgeworth' should be proud of of [*sic*] having sent forth such an ornament to society." For Bessie, being sent forth was still in the future, and she preferred the women at Edgeworth to any thought of leaving or of what one might find in the world to ornament. Learning the rules of etiquette from the strict Miss Brown, Bessie was far more interested in whether the cool Yankee teacher would "win the hearts of the warm-hearted Southerners" than she was in how "gait, manners, and general appearance" would figure in her womanly duties beyond the academy. And though she sent several letters a week to family and friends, she also enjoyed asking her teachers to read them first, which many times "led me to feel calm." It seemed that Edgeworth would take care of anything, let her meet any requirement or define any attitude. And Bessie came to love even the routine she once found restricting. She applied to academy life the resources the school intended for the larger world. The fourteen-year-old girl who wrote letters listing what she learned ("the principal things of Geography such as the bodies of water, the globe, the rivers, capes, mountains, islands, capitals, subdivisions and provinces") two years later became the young woman whose knowledge was not in lists but in a perspective essentially schooled, rhetorical. The strain of early studenthood gave way to a comfortable expressiveness. "Nightly the grim skeleton of an unfinished composition visits my bedside," Bessie wrote Drury, amused at her accumulated work. "As soon as one study is finished and ready to be laid aside for examination, another springs up in its place, like the Hydra." No matter the quick succession of metaphors; in "leading out" Bessie's mind, Edgeworth had led her further inside its community.[14]

"I wish you were acquainted with my teachers, the Misses St. Johns," Bessie wrote her father in early 1848. "They are so kind and good to me. Miss Julia lets me come and lay my head on her shoulder and cry whenever I want to. We . . . go to their room and read on Friday and Saturday evenings. We spend more happy evenings there together, and it will be no small effort for me to wean myself from Edgeworth next Spring." Drury Lacy's worst fears about the schooling of young women were not confirmed by Bessie's tenure at Edgeworth, yet he made it clear that she must leave by 1848, probably because of the expense. Drury decided that Bessie would attend the school at Hampden-Sydney, Virginia, run by his cousin Moses Drury Hoge, and that she would board with kin there. Although she apparently did not strongly object to the change, the next year was a difficult one for Bessie. Not only was leaving Edgeworth a sad prospect, but by mid-1847 she began to doubt her faith in Christ and the church. It seems that she did not write at length about this crisis to her father, possibly because she found her doubt inextricable from his own ministry and from her fear of leaving the academy. She did write more about loving him, however, and this touched something in both of them. "You said in yr. last letter that no one ever loved you one hundred times as much as you loved them," Bessie wrote. "Oh, Father, you don't know how very, very much I love you—almost too much, I'm afraid."[15] Bound up with these doubts and confessions were questions about what she would do when schooling ended altogether. As she took long afternoon walks at Edgeworth, alone or with her "bedfellow" Maggie Morgan, Bessie found herself thinking more about what she might do or be as a woman. She and Maggie felt that their music and conversation and the female intimacy of the academy somehow had to be planted outside Edgeworth. They decided that they had found their life's work in teaching, and declared themselves—lightheartedly but with purpose—immune to the love of men. "Maggie Morgan and I have laid out all our plans for the future," Bessie told Drury as early as 1847.

Our hearts are impenetrable to the keenest arrows of Cupid. Consequently we have concluded to spend our days in single blessedness, or to use a homely phrase, we will be *old maids*. We are going to pursue our studies with the greatest diligence and are going to some of the Southern states or somewhere, and establish an institution for young ladies. We were speaking this morning [of] how happy we would be in our snug little room.[16]

No doubt Drury took this as the wish of a fifteen-year-old. But two years later, Bessie still was saying much the same thing, though by now she was trying out other suggestions with varying measures of playfulness and broad hint. She wanted to work, perhaps to be domestic. But where, and with whom? To Horace she wrote excitedly, "It really seems strange to think that . . . you . . . are almost a man(!!!) Soon you'll go to college, and then come home and frisk about awhile and get married. Don't you want me to come and keep house for you when I get to be an old maid?" With Drury, too, Bessie saw herself as a kind of wife, promising him that "your harum-scarum daughter" had become "a *good economist* [and] a *good housekeeper*" and that she would "make your coffee just as strong, your tea just as sweet as you like. I will bathe your head when it aches and comb your hair as long as you wish. I will cry with you when you are sad, laugh when you are merry, read poetry and sing songs." Even in professing her maturity, Bessie envisioned a kind of Edgeworth intimacy with her father, a closeness of song and poetry joined not awkwardly to sound domestic economy. There was enough urgency in Bessie's tone to preclude an altogether light reply, and Drury responded soberly if not sternly. She would go to Virginia; it was too soon to think of anything beyond that.[17]

Bessie seems to have been pleased enough by her new surroundings with cousin Moses Hoge, and pleased with herself at fitting into the new academic institution as if she had always belonged. Yet her doubts continued in 1848; separated even more distantly from her father, Bessie presently heard from him that his proposal of marriage to Mary Rice Ritchie had been accepted and they would marry the following year. It is not clear whether Bessie had known Mary Ritchie well or at all, and her response to her father's engagement is lost. It can be supposed, however, that at the very least the impending marriage of her father stirred old memories even as it closed off certain imagined futures. After learning of the engagement, as she was trying to settle into her new routine and also work as a tutor, Bessie established a correspondence with Maggie Morgan which kept alive their hopes and love. Indeed, the image of a shared past and future happiness was a powerful force in the lives of both young women. Maggie's letters were love letters, conventionally caring and seductive, which conjured times each hoped were not over.

[I] sit and think of Bessie, fancy her by me with that sweet hand in mine and her soft cheek laid close by mine and then I could almost

hear your sweet voice. . . . I have been thinking much lately about
our *school.* You wanted to know if I had forgotten about our great
plans. Why, I have been maturing them. I have pictured the house,
furnished *our* room throughout and throughin; we must get a pretty
carpet; in one corner we must have a large library. Then we must get
a great big mahogany bedstead, where we will sleep like *we* always
do.[18]

Something in Maggie Morgan's letters suggests that if these plans
never came true neither woman would be wholly surprised. But if their
school was only a dream their love was not, nor were the images of
what Bessie was missing by leaving Edgeworth. Maggie *knew* Bessie,
and her letters asserted an unbreakable bond:

> I do wish you were here this winter to sit by me in church. You used to
> keep my hands so warm under your cloak. I miss you amazingly on
> all sides, at home and abroad. Don't you remember how I used to
> whip you and make you go and wash your face to put you in a good
> humor? I think my whippings used to do you a heap of good. . . .
> The reason I love you darling is that I can't help it and the reason I
> can't help it is that you are the strangest little being I ever saw, one
> minute a little bundle of temper, the next a little bundle of perfec-
> tion.[19]

To be loved by Maggie was to be transfigured into the most alluring of
fictive females, the wicked saint. Rhetoric and memory fed on each
other, and Bessie kept Edgeworth alive through Maggie, who finally
told her uneasy news. "You wanted to know who I slept with, who I love
most, who is my Bessie now-a-days. Well, I sleep with, I love, the sweetest girl in school—Flax Reid. She is so like and yet unlike you." Maggie's
Edgeworth continued to be a place of warmth and intimacy where a
young woman could find "a loveable creature" like and unlike herself.
Yet it was a place, and a time as Bessie learned by 1849, where intimacy
might be lodged forever and lost. Should she be happy or sorrowful
that she had been succeeded by Flax Reid?[20]

This intense correspondence continued into 1850, as Bessie pursued
her studies at Hampden-Sydney and at Richmond. She made at least
two visits to Raleigh during this year, finding that she liked her new
stepmother but still filled with doubt over her faith in God. Her father
seems not to have pressed her to join his church, but rather she herself
felt unable to profess the faith a young woman needed to become truly
feminine. The full power of womanhood, its social reach and individual
promise, was diminished as long as faith was tacit and denomination
undeclared. Bessie returned to Edgeworth as a teacher in early 1851,

after Maggie had left the school. But with a new group of girls and few old acquaintances, Bessie found that life was not the same. Doubts about her ability to teach and to train younger women seem to have undercut her delight at coming back to the academy. As she lived with these various emotional tides—her faith, Maggie, her family, her vanishing childhood—Bessie was courted by at least two men, and favored by 1851 the son of a local planter, Thomas Webber Dewey.[21]

Bessie entered into her courtship with a focused energy, an energy lacking in her struggles with religious faith and absent from her teaching. This is not to say that her courtship was initially more important or occupied more of her time; indeed, her ability to compose a letter to Thomas Dewey, copy it over onto embossed paper, seal it into a small monogrammed envelope, and then wait for the inevitable pleasant reply did not take up much of her time at all. But courtship ritual was more satisfying than puzzling out the ways of belief and work. It was under her direction and had predictable consequences, or so it seemed in 1851. Thomas was a brother of two of her Edgeworth friends, and Bessie had known him for at least two years before he asked to correspond with her. He seemed a serious, ambitious man, aspiring to local political office and helping his father at the plantation. She assented to an exchange of letters with him, and when she returned to Hampden-Sydney in late 1851, Thomas continued to write. In her letters to him, Bessie easily mastered the sweet, cool voice a woman reserved for suitors alone. She accepted gifts, but wrote of his soul; she wrote in her best hand the sentiments of a young woman following herself into love:

> Thank you, Mr. Dewey, for your beautiful present. I will always think of you when I read it. But with far deeper interest will I remember you when my eyes fall on the pages of the Book of Life. . . . I fear you will think I take an unwarrantable liberty in thus writing to you; but I beg you *permit me*, as your *sincere friend* to ask you once more to give your careful and prayerful attention to your soul. . . . Forgive me, Mr. Dewey, but my pen will not refuse to write what my heart so earnestly prompts. If you *really are my friend* have regard to what I now ask, even if you have no desire to be a child of God . . . pray to God to give you that desire.[22]

Turning his gift of a book into a concern for his spiritual well-being, Bessie turned her own religious doubts aside. Here was a new voice, a woman's at her pastoral best, with none of the ragged exclamation or passion in her letters home or to Maggie. The orderliness itself seems to have calmed Bessie; it allowed her to take on the careful romantic evangelism of a courted woman whose neatly copied letters were so simply dispatched yet so eagerly sought. While continuing to write loving or confused letters to her father and brothers, full of misspellings, cross-hatchings, and hasty grammar, Bessie wrote carefully to Thomas, making a cool, mature place in her day. She knew he would think about his soul if she asked him to; he would respond each time she wrote.

Thomas kept her letters, quoting them back to her, not letting many days pass before she heard from him. Gradually, by the spring of 1852, Bessie wrote less of his soul and more to the point. She began to flirt, telling him of the attentions of Mat Lyle, for instance, who could not be dissuaded from calling on her at her grandfather's. Mat was a cousin, she told Thomas; otherwise, she would not be obliged to be so agreeable. He was "so excitable in his nature and so violent in his feelings" that she sometimes wished she did not have to receive him so often. But Thomas should not worry, she added slyly, for she had told Mat that her correspondence was settled with another, though "I have corresponded with [Mat] for four or five years and it is the hardest thing in the world to break right off."[23] Bessie loved to play at courtship, to find herself saying such things, and by the spring of 1852 she was writing Thomas almost daily letters. Flirtation edged closer to familiarity, and the epistolary game of naming a lover let Bessie talk about the boundaries of their courtship:

> I wish I had a name for you. Tom sounds very disrespectful. Mr. Dewey sounds as if I did not love you—it sounds icy. "Old Tom" suits when I can say it with my lips . . . but I can't write it. But it makes no difference. You know, Mr. Dewey, that no icy words could make my heart cold—and you know "Old Tom" that for you I have a respect so high and pure that it almost amounts to reverence and you know Tom that there is a love within me which I pray may never grow into idolatry.[24]

Beginning with a simple wish, she drew it out into a lover's serious prayer. She called Maggie Morgan "Pug," but Thomas Dewey was not so comfortably named. She played with three names, he required three, not only because it made for a more delightful game, but also because the aim of such play was to be the one who invented the relationship. She had now written it down. He could choose one of his names, or accept all three, and certainly he would not miss his chance to become an idol even as Bessie foreclosed it.

By summer, Bessie began to see herself and her correspondence with Thomas in a way different from the formal, light-and-dark rhetoric of her early letters. Though hardly ever seeing him face to face, Bessie began to risk confessions, revelations about herself and her days as a young woman which were not outside the romantic style exactly, but not pure flirtation either. She began to give him glimpses of her routine life, of who she was instead of how she appeared. She wrote tentatively of what she would like to become. She confessed, for instance, to a dislike for "behaving all the time—I get mighty tired of it." Dreaming, she told him, was the nice antidote to being a well-behaved lady. "While I am sitting up straight and knitting my thoughts take long jaunts in dreamland; these still soft, hazy days, too, lend new wings to my imagination." On another spring day she wrote him, "I wonder what sort of nature I have. Everybody thinks it is so happy and joyous and full of glee. Well so it is. But I always love mournful music most and still, dark pictures and books wild and mysterious." Wondering out loud to a lover was a part of making love, but Bessie went a step past flirtation, hinting at real self-doubt in questions less rhetorical than truly curious. "I'm half afraid yet you would not love me if you knew me very well," she wrote. "If you knew what a strange sort of head I have with nothing developed but ideality, and what strange visions come to me and pictures; and what music sometimes whirls and rushes through my brain." Though these thoughts, too, might perhaps be depended upon to enchant a man, Bessie also wanted to know Thomas, asking him, "Do all these things trouble your head as they do mine?" Newly intimate, or trying to be, Bessie wondered about Thomas's life as a man. Did he, like herself, Maggie, and other women, sometimes doubt his own senses or his own ideas? She asked him once, in a postscript, "Do you dream away your life?" She talked to him many times of her visiting, her work, but always of her dreaming and its suggestive power. She loved to dream but worried about its influence apart from the academy sisterhood. "I always wake up from a tour of this sort vowing against soul-excursions and seeing fully the unprofitableness of such journeyings. But there is a fascination in such a set of thoughts. . . . There never was a poor child born with such a wandering spirit as I have and were I not a woman I believe this moment I'd be in Africa or Japan . . . in some almost inaccessible place."[25]

Wishing herself somewhere else as she wished that Thomas was there in Virginia with her, Bessie imagined him daily; he took his place in her soul-excursions. Sometimes he seemed to give her the answers she wanted, glimpses of his feelings, but more often she felt that she could not reach him; the bright patch of intimacy clouded over and she felt she did not know him. So she flirted and entertained. It is not clear what Thomas was doing in the spring of 1852, but he seems to have been running for local office and establishing business ties. He traveled about, sometimes not writing when she expected, and a few times writing to reprove her. "Why didn't you write, Mr. Dewey?" she asked him on one occasion, reverting to the icy name for him. "I will not believe that you love me any the less—for I judge thee by myself and such a thought is treason." Bessie could in fact do nothing else but imagine what his feelings were—to judge him by herself and believe that he was as she imagined him to be. He was strained, then loving, by turns. He told her what he as a man knew best, to leave off dreaming, to become her schooled, ladylike self. Bessie responded at these times by pulling back from the intimacy she invited, back into the sure ground of court-ship ritual. And she acceded to his wishes. "I will stop dreaming," she promised. "I am getting over my almost frantic love for music. I can do anything *for your sake*, and you must tell me always when I do or say or write anything that you disapprove. I am yours now and you can mould me as you please. You must mould me."[26]

As she struggled with the intimacy her courtship seemed both to offer and preclude, Bessie also began to worry about another matter. After more than four months of courtship, sometimes with Thomas present but more often by letter, Bessie still had not told her father of Thomas's privileged place. Mat Lyle and others might still call on Sundays when Thomas was a state away, but it was Thomas who received the daily notes, the best stories, the flirtatious complications, the embossed stationery. Bessie's kin in Virginia began to suspect, she told Thomas, that something more than a friendship was taking place. Once, writing all afternoon to family and friends, Bessie saved Thomas's letter for last and felt her head swim as she tried to finish it. A few days later, she wrote him, "Aunt Mary saw me [writing] just now and said I must stop as I'd be sick again. . . . They all watch me while I'm writing lest suddenly for the amusement and edification of all concerned I should take a fancy to a fainting fit." Was she being coy with Thomas? Did he wonder who might guess what sort of letter was being written, or perhaps even have already guessed? Whatever the drama in her writing and fainting, Bessie finally asked him directly about the propriety of their courtship. In the same spirit in which she told him about her woman's ways she wrote, "I wonder if it is right for you and me to love each other as we do and write to each other without telling Father. My conscience hurts me on that question sometimes. Tell me your views—do you wonder, too?" Thomas apparently suggested that they go on as before, for a month later Bessie raised the issue again more urgently. She felt the pressure of her father's love, and told Thomas that "I am beginning to have in my heart the deep, true love and a sincere respect that a child ought always to have for a parent." She had fallen in love with Thomas and five months of letters had passed between them. They had arranged meetings through Bessie's cousin Jenny McPheeters which apparently were unknown to Bessie's uncle and were unchaperoned except by the sympathetic Jenny. Bessie began to feel that she had seriously breached morality, and by June 1852, even while longing for Thomas to be with her as she dreamed in her father's orchard, she laid the ground for disagreeing with her lover. "I do not know what to tell you about what you wrote me of telling Father," she said after Thomas had again counseled delay. "I believe you are right, but I detest deception and would not for the world wound my Father's heart by doing anything he would disapprove." She was even stronger in her terms only a month later, finding her own happiness at risk in their deception. As their correspondence continued, secret only from the older folks but not from friends and confidants, Bessie sometimes felt "a drawing back from marriage." Although her letters as well as his had fueled the romance, and though her intense search for his image, his name, and his feelings had driven her to keep the courtship alive in spite of his opaqueness, Bessie slowly began to see the larger view of how far she had come. "[I]t is a hard thing to leave Father and Ma and all that the heart has treasured since childhood. . . . It is removing myself from my Father's immediate love that I dread. I owe him such an immense load of gratitude that it seems I ought to stay with him and make the rest of his days as easy and as happy as I could," she told Thomas. And even though she considered their correspondence a pledge, "When I engaged myself to be yours I thought more of loving you than marrying you and thought not what a solemn covenant I was making. I would not break that covenant for anything save one—my Father's request that it should be dissolved." These words doubtless leaped out at Thomas; "covenant" was not a lover's word, and Bessie's voice here had none of her usual tone of sly flirtation concealing open embrace. Instead she plainly stated what she thought about the place where courtship had brought her. When she concluded, 'You have won me. Win Father and I am thine whenever you claim me," her lapse into literary idiom did not soften the ultimatum. Drury Lacy, his daughter decided, had to be brought into her love story where he belonged.[27]

In November 1852, Thomas Dewey gave in and wrote what can only be described as a model letter of request for Bessie's hand in marriage. As Drury Lacy read the first sentence any suspicions he may have about Bessie and Thomas were doubtless confirmed. "My object in writing this is to approach you upon a delicate ma[tter][and] a subject of deep interest to you and of moment to me," Thomas's letter began in the finest conventional style. Turning Bessie's demand upon him into the rhetoric of a manly suitor, Thomas continued, "It is in regard to a matter in which every feeling of honour and propriety dictates to me the necessity of perfect candour and frankness with you. I fear that I have already been silent with regard to this too long. . . . For sometime past, as you have doubtless perceived, I have cherished an at-

tachment for your daughter Miss Bessie. That attachment only requires a father's sanction, a father's approbation, to be fully returned as
I could desire." This statement, of course, was more accurate than conventional form implied. Thomas asked Drury's "consent to our union,"
asked that the Lacy family consider a son gained and not a daughter
lost, promised to be a son to Drury should the older man consent, and
closed by asking to "visit your daughter with your app[robation]." It
was, in all ways, a letter drawing upon courtship ritual to strengthen
this particular suit; certainly Bessie could not have been displeased. Yet
in view of the emotional turmoil that followed, it is important to appreciate the pass at which Bessie found herself by late 1852. She had spent
a year entering ever deeper into a courtship concealed from her father
as she pursued studies and work under the care of family. Her desul-
tory experience with teaching and her disheartening bouts with religious faith were eased by her relationship with Thomas and her imagination of him; she was drawn to the delights of controlling love. Yet
after the first few months of directing Thomas in his lover's performance, Bessie began to pursue the kind of emotional intimacy she had
known in the academy, this time with a man. Most of her letters seemed
to reach for a closeness she did not find. He was her lover; their letters
said so. But where was the confident, all-involving relation she had had
with Maggie Morgan? When Bessie worried about the "unprofitableness" of her dreams, it was not a woman's loving voice she echoed, but
a man's calculations; the sensuous images of happiness she had shared
with Maggie did not appear in her letters to the man she might marry.
Instead, stories of cousin Mat and fainting fits honed his jealousy as
they sharpened her love. If Bessie's desire for closeness with Thomas
was neither fully uttered nor denied, she was at least able to move her
courtship in a moral direction by repaying her father's trust in her. In
this, she got exactly what she wanted from Thomas, though her act of
daughterly responsibility balanced, perhaps replaced in some way, her
desire for a lover's intimacy. On the surface, Bessie appears to have left
the turning point of her courtship up to a classic, formal encounter
between father and lover. But hers was no passive surrender. The distance between herself and Thomas had not gone unnoticed, and her
attention to filial obligation was in part an effort to establish her firm
footing on ground she could defend—her father's love and family
support. If Thomas would do *his* duty, all the better; but if he failed, she
was prepared to make his shortcoming ritually obvious and not be left
without emotional resources of her own.[28]

During the four months following Thomas's proposal, Bessie discovered a new map of courtship, one that placed her between a vast need
for Thomas to love her and a precise desire to mark out the terms of

impending marriage. Her letters to Thomas took on startling variations of language and form, and can scarcely be seen as other than a sign of her struggle between aspirations and distress. Drastic shifts in her social and family circumstances contributed to her changed feelings. In the first place, despite some manifest but inexplicit misgivings, Drury Lacy consented to his daughter's engagement, throwing open the love affair to the full scrutiny of family and friends and making Bessie responsible for the public appearance of a betrothed woman. A month later, Horace, at seventeen, took ill with fever and vomiting, followed by a skin eruption doctors diagnosed as smallpox. In less than a month, he was dead. Shocked at not seeing him alive for a last time, Bessie returned to Raleigh for an emotional reunion with her father and stepmother and decided to stay. This decision not only meant a return to her childhood home and her father's immediate presence, but also gave her frequent occasions to see her fiancé, something that her courtship had not so far allowed. Finally, in February, Maggie Morgan wrote to say she would marry, and this decision, too, must have unsettled Bessie's world.

In new proximity to Thomas, Bessie wrote shorter letters, but as frequently. She sent them to him by way of slave messengers and Thomas did the same, usually by a man named Zack. Her letters, now often no more than notes, unsigned and unaddressed, became more intimate, or at least more spontaneous. She chafed somewhat at her public engagement, writing to Thomas in January 1853, that "it seems like a very long time since I saw you all by myself. . . . If we ever do see each other again in our old-fashioned way it will be so much the more delightful." Her attempts to write about herself gave way to urgent notes wanting him to come to her; she wrote him on the spur of the moment, a new neediness counterpointing her new status as a fiancée. "I am going to commit an unheard of piece of audacity now," she wrote eagerly in February. "And what do you guess it is? Come here tonight if you have no engagement to prevent. . . . Write on a scrap of paper *yes* or *no* [and] don't tell Uncle Zack for I don't want anybody to know that I wrote this." At these times she was pleased to be conspiratorial, though there was an edginess to many of these hasty plans, and a keen disappointment when she felt Thomas did not attend to her because some male business prevented. Then she was seized by loneliness, puzzled at her lover's political pursuits which she either did not understand or else felt should be secondary. Thomas, his time increasingly taken up with politics, lost an election for the state legislature, and in the meantime decided that he would not pursue on-again, off-again plans to prepare himself for the ministry. He apparently felt Drury Lacy did not wholly approve of him, and there were intimations that Drury and Thomas's father had been at odds over some matter or other. Bessie found Thomas preoccupied and distant, and her need for him in the spring of 1853 often was desperate. She adopted a lover's forlorn vernacular, sometimes relapsing into the third person, begging him to take on all responsibility for their almost joined lives. In one such letter she implored, "Mr. Dewey, touch the sceptre and say '*live.*' Say to me come, say to me speak." She wanted him to

> forgive Bessie for all she does wrong, that you will ever bear long and patiently with the wicked child. . . . Think of me as your Bessie, think of her as loving you so entirely that you have the power of moulding her yourself. Think of the poor little child as stealing off from all and dreaming fond dreams of you—saying to herself words you have said to her, counting days and hours for your letters, and love her. For her whole heart is yours, she is your Bessie alone, your Bessie entirely and forever. *I plead for her.*

Never before had her letters been so stricken, nor such obvious first drafts. Her dreaming ways came up again, but with no sense that Thomas might share them. Rather, she wanted him to fulfill a dream, to save her. She wanted to make her dependence into a strength. Absent in these letters is Bessie's edge of self-control which earlier had permitted her to direct the correspondence even as she indulged herself in romantic rhetoric. Though her begging showed perhaps some calculated self-indulgence, these letters nevertheless put the power to shape affairs into Thomas's hands.[29]

It was not quite that simple, however; for alternating with her imploring, childlike voice was another, wholly different one. She became directive, even assertive. As Thomas also appears to have suffered emotional shifts, Bessie placed firm demands upon him. She constantly tested his commitment to the formal engagement, telling him that if he changed his mind to "never let a strict and high sense of honour cause you to profess what you do not feel." Bringing up the possibility, of course, did little to put either lover's fears to rest. She began to criticize openly his emotional fluctuations and his impatience with the advice of family. "I shall look for you this afternoon at the time appointed," Bessie informed him in February. "And never, never again submit yourself to one of your 'curious fits.' They are unendurable and needless I assure you." On another occasion she wrote in a similar vein, "I will expect you tonight in one of your best humours; if you look as solemn and cross as you did last night I will make you go right straight home again, so you had better practice a smile all day. I would write a great deal more but this pen and this ink say 'I won't.' " Like a lover early in a courtship, Bessie animated her pen and ink, but with an altogether different purpose. Instead of the "adventurous pen" that pushed lovers to express their love, Bessie's coolly shut off the flow of words at just the point at which she had uttered her needs. She knew what she was doing, she said, and even suggested to Thomas that he might want to think her "very bold, forward" or "too severe and . . . too punctilious." She invited him, that is, to think of her as neither ladylike nor dependent. If this sort of challenge was not enough to signal a sharp angle in their romance, Bessie's new, assertive voice speaking in near unison with her childlike, beseeching one gave her letters the sense of having been written by more than one person during this spring and summer. More confusing, from Thomas's point of view, were the shifts in usage and form, as when she insisted that she address him as "friend." Emotion—who possessed more of it and how much was enough—became an issue of debt between them, and ultimately implicated their entire courtship. "Let me say *friend*," Bessie wrote him. "It does not come from a *cold heart* and is not a freezing word as you would have it. I mean as much as if I said *dearest* and that I can't say—it wouldn't be right in me. But it is *your duty* to say *dearest* and feel dearest, too." She felt that he did not desire a love like hers which "comes too directly from my heart," and that he preferred that "feeling should pass thru a purifying alambic before it is given to you." This judgment hardly could have been predicted from a woman who a month earlier had passionately invited him to join her in "a piece of audacity," and it was far from the girl who had begged him to shape her desires and ways. There is no way, of course, to untangle all of the knots of fear and desire, and no need to. The point is that by the summer of 1853 Bessie found herself vacillating wildly in her feeling toward Thomas, in her commitment to him and to marriage, and indeed in her sense of the power and place of love itself. Although her childlike imploring kept alive a hope that her courtship would yet permit her to find a new parent, someone who would love her like mother and father or even more completely, Bessie struggled with the limits of her closeness to Thomas. She slowly turned away from the world of young women and set about drawing the boundaries of a mature woman's sphere. A search for dreams and intimacy, nourished by loving parents, Edgeworth, and days alone under the trees, had to be trimmed to fit the terms of a marriage.[30]

As Bessie and Thomas contended with their feelings, they thus confronted the social alienation between the sexes, the tension between love and marriage, and the end of childhood. Their families and friends played a crucial role in this hard-fought passage. Though it is impossible to know everything behind Bessie's fear that marriage would close off "all that the heart has treasured since childhood," it is obvious that the mere propriety of marriage counted for little in itself. Foreboding became the central theme, not duty. Her fears were credited by her family and friends—and attacked by Thomas's intimates. The courtship did not break up in the altogether partisan commotion of the summer of 1853, but the involvement of kin and friends added to the social tensions of what was not merely a lovers' quarrel. Something generally important was at stake: the settling of a man's place and a woman's place as husband and wife, which (so the partisans believed) would anchor Bessie and Thomas among their kind for the remainder of their lives.

Courtship's final terms, implying the relative powers of wife and husband, were on Maggie Morgan's mind when she wrote to advise Bessie in the spring of 1853, and to say goodbye. Although their letters carried less passion than eighteen months before, the two women had remained correspondents. It was the shift in their relationship from academy friends to almost-wives that explains Maggie's last "single" letter to Bessie, a letter that is as remarkable for its remoteness as for its irony toward her impending marriage. Maggie managed to combine amusement and resignation, even veiled warning, as she studied her own momentum toward the wedding day:

> My time is so filled with what the Physician [i.e., her fiancé] calls "feminine gear" that I wish very much to find a little moment to write *once more* to all my friends before that great event takes place by which I am to "lose my identity." I got a letter today from the Dr. in which he makes great promises—I wonder if he will fulfill them all! Here I could easily go off into a dissertation on "the joys of childhood's happy hour" . . . but it is too near the reality. I must grapple now with the *thing* not its vision. . . . I, too, am sometimes taken with aversions. . . . If I am unhappy in my married life, my great hope will be that I may by it be drawn closer to God and taught by bitter daily experience to look away from earth to heaven. But I think I shall not be unhappy. I am not looking for *bliss*.[31]

She is a realistic observer gazing on her own affair, with a slight nod to the days, only four years past, when she and Bessie wrote academy essays together. Now they are "too near the reality." She has settled in her own mind what she will discover: there will be promises, there will not be bliss; a belief in something greater than the "great event" will sustain it all. Despite her protective quotation marks, Maggie clearly thought of marriage as a loss of identity—not an exchange, an actual loss. She gave Bessie her last words in the life they had known together, and then like a voyager she turned to what lay ahead. She concluded mundanely; but in these words, too, she touched the essence of their shared fate as women. Thinking that Bessie would be interested in the latest "marrying etiquette," she noted that a friend had received silk dresses, riding dresses, and money from her fiancé, maybe even her linen. "Did Tom do that much for you?" Maggie asked. "Dr. didn't for me, but then we were not necessitated—that makes all the difference. But I ought not to talk so—it is wrong." Wrong or not, Maggie brought out the final motif of courtship: money, possessions, and sexual relations. What could Bessie have made of it? In the following months, when she began in earnest to test Thomas and her own emotional balance, Maggie's summation may well have reappeared in Bessie's own attempts to control the slide into marriage.

Maggie Morgan's voice definitely appeared in Bessie's letter to Thomas in which she called herself a "bundle of contradictions," not in play as with Maggie but out of frustration with her own gyrating emotions. In an effort to steady the affair, Bessie reached out to her father and friends, wondering whether the time had come for "kicking" the engagement. Drury Lacy, despite Thomas's dutiful proposal, apparently still felt the match was not quite right; yet he was not so convinced that Bessie could act one way or another with certainty. A cousin, Tucker Lacy, who had himself paid some attention to Bessie in the past, wrote in answer to her plea for suggestions and advice. Did Tucker know if her father truly opposed Thomas and was only sparing her feelings? Did Thomas's father, who apparently also had a dim view of the couple, mention anything? What did the turmoil mean for her future happiness? Tucker (who was perhaps not disinterested) replied with measured advice: "As to your father not being pleased, or the old gentlemen on both sides not being particularly congenial, it does not strike me as imposing any insuperable barrier—for I do not infer that your Father's opinion amounts to decided opposition. If it does I would advise the dismissal of the whole affair upon *that ground*." A father as "kind, prudent and loving" as Drury Lacy deserved no less, Tucker told her. And so even as she sought some new vantage point on her father's place in all this, her young cousin quoted smooth morality back to her. And he did more; he allowed that the whole affair had sobered him. Few men and women, it seemed to Tucker, were destined for happiness despite what lovers thought, and "Were it not for a restless feeling and a desire to have a *home* in the world, I believe I would not run the great risk of marriage."[32]

Thomas, too, sought intervention and information from others. He asked them what they thought of Bessie, and what they knew of her wishes. One mutual friend, Alexander McPheeters, stepped carefully through the breakage of the courtship to warn Thomas. "I am going to speak plainly," McPheeters wrote. "I like Miss Bessie *much, very much,* but she has some strange, passing strange 'ways' and I tell you honestly that if her feelings do not undergo a radical change for you it will be sealing the misery of both of you to marry." Like other friends, McPheeters did not see the dispute as trivial. Like others, he stressed the lifelong bond of marriage, the irretrievable happiness lost in making the wrong choice. McPheeters added, gaining confidence, that if Bessie "loved you as she ought, as you have a *right* to expect she does, she would not—*could not*— *trifle* with yr. feelings as she has done." Courtship, McPheeters told his friend, established certain rights between lovers, which he saw Bessie dismantling. Indeed, McPheeters knew ("I have it from the best authority") that even Drury Lacy felt that Bessie "has treated you shamefully." Having said this, McPheeters may have feared going too far in giving a bleak picture of his friend's (perhaps) future wife, and so he bolstered the positive by complementing Bessie as a "noble woman" though "singular," and concluded that in such matters "it is hard to know without loving." On top of such advice, Thomas heard from Bessie's family and from his own, kin upon kin, drumming into him what to think and do. From Mary Lacy came a bantering letter with a sharp edge, assuming without argument that the wedding would take place. Amid some levity, Mary made her loyalties clear: "If you feel disposed to complain of [Bessie's] short letter now or any others recently I must tell you how busy she has been getting ready for the important change. However much to blame for remissions on former occasions, I think at present she is quite excusable. I wonder how near of kin you and I shall be when you marry Bessie? We'll cipher that out one of these times. If you are not good and *forbearing* towards Bess you and I shall quarrel certainly." Like the daughter, the mother told Thomas that it was his duty to hold Bessie dear—and to say it, too. But from his own family, Thomas received nothing but support. He had been badly used by a temperamental coquette, his sisters told him. Beyond this, they dreaded his departure after marriage. His sister Mary, mentioning a long talk between Drury Lacy and the eldest sister, Sarah, reported that Drury "blames Bessie very much but praises you to the skies." Mary thought it evident that Bessie's "love cannot bear the test of absence," and added, "It makes me so mad to think of it. She is not worthy of your love. Tom forgive me if I hurt your feelings in writing this but you know you are very dear to me and the idea of any woman trampling on your love makes me mad. . . . I think any woman might be proud and feel herself honored to get you." In fact, his sister thought Thomas would never find the mate he deserved. "I never saw the woman in my life that I think is good and clever enough for you," she told him. "I want you to have an extraordinary wife."[33]

Dependency, worthiness, duty; families on both sides of the quarrel summoned the final words of the ritual to their advantage. Though Drury Lacy may have felt that Bessie had overstepped certain boundaries, he continued to write lovingly to her, and her stepmother was a firm ally in her trouble. Thomas, while not giving up his suit, could scarcely have brushed off his sisters' passionate clasp. The language of loss and finality closed out this courtship—did not end it, but sent it into a final crisis from which a marriage was born. No hearts and flowers, little playfulness, and no sense of families uniting in calm good sense or celebration. Though the wedding date continued to draw near unhindered, Thomas's family fixed his view on what was falling away behind him. "Tell me when the wedding is to be," sister Sarah wrote in late August. "You must stop a day in Greensboro as you go down so that I can bid you a final adieu. I shall feel like you were dead and will grieve very much over *my loss.*" Though she wrote at times in an oblique, ironic voice, this time Sarah was not to be misunderstood about the enormity of her brother's transition. "I want you to write to me," she demanded of Thomas. "That is my aim. And I want you to remember it *even after you are married—write to me.*" In a strange last act to the courtship, someone sent a letter to Drury Lacy, addressed to Bessie, in which Thomas was charged with being constantly drunk since coming to Charlotte. Drury did not show the letter to his daughter, but wrote to Thomas to ask "on your honour as a Christian" whether there was "a foundation for such an insinuation." Thomas denied it, and Drury was satisfied. The wedding took place a few days later, and Bessie returned to Charlotte with her husband.[34]

Although an anonymous attempt to sabotage the courtship was rather more extreme than usual, most of the tension between Bessie and Thomas in their passage into marriage was completely within the scope of courtship ritual. Indeed, the ritual accounted for most of it. Yet because the tension was so high-strung by the October 1853 wedding, it might be expected that the first year of marriage would continue the conflict. Quite the opposite seems to have been the case, however, and it is important to bring the story of Bessie Lacy a bit further into her coming of age to attempt to understand how the rapids of her courtship emptied out into her sense of being a wife. In doing so, we are hampered by a relative lack of correspondence; Thomas's position as manager of a Charlotte bank and overseer of his father's interests kept him close to home between October 1853 and July 1854, thus erasing the need to write his wife. After July, however, when Bessie returned to her father's in Raleigh to be in familiar surroundings for the birth of her first child, the letters with Thomas resume, giving a sense of how their married relationship differed from, yet drew upon, their relation as lovers. Bessie's new sense of herself as a wife and mother anchored firmly in a new region of the woman's sphere, emerges in several ways. The loss of childhood and family did not leave the terrible void Bessie had feared. Certainly there was loss; Bessie left her family and they missed her, just as Thomas's sisters longed to see him. As Bessie's nine-year-old brother William wrote sadly, "I miss that wink of your eye and that graceful turn and hop when coming to the table." And Bessie, too, felt detached from all that was familiar, but not in the drastic, tearing way she had supposed. The tensions of her last weeks of courtship left her feeling lightheaded, and instead of loss she felt a kind of timelessness. "I can hardly realize that it has been only twelve days since I left Raleigh," she wrote Drury. "It seems to me that I have been married six months." She thought that this feeling was not so bad and was rather proud of herself; the first few days of married life were not unlike the pleasant dreaming state she had treasured as a girl. Moreover, Bessie found that her changed status brought changed relations with friends which gave her new authority and new insight. Bessie's friend Priscilla, for instance, who in the past had helped her when "I thought I was a hypocrite and no Christian," now wrote asking Bessie's view from the other side of marriage. Only half-bantering, Priscilla wrote,

> Is marriage the awful event I think it is? . . . Whenever I think of the *crisis*, the winding up of affairs, I am taken with such a shuddering horror that if it wasn't a sin I'd wish I were dead. . . . Is matrimony then that blessed state which Poets speak of, that blissful existence of which one dreamed in youth, and to which young eyes are more eagerly and hopefully cast, I may add less prayerfully, than older ones[?] . . . I really want your experience before I take the fearful plunge, which is awfully solemn to me as death—*Doom*, do you remember that night?

Bessie responded and found herself rising to the challenge of speaking as a married woman in a calm, authoritative way.[35]

Of deeper importance to her, in view of the dread with which she had contemplated losing him, was a new closeness to her father. Somewhat to Bessie's amazement, father and daughter wrote to each other frequently in the aftermath of the wedding, he confessing openly his love for her in the language of a man who had found a new way of addressing his child as an emotional equal. Drury now admitted, with an air of discovery, that "in the love of a *father* for his children there is often some measure of *reserve*—as if the full expression of it all were allied to weakness." He allowed that such love was not the less constant for all its momentary ebbings. Even if a father's love had "too much of the world about it," it was still allied more with God than human weakness. But Drury did not content himself with a discourse on love; he opened new vistas of a father's doubts now settled by Bessie's coming of age. "Years ago," he admitted, "I used to think sometimes that you did not think I loved you as much as I ought—that I was often cold and distant, if not harsh and austere, that I did not cherish a tender and forbearing spirit towards yr. foibles . . . [that] I did not hug you lovey you up as often as you wished it." He could see the nature of his love and say it, now that she had become a woman and was gone. He was not seeking forgiveness, exactly, but a new openness between them, and Bessie responded in kind, finding unexpected intimacy in her new status as another man's wife.[36]

As she saw that old ties did not disappear with marriage, and that her fear of losing everything had been part of the bottleneck of courtship, Bessie also faced an even greater transformation. She suspected in January 1854 that she was pregnant, and by February she was certain of it. Seated at her writing desk in their rented Charlotte home, she felt the quickening of the child as she wrote letters to father and friends. It was an "important event," as women said among themselves quite without irony, and by early spring Bessie attempted to quell her mounting anxiety by planning a return to her father's for the birth. By May she was completely absorbed with her physical condition and arrangements for the birth. The summer promised to be a busy one, for Mary Lacy, too, was pregnant and expected to give birth within a month or two of her stepdaughter. The two women found a new closeness in sharing preparations for the births, though, interestingly, Mary was of the opinion that Bessie, who had not before witnessed childbirth, would be better off not seeing one just before her own. "Come when it suits you [but] I think it would not be well for you to know the fuss I make," Mary Lacy wrote her. "And if Mr. Dewey is here he will have to vacate the premises or put cotton in his ears! . . . It would be remarkably unpleasant to all parties for you to drive up just at the moment I was 'lifting up my voice.' " The timing of her letter to Bessie was as apt as her minister's figure of speech; two days later she safely delivered a son. And two weeks after, despite her own convalescence, her stepdaughter came home to her care, assisted by Thomas's sister Mary who had so opposed the wedding. Bessie became entirely focused on the coming event, but was able to write at great length to her husband about it, freely and without the slightest trace of device and obscurity which had marked her final turnings in courtship. This, as Maggie Morgan had said, was the thing, not its vision. The timing of the birth, not knowing when, concerned Bessie the most. "Ma prophecizes that I will be sick [i.e., give birth] a month from today," she wrote Thomas in July. "Because I have been a little sick all day and people are often threatened just a month before the right time. Last night I took one of my little Gibbon opium pills—I think they have strengthened with age." Her writing became wholly concerned with *when.* "You don't know how scared I get whenever I see the Dr.," she admitted to Thomas. "Oh! I dread, I dread, I dread—do you know it is less than a month now before my apprehensions draw to a focus." Five days later she wrote, "I am getting mighty scary now—my illness is so near—*four weeks at the farthest.* I hardly ever go to bed without thinking 'maybe before morning.' "[37]

Bessie's pregnancy and the ways she worked to come to terms with her fears opened a new conversation with her husband. Her letters to him reveal a developing relationship that, if not without emotional awkwardness and distance, showed a new concreteness as the weeks passed. Bessie was not entirely content to have Thomas remain in Charlotte, but for the most part she supported his reasons for tending to business and letting the women of the family midwife the pregnancy. She wanted him to "comfort my heart and fill me with courage," but found that in his absence his letters did so, and he wrote frequently. "I think a great deal more of your letters now as a husband than I did as a lover," Bessie told him in August. She wrote when she was lonely, with just a trace of the little-girl Bessie lingering in some of her words, but she found that writing about it released it to him and his care. "Last night I came near to having a hard spell of crying for my husband than I have in a long time," she told Thomas. "I felt so badly. I wanted somebody to pet me a little and kiss me and love me. Everybody was too busy here, and my petting desires were all in vain." But her expressions of love were also playful as never before, and sexual to a degree not confided to paper during her courtship; indeed, Bessie recalled with pleasure times in their courtship when "you kissed me and loved me over again" and yet now the sexuality was not so much romantic as domestic, a remarkable transformation. She used their pet names for each other not as a figure in courtship but as a bond of domestic intimacy: she called herself his "blanket saver" in bed on freezing nights. There are passages of comfortableness and unaffected sexual playfulness. "Goodnight sir," she wrote from Raleigh. "Now just imagine that I got up and leaned on my elbow and gave you one of the sweetest of all kisses. Did you see . . . the story of the little girl who wanted a baby so much and prayed 'Lord, please give me a baby—a *meat* baby.' Well, I feel about kisses very much as the little girl did about her baby. I'm tired of flimsy, imaginary kisses—I want sure enough *meat kisses.* Goodnight, love. Don't give away *too many* of your kisses. I will want a great many when I am with you again." She could tell him, and it was enough, "I am a very happy wife, Tom, I assure you."[38]

The birth of Charles Dewey in September was the conclusion of the most dramatic event in Bessie's first year of marriage, brushing away the traces of courtship and loss at least for a time. The boy apparently was born healthy, though Mary Lacy alluded to a "screaming fit" seizing Bessie after the birth. Bessie filled her letters to her husband with accounts of their child after Thomas had returned to Charlotte from seeing his son and Bessie remained in Raleigh to convalesce. She nursed her child, and a slave woman Narcissa and another named Betsey attended to her needs. The new son and grandson and the recovery of the mother were the topic of family correspondence for a time. "Charlie is awake and opening his mouth for me," Bessie would write. Or, "Little Charley has no pity. He roots like a little pig and has the most don't care defiant look in his blue eyes when he is pulling the hardest." "I have a great deal of milk, but no more than little Charles *Breastpump* Dewey can draw out."[39]

Bessie Lacy had gained a new voice, at ease and frankly descriptive. She looked to her child and looked forward to going home. She returned by November 1854, a young mother and wife whose first child was the talk of her growing circle of friends. Sometimes, in letters to her father, the young Bessie reappeared, but for the most part after 1855 she inhabited the woman's sphere and saw it as her own. There would be severe trials: little Charles would die of illness while still a child; the war would shred the Lacy finances and claim Singleton, who would die of typhoid outside Petersburg in 1862; postwar society would test the ability of all to trust that good intentions and godly carefulness sufficed. Yet whenever the woman Bessie spoke, she spoke in the voice that had emerged from her schooling and courtship and had settled her marriage. She spoke as a woman who knew something about emotional extremity and resolution, as a woman ought, and about how keeping up appearances was more than a false front. Appearances delayed the need to make decisions. And when decisions no longer could be put off, the facade one had created helped to explain how to choose.

Extremity, resolution, and choice were the stuff of ritual in an individual's life. Embracing the rituals of young womanhood, Bessie Lacy first eased herself from her childhood home by discovering the emotional closeness among academy women. Though never cut off from her parents and their visions of womanhood, Bessie learned new ways to define intimacy and express love. These ways were lodged, as everyone knew, in a temporary, hothouse institution; but they were ways that became obvious standards for the continuing tie to family and, finally, for the quite different love between women and men. The strength of Bessie's attachment to the academy and to the love between women was counterpointed in its intensity by a courtship that seemed to promise control but delivered another formal challenge to her needs. Her love affair, in drawing upon convention yet resisting it, taught her about the seriousness of appearance and the artfulness of "sober reality." Once she was married, those extremities of schooling and courtship receded. But they left her with a sense of how she might manipulate appearance, this time as a wife, into a solid, woman's claim on the social world: as adviser to single women friends, as confidante to her father, as a mother. Bessie first acted as a wife, as she had initially played schoolgirl and lover, and then came to believe it. Having tested a woman's opportunity for self-indulgence and self-control opened by ritual, she came of age.

CHAPTER VI

THE KINGS:
WAITING FOR FATHER

For Thomas Butler King, the life worth living was a life of challenge and possession, a life, as he frequently said, of "manly éclat" and timely decision. As he entered his fortieth year in 1839, the possibilities for accomplishment were just opening. Everything had come in its time. King was a successful sea island planter at St. Simons, Georgia, owning several thousand acres of land at three planting sites and working more than three hundred slaves. He had recently been chosen to represent Glynn County, a fertile area with the lowest ratio of whites to blacks in the state, in the United States Congress. His election, and the exciting prospect of traveling to Washington, D.C., to make policy on coastal trade and railroads, followed surely upon five years as a state legislator and dedicated work at canvassing and furthering his district's economic interests. He had built the prerequisites of an honorable career: law degree, legal practice, contacts with other local men of property, and finally, in 1824, marriage to Anna Matilda Page who brought with her the centerpiece plantation Retreat. Two years older than her husband, Anna King was a woman of strong religious feeling and gentle good looks. Educated in Philadelphia in the French fashion, Anna Page married Thomas after a year's courtship and during the following fifteen years bore eight living children.[1]

The subsequent twenty years of their marriage, those following upon Thomas King's first term in Washington in 1840, is a story of a marriage typically—and uneasily—grounded on actual distance between spouses and the ideal of a unified couple. The Kings' marriage, somewhat more marked by physical separation than most, sharply reveals not only the shape of conflict and reciprocity between husband and wife, but also the remarkable tenacity of ideals belonging to gender—ideals constantly reinvented by Thomas and Anna through their letters. His commitment to manly effort and hers to an elusive

intimacy became the divergent themes that, paradoxically, characterized a long-lived union. It is a story, too, of how the Kings' children came
of age, learning the terms of desire and duty in the split worlds of
mother and father, and grasping the meaning of intimacy and authority. The experience of Thomas Butler King, Jr., especially, is important
in this regard, for his place as eldest son put him singularly in the gap
between his parents. As his father's namesake and his mother's dearest
companion, he was forced to sort out the tensions of gender and class
in a most obvious way, choosing some combination of his parents' very
different worlds. Thus this chapter concerns another alignment of the
cultural themes of planter-class family life—sex, mastery, and the
power of personal values as a social force. It concerns the struggle of a
family to be happy and to love while in the grip of what they perceived
to be unchangeable imperatives of honor and obligation that no
worthy family could deny.

Friction between Thomas and Anna King was apparent even before
he went away to Congress, but they had ways to avoid its worst effects.
She sometimes complained about his political travels about the state,
but praised him for attending so shrewdly to planting when he returned
home. He did not regularly attend church, but neither did he chafe at
her ever prompt and unwavering devotion to religion. She criticized
him for the "biblious [sic] habit" which he contracted each summer,
and he promised that when the fever subsided his drinking would also.
They mostly agreed on important matters like the need to retain the
Dunham brothers as overseers and the desirability of a thorough
academy education for their sons and daughters. Thomas chaired the
board of trustees of a boys' academy at Waynesville, Georgia, and
planned to enroll there his oldest sons, Thomas Butler King, Jr., called
Butler, eleven years old in 1840, and Henry Lord, called Lord because
his mother liked the name, then nine. The oldest child, Hannah, who
was fifteen in 1840, was sent to school in the North despite a plea from
Episcopal Bishop Stephen Elliott for his own Montpelier Institute in
Savannah. Politely ignoring the bishop's warning about the "love of
display that takes the edge off delicacy," Thomas and Anna King were
swayed by the very "ornaments and brilliancy of Northern schools"
Elliott cautioned against. Northern colleges, too, were deemed better.
Both he and Anna aimed to push Butler and Lord out of the academy
and into Harvard University as soon as possible.[2]

Thomas's first term in Congress changed how plans and decisions
were made in the King family, however, and the emotional center of
the family began to shift. His first term began an almost constant separation from his family, a reality that came to mark his life and his most
important familial ties. Anna King demanded detailed letters from her

husband, but more often than not he wrote only to inform her of snarled travel plans or to compliment himself. "I never was more distressed and perplexed at being delayed on my [way] home than I am now," Thomas wrote her in the fall of 1842 in words that became almost rote. "I trust however that I can explain all my dearest and best of wives when I see you." Clearly articulated was his enjoyment of his successes on the political circuit and the "disposition of all parties here to toast and feast . . . my humble self." King doted on the attention a congressman received, and enjoyed even more the competition among men that gave an edge to friendship and a savor to political achievement. By the end of his first year in office, however, Anna found his political attainments no substitute for his presence at the plantation. She pressed him to consider his duties as a father. "I think Butler and Lord still feel the influence of your late *visit* at home," she wrote in early summer of 1842. "They do not give me quite so much trouble." She admonished him to "keep your calmness and firmness and . . . your health may be spared," admitting that "it is of no use my preaching to you, but if you have any value for your life or reason *let self* for once *be your cure.*" Anna probably had her husband's drinking in mind, but she also began to see politics, too, as a kind of intoxication. Amid her accounts of visits made and received at Retreat, of slave illness, and of which young man had been seen in church with which young woman, Anna King counseled her absent husband to remain calm, not to let the engine of politics drive him beyond a good man's self-possession. When the younger children wrote to Thomas, Anna's hand guided their pens. "I wish congress would make haste and adjourn," seven-year-old Georgia wrote him. "As I feel your long absence more and more every day[.] Please as soon as you can come home for we all require you here very much. If you do not come home soon you will not know little Tip. Mamma has put short frocks on him and he looks very sweet."[3]

Little Tip was Richard Cuyler King, Anna's last child, born just before another turning point in the family's life which equaled in importance Thomas's election to the state's political elite. In July 1841, overseer John Dunham reported to King that "cotton lice" covered the fields at Retreat and that the already too abundant rain would combine with the insects to destroy the season's crops completely. This disaster occurred shortly after high winds had ripped up crops at his other planting sites. By late 1841 a major economic misfortune had befallen King, and he turned to his brother Andrew for a loan after exhausting other lines of credit. To his alarm, Thomas found his brother in debt to the amount of $17,500 at 18 percent interest and desperately needing to borrow. In a financial chain reaction all too common in planter finances, the Kings, their debtors and creditors, all staggered under the blow. Thomas was compelled to sell scores of slaves to save himself from selling land. Anna found herself presiding over the breakup of a slave force who had worked well for her; she was amazed that her husband spent only a few days overseeing the transition before returning to Washington. Anna tried to make the best of their stripped down, though still substantial, holdings. She organized new household economies, keeping the pantry keys to herself and finding that by doing so she scolded servants less and knew exactly her supplies and expenditures. But she also complained of shortages and the general bleakness of the sudden financial restrictions. She impulsively, and without consulting Thomas, wrote to a wealthy cousin in Alabama asking him to make her husband a loan. "In adversity we should act philosophically," was her kinsman's dryly polite response. "I am sure if Mr. King is possessed of the business habits and capacity that he is represented to have he will never let you nor your children suffer." Thus confronted with her husband's own honor as a barrier to her rescue, Anna unsuccessfully implored an annoyed Thomas to "*not lose so important a friend to your wife and children by want of a little civility on your part.*" She wanted him to initiate a correspondence with her cousin (as the cousin had rather grudgingly suggested) which might lead to a loan. But Thomas would not, despite Anna's avowal that here was a man who "*has made his fortune* and knows how to turn one penny to make it grow into a pound."[4]

Thomas King was not unconcerned with his planting reverses, of course, but unlike his wife he searched for a single solution, a dramatic move that would put them beyond their troubles. When Thomas came home, he talked with Anna about moving west, perhaps to Alabama. The two of them would walk up and down the porch talking, and Anna began to like the idea. But Thomas King's main chance, as he saw it, was political fame. Rising above the mass, and then above his fellow legislators, was his dream. He knew that he could do it, he told Anna. Complete strangers wrote to him, asking for his opinion on the navy, or on the matter of new territory in the Far West. King was a Whig, enthusiastic about Henry Clay, and envisioned an America that transformed factions into a powerful prosperity. And although he devoted attention to his constituents, writing tedious letters regarding this problem with a boundary or that part of the tariff law, his political gaze was fixed not on the close work of democratic push and pull, but on the horizon of glorious achievement. Ultimate challenge and competition were all. The Democrats, the "Locofocos," were "the enemy," and railroads were salvation. The image of a powerful America, slave and free notwithstanding, fueled his politics and drove him past the emerging sectional quarrel as so much petty carping.[5]

Thomas's political ambition found personal meaning in the psycho-

logical refreshment of being "fairly in the political saddle," as he wrote
Anna in 1842. Despite the sobering news from home, indeed because of
it, King renewed himself by leaving Retreat for the hallways of politics.
There he fondly recalled home. "I find that . . . the reception I met
with in Sav[anna]h has given me much éclat!" he excitedly wrote Anna
the day after Christmas, 1842. "Much do I care for it!! I would thousands of times prefer my quiet home, my dear wife's society and the
noisy romping of our dear children. This house [a boarding house in
Washington] is full of people, and really I am treated with more deference than I desire or is comfortable."[6] And as discomfiting as too much
deference was, none at all was worse. Denied reelection to Congress in
1842, King morosely reflected how he and other fallen legislators
would soon "mingle once more with the masses and be forgotten." In
mourning his career, he made extravagant promises to Anna:

> I am as sensible as you can be, my beloved wife, that my presence
> would be of service to our dear children, and I am resolved never
> again to do anything that will separate us. Hitherto Fate seems to
> have driven me on. I know that arguments are useless against the
> decrees of Fate. But . . . had I forseen the disastrous results which
> have attended my efforts for the last six years, as a planter, I should
> never have continued in politics. My object was to make a fair name
> and fame for my dear family, supposing we had enough of pecuniary
> means to satisfy our ambition; and to enable me to bring my fame
> thru with me. Fate has decided otherwise in regard to money. I shall
> now conform my actions to his decrees.[7]

She was right, he told her. His loss brought to the surface a sense of
having been pushed about by fate. The image of his family had pushed
him on, too; it was "our ambition" he was pursuing, and all of their
names he wished to polish. Yet Thomas's seeming passivity before fate
only waited a new opportunity to "bring my fame thru with me." He
was once again elected to Congress in 1844, and once again he exul-
tantly scribbled off a letter to his wife, recanting his discontent of a year
before. Writing from New York City, Thomas wasted no words on fate,
but spoke of men and audiences:

> I . . . see how proper it was for me to come. A man must not allow
> himself to be thrown into the shade or forgotten by his political asso-
> ciates. I am invited to address the people in many places. Last night I
> was conducted by a committee of 7 gentlemen to Brooklyn and
> made a speech to about 3 or 4000 people and was then carried to a
> most splendid entertainment where about one hundred gentlemen—
> the first merchants of both cities [i.e., Brooklyn and New York]—
> made speeches, drank toasts and sang songs until 1 a.m.[8]

Instead of being pushed about, he was carried on a tide of comrades, men who like himself enjoyed a toast and a victory. Throughout the 1840s, Thomas wrote in this way of his triumphs, punctuating his few long letters with short notes telling Anna of his whereabouts and his travel plans. He wrote of the pleasures of Washington society, of dinners and drawingrooms. Sometimes he revealed more than he knew, as when he commented at length on the "sad business" in which an eighteen-year-old belle, married not even two years, had separated from her husband and was now seen all about town. King found it distracting. "Who believes she will live without a husband?" he wrote Anna. "She ought to be divorced, or re-united with her husband if he be the [vilest?] brute alive." He added, "I am crazy to be with you." Anna found the image of eighteen-year-old belles disturbing, and Thomas was quick to say in his next letter, "How few of my ilk make good husbands! . . . *Faithful* and *true* I surely am, and when I observe the conduct of some men, I think this is something." These words did not set Anna's mind to rest, nor did the fact that King became a principal in a duel in early 1845 in which two shots were fired by each antagonist, but "*no mischief done.*" (King's opponent, after the exchange, declared that his words had been political, not personal, and then "all the parties dined together and had a *jovial time.*") But it was all part of being a man, King pointed out. In any event, belles and duels did not often interrupt the grueling political work necessary to his fame. Yet King's letters to fellow legislators, and their replies and accounts of their meetings, mostly suggest the pleasure, rather than the drudgery, of men working for power and money. King strove for greatness, and other men told him that it was drawing near. They spoke his language: public policy and personal honor combined into urgent phrases of manly work: "the publication of your correspondence concerning our Harbour has been of great benefit to you, personally, in this City," an associate typically wrote King from Savannah. "Persevere in these efforts, for you are openly applauded by democrats as well as whigs—and especially among the active men. If you can obtain success . . . you will receive (I hesitate not to make the prophecy) some marked tribute of respect from our Citizens *of all parties*. Rely upon it, they all feel kindly to you and now is your day to *work, work,* and *keep working.*"[9]

More than anything else, if time and effort is the measure, Thomas King loved being among the active men. Anna tried to make his stays at home as harmonious as she knew how and then saw him pace restlessly about, talking politics under his breath. She reminded him that his sons, especially Butler, would soon be of an age when they could help him, "should you continue to be a planter." She wanted him home, or she wanted to move their home somewhere else, as if politics could be escaped in the West. Still thinking about a move to Alabama as late as 1844, Anna urged her husband to settle his debts by selling seventy slaves, and, with a rare assertiveness, added, "I wish we could get rid of *all* at *their value* and leave this wretched country. I am more and more convinced it is no place to rear a family of children. . . . To bring up boys on a plantation makes them tyrannical as well as lazy, and girls too. . . . Oh my husband my heart is sick from trouble. It seems to me I have no comfort. If you do get home safe it will be but to leave me again. I know it can't *now be helped*. I also know there is no use to repine. So I will stop—." The loneliness was the worst of it, not entirely offset by the presence of her children or visits by friends and travelers. Anna made the decisions brought to her by overseer or cook, but she made them with an authority she neither truly felt nor relished. It was not that she wished to give over everything to Thomas, but she did wish to share the rearing and the growth of their children: Tip in his new frock, Butler riding about with his new boots and crop. At times she wrote in anger to Thomas, telling him in 1848, "You pass over my question whether or not you intend to be a candidate. I do *not like your silence.*" Yet she was unable to make a final critical judgment that dismissed her husband's preoccupations. Men were vexing in their ways, she admitted, but she could not see Thomas as simply "a man" and get on with her own, womanly satisfactions. Her sister-in-law, in contrast, wrote of her own husband from an ironic distance: "He sometimes threatens to sell," she told Anna. "But this is *all* talk. I often ask him why it is that he harrasses [*sic*] his mind so much. He says, to make money for *our children.*" Louisa King knew that even if this reply was merely a dodge, it was one not likely to be abandoned by her husband and so must be tolerated by a wise woman. Anna, however, was hurt anew each time her husband postponed a trip home, and, indeed, each time she realized how mysterious his strivings had become. "How is it the 'Falcon' brought me no mail from you?" she wrote immediately upon returning from the steamboat landing. "I cannot conceive it! Were you sick my beloved and unable to write? God forbid such a misfortune!! . . . I am more distressed than words can express." She worried that he was somewhere "surrounded by everything that is strange—strange scenes—strange faces—nothing that you love" without understanding that Thomas King loved just that: being welcomed to strange places and having his honor recognized and his name pronounced as if for the first time.[10]

Anna almost never responded to Thomas's tales of being feted and admired; instead she continued to see his politicking as a kind of derangement, one he had to account for. "You *promised* me you would not consent to be again put up to be a *target to be shot at*," she wrote Thomas after hearing from a neighbor that he would be the Whig candidate once again in 1848. "And I believed you! Oh! my husband, you cannot feel our constant separation as much as I do or you would not think of going again." She worried about the practical things: how would he go on the canvass with too few horses and no means to buy new ones? She persisted in seeing their trials since 1842 as economic, pushed close to disaster by Thomas's willful pursuit of nebulous glory. "You say my beloved that you 'are working hard for myself [i.e., Anna] and the children.' You have certainly built up a *proud name for yourself*, but I fear that will be all. You see my own dear husband, I have much time to *think* and . . . I can see no way open to escape from our difficulties." No way, she added, except to make a clean break and move away from Georgia. At home each day, handing out smaller portions to the servants, coping with broken tools and housewares, deciding whether Butler was old enough to be ordering about male slaves, Anna King did not have time to think as much as she had the compelling, immediate reason to think hard about the future. If she softened her attack on Thomas, it was not because she feared questioning his paternal leadership. It was that finally she could not believe that he could see things so differently than she. "I have said all this before," she wrote. "And I would not repeat, but think you must have forgotten." To read this as sarcasm would be to underestimate the depth of Anna's puzzlement; sarcasm was not one of her devices. Trusting her husband, knowing that he was *said* to be great, seeing him less and less, she could find no other explanation for his obscure political sojourns than that he must have forgotten his helpmate's best advice.[11]

Anna King's mixed anger and need, her speaking in italics but nevertheless permitting her husband many exits from her accusations, was the voice of a woman stranded in a marriage relation whose difficulties went to the heart of being a planter-class woman and wife. In the face of frustrations in the 1840s, she continued to cherish the idea of a helpmate based on the powerful gender ideal that stressed the social position of each sex over personal satisfaction. Her letters to Thomas made full, persuasive use of her position as wife, plantation mistress, and mother. But they ultimately succumbed to the absence of the man whom she wanted at home; she found herself with only an image, a sequence of short letters. Yet so strong was her emotional need for the man she pictured—the ideal Thomas who would live up to the ideals she pronounced—that the failure of her letters to create such a man did not stop her from trying to create him, year after year. Her letters became a kind of essay on wifehood, all the more revealing for being repetitious and broken.

As Anna's two oldest sons matured, many of the emotions raised by her predicament were transferred to them as well. Anna saw them much more frequently than she saw Thomas, of course, but she just as intensely implored them as mother and woman whenever they were apart from her. When seventeen-year-old Lord traveled to Cambridge, Massachusetts, for instance, to take the entrance examinations for Harvard University, Anna wrote urgently to him, commending the very masculine ways that confounded her:

> If you have been so fortunate as to stand the [entrance] test I hope and trust your whole mind will be bent on study—so that in the end (if God in his mercy spare your health and life) you may come off with honor to yourself and oh! my son with deep heartfelt gratification to your parents and friends. I believe my dear son you have ambition enough to try for this, but I fear you love pleasure too. Yet I trust you will not forget that the world is now before you and that it depends on yourself whether you will rise among the greatest or sink with the lowest.[12]

When Lord failed the entrance test (he subsequently went to Yale University), Anna's disappointment was swept away by her continued exhortation to greatness. She told Lord that *she* knew he could succeed and would some day prove to "*those gentlemen*" who had turned him down that he was better than they. "You have the *capacity*," she wrote him. "And I know my own beloved boy you will put 'your shoulder to the wheel' and not give up." He would be, she fervently knew, "the *pride* and joy of your devoted Parents. Lord! you little know how much I love—I dote—on you." In the mother's vision, focused by her own discontent, the son became the embodiment of a masculine effort that would please her. It is ironic, and poignant, that Anna's love for Lord turned on the same ambition, pride, and terrible male fear of either sinking or rising that took her husband away from her. She fed male ritual even as she resisted it. Lord King responded to his mother's urgency as the son of driving desires. "I hope . . . to be a great man," he wrote. "A Washington, or a Napoleon, a Bishop or Tom Paine." In any contest, he promised that he "won't be last on the list." Even at eighteen, Lord was fascinated with his father's political maneuverings, and became a confidant in some of them. Other family members saw him as the rising public man, and told him so. Younger sister Georgia relayed some praise by quoting a wise slave: "When *Mom Lady* heard what Father said about you, all that she said was, '*I knew* [he] was *too good* for St. *Simons.*' "[13]

Butler King was a more complicated figure than his brother Lord in this family drama. Though the eldest son, Butler possessed a gentleness in marked contrast to Lord's ambition. Whereas Lord wrote letters of flourish and male hyperbole, Butler wrote both his mother and father in a way almost feminine in its detail. Thomas King at first pushed Butler, too, to apply to Harvard but gave in to his son's wishes to stay in the state and attend classes at Franklin College in Athens. Butler kept in close touch with his parents, writing letters more than twice a week which were calm, almost placid, in their unself-conscious direct-ness. He had something of his mother's intellectual bluntness which avoided the entanglements of epistolary style even if it did not flower into a sustained interpretation of life or events. Initially Butler was not fond of college, preferring a tutor who "combines the schoolmaster and the companion." He took some pride in manly accomplishments, however, and liked relating them to his father, as when he wrote of his success in ordering slaves about, of his interest in a company of horse militia, the "Glynn Rangers," or of spending afternoons practicing ma-neuvers from "Ben's Cavalry Drill." Unlike his mother, Butler was ready to find excuses for Thomas's delays and his lack of long letters. "I do not wonder at your not being able to find time to write to *me*," Butler told his father in early 1848. "For as the old saying goes 'a willing horse is always in the harness'—because you are willing to work, everyone comes to you." Thomas must have been satisfied when he read this; his son credited his work as hard labor, one man to another. Yet Butler from about the age of nineteen mildly but persistently let his father know that he found the tumble of politics less than satisfying. No budding Washington or Napoleon, Butler asked Thomas to teach him about cotton, weather, slave management, and arrangements with agents. "You are well aware that I have always had a great taste for planting," he explained. "And I find that the older I grow the more this taste increases." Butler was not above manipulating his mother by cit-ing his father's authority (more than once Butler and Lord requested some freedom or favor from Anna by referring to their absent father and trusting that "you will indulge us as our Father did"), but most of his correspondence with Anna was wholly conversational and direct. They wrote each other of planting and management, of Butler's up-country sweetheart ("No doubt you were somewhat astonished at the way she spoke of young gentlemen," Butler wrote Anna. "That is, when she likes them confessing it so openly!") and increasingly of Thomas's separation from home. Through the next decade, their relationship to this absent center would become the substance of their bond. As early as 1847, Butler was aware of how Anna suffered when Thomas de-parted. With boyish openness he wrote Thomas from Athens, "I got a long letter from Mother the other day and I was not less surprised than pleased to see how well she bore your absence. I am only sorry it is not so that I could be at home to fill in some degree your place—to try to take some of her trouble on myself, which by the way my dear Father, you know she augments very much in her own mind unless she has someone to help her." To fill his father's place and take his mother's trouble on himself would become Butler's work and would give the King's family life its direction after Thomas went even farther from them in 1849.[14]

Throughout the 1840s Congressman King felt his political energies directed by his belief in an economic nationalism, a belief that hardly excluded his own economic gain. His support in the 1830s for a railroad linking Brunswick, Georgia, with points as far west as Mobile and as far north as New York shifted in the next decade to an intense interest in a transcontinental railroad. While in Congress, King acted as chairman of the House Committee on Naval Affairs, and became something of an authority on the coastal trade, steamship design, water route negotiations, and trade with Cuba and the West Indies. He ultimately hoped to promote his own steamship line to Europe. He advocated an aggressive stance on the Oregon Territory, and supported the war with Mexico, though not Polk's prosecution of it. The United States, in King's view, was destined to rule the continent, and the nation's driving economic power would melt the chill of sectionalism. During the secession crisis of 1850, he advised his political friends to oppose any radical disunionism and to trust that the mutual economic interests of both sections would pull them through the political crisis. Ideology, he felt sure, would finally have to bend to the overwhelming prosperity and power implicit in the American nation.[15]

With his political ambitions tied to what he saw as the long view, King was an early supporter of Zachary Taylor for president and put himself up for election to Congress as a Taylor man in 1848. When the Whigs won, himself included, King fully expected to be appointed secretary of the navy and was deeply disappointed when Taylor had other plans. The president sent King as his personal (and many said Whig) representative to scout out the political and economic situation in California. Although King denied it, Taylor's foes saw the Georgia congressman as an advance man for a Whig constitution should California become a state. King's broad assignment to tour the state and report on any and all things of interest did little to quiet rumors that his mission was a partisan one. He began his journey to the Far West in May 1849 by way of Panama, which greatly excited him as a site for an isthmus railroad and a prime trade route. During the previous twelve months, King had spent only about six weeks at Retreat, and left on his journey about the time Lord traveled to Yale and Anna was fretting over plans for Georgia's gay season and whether or not Mallory, sixteen, should also apply to Yale. Butler, who had been for some months shyly courting an Athens woman, Fannie Grant, surprised everyone by insisting that he accompany his father and felt quite "provoked" when Thomas demurred. "If he goes there again," Butler wrote Anna, "I know who *will* go too." Later he was glad he was home with Anna when word reached them, by newspaper it seems, that Thomas was laid low with a serious illness (probably typhus) in Sacramento in the late summer. Anna was frantic with worry, but finally Thomas wrote to reassure her and to tell enthusiastically of the almost unlimited potential for business ventures and political prominence in the raw towns of northern California. Convinced for some months that his glory lay in this new country with its exquisite dry air and mild climate, King resigned his seat in Congress in September 1849, and sought election as United States senator from the new state. When he failed to win, however, he protested his love for Georgia all the more. Georgia, like family and Retreat, would thereafter always be closest to his heart, he said.[16]

However genuine his feeling, Thomas Butler King saw little of his home state and home after 1850, a fact that would importantly shape his family life until its near collapse nine years later. When he returned East from California in the late summer of 1850, Anna King rejoiced but learned a few days later that her husband had reappeared only to accept an appointment from President Fillmore as collector for the Port of San Francisco (and doubtless to continue as a political operative). King's salary would be $10,000 annually, which he hoped to use to subsidize his planting and to enable him to flush out investment possibilities out West. Leaving once again for California in November 1850, Thomas was accompanied this time by Butler, a decision almost incomprehensible in one sense, given Anna's reliance on Butler for help in planting. King apparently believed that the combined efforts of his wife and his longtime overseers would make up for Butler's absence, and that Butler would be far more useful as the daily manager of the customs office, freeing Thomas to test the political winds and plot his many courses. It was the beginning of a two-year sojourn in the West, to be marked by new railroad schemes, a disastrous fire at the customs house in 1851 (and subsequent questions about King's management of customs duties, office rent, and his own salary), and another unsuccessful run for the Senate. These two years would put the seal on relationships in the King family and the words they uttered to one another about their lives apart and together.[17]

The passage of letters from California to Georgia took about a month. For the most part, Thomas relied on Butler to keep Anna informed of events, telling her that pressing duties kept his letter-writing time to a minimum. The letters Thomas did write began to fall into a pattern even more pronounced than before, a pattern marked by silences. He almost never asked Anna for specific information about planting, though he grew anxious if she did not mention the status of the crops. He almost never varied his conventional expressions of love for her, beginning each letter "My Dearly Beloved Anna!!," one of several constant figures that give his affection a stop-time quality, beyond change yet somehow unassuring, even rote. His interest in happenings at Retreat broke through most strongly when his children's education periodically concerned him. He was, he said, generally confident that Lord would excel at law, but wrote Mallory admonitions (by way of Anna) to concentrate and to study harder. Anna continued, in his mind, to be his competent deputy, but in order to perceive her this way he had to ignore her longing and her accusations. When sixteen-year-old Georgia wrote him that she had never been outside the "three counties" and that she had hoped to travel to Savannah "for the first time with *you*," Thomas relied on Anna to break the news that he would not be home, and told Anna to look into the relative merits of northern and southern academies. "Do not hesitate a moment to act in this matter promptly if necessary," he implored his wife. "Do not permit our children to be neglected or imposed on." The only instance in which King himself initiated something specific on his children's behalf occurred in the spring of 1852, when he received an anonymous letter informing him that Florence, distracted by homesickness, had threatened suicide while at school in Philadelphia. King instructed Lord to go at once to that city for "*perfect*, personal knowledge" about the affair. And even before hearing from Lord that Florence was now settled into the academy and happy, Thomas wrote her moral advice about youth's trials, supposing that an unhappy flirtation was at the root of her disquiet. He pushed ahead in a broad, jocular fashion, suggesting that she might be "*lovesick* and consequently very unhappy, as all young ladies are when suffering for the first time from this very common complaint. . . . Don't keep it a secret!! Tell your sisters confidentially—they will blat it to your mother and myself. . . . We will help you on in your love affair, and if it is a mistake you are making, you will kick it to the dogs without our assistance." But he found the distant situation troubling enough to conclude his letter to Florence quite seriously, asking her to confide in him as a friend, even if she felt she had been foolish: "I have seen much of young people. I think I know them well."[18]

For the most part, Thomas's letters flattened out even more during his California years. He almost never mentioned the exciting scenes of feasts and electioneering that he loved to relate in the past decade, perhaps in part because the days of intimate Georgia politics were over. But although he still was heavily engaged in the masculine world, he did not share its images with Anna. Moreover, the previous tension in his letters between the playfulness of politics and its drudgery now leaned toward the latter in a portentous, abstract way. In fact, it is impossible to tell from King's words to his wife just what he was doing. He spoke in masculine, elevated generalities. He spoke to his wife of putting "the wheels in motion" and of unspecified plans which would be greeted by "a genial sun of a new day." Specifics, never his strong suit, disappeared completely from his accounts of his work. It is as though Thomas had at last despaired, perhaps unconsciously, of ever recruiting Anna's informed support of his efforts, so instead he depended on pleas to wifely duty rather than to her understanding. His reports to his family from the outside world became the repetition of bright key phrases and loaded images of toil. Though on rare occasions he gave glimpses of himself and his doings ("I write or read in the evenings and then go growling to my lonely bed") his paternal self-image became almost entirely disembodied. News about himself quickly slid into a generalized characterization of manly duty and self-assurance. He was, he told Anna, "proceeding prosperously in the accomplishment of the object for which I came here. I have every reason *now* to hope that I shall return perfectly successful." He added, in phrases which became interchangeable in his brief missives home, "I am distressed that I have not time to write a long letter but so it is. . . . My efforts and privations are all made and encountered on your and [the children's] accounts." His temper and voice were nearly unchanged by three years of effort, and he wrote Anna near the end of his California stay: "I examine my heart and conduct and find *all safe*. I doubt not you can do the same. I find the trial of this long and cruel separation set surely upon me. Nothing but my sense of duty to those whom it has pleased Providence to make us the instruments of bringing into the world could induce me to submit to it."[19]

Rising to such paternal heights, Thomas King used his drive to excel as a part of a ritual self-indulgence. His denial of his wife's longing and his children's actual lives was inextricable from his desire for honor, fame, and wealth. Yet it would be mistaken to see this state of affairs as wholly under King's control. It was instead the consequence of a long, slow process in which flesh-and-blood family members were replaced by his image of them. King was indeed self-centered in his vision of his family's needs and expectations, and quite able to screen out much of what they actually said to him, but it was a vision that held him captive as well. His family became as disembodied in King's life as he was in theirs, but as such it became part of a powerful myth. In a world of prospects, deals, and money to be made, the mythic family became the unchanging backdrop against which the male drama was played. King's paternalism was not so much an inclusive dominance as it was a kind of exclusive vision; or, rather, the two were joined. His strength as a planter-class father was his ability to invent his family and bend his work—and theirs—to fit that vision.

Much of Anna King's dismay at Thomas's going to California stemmed from her inability to penetrate her husband's fiction—the sustaining myth of his distant, waiting family for whom all toil was suffered. Anna's competing vision, expressed as mixed anger and pride with regard to men's strivings, and as a kind of puzzled skepticism at masculine values, implied a family life much closer to the ideal of popular culture. She wanted the sexual spheres and their complementary differences to be a part of her daily routine, with women and men in family relation sustaining each other with their peculiar talents and judgments. Never happy with Thomas's frequent absences, Anna was appalled at his California journey. With Thomas farther away than ever before, Anna implored him even more strongly to write to her. She made letters the single moral bond of their marriage. It was, she said several times, "against my conscience to send you blank paper" and so she would fill both sides of a sheet even if she had written only three days before. "I can't put down my pen and yet I can't find anything to say," she wrote one warm June day seven months after Thomas and Butler had departed. "In mercy write me as often as you can. . . . I trust you will be able to write long letters." For the first time in her correspondence, Anna King portrayed her life, which she had earlier seen as shifting and unstable, as dauntingly static. She began to feel even more deeply her isolation on the sea islands, the days spent seeing no one but family, the afternoons she found herself searching the low horizon of trees and fields for a moving human figure. She began to hear, in the midday, a persistent roaring in her ears. She began to consult with a slave "prophetess" about the safety of her husband and the prospects of the harvest. She begged Lord to make the decision about Florence's request to attend a party in Philadelphia, because she, Anna, "has been so long out of the world" that her advice would miss the mark. Yet the sameness of her days spent without Thomas did not blunt the suspense she felt when she thought of him; in a way it sharpened it. "It is indeed a terrible sacrifice this of being so far separated," she wrote him. "This *looking forward* . . . for the time I may *hope* to see you is terrible. . . . Oh! when will you remain at home? The subject I will drop, as it is useless. I will do all I can to rear your children."[20]

She continued to criticize Thomas's political ambition, but in a way that made her words a statement of hope rather than a direct challenge to his authority. "Hard, hard have you labored for a reputation to leave your children," she told him in June 1849. "But that will not *give them bread*. Surely some more substantial reward is in store for you." She longed for her husband, wherever he was and whatever his hard labor.

She was jealous, even of her sons, once writing sharply to Thomas that his recent gift to Lord was generous, but "there are eight others at home equally entitled to your remembrance. For myself all I ask *is for my lawful share in your affections.* Bring me back your heart unchanged and I ask no more." She wished he would change his ways, but not his heart. Her words to him always came back to a need for intimacy and love, an erotic bond in which Thomas emerged as the much-desired but silent lover of fiction's doomed courtships. That same spring she told him, "If you would write *once a week* there would be some relief. . . . You will perhaps say 'we are too old to talk love to each other.' If that be your opinion, I differ from you. I feel as much pleasure in writing to you now as the most love-sick damsel of 17 would to her lover. More—a great deal. No woman can love lover or husband more ardently, tenderly than I do you." When his letters came, she placed them beneath her pillow.[21]

Nevertheless, Anna and Butler were the ones who exchanged weekly letters, and the relationship between mother and eldest son articulated the King family life more fully than any other. Though previously self-deprecating in a way that sometimes went beyond conventional modesty, Butler asserted himself in California to become his father's right hand. Before the trip, Butler had not seen much of Thomas for five or six years, relying instead on correspondence and Anna's reports. Six months before joining his father on the journey, Butler wrote Anna that "I am most happy to hear that Father has such a good opinion of Lord and myself. I am afraid he thinks well of me because he does not know enough of me to form much of an opinion. And as for yourself, dear Mother, your opinion is much biased by love." In the initial months of travel and settling into San Francisco, Butler came to admire his father, seeing in his frenetic politicking "the course of greatness," and reporting each time Thomas was distinguished in some way or asked to dinner. "He is looking well, though I can't see how he keeps from worrying to death," was typical of Butler's characterizations of his father, and he took elaborate note of the few times they enjoyed intimate fellowship. But for the most part, Butler seems to have managed the daily affairs of the customs office and appreciated Thomas from afar, keeping the books and answering the mail. Intimacy, when it came, seemed to surprise Butler as much as delight him; it seemed beyond what a son might expect. "Oh! it does me so much good when he has had a comparatively easy day," Butler confided in Anna in 1852. "When we sit down to dinner and talk of old times—not as some sons and fathers would but freely and with unashamed confidence which can only exist between a noble, highminded, generous Father—and a son who has been brought up as I have been—to treat my Parents with

love and confidence." He cherished times of "freedom of conversation" when Thomas bent a bit and talked of personal things. Yet these
times have the quality, in Butler's open and conversational prose, of
swift, odd moments in what was usually a deferential relation to a great
man.[22]

Even so, Butler's relationship with his father was sufficiently novel
to inspire letters to his mother, as was his increasing receptiveness to
young women and love. Butler's balky courtship with the young
woman in Athens had come to nothing, and previously he was more
likely to write Anna about Lord's winning ways with women than to
reflect on his own marital prospects. Thus his mention of women and
memories of women in his California letters was something new. San
Francisco was not a real city, but neither was it the Georgia sea islands.
Butler was taken with the dry air, the cool nights, and the "dark"
women of northern California. Though he often laughed at himself, his
letters to Anna sometimes seemed to get out of hand, blending the girls
he saw on the muddy streets of the bay city with fantasies of who might
someday be his girl. And San Francisco was free from the courtship
ritual Butler had found so embarrassing. In San Francisco things
moved quickly and invited realism about marriage: "If you go to see a
young lady *once* a week, people have you in love. . . . I like the variety.
Sister [Hannah] says in the last letter 'if you bring home a wife, let her
be one who I can love.' Good Heavens! The idea of bringing home a
wife—I would much rather bring home a *big stick* to beat me over the
head with. No wife for me this year." But in San Francisco girls need
not become wives. It was exhilarating, he confessed, to wander unin-
vited to a dance, waltz with "a baker's daughter" and discover "such a
mouth and yes, how sweet it would be to *kiss her.*" Butler joked with
his mother that his old sweethearts in Georgia would be married by the
time he got home. When one named Louisa was married, Butler imagined being there and proving that if he were by her side, even at her
wedding, her husband would defer to him. Butler's desires wavered
between real opportunities to kiss bakers' daughters and fantasies
about reclaiming former sweethearts; he wished to do something sexually decisive, but also to hear from Anna that being home was best.
Commenting again on Lord's flirtations, Butler wrote her in the fall of
1851, "I tell you what, my dearest *Ma*—I am the smartest child you
have, in that line. I can take a pretty girl right through [and] be not one
bit the worse for it myself." Yet he wondered about the old ideal: "Is
there never to be any more pretty girls on St. Simons? I do wish some
old sick fellow with two pretty daughters would get a place on the
Island—so when I come home I would not have to go off to have fun."[23]

But despite coming of age in love and work, coming home became the dominant theme of Butler's letters. It combined his own deeply felt domesticity with his growing intimacy with Anna and concern for her health. The customs house fire in the spring of 1851 diminished Butler's enjoyment of California. It started in the afternoon, no one knew how. Butler, in charge in his father's absence as usual, was slightly burned as he attempted to save documents and furniture; but Thomas's first response was to censure him. "When Father came he found *a great deal of fault* because I did not do more," Butler wrote Anna. "When everyone here knows how I acted. Well, he was not here—so he knows nothing." It was a rare judgment on Thomas's habits of command. Yet anger at his father, or even dismay at the loss, was not the first thing Butler recounted to Anna. Family and home loomed the largest the morning after the fire, he said. "I thought if I could have you or one of the girls to rub my head—though I did have a very pretty young lady to do the same thing, I don't love her." After the fire, Butler took a dimmer view of the importance of things like customs duties, tonnage records, and bribes from importers. The formerly exciting world of men and deals began to go flat, and Butler longed for southern vistas and southern values. "Some people think Customs House officers are perfectly right in stealing everything they can," he admitted to his mother. "But I am not such a *yankee*. . . . Tis strange how large a majority of the respectable people in this world love to lie & steal." The ways of money and profit, he decided, had led him back to his belief that "after all a planting life is the pleasantest, and if they would only make this a slave holding state I would be willing to live in it—but I won't without. The lands are so rich here it would be pleasant to see some good Georgia '*niggers*' make them produce as they should—and have *me* for their boss." But he would have to go back to Georgia for that, and he looked forward to the day of his return.[24]

Georgia mingled with Anna in Butler's mind, and with the recalled happiness of Retreat. Throughout his stay in California, Butler again and again worked to knit the family together. Filling out his father's brief general remarks, Butler wrote lines, as well as entire letters, to each sibling. He sent miniature straw hats to his younger sisters, and exchanged brotherly jokes with Lord and Mallory. He kept up with Florence's education, and wrote Georgia about helping Anna and about her young men. Unlike his father, Butler wrote regular "howdies" to certain slaves, and often included words from his slave Davy to Davy's wife. Indeed, Davy occasionally emerges as a figure in Butler's writing, seen not with affection so much as familiarity. Compliments were racial and backhanded, but hint at genuine feeling. "Davy is as usual true *nigger*," Butler wrote lightly in 1852. "He never cleans boots that are mates, always brushes the coat you are not going to wear. . . .

However he is sober and honest and never lets a washer-woman cheat him." Butler was sharper than Anna, who usually projected her longing onto the slaves. "Servants send many 'huddys,' " she typically wrote. "Poor things they are so anxious for your return." Butler even managed to be wryly philosophical when Davy ran off, surprised at being deserted, but not really expecting gratitude from a man kept in slavery.[25]

Underlying all of Butler's efforts was his love for his mother. In the earlier months, Butler sometimes echoed his father's rather conventional regrets over the "distressing separation" from Anna. But by 1852 he went beyond this to promising her he would allay her distress. "My dearest Mother please don't allow yourself to be low spirited on account of our long separation," he wrote in May 1852. "Don't Mother—& I will give you such a sweet kiss when I get home, and stay with you a long time." He began to realize that his constant letters recorded his own unusual sensitivity to emotion and to Anna. "You say 'our mutual affection has been remarked [upon],' " he observed. "I feel so confident of it that I care not whether others know it or not."[26] "Others" included Thomas, with whom Butler began a veiled but definite competition. Butler increasingly pictured himself to Anna as the force behind his father's expressions of love, and therefore as knowing her needs better than her husband. He wrote in May 1852 with a joking archness not quite covering his self-advertisement:

> F[ather] told me this morning that he would write to you himself. Now I know it gives you the sweetest pleasure in the world to get his letters, and I am perfectly willing that he should get all the credit for giving you said pleasure. But . . . allow me in the most delicate manner to insinuate to you privately that I—*capital I* am the small individual who takes the responsibility of . . . say[ing] unto him "Pa, don't you want to write my *Ma?*" So you can credit me by so much.[27]

It was Butler's way to tell of small deeds; but not far beneath was his wish to be the capital I in his mother's life. That he did not finally fill his father's place, even though his father needed his prompting, cut Butler deeply. In a rush of feeling at Christmastime 1851, when Butler found himself missing Retreat and wishing he could arrive home by surprise ("how the negroes would open their eyes and I *my heart*"), he confessed to his mother how her letters made him weep with happiness "in this far country [where] the true feelings of the heart and promptings of nature are untrammeled." But he also recalled a time when he had returned home by surprise from Athens: "Oh! how well I remember that night—you were expecting Father and were so much disappointed at not seeing him, you said to me—when my heart was overjoyed at seeing you—'it is *only* you.' Of course my dear Mother such an expression of your disappointment was only natural. But *I* never shall forget how *I felt*." Butler lamented her distance from him, as a lover might, and as a lover he gave her vivid images of herself. There was the time when the two of them crossed the inlet in a boat to Fancy Bluff, "when it was a little rough and as we had to pull against a south west wind it made the boat take in the spray very freely. Don't you remember you would not let me wipe the salt water off your face for you said you liked it—you would not let me move." This sharp picture of Anna is not to be found even in her own letters, not to mention the letters of her husband. Butler's images of her were intimate and close, courting her response. And like a courtship, his relation to her promised absolutes. "I feel that if I ever get back to you again I will never leave you," Butler wrote six months before he and his father left San Francisco. "I always felt as if it was my place to stay with and take care of you—for I know I love you better than all the others do."28

Thomas and Butler at last departed California for the East on December 16, 1852, arriving on the thirtieth in Panama where they missed the steamer to New Orleans by a few hours. Apparently, Thomas had decided that it would take further travel to secure his business interests in railroads. His schemes for western and transcontinental lines, backed in the past few years by Anna's work in planting, had by now outstripped his immediate resources. Father and son arrived in Washington, D.C., in late January. Although away more than two years from Retreat, Thomas did not stop in Georgia (Anna was shocked when Butler informed them of their arrival in Washington) but immediately arranged for a trip to London to seek financial backing for a railroad and a gold-mining operation in northern California. Anna King would have been further amazed could she have foreseen that her husband would not be home for yet another year, coming back for a few days only in December 1854. With Butler now back in Georgia, Thomas wrote somewhat more frequently to his wife and eldest son, including notes to his other children. He continued to refer in only the most general way to his activities, and the most concrete concerns in his letters continued to be those regarding his children's education. He corresponded with seventeen-year-old Virginia in the fall of 1854 about her desire to travel to Charleston to "finish off." He lectured his youngest son Richard, who had probably only seen his father two or three times in his life, about learning to write properly, returning one of the boy's letters to him for its poor penmanship and spelling.29

Butler had his mother to himself. Arriving at last in Washington, within a few days' journey to the sea islands, Butler could scarely wait to be home. He was, he told Anna, "the *home son* of the family," and reflecting on his service to his father and the federal government in the

Port of San Francisco he concluded, "Confound the *world*—I have had enough of it." He did not want praise (though his parents often praised him); it made him "feel quite small" when he heard it. He wanted peace and planting. He wanted to do his work at home, and "you will say 'good boy,' " he wrote in his transparent, half-joking way to his mother. "That is all I can ask of you."[30]

Anna King was relieved, of course, to have Butler back with her, though she had managed well enough in his absence with the help of the Dunhams and her son-in-law William Couper. Though Butler remained somewhat involved in Thomas's dealings, traveling to Washington and New York once a year or so on "California business," he disliked it and remained home most of the time. Still the absence of her husband weighed upon Anna as nothing else did. Worrying about Floyd's schooling and Lord's term at Harvard Law School, Anna told Butler of the dragging necessity to make every decision about her children alone. "I want advice," she told him. "I want someone to help me." After 1854, Anna seems to have become more angry but also more resigned to the strange course her marriage had taken. As never before, she wrote Thomas the blunt truth as she saw it, but even frontal assaults seemed wasted. "I must *insist* on your returning home, when you have accomplished your present mission," she wrote him in 1853. But it made no difference; Thomas was off to England. Anna wrote her children instead. "*No benefit as yet has come from* all this hard work of your Father's," she wrote Lord in Cambridge. "And in my opinion *none ever will*." But nobody else seemed to care as much as she that, despite running every risk and working like a "galley slave," her husband had gained no reward. She spoke with a feeling between exasperation and despair. She told her husband *facts* about his efforts and he ignored them. She struggled for the calmness simply to state to him that his labor was fruitless and his excuses old.[31] "Your *three* weeks are lengthening sadly my dear husband," she told him in early 1855, watching a familiar, dreary tale unfold:

> I know from no fault of yours but certainly your misfortune. Oh! my husband I sadly fear no benefit is ever to result from all this labor— all this waste of time & money. Give it up dearest—come home & take better care, than I can, of the little that we have. . . . I may be wrong in writing this to you, but it is just as I feel. You and Butler tell me nothing, whether all is failure or whether any substantial proof of success has been yours. I have but my fears to dwell on—[32]

Everything had gone wrong with her world; it had all slipped away since the ruinous harvest of 1841–42, leaving her "so long *hoping* the hard labour you have been undergoing . . . would end in some reward, but the longer you strive the worse off you seem." Not only for herself, but for Butler, Anna wished that Thomas would come away from what she increasingly saw as a generic male insanity (writing to her daughters of Thomas and his brother, she observed, "How queerly men are now acting!" as though everything could be understood by sex). Butler should be settled for himself, she told her husband. Such a "fine noble fellow" should be free to find a wife and start his own family.[33]

Thomas King's brisk, manly responses continued to pass over his wife's words and her needs. Whereas she saw the family blowing apart ("Children scattered far & wide—all, all like ships cast on the wide ocean without a chart!!!—") he continued to work for the tightly knit group God in his wisdom had given to his and Anna's care. All deprivations were on this account. Was there to be no reward as Anna said? "I hope and believe that this is the 'dark hour before the break of day' " he replied to Lord. "And that ere long we will be blessed with the light of a genial sun." It was just this lack of substance, this reliance on abstractions, that so puzzled Anna. Thomas offered nothing else because no other way of phrasing his work seemed to be as inclusive and yet succinct. Retreat, home, family maintained their timelessness in his letters. It was as though everything, even the present letter-writing moment, was either past or future. "What a dear old place [Retreat] is," he wrote fondly. "How many of the dearest recollections of life are associated with it." Yet, once again, he did not go there. "I shall . . . proceed direct to New York. This I am compelled to do to set the *wheels in motion.* It is certainly a severe trial to pass so near home and not visit it, but the stern demands of fate seem to forbid it." It is too reductive to see this stance as simply a facade. In part, of course, his attitude was a rationalization, a story he told to justify his paternal care to a family he rarely saw. But the fact that the rationalization worked is precisely the deeper meaning of King's mixture of care and separation. The two were joined without fatal contradiction, violating no moral precept in his own view. King believed his own story, and home, wife, children all became more dear as he was driven beyond them by fate. Fate and family ultimately were equal in the balance of his ambition, and his home slowly became something he invented. Its strongest image lay not in the tortured words of his wife or in the reports from sons and overseers, but in the "dear old place" of memory. The rough-and-tumble masculine world was thus founded on a wish and a memory, the combined energy of which—rhetorical and social—drew upon the spheres of gender and class dominance to sustain a family over time and distance.[34]

Therefore, just as it would be a mistake to see Thomas King's love for home as less than the powerful image it was, so it would be too one-dimensional to see in Anna's mounting criticism her escape from the dreary cycle of suspense and separation that her emotional life had become. In important ways she, too, believed the story. Her need for her husband—an erotic as well as economic need sharpened by her loneliness and his promises—surpassed her recognition of his failures. On the rare occasions that he wrote lovingly to her after 1850, her response absolved him of blame. "It is a sweet, beautiful letter dear husband, I glory in possessing the love of such a man," she told him in 1857. "I wish for your sake I was young & beautiful & accomplished, etc., etc. . . . [but] we have loved and been faithful to each other for 32 years 7 months & for this I am thankful & should be content." She did not say she *was* content; but the slightest word of love from Thomas set her to counting the months of their marriage. Beyond their actual relationship, a sexual ideal still had life, an ideal in which women were beautiful and accomplished and men tender. Butler, too, found in his father's words occasion to praise the absent hero, this paternal giant whose stature strangely grew as he receded from their lives. "My name has always been my *ticket*," Butler told Thomas proudly in 1857. "You have given me more in it, than you would have could you have given me a fortune. I never have been asked more than once what my name was." In a way, reputation, honor, words of praise, and the love of wife and son did matter most of all for a planter-class man. If a word of love could release Anna's emotions and overshadow her criticism with expressions of love, if a letter of praise could make Butler respond that fortune paled beside the name King—then why should not a man feel that honor was indeed all, that name and fame worked a kind of magic in all the relations of life? [35]

So it was not criticism, broken promises, delays, and obscure arrangements that could bring it all down, or finally even misdirected letters and misunderstood directions. Only death could change it. Like the ritual kisses Thomas always sent to his children, he and Anna traded fears of each other's death, fears that doubtless concealed a wish. Anna had dreams of his death, picturing boats colliding on the Mississippi River and Thomas going under the fiery water. Thomas could become truly alarmed when the looked-for note did not arrive and he was left to "picture to myself a thousand calamities." But then the real calamity came. Butler fell dead in the fields one day in January 1859. He had the previous year suffered no worse than a broken courtship, and had seemed a healthy, strong thirty-year-old not at all unhappily committed to be his parents' planter. His sudden death undid Anna King. She brooded over images of Butler's "noble, beauteous form . . . mouldering in the cold grave," and was distracted by memories of "how he did his duty to his parents, sisters, brothers, servants, neighbors—of his honesty, truth & almost perfect character." In death, Butler was at last acknowledged as "our best & noblest." "We have other beloved sons," Anna told Thomas. "[But] *they can't fill the place he did.*" In the weeks following the burial, Anna seems to have run out of words, her letters to Thomas (now back on the road) dwindling but becoming thickly religious. Seven months after Butler's death, Thomas once again sought election to the Georgia legislature, finding cause to challenge an opponent to a duel and sending Anna his usual itineraries and flowering prospects. Her criticism of him drained to its last, Anna wrote nothing about his affairs, and very little of Retreat. She died at age sixty in September 1859 while Thomas was away in the upcountry taking the cure at a hot springs. The family was staggered. Thomas won his election but found no savor; Lord surprised everyone by joining the church. Though diminished, the family regained itself. Georgia King became mistress of Retreat, with Lord looking to practice law in the state. Thomas would locate his work in Augusta, miles away but close by in view of his past decade of travel. Anna and Butler were gone, but remained with the family always. "It has now pleased Almighty God to remove her from us," Georgia wrote young Richard. "And we must live without her for a few more years—until we are permitted to rejoin her & our darling Buttie. . . . It will be impossible for me to write you as she did, but I will try."[36]

Looking at personal relationships has often seemed to threaten historical interpretation with a kind of paralysis. When we move away from solid structures into a realm of subjective experience the intricacies of personal happiness and fear seem to defy our ability to say what counts as reliable evidence. But the solidity of cultural structures is itself a kind of illusion, just as the wishes and fears of individuals are far more structured than we once supposed. Marriage and the family are not timelessly ordained, as the planters believed, but defined and redefined throughout peoples' lives. The Kings' union, like others', took its fundamental shape from what they *said* it was; we are guided in our interpretation by the very insights that guided them, and, in different measure, guided the Gastons and the Lacys: individual honor, social leadership, reciprocity within separate sexual spheres, perseverance through ritual renewal. The union of the King family lasted because its definitions, shaped by ritual, remained intact. It lasted, despite considerable tension, because common understandings withstood the shocks of disappointment, separation, death. It lasted because of the profound ability of each member to reinvent meaning within the family and to put up with—even cherish—the knot of intimacy and authority at the heart of their lives together.

Although Anna and Thomas King spent less time in each other's company than most elite couples, their lifetime pattern of married separateness was the general pattern of their peers. Men's mobility and scope, women's attention to detail; men's public flair and authority, women's devoted conscience—the Kings embodied the ideal sexual division of labor and worth. Indeed, the Kings' marriage was in this sense a model one in spite of its extremities. Personal separation was explainable, if not enjoyed. If anxiety, waiting, and fleeting happiness too often punctuated their days, these, too, were funneled into conventions which soothed, explained, inspired.

To an outsider's view, then, the Kings had a true marriage; it worked well. Harvests came and went, children were born and reared, Thomas possessed honor in Glynn County and beyond, Anna managed a household and slave force with shrewdness and care. Yet at the core of this marriage was a paradox everyone saw but no one avoided: the divisions and separations that permitted the Kings to meet their social duties in fact stunted other, personal needs which, unmet, did not disappear. For Thomas, man's work required more justifying to his family than he had expected; certainly more than he desired. As the years passed, he relied less on touting his manly pleasures and more on simply declaring that he was doing his duty and that he trusted others were doing theirs as well. His ties to Anna and the children (Butler for a time excepted) were increasingly less grounded in the shared experiences that become the much-loved touchstones of intimate life. Instead, the image of his family became his family in fact, abstract and sentimental. His children received their paternal care by way of their mother, leaving her fallibilities open to view and Thomas's authority distant, intact. For her part, Anna was forever giving and forgiving. She constantly was in need. No matter the social uses of the separate spheres, Anna's desires and discontents continued to orbit around her love for her husband. For her, the spheres might be separate in task but should be united by the daily, mutual presence of husband and wife. She remained alone, however, and the work she had to do alone, as slaveholder, planter, and mother, constantly postponed her need for love and ultimately undercut even her ability to define what it was she needed or how Thomas had failed to give it to her. Though she told him that his years of risk and speculation had brought no reward, telling him neither answered her needs nor allowed her to formulate a critical perspective on her dependence and isolation. Being "so long out of the world" was not, finally, a worldly situation for Anna; rather it was a matter of forbearance and faith. If her life was without a chart, as she once despaired, she did not conclude that Thomas, gender, or class was to blame for withholding it.

Separation, few alternatives for other work and achievement, faith in God and children all underlay the planter family. The Kings inhabited the cultural conventions of knowledge, love, and duty that created family feeling from these roots. Convention is seen in the passionate, yet wholly typical, protests of hard labor from Thomas. It is seen, too, in the way Anna's complaints were tamped down into a few long-suffering phrases. But it is seen perhaps most clearly in the choice young Butler had to make between two worlds. As a male he had the power to choose, but his life therefore was not less difficult. Though a gentle man, Butler nevertheless was drawn to the authority of manly reputation. Butler learned that his father's honor rested on the *way* he strove for fame rather than on material gain. Thomas King's only substantial economic asset at the end of his life was Retreat plantation, brought to him by Anna and largely maintained by her thereafter. It was his visible display of his honor in a world of men, related to his family in his letters and invented by them in theirs, that was at the heart of their admiration for him. When Butler chose between politics and planting, in a sense between the masculine and feminine worlds, he decided that despite his father's honor the male world was one of deceit and aggravation. He did not openly reject Thomas, but in effect he decided against the manly equation of character with social authority and limitless ambition; he sidestepped the elite propensity to mistake master-class interests for the general good. But it was even more complicated. In staying home and farming, and to this extent turning his back on grandiose masculinity, Butler postponed other things that signified full manhood: a wife and children of his own, for example, and his independence from siblings and mother. He told himself that these things could wait, especially separation from Anna. His decision for planting thus was all the more compelling because it was a choice not only between working worlds and their values, but also between parents whom he might deeply love. To choose planting was to choose to live with his mother and be the helpmate she wished his father to be. If the choice was clear, the distance between alternatives was no less harrowing.

CONCLUSION

In this study I have described aspects of a people's culture and, through these, have explored their consciousness. I have attempted to follow the planter elite's own struggles to be worthy, to know, and to love. In part, therefore, this study has aimed to demonstrate certain things about the inner workings of planter-class culture, to discover the anatomy of its rituals, and to test the sinews of its common-sense expectations. In this regard, the shared style and values of the planters can be traced with considerable certainty. But this study has also aimed to suggest the particular puzzles and intensities individuals encountered because they inhabited this culture. The difficulties of reconstructing a past culture make it impossible to do more than suggest how a particular life bent culture to particular needs. Yet plausible suggestion in these matters is as important as being able more surely to demonstrate the functions of culture at a collective level.

The attention here to the language of ritual and daily routine has, I hope, plotted a way to study the planters' consciousness and, inevitably, to reflect on our modern (often mythic or ironic) consciousness of them. If the term *class consciousness* is to mean anything in cultural history, both words must alternately be stressed, and in emphasizing class our conclusions must be about those features of cultural life which made the planters a defined and powerful minority, a "class-for-itself," in Eugene Genovese's phrase. In stressing consciousness, on the other hand, our conclusion must concern the personal content of this social power, the ways power became cultural authority as individuals persuaded themselves and others that their reality was *the* reality, and if persuasion failed, produced that reality at all costs. Because this book has looked at class consciousness as a historical setting, not as a sequence of events, the conclusions do not concern specific causes and effects but rather reflect on the potential for change and cohesion in the planters' world. The conclusions are thematic because the layers of culture themselves formed themes, conceptual and emotional, that gave shape to the planters' purposes and texts to their desires.[1]

The dominant themes can be gathered into two broad sets, though there is nothing inevitable about this grouping. Certainly the complexity of the culture examined here lends itself to more than one way of summarizing its limits and its insights. But for reasons of economy and contrast, a duality seems useful. The first set concerns the fundamental structure of elite culture and the second has to do with the dynamics of cultural process. Central to the first was a celebration of hierarchal schemes of love, authority, and moral belief. A sense of the social world as vertically stacked, as a sustaining but often restrictive rank order, was not merely tolerated by the planters, but enjoyed and cherished. This delight in hierarchy was not without its tensions. The tiers of worth, knowledge, and love made personal intimacy a quality without a sure-footed language, for example; it made differences between the sexes and the generations ripe with the possibility for transgression and collapse. But the planters could celebrate even the tensions of this worldview. What was an affair of honor but a high-strung drama of men's equal standing atop the social hierarchy? And what was courtship but the pleasure of "losing" oneself or "falling" in love? Moreover, personal relationships came to be judged by their place in the order, giving the elite a sense of social permanence. Unlike the busy, abstract hum of egalitarian theory, an obvious hierarchy meant that some events and relationships were not amenable to acquisitiveness, leveling, or striking a bargain. Here was something to be leaned upon, whether in the heated, ambitious style of Thomas Butler King looking for the ultimate railroad venture, or in the cool, almost mournful fashion of William Gaston pondering the silence that fell over families as they matured. The push and pull of Jacksonian America notwithstanding, the southern elite drew satisfaction from the hierarchy of all values and habits.

Also immutable, in the planters' view, was another crucial aspect of the structure of cultural life, the organization of gender into divided worlds. The planters' sense of gender might be seen as another instance of hierarchy, but the "sexual spheres" were a unique kind of rank order. Sexual priorities were thereby established, to be sure, but more important the sexes discovered their respective tasks and identities jointly within their class. Though far from equal in most respects, men and women shared elite standing which appeared to give them a similar stake in the survival of elite authority. Gender values lent the force of biology to this cultural arrangement, while at the same time permitting the planters to contain sexuality by locating it in two cultural worlds instead of a single biological one. Thus the power of sexuality was not denied so much as it was divided, and the revelations and pleasures of sexuality were always in some measure "over there" in the other

sphere, locked up and strange. If courtship ritual's sudden shifts between despair and exaltation could be a lover's undoing (as it almost
was for Bessie Lacy), it remained, almost paradoxically, a unifying vision of human nature which bolstered the planters' explanation of
what mattered in life.

Pervasive and nearly beyond question, the planters' deep belief in
the structures of hierarchy and gender sustained their daily lives as it
focused their vision of the world's order. But to look at culture only as
structure is too static a view; it requires some movement, a feeling for
consequence and process. Thus it is also necessary to conclude something about the planters' opportunities for flexibility and cohesiveness,
their chance for shared identity in the face of conflict, their capacity for
happiness. One dynamic that has appeared throughout this study,
whether in the rigors of a duel or in the passage of a youth from home
to the academy, is the close correspondence between personal self-
esteem and the social order. Southerners themselves liked to say that
the social world was an organism, and the correlation of the personal
and the social was a part of this romantic allegiance. But this observation is too metaphorical; the plain point is that the elite perceived personal character to represent collective order itself. The most personal
concerns were neither private nor atomized; they were swollen with
general significance. A challenge to an upper-class man was felt as a
shock to the society; the acquirements of a woman in love or in school
were not only her own private satisfaction but a mirror of much wider
scope. The tight link between the personal and the social accounted for
much of the tension the planters felt when "on display"; it also gratified
them enormously. It shaped their worldly prospects and their relations
with family. William Gaston was unable to expect anything from himself or his children without looking abroad to society, to what he "ought
to expect." Thomas King, laboring away at his financial schemes like a
good capitalist, nevertheless shunned the clean language of finance for
the clotted words of a paterfamilias. The affair of honor was the epit-
ome of the link, as were the openly social gestures of lovemaking. In
short, the planters found themselves living their lives as if always in
view; their words, private and family bound, were never without an
echo in the world outside. Indeed, there was really no "outside" if one
took one's elite standing seriously; and if one did not, a risk threatened
everyone implicated in mastery.

Mastery was, after all, the final measure of things. And along with
the equation of personal esteem and social order was a second dynamic of elite culture, the relation between what might be called the
substance of cultural life (the bedrock realities of moral striving, love,
work, and meaning) and the desire (or necessity) to display it. To believe

they mattered, indeed to survive as an elite, the planters had to move beyond expression to exhibition. Theirs was a culture in which quiet satisfaction in one's personal worth was a kind of ineptness. Culture was plumage for display; consciousness had to be made manifest, to appear "to an advantage," as the phrase had it. We have seen this dynamic in the elevated showiness of the affair of honor, in the formal salience of courtship, in the conviction that knowledge was useless without a voice and a forum. This dynamic, too, was full of tension. When it worked smoothly, women and men felt a deep unity of image and action, personal belief and social influence. When it went awry, it flaunted its falsehoods, mistook ambition and desire for a social landscape, and ran the risk of exposure: by one's "lessers," by sharp Yankees, and worst of all, by armies of slaves. Keeping up appearances, then, was not trivial because it was always attractive (and often necessary) to believe that appearances were real, as real as anything else that the master class could make.

It bears repeating that certain familiar themes in the history of antebellum life were nearly absent from the main themes of planter-class culture expressed in their words. For example, the possibility for change in family life or in the definition of personal achievement was not evident in any systematic way in the elite's worldview, whether change was seen as either disruptive or excitingly "modern." Unlike the northern middle class, the planters did not trim honor to fit law, place courtship into the hands of lovers alone, or divert education from its association with true character. Indeed, the rituals of courtship and honor, womanhood and manhood, parenting and autonomy, changed very little over the antebellum years, revealing a remarkable degree of continuity in elite habits and values. This constancy must balance what we know of the comparatively rapid changes that characterized the South's place in national politics and economic production during the years 1820–60.

Even more striking is the almost complete absence of black people in white accounts of ritual and daily routine. We know that slaves tended white children, delivered white love letters, and accompanied white academy youth to school. We know, too, that slavery in these years increasingly influenced public writing on labor management, economics, government policy, and personal morality. How to assess the only marginal appearance of blacks in white accounts of family life deserves a study of its own. It is important that the planters used the bodies of black people, profited from their labor, and confided personal affairs to their agency while seldom characterizing them as persons. There is little question that most masters perceived a kind of personhood in blacks, but the culture of white family life indicates a capacity for ignoring it that must be seen as a profound dimension of white racism. Moreover, the accounts of family life indicate that the planters did not permit themselves to worry about this aspect of their mastery. They might worry about economic ruin or political disaster, but as far as family life was concerned, the framework of hierarchy (including paternalistic control of slaves) and gender (involving white women in slave mastery) would suffice to keep blacks down. And the showy, public nature of whites' personal lives would further intimidate them.

Some fifteen years ago, C. Vann Woodward, writing of the "Old South drama," called for the study of "the institutional setting in which [southerners] performed—the patriarchal tradition, the caste system, the martial spirit, the racial etiquette, the familial charisma—all deserve attention from the historian of the Southern Ethic."[2] This study and others cited here have attempted to do a piece of this work. If the planter family and its rituals shared certain conventional wisdoms with other white, propertied Americans—the divided world of sex, the sentimental view of children, the perfection of success—the main themes summarized here deserve to have their southern accent noted. The themes of elite family life had a southern slant recognized and acted upon as such: the celebration of hierarchy, the intense formality between men and women, the powerful translation of the personal into the social, the conflation of image with substance. All were manifestly distinct from the egalitarian, fluid, privatized, calculating style emerging in the homes of the northern well-to-do. Of course a full understanding of the "Southern Ethic" must involve a comparison with the North. It must involve further understanding of the ties of white culture to black, especially in terms of each race's Christianity. If this book offers a picture of elite, secular culture, it also offers a map for the comparative studies that will further reconstruct how antebellum southerners made their lives from circumstances and relations not always of their own choosing.

NOTES

Introduction

1. Looking at the culture of everyday life should not imply that it was more "real" than formal intellectual life, nor do I intend to say that what people *think* their lives are about is more revealing than what they *did* with their lives. However, because the planters' common sense has generally gone unexamined, the ordinary routines they cherished have not been taken so seriously as the great events that disrupted their world. Attempting to dig up the pattern of these routines has led me on an intellectual journey into historical method that can be documented only in part in these notes and in the Bibliographical Essay. I have tried to include those people and works which have most influenced my study, and those which are especially contentious, in hopes that others will be drawn to them as I was.

2. C. Vann Woodward, "The Irony of Southern History," in his *Burden of Southern History* (New York: Vintage Books, 1960), 170, 167. William R. Taylor, *Cavalier and Yankee: The Old South and American National Character* (New York: George Braziller, 1961), remains the best analysis of the Old South myth as a cultural force. A moving personal account of growing up under the myth—and struggling rather successfully against too much irony—is Lillian Smith, *Killers of the Dream* (New York: W. W. Norton, 1949).

3. The observer is Henry Benjamin Whipple, quoted in Clement Eaton, *The Waning of the Old South Civilization* (New York: Pegasus Books, 1969), 29–30. The historian is Eugene D. Genovese, *Roll, Jordon, Roll: The World the Slaves Made* (New York: Vintage Books, 1976), 96–97.

4. The tension between myth and irony is essentially a moral one, as Stanley Elkins discovered in 1959, when he sought to place the debate over slavery and the Old South in the cool light of social science but instead touched off the fiercest moral debate over the southern way of life in twenty-five years; see Elkins, *Slavery: A Problem in American Institutional and Intellectual Life* (New York: Grosset & Dunlap, 1959) and Ann Lane, ed., *The Debate over Slavery: Stanley Elkins and His Critics* (Chicago: University of Chicago Press, 1971). Three important recent studies that variously take up southern myth and irony are Bertram Wyatt-Brown, *Southern Honor: Ethics and Behavior in the Old South* (New York: Oxford University Press, 1982); Dickson D. Bruce, Jr., *Violence and Culture in the Antebellum South* (Austin: University of Texas Press, 1979); Drew Gilpin Faust, *James Henry Hammond and the Old South: A Design for Mastery* (Baton Rouge: Louisiana State University Press, 1982). Historiographical sources for planter-class culture are discussed in the Bibliographical Essay.

5. "While it is still debated whether or not the slaveholding planters controlled the society of the South, it is not much debated," Joel Williamson has observed. "Rather clearly they were the elite, they set the tone of the culture . . . [and] many people who at first glance might seem to be only ministers, lawyers, or city businessmen will, upon investigation, be found to own plantations and slaves." Williamson, *New People: Miscegenation and Mulattoes in the United States* (New York: Free Press, 1980), xiii–xiv. For varied comment on the political exercise of the planters' social authority, see Michael P. Johnson, *Toward a Patriarchal Republic: The Secession of Georgia (Baton Rouge: Louisiana State University Press, 1977); Steven A. Channing, Crisis of Fear: Secession in South Carolina* (New York: W. W. Norton, 1970); John Barnwell, *Love of Order: South Carolina's First Secession Crisis* (Chapel Hill: University of North Carolina Press, 1982); J. Mills Thorton, *Politics and Power in a Slave Society: Alabama, 1800–1860* (Baton Rouge: Louisiana State University Press, 1978); Michael P. Johnson, "Planters and Patriarchy: Charleston 1800–1860," *Journal of Southern History* 46 (1980): 45–72.

6. C. Vann Woodward, *American Counterpoint: Slavery and Racism in the North-South Dialogue* (Boston: Little, Brown & Co., 1971) remains an excellent window onto the question of southern distinctiveness. A balanced, concise discussion is Carl N. Degler, *Place over Time: The Continuity of Southern Distinctiveness* (Baton Rouge: Louisiana State University Press, 1977). Regarding the lack of mention of slaves in whites' correspondence, Jan Lewis found much the same thing in the letters of Virginians in the late eighteenth, early nineteenth centuries: "Slaveowners in their private correspondence almost never discussed slavery as an institution and rarely mentioned their own slaves." Lewis, *The Pursuit of Happiness: Family and Values in Jefferson's Virginia* (New York: Cambridge University Press, 1983), 141. Jane Turner Censer also found almost no mention of slaves in the letters of North Carolina planters, and she concludes that a severe emotional distance marked interracial relations despite the lore of the planters' "black family"; see Censer, *North Carolina Planters and Their Children, 1800–1860* (Baton Rouge: Louisiana State University Press, 1984), esp. chap. 7.

7. J. G. A. Pocock, *Politics, Language, and Time: Essays on Political Thought and History* (New York: Atheneum, 1971), 29.

Ritual: Between Indulgence and Control

1. I have found the following works on ritual particularly useful for thinking about the historical significance of such elevated experiences in the run of ordinary days: Victor Turner, *The Ritual Process: Structure and Anti-Structure* (Chicago: University of Chicago Press, 1969); Mary Douglas, *Natural Symbols: Explorations in Cosmology* (New York: Random House, 1972); the now seminal (especially for historians) two works by Clifford Geertz, *The Interpretation of Cultures* (New York: Basic Books, 1973) and *Local Knowledge: Further Essays in Interpretive Anthropology* (New York: Basic Books, 1983). See the Bibliographical Essay for other works on ritual and family.

2. Nancy S. Struever, "The Study of Language and the Study of History," *Journal of Interdisciplinary History* 4 (1974): 413. Looking at the cultural setting of historical events, tracing their sequence, raises the risks of anchronism. But the rewards of anchronism are at hand as well. The historian, as Margaret Leslie

has written, "is committed to making this unfamiliar world [of the past] intelligible to himself and his readers, and how can he do that without reinterpreting it, using anchronistic modern concepts to grasp it with, and in the process adapting and enriching those concepts themselves? . . . The perception of similarity in otherness, of unity in difference, is the very life-blood of analogical thinking, one of the commonest ways in which we extend the limits of our thought." See Leslie, "In Defence of Anchronism," *Political Studies* 18 (1970): 441–42. Issues of language and historical interpretation are further considered in the Bibliographical Essay.

3. For good introductions to these aspects of language, see Dell Hymes, *Foundations in Sociolinguistics: An Ethnographic Approach* (Philadelphia: University of Pennsylvania Press, 1974), and Gordon Allport's classic *The Use of Personal Documents in Psychological Research* (New York: Social Science Research Council, 1942).

Struever, "The Study of Language," is an excellent place to begin plumbing the historical importance of language and expressive forms. Some of the writing on the nature of speech as action is relevant here, for example, the venerable J. L. Austin lectures, *How to Do Things with Words* (Cambridge: Harvard University Press, 1962). For an extension of Austin's thinking, see P. F. Strawson, "Intention and Convention in Speech Acts," *Philosophical Review* 73 (1964): 439–60 and see also Austin's critic, L. Jonathan Cohen, "Do Illocutionary Forces Exist?" *Philosophical Quarterly* 14 (1964): 118–37. On meaning in language, see John R. Searle, *Speech Acts: An Essay in the Philosophy of Language* (New York: Cambridge University Press, 1969); H. P. Grice, "Meaning," *Philosophical Review* 66 (1957): 377–88; Paul Ziff, "On H. P. Grice's Account of Meaning," *Analysis* 28 (1967): 1–8. See the Bibliographical Essay for additional useful sources.

4. Hymes, *Foundations in Sociolinguistics*, 8; Canby, quoted in John Fraser, *America and the Patterns of Chivalry* (New York: Cambridge University Press, 1982), 203.

5. Edward Sapir, "The Status of Linguistics as a Science" in *Culture, Language, and Personality: Selected Essays*, ed. David G. Mandelbaum (Berkeley and Los Angeles: University of California Press, 1949), 69. In recent years, many "structuralists" have elaborated upon such analysis. Though often polemical, and sometimes incomprehensible, structuralist interpretations sharpen the sense of how cultural habits and expectations assume a characteristic shape in people's affairs. For useful introductions to structuralism as a way of cultural analysis, see David Roby, ed., *Structuralism: An Introduction* (Oxford: Clarendon Press, 1973); David Pace, "Structuralism in History and the Social Sciences," *American Quarterly* 30 (1978): 282–97; Hayden White, "Structuralism and Popular Culture," *Journal of Popular Culture* 7 (1974): 759–75.

6. A sustained analysis of the letter form as historical evidence is hard to come by. Allport, *Personal Documents*, does not have much to say about letters, but raises general questions about "personal" writings. Janet G. Altman, *Epistolarity: Approaches to a Form* (Columbus: Ohio State University Press, 1982), is suggestive, though her subject is the use of the letter form in fiction. For histories that make some comment on the nature of letters and letter-writing, see Elizabeth Hampsten, *Read This Only to Yourself: The Private Writings of Midwestern Women, 1880–1910* (Bloomington: Indiana University Press, 1982);

Paul Fussell, *The Great War and Modern Memory* (New York: Oxford University Press, 1975); Marilyn Ferris Motz, *True Sisterhood: Michigan Women and Their Kin, 1820–1920* (Albany: State University of New York Press, 1983); for a different view from Motz's, one that stresses difference between women and men as writers, see John Mack Faragher, *Women and Men on the Overland Trail* (New Haven: Yale University Press, 1979).

Chapter 1. The Affair of Honor: Character and Esteem

1. Mary Douglas, *Natural Symbols: Explorations in Cosmology* (New York: Random House, 1972), 8; Georges Balandier notes that political ritual "is seen as a means of expressing conflicts and, at the same time, of transcending them by affirming the unity of the society." See *Political Anthropology* (New York: Pantheon Books, 1970), 18. Authors who wrote immediately after the Civil War about the affair of honor or the duel tended to treat the subject with seriousness; see, for example, John S. Wise, *The End of an Era* (Boston: Houghton-Mifflin, 1899). As decades passed, however, anecdote, comedy, and moral disapproval attracted writers to the duel, with mixed results for scholarship. See Thomas Gamble, *Savannah Duels and Duellists, 1733–1877* (Savannah: Review Publishing & Printing Co., 1923); Don C. Seitz, *Famous American Duels* (1929; Freeport, N.Y.: Arno Press, 1966); William O. Stevens, *Pistols at Ten Paces: The Story of the Code of Honor in America* (Boston: Houghton-Mifflin, 1940); Harnett T. Kane, *Gentlemen, Swords and Pistols* (New York: William Morris & Co., 1951); Henry W. Lewis, "The Dugger-Dromgoole Duel," *North Carolina Historical Review* 34 (1934): 327–45. In the storytelling mode, but still useful and gracefully written, is Jack K. Williams, *Dueling in the Old South: Vignettes of Social History* (College Station, Tex.: A & M University Press, 1980); see also W. Conard Gass, " 'The Misfortune of a High Minded and Honorable Gentleman': W. W. Avery and the Southern Code of Honor," *North Carolina Historical Review* 56 (1979): 278–97. Students of the duel and the affair of honor have recently begun to piece together their cultural meaning, whether as drama, ritual, or psychological crisis, beginning with John Hope Franklin, *The Militant South, 1800–1861* (Cambridge: Harvard University Press, 1956), esp. chap. 1. Dickson D. Bruce, Jr., *Violence and Culture in the Antebellum South* (Austin: University of Texas Press, 1979), esp. chap. 1, perceptively sees the duel as a consequence of men accusing one another of being out of control in society. Bertram Wyatt-Brown also stresses the communal nature of the duel, and sees its roots in individuals' anxieties (though he probably overemphasizes the cross-class appeal of the duel); see *Southern Honor: Ethics and Behavior in the Old South* (New York: Oxford University Press, 1982), 350–61. Also suggestive are Kenneth S. Greenberg, *Masters and Statesmen: The Political Culture of American Slavery* (Baltimore: Johns Hopkins University Press, 1985), and Guy A. Cardwell, "The Duel in the Old South: Crux of a Concept," *South Atlantic Quarterly* 66 (1976): 50–69. For essays that place the duel and male honor in the contexts of law, self-esteem, and political values, see Charles S. Sydnor, "The Southerner and the Laws," *Journal of Southern History* 6 (1940): 3–24; Michael P. Johnson, "Planters and Patriarchy: Charleston, 1800–1860," *Journal of Southern History* 46 (1980): 45–72; James Brewer Stewart, " 'A Great Talking and Eating Machine': Patriarchy, Mobilization, and Dynamics of Nullification in South Carolina," *Civil War History* 27 (1981): 197–220; Lawrence T. McDonnell, "Struggle against Suicide: James Henry Hammond and the Secession of South Carolina,"

Southern Studies 22 (1983): 109-137; Steven M. Stowe, "The 'Touchiness' of the Gentlemen Planter," *Psychohistory Review* 8 (1979): 6-15.

2. On the historical roots of the antebellum affair, see Lorenzo Sabine, *Notes on Duels and Duelling* (Boston: Crosby, Nichols & Co., 1855), 5-49; Williams, *Dueling in the Old South*, 6-7, 100-101; Franklin, *Militant South*, 44; Wyatt-Brown, *Southern Honor*, 352-53; Bruce, *Violence and Culture*, 27, 42. See also John Lyde Wilson, *The Code of Honor; or the Rules for the Government of Principals and Seconds in Duelling* (Charleston, S.C.: Thomas J. Eccles, 1838). Antidueling sentiment and the general inefficacy of the law are noted in Williams, *Dueling in the Old South*, 61-67; see also Sydnor, "The Southerner and the Laws," passim, and Rosser H. Taylor, *Ante-bellum South Carolina: A Social and Cultural History* (Chapel Hill: University of North Carolina Press, 1942), 45-47. The important point is not that dueling stood outside the law, but that it stood alongside it in a separate realm. Satisfaction, not justice, was rendered; questions of self-esteem, not questions of interest, were most closely involved. Jack K. Williams cites a "Southern gentleman" as recalling how the code of honor "towers above the cloud of laws that blanket and hold in place the lower orders" (*Dueling in the Old South*, 72). Though Harriott Horry Ravenel disapproved of the duel she noted that it "brought constantly to a man's mind, not as a menace but as a principle, the belief that his words were part of his character and his life. False or cruel speech was to be answered for, as was an evil act; it, therefore, was held *to be* an act, not mere empty breath" (Ravenel, *Charleston: The Place and the People* [New York: Macmillan Co., 1906], 414).

3. Wilson, *Code of Honor*, 3-4. Most contemporary observers of America, of course, did not share Wilson's elevated views. Most detached was Tocqueville, who commented that "honor is simply that peculiar rule founded upon a peculiar state of society, by the application of which a people or a class allot praise or blame." Baron Klinkowstrom thought that duels "testify to an unruliness in the American character," an observation not credited by Harriet Martineau. She wrote that the "hubbub" of dueling "is occasioned by a false idea of honour, and not by fault of temper," stressing the amiability of most Americans when they were obliged to wait for a late coach or stalled legislation. Martineau explained dueling in the South by the slave system: "In the south, where labour itself is capital, and labour cannot therefore be regarded with due respect, there is much vanity of retinue, much extravagance, from fear of the imputation of poverty which would follow upon retrenchment; and great recklessness of life, from fear of the imputation of cowardice which might follow upon forgiveness of injuries. Fear of imputation is here the panic, under which men relinquish their freedom of action and speech." See Alexis de Tocqueville, *Democracy in America*, 2 vols. (New York: Vintage Books, 1945), 2:243; F. D. Scott, ed., *Baron Klinkowstrom's America, 1818-1820* (Evanston, Ill.: Northwestern University Press, 1950), 79; Harriet Martineau, *Society in America*, 3 vols. (London: Saunders & Otley, 1837), 3:60, 11-12.

4. Wilson, *Code of Honor*, 3-4. Bertram Wyatt-Brown aptly observes in this regard that the sense of honor "made the opinion of others inseparable from inner worth." *Southern Honor*, 45. For perspective on how honor was related to questions of social justice, see Edward L. Ayers, *Vengeance and Justice: Crime and Punishment in the Nineteenth-Century South* (New York: Oxford University Press, 1984).

5. Wilson, *Code of Honor*, 5. See Bruce, *Violence and Culture*, 67–70 for a discussion of the southern sense of fragile social relations.

6. For a thoughtful characterization of the yeoman's attitude toward his elite countryman, see Steven Hahn, *The Roots of Southern Populism: Yeoman Farmers and the Georgia Upcountry, 1850–1890* (New York: Oxford University Press, 1983), 50–51, 84–89, 91. Elliott J. Gorn suggests that both yeoman and planter saw personal violence among poorer, backcountry whites as significantly different from elite affairs of honor. See Gorn, " 'Gouge and Bite, Pull Hair and Scratch': The Social Significance of Fighting in the Southern Backcountry," *American Historical Review* 90 (1985): 18–43.

7. Wilson, *Code of Honor*, 4.

8. Ibid., 6–11.

9. Ibid., 11–13. Through most of the antebellum years, dueling pistols were smooth-bore, carried a special shot, and were loaded at the muzzle. Older flintlock types, prized for their traditional value, had to be primed at the pan as well. See Stevens, *Pistols at Ten Paces*, 134–36.

10. Wilson, *Code of Honor*, 6. Silence and a more general passionlessness were seen, of course, as a sign that self-defense and not aggressiveness ruled behavior.

11. Ibid., 7.

12. Ibid., 11. However, as with many other aspects of the ritual affair, certain "correct" behavior could suddenly shade over into insult. Alexander Mackay witnessed in Richmond how "even a coolness between parties is dangerous, as having a fatal tendency speedily to ripen into a deadly feud." Mackay, *The Western World; or Travels in the United States in 1846–47*, 3 vols., 3d ed. (London: Richard Bentley, 1851), 2:75–76.

13. Wilson, *Code of Honor*, 5–7, 14.

14. Ibid., 6–7.

15. Ibid., 7, 11–12.

16. Ibid., 6.

17. Ibid., 9.

18. Ibid., 6, 8–10. Wilson was speaking about the propriety of substituting a second for a principal in cases in which the latter was judged "unequal." For a duel that involves such a substitution (though not an orderly one), see the Cilley-Graves conflict later in this chapter.

19. Regarding failed reconciliation, Wilson's chapter 3, "Duty of Challengee and His Second before Fighting," begins: "After all efforts for a reconciliation are over" without having mentioned any effort at all beyond a general desire to track down "misapprehension." For examples of written reconciliations, see Williams, *Dueling in the Old South*, 45–48, and Gamble, *Savannah Duels*, 238–40.

20. "A Southron," *The Code of Honor, or the Thirty-nine Articles* (Baltimore: William Taylor & Co., 1847), 22.

21. Ibid., 38.

22. Ibid., 23.

23. Ibid., 23. Farce and tragicomedy always were possible in an affair, given its pretensions. One or both surely befell the hapless Reverend J. H. Ingraham of Georgia, reputedly a duelist, who killed himself when his pistol accidentally discharged while he was adjusting his clothing before conducting church services. See Williams, *Dueling in the Old South*, 34.

24. Southron, *Code of Honor*, 23.

25. Ibid., 24. This setting was by definition social. If an insult was given among a group of people, that same group should witness the apology or explanation, partly because of the practical need for witnesses. But the fully social nature of offense, explanation, apology, and possible challenge more deeply reflected the communal nature of honor itself. See also Southron's articles 4, 11, and 31, pp. 24–25, 30.

26. Southron, *Code of Honor*, 24; and see also "hint" 8, p. 35. For representative insults, see Williams, *Dueling in the Old South*, 22–24; Seitz, *Famous American Duels*, 129.

27. Southron, *Code of Honor*, 29.

28. Ibid., 24–25.

29. The momentum of a duel reveals the ritual as being something more than a shadow of the social order. Rather order was collapsed into the ritual and there condensed. As Mary Douglas remarks, this process argues for "the power of symbols generated in a particular social set up to control it. The symbols themselves lash back at the people and divert their attempts to change their lot into channels which do more to symbolize than to improve it." Douglas, *Natural Symbols*, xiv.

30. Southron, *Code of Honor*, 25, 29, 27. Southron refers to the "advantage" of being the challenged party, but does not elaborate. Apparently, unlike Wilson, he believed that the challenged man had the right to choose time, weapons, or place, or come combination of the three.

31. Ibid., 27–28. Students of the South have taken note of this tension between ambitious individualism and shared class authority in a number of ways. J. Mills Thornton remarks of Alabama politics, "The necessity for reconciling an antisocial ideal [of individual autonomy] with the obvious imperative for communal cooperation induced the fascination with symbols which we have encountered so often in political propaganda. Observers focused their comments so intensely upon the symbolic issue or verbal formulation that the issue or formulation could pass beyond a mere hint at truth to the substance of truth." Thornton, *Politics and Power in a Slave Society: Alabama, 1800–1860* (Baton Rouge: Louisiana State University Press, 1978), 219. See also Johnson, *"Planters and Patriarchy,"* passim.

32. Southron, *Code of Honor*, 28–29.

33. Ibid., 38, 35.

34. Ibid., 36. The extension of male self-esteem to every corner of social life put enormous strain on men. This aspect is misunderstood by observers who see such extreme self-projection as merely ridiculous, as in duels fought over who was the better poet or over one man crushing and tossing away the letter of another man's sister. The point is that men felt driven to be responsible for everything. See, e.g., Sabine, *Notes on Duels and Duelling*, 35–37, 379–84.

35. In his survey of dueling, Jack K. Williams concluded that "the duel was a regular and violent occurrence" throughout the antebellum period, though it appears to have declined somewhat after the 1830s; Williams, *Dueling in the Old South*, 9, 78. Concurring in the regularity of dueling is Bruce, *Violence and Culture*, 4–5, 26–27.

36. William Henry Trescot to Thomas Butler King, January 30, 1849, King Papers, Southern Historical Collection, University of North Carolina, Chapel Hill (hereafter cited as SHC).

37. James Robertson to William Gaston, July 31, 1832, Gaston Papers, SHC.

38. Planter-class men disposed to duel took delight in the mixture of fiction and social reality in the "chivalric" affair. John Fraser remarks upon American, especially southern, fondness for the chivalric's "curious resistance to irony. . . . In the chivalric transmissions and incarnations, life and letters . . . interpenetrated from the outset" and became self-sufficient guides for both imagination and action. See Fraser, *America and the Patterns of Chivalry* (New York: Cambridge University Press, 1982), p. 54.

39. James H. Hammond, like other politicians, took great care in his preparations for office-seeking. In a draft of a letter to an unnamed man, Hammond cautiously noted that the two might be preparing to run for the same office and asked if his respondent was in fact thinking of doing so: "I do not wish to be in your way. And by giving me an early intimation of your views I shall [here Hammond also writes "may"] be able to check my friends and save myself probably from the mortification of a defeat, and you the mortification of being the cause of it." Every quality, from glory to mortification, had to be spread evenly around. Failure to do so left many men feeling alone and friendless. Drew Faust has shown how "recurrent bouts of depression and gloomy introspection" characterized members of "a sacred circle," and Robert Brugger has noted much the same thing. Loss of friendship and intimacy is a constant theme in men's letters. See Hammond, Diary, July 20, 1837, James H. Hammond Papers, Library of Congress; Drew Gilpin Faust, *A Sacred Circle: The Dilemma of the Intellectual in the Old South, 1840–1860* (Baltimore: Johns Hopkins University Press, 1977), 18 and esp. chap. 2; Robert J. Brugger, *Beverley Tucker: Heart over Head in the Old South* (Baltimore: Johns Hopkins University Press, 1978), esp. chap. 2.

40. James H. Hammond, MS memorandum, September 6, 1847, Hammond-Bryan-Cumming Papers, South Caroliniana Library, University of South Carolina (hereafter cited as SCL). For the Hammond-Hampton quarrel, see Drew Gilpin Faust, *James Henry Hammond and the Old South: A Design for Mastery* (Baton Rouge: Louisiana State University Press, 1982), 241–45.

41. James Wyche to William Gaston, January 1831, Gaston Papers, SHC.

42. L. D. Henry to William Gaston, December 30, 1831, Gaston Papers, SHC.

43. E. D. Stockton to Alfred Cumming, October 18, 1851, Hammond-Bryan-Cumming Papers, SCL.

44. Samuel Townes to George Townes, September 13, 1831; Henry Townes to George Townes, November 3, 1831, December 1, 1831; Samuel Townes to George Townes, November 25, 1831; Townes Papers, SCL.

45. Samuel Townes to George Townes, November 25, 1831, December 11, 1831, Townes Papers, SCL.

46. Preston Brooks to Milledge Bonham, July 14, 1849, Bonham Papers, SCL. The two men were cousins and well known to each other.

47. Milledge Bonham to Preston Brooks, July 13, 1849; Brooks to Bonham, July 14, 1849; Bonham Papers, SCL.

48. Milledge Bonham to Preston Brooks, July 16, 1849, Bonham Papers, SCL.

49. Preston Brooks to Milledge Bonham, July 17, 1849, Bonham Papers, SCL.

50. Milledge Bonham to Preston Brooks, July 18, 1849 (noted as "No. 3" on reverse); Brooks to Bonham, July 18, 1849; Bonham Papers, SCL. At this point,

there was the likeness between marrying and dueling seen by Sen. Lewis Linn of Missouri: "The more barriers erected against it, the surer are the interested parties to come together," quoted in Kane, *Gentlemen, Swords, and Pistols*, ix.

51. Milledge Bonham to Preston Brooks, July 19, 1849; Brooks to Bonham, July 19, 1849; Bonham Papers, SCL.

52. Milledge Bonham to Preston Brooks, July 20, 1849; Brooks to Bonham, July 21, 1849; Bonham to Brooks, July 25, 1849; Bonham Papers, SCL.

53. Milledge Bonham to Preston Brooks, July 26, 1849; see drafts of letters in James H. Hammond's hand, July 26, 1849; Brooks to Bonham, July 26, 1849; Bonham Papers, SCL.

54. Charles Fisher, "To the Public," pamphlet, n.p, [1833], 1, New York Public Library.

55. Ibid., 1–2.

56. Ibid., 1.

57. Ibid., 2. There is some confusion over the dating of the conflict. This reproduced letter is dated August 10, 1833, and Fisher says he replied "Saturday evening, August 10" although he later says, erroneously, that August 10 was a Monday.

58. Ibid., 3.

59. Ibid., 4.

60. Ibid., 5.

61. Ibid.

62. Ibid.

63. Ibid., 6.

64. The first account of the Cilley-Graves duel is in House of Representatives, *Report of the Committee of the Late Duel*, April 25, 1838. The encounter is mentioned in some of the histories of dueling, including Stevens, *Pistols at Ten Paces*, 219–27; Seitz, *Famous American Duels*, 206–69, and also 253–57. The complete correspondence and the congressional committee report are in Sabine, *Notes on Duels*, 89–108, from which this account is drawn.

65. See, for example, Sabine's observation that Cilley had shown great esteem for his "lineage of an ancient and honorable family." Sabine, *Notes on Duels*, 90–91.

66. Ibid., 90.

67. Ibid., 92.

68. Ibid., 93.

69. Ibid.

70. For a man to invoke congressional privilege when he was accused of giving personal offense was considered by many men to be a questionable exercise of the privilege. Southron's code indicates that it was often invoked, but was at best a cause for wry humor. Thus Graves was not suggesting a wholly unclouded course of action. See Southron, *Code of Honor*, 23.

71. Sabine, *Notes on Duels*, 94.

72. Ibid.

73. Ibid.

74. Ibid., 95–97.

75. Ibid., 97–98. The committee investigating the duel strongly implied that Cilley's added words, "the highest respect and the most kind feelings," were especially good grounds for the affair to have ended there. See ibid., 89 and 103.

76. Ibid., 98–99.

77. Ibid., 99–100.
78. Ibid., 100.
79. Seitz, *Famous American Duels*, 266. The seconds' statement is reprinted in full here.
80. Ibid., 263.
81. Sabine, *Notes on Duels*, 107, 89.
82. Ibid., 102.
83. Ibid., 102, 105. In contrast to the honorable actions of Cilley, the committee noted that editor James Webb, almost forgotten in the affair, had behaved reprehensibly by declaring in print that he had attempted to find Cilley before Graves did in order to challenge or shoot him if the challenge was denied. See ibid., 100.

Chapter 2. Courtship: Sexuality and Feeling

1. Among the better older studies that at least mention courtship (interestingly weighted toward the eighteenth century) are Julia C. Spruill, *Women's Life and Work in the Southern Colonies* (1938; New York: W. W. Norton, 1972); Arthur Calhoun, *A Social History of the American Family from Colonial Times to the Present* 3 vols. (Cleveland: Arthur H. Clark Co., 1917–19); Edmund S. Morgan, *Virginians at Home: Family Life in the Eighteenth Century* (Charlottesville: University Press of Virginia, 1952), Chap. 2; Rosser H. Taylor, *Ante-Bellum South Carolina: A Social and Cultural History* (Chapel Hill: University of North Carolina Press, 1942), 58–63; Guion G. Johnson, "Courtship and Marriage Customs in Ante-Bellum North Carolina," *North Carolina Historical Review* 8 (1931): 384–402.

2. For a view of eighteenth-century courtship and marriage that heavily stresses kinship and property as values, see Morgan, *Virginians at Home*, chap. 2. Daniel Blake Smith emphasizes individual feeling and choice; Smith, *Inside the Great House: Planter Family Life in Eighteenth-Century Chesapeake Society* (Ithaca: Cornell University Press, 1980), 140–48. Jan Lewis, *The Pursuit of Happiness: Family and Values in Jefferson's Virginia* (New York: Cambridge University Press, 1983), chap. 5, shows how love was a predicament for Virginians in the eighteenth and early nineteenth centuries. For the antebellum years, kinship and property figure heavily in Bertram Wyatt-Brown, *Southern Honor: Ethics and Behavior in the Old South* (New York: Oxford University Press, 1982), esp. chap. 8.

3. What young people learned about romance, marriage, and the standards of womanhood and manhood was, of course, rooted in their own families and, increasingly by 1830, in the social life of single-sex academies for youths aged twelve to eighteen. Some of this social context is examined in chapter 3, but for the present my concern is with the ritual of courtship itself: the social activities and personal perceptions supposed to lead women and men to marriage. Though path breaking in its attention to the family, Edmund S. Morgan's view of eighteenth-century courtship is slanted rather briskly toward the "business" of getting married and does not attempt a thorough analysis of the place of emotion and impulse in formal ritual. For the same century, Daniel Blake Smith finds that the "obsession with balance and a well-ordered family" in courtship "gradually gave way . . . to a view of family life that prized intimacy, affection, and even a measure of passion." Smith's discussion of the ritual itself is minimal,

however, and he reserves his fullest treatment of conflict and harmony between the sexes until after marriage. Jan Lewis, finding intimacy much more of a problem, discusses love in general rather than the shape of its rituals. But she insightfully sees that Virginians' increasing reliance on love rather than material calculations did not "free" them from courtship's demands; it only changed the nature of the demands. See Morgan, *Virginians at Home*, 29–35; Smith, *Great House*, 141; Lewis, *Pursuit of Happiness*, 178–79. Somewhat surprisingly, the discussion of courtship in the antebellum period has been less detailed than that of the preceding era. Ellen K. Rothman excludes the South from her fine survey of courtship in America. Anne F. Scott has little to say about courting, and curiously concludes that "pragmatism or impulse or necessity for the most part outweighed romance in the marriage market." With a different but brief look at women's courting, Catherine Clinton describes it as a time "filled with fun and frivolity" in grim contrast to the subjection that followed. But Clinton, too, has little to say about ritual of courtship as a drama of sexuality, and almost nothing to say about men and their perceptions. Perhaps the most inclusive pictures of courtship are those of Bertram Wyatt-Brown and Jane Turner Censer. The former is concerned with the broad economic and kinship strategies, however. Censer orients her interpretation to feeling and sexuality (and corroborates the finding that planters tended to marry other planters, often cousins) but emphasizes harmony and good feeling perhaps overmuch. See Rothman, *Hands and Hearts: A History of Courtship in America* (New York: Basic Books, 1984); Scott, *The Southern Lady: From Pedestal to Politics, 1830–1930* (Chicago: University of Chicago Press, 1970), 25–26; Clinton, *The Plantation Mistress: Woman's World in the Old South* (New York: Pantheon Books, 1982), 62; Wyatt-Brown, *Southern Honor*, chap. 8; Censer, *North Carolina Planters and Their Children, 1800–1860* (Baton Rouge: Louisiana State University Press, 1984), esp. chap. 4.

4. The planters' values—the expectations and standards they attached to their world—thus shaped the very terms of change in relations between the sexes. "Values are not 'imponderables,' " E. P. Thompson reminds us, "which the historian may safely dismiss with the reflection that, since they are not amenable to measurement, anyone's opinion is as good as anyone else's. They are, on the contrary, those questions of human satisfaction and of the direction of social change, which the historian ought to ponder if history is to claim a position among the significant humanities." Thompson, *The Making of the English Working Class* (New York: Vintage Books, 1966), 444.

5. In this sense, courtship like the duel was a kind of *work*, an effort to produce a set of values and their supporting social and intellectual forms to which everyone who mattered would refer—and defer. In interpreting the meaning of such works, as Alasdair MacIntyre has said, the actors' own explanation of them has a "privileged position," not because it is more accurate, but because it supplies the language of description which "assigns some purpose to the action. And descriptions are public property," changing historically like other cultural artifacts. See MacIntyre, "A Mistake about Causality in Social Science," in *Philosophy, Politics, and Society*, ed. Peter Laslett and W. G. Runciman (London: Oxford University Press, 1962), 58–59.

6. For the older style of moral advice in planters' libraries and academies, see Hannah More, *The Works of Hannah More*, 2 vols. (New York: Harper &

Brothers, 1846–47); Hester Chapone, *Letters on the Improvement of the Mind: Addressed to a Lady* (Boston: James B. Dow, 1834). For popular advisers in the newer style, see James M. Garnett, *Lectures on Female Education* (Richmond, Va.: T. W. White, 1825); Charles Butler, *The American Lady* (Philadelphia: Hogan & Thompson, 1836); Margaret Coxe, *The Young Lady's Companion: In a Series of Letters* (Columbus, Ohio: I. N. Whiting, 1839); Virginia Cary, *Letters on Female Character, Addressed to a Young Lady, on the Death of Her Mother* (Richmond, Va.: A. Works, 1828). For recent interpretations of the Intellectual context of this literature, mostly in a northern setting, see Ann Douglas, *The Feminization of American Culture* (New York: Avon Books, 1977), esp. chap. 2; Kathryn Kish Sklar, *Catharine Beecher: A Study in American Domesticity* (New Haven: Yale University Press, 1973), esp. chaps. 6, 9; Joan Jacobs Brumberg, *Mission for Life* (New York: Free Press, 1980), esp. chaps. 4, 5.

7. Coxe, *Young Lady's Companion*, 51–52; Chapone, *Letters on Improvement*, 22–23.

8. Chapone, *Letters on Improvement*, 23.

9. Coxe, *Young Lady's Companion*, 52.

10. Ibid., 52–53.

11. Chapone, *Letters on Improvement*, 88 (see also 85–86); Coxe, *Young Lady's Companion*, 191–92; More, *Works*, 1:379–80; Coxe, *Young Lady's Companion*, 191; More, *Works*, 1:381.

12. Charles Butler, *The American Gentleman* (Philadelphia: Hogan & Thompson, 1839), passim. E. Anthony Rotundo wrote an excellent study of northern masculinity: "Manhood in America: The Northern Middle Class, 1770–1920" (Ph.D. diss., Brandeis University, 1982).

13. Butler, *American Lady*, 115–16; More, *Works*, 2:472; Coxe, *Young Lady's Companion*, 195. Interestingly, Virginia Cary, one of the most vigorous proponents of female submissiveness, notes that, in moderation, novels could aid a girl's education. She herself read "Scott's romances (some of them) with great Pleasure by way of recreation: they relax the mind pleasantly, after long tension." See Cary, *Female Character*, 125–26. Along these lines, Steven Mintz notes that no less a moral figure than Lyman Beecher found his wariness of novels overcome by reading Walter Scott. Beecher determined that Scott, in balance, elevated and refined feminine sensibility. See Mintz, *A Prison of Expectations: The Family in Victorian Culture* (New York: New York University Press, 1983), 24.

14. Coxe, *Young Lady's Companion*, 51–53; Butler, *American Lady*, 201–2. See also Cary, *Female Character*, 147.

15. Cary, *Female Character*, 152; Coxe, *Young Lady's Companion*, 249–58; Chapone, *Letters on Improvement*, 89; More, *Works*, 1:389–91; Chapone, *Letters on Improvement*, 74. See also More, *Works*, 1:383; Cary, *Female Character*, 145–46 and Butler, *American Lady*, 189 ff.

16. Butler, *American Lady*, 202–3; Chapone, *Letters on Improvement*, 23; Coxe, *Young Lady's Companion*, 53; More, *Works*, 1:383; Cary, *Female Character*, 99, 89.

17. A late antebellum physician who raised some of these questions and criticisms was William A. Alcott, *The Moral Philosophy of Courtship and Marriage* (Boston: John P. Jewett & Co., 1856), 17, 22, 33–35, 151–54.

18. The letter-writer guides are ancestors of certain twentieth-century

books that use love letters both as an amusement and as a means of yearning for days gone by. See, e.g., C. H. Charles, *Love Letters of Great Men and Women from the Eighteenth Century to the Present Day* (London: S. Paul & Co., [1924]), and John Fostini, ed., *Love Letters* (New York: R. Speller, [1961]).

19. Thomas Goodman, *The Young Secretary's Guide* (Boston: T. Fleet, 1730), 3-4, 17-19. For other examples of the earlier style of these guides, see *The American Academy of Compliments; or, the Complete American Secretary* (Philadelphia: Printed by Godfrey Deshong and Richard Folwell, 1796) and *The New, Complete Letter Writer; or, the Art of Correspondence* (New York: John Tiebout, 1800). For examples of antebellum guides, see *The New Universal Letter-Writer* (Philadelphia: D. Hogan, 1850); *The Letter Writer* (Boston: G. Gaylord, 1831); R. Turner, *The Parlour Letter-Writer and Secretary's Assistant* (Philadelphia: Thomas, Cowperthwait & Co., 1845); Daniel Harrison Jacques, *How to Write: A Pocket Manual of Composition and Letterwriting* (New York: Fowler & Wells, 1857).

20. Turner, *Parlour Letter-Writer*, 95.

21. Ibid., 95-96.

22. Ibid., 97-98.

23. *Universal Letter-Writer*, 58.

24. Ibid., 59.

25. Ibid.; cf. Turner, *Parlour Letter-Writer*, 103-4.

26. *Universal Letter-Writer*, 59-61.

27. Ibid., 62-63; Turner, *Parlour Letter-Writer*, 107-8.

28. See, e.g., *Universal Letter-Writer*, 64-65, 70-92, 107-11, 117-20.

29. Ibid., 111-12; *American Fashionable Letter-Writer* (Troy, N.Y.: Merriam, Moore & Co., 1850), 81.

30. *American Fashionable Letter-Writer*, 89-92; *Universal Letter-Writer*, 111, 107-8.

31. The definitive work for nineteenth-century American women writers and their world is Mary Kelley, *Private Woman, Public Stage: Literary Domesticity in Nineteenth-Century America* (New York: Oxford University Press, 1984). Book reviewing and reviews are interestingly handled in Nina Baym, *Novels, Readers, and Reviewers: Responses to Fiction in Antebellum America* (Ithaca: Cornell University Press, 1985). Also useful is Nina Baym's *Woman's Fiction: A Guide to Novels by and about Women in America, 1820-1870* (Ithaca: Cornell University Press, 1978). On specific writers see Ann Douglas Wood, "Mrs. Sigourney and the Sensibility of the Inner Space," *New England Quarterly* 45 (1972): 163-81; Brumberg, *Mission for Life*, 122-40. Tying women's literature to the historical South are Anne Goodwyn Jones, *Tomorrow Is Another Day: The Woman Writer in the South, 1859-1936* (Baton Rouge: Louisiana State University Press, 1981); John Carl Ruoff, "Frivolity to Consumption: Southern Womanhood in Antebellum Literature," *Civil War History* 18 (1972): 213-29; Steven M. Stowe, "City, Country, and the Feminine Voice," in *Intellectual Life in Antebellum Charleston*, ed. Michael O'Brien and David Moltke-Hansen (Knoxville: University of Tennessee Press, 1986); Harland D. Hagler, "The Ideal Woman in the Antebellum South: Lady or Farmwife?" *Journal of Southern History* 44 (1980): 405-18; Harriet E. Amos, " 'City Belles': Images and Realities of the Lives Of White Women in Antebellum Mobile," *Alabama Review* 34 (1981): 3-19; Kathryn L. Seidel, "The Southern Belle as an Antebellum Ideal," *Southern*

Quarterly 15 (1976–77): 387–401. For older collections of works and biographical sketches, see George A. Wauchope, *Writers of South Carolina* (Columbia, S.C.: State Co., 1910); Mary T. Tardy, *Southland Writers: Biographical and Critical Sketches of the Living Female Writers of the South,* 2 vols. (Philadelphia: Claxton, Remsen & Haffelfinger, 1870); John S. Hart, *The Female Prose Writers of America* (Philadelphia: E. H. Butler & Co., 1857); Julia Deane Freeman, *Women of the South Distinguished in Literature* (New York: Derby & Jackson, 1861). The literary criticism of women's fiction is vast, and I cite only those works I found most useful as a historian. A watershed general work is Elaine Showalter, *A Literature of Their Own: British Women Novelists from Bronte to Lessing* (Princeton: Princeton University Press, 1977). Making a persuasive argument for the power inherent in fictional femininity (and linking aesthetic form to social values) is Nina Auerbach, *Woman and the Demon: The Life of a Victorian Myth* (Cambridge: Harvard University Press, 1982). Quite different is Françoise Basch, *Relative Creatures: Victorian Women in Society and the Novel* (New York: Schocken Books, 1974); Basch sees fiction and social life as rather more distinct. Also useful are Helene Roberts, "The Inside, the Surface and the Mass: Some Recurring Images of Women," *Women's Studies* 2 (1974): 289–308; Elizabeth Janeway, "Who Is Sylvia? On the Loss of Sexual Paradigms," *Signs* 5 (1980): 573–89; Janice Radway, *Reading the Romance: Women, Patriarchy, and Popular Literature* (Chapel Hill: University of North Carolina Press, 1984).

32. Jones, *Tomorrow,* 71. As Jones notes on p. 52, women's novels were attacked by both feminists and conservative moralists—the former seeing them as insipid and the latter as risqué. The dispute more or less continues up to the present, and the "ambiguous and contradictory truths" that Mary Kelley finds in domestic novels is perhaps the most complete assessment. Fiction reflected women's predicament so well that, for many women, it influenced resistance to it; see Kelley, *Private Woman,* 251.

33. Caroline Gilman, *Recollections of a Southern Matron* (New York: Harper & Brothers, 1838), 20; Alice J. Graves, *Girlhood and Womanhood; or, Sketches of My Schoolmates* (Boston: Carter & Mussey, 1844), 51–52, 70; Mary Howard Schoolcraft, "The Black Gauntlet," [1860], reprinted in *Plantation Life: The Narratives of Mrs. Henry Rowe Schoolcraft* (New York: Negro Universities Press, 1969), 132; E.D.E.N. Southworth, "Sybil Brotherton; or, the Temptress," in *The Wife's Victory and Other Nouvellettes* (Philadelphia: T. B. Peterson, [1854]), 92–93.

34. Susan Petigru King, "A Coquette," in *Crimes Which the Law Does Not Reach* (New York: Derby & Jackson, 1859), 298; Susan Petigru King, *Lily* (New York: Harper & Brothers, 1855), 125, 90; Schoolcraft, "Black Gauntlet," 132, 20.

35. Southworth, "Sybil," 92–93; King, *Lily,* 150.

36. Caroline Lee Hentz, "The Beauty Transformed," and "The Pet Beauty," in *Courtship and Marriage; or, the Joys and Sorrows of American Life* (New York: F. M. Lupton Publishing Co., [1870]), 305, 48.

37. Gilman, *Southern Matron,* 110.

38. Hentz, "Pet Beauty," 28; see also King, *Lily,* 180.

39. King, "Coquette," 294–95; see also Hentz, "Pet Beauty," 28; E.D.E.N. Southworth, *Love's Labor Won* (Philadelphia: T. B. Peterson & Brothers, [1862]), [1].

40. Caroline Lee Hentz, "Three Scenes in the Life of a Belle," in *Love After*

Marriage and Other Stories of the Heart (Philadelphia: T. B. Peterson & Brothers, [1870]), 136–37.

41. Louisa Tuthill, *Reality; or, the Millionaire's Daughter: A Book for Young Men and Young Women* (New York: Scribner, 1856), 73–76; Caroline Lee Hentz, "The Red Velvet Bodice," in *The Lost Daughter and Other Stories of the Heart* (Philadelphia: T. B. Peterson, 1857), 100; King, *Lily*, 179–80, 90; King, "Coquette," 298; Hentz, "Pet Beauty," 55.

42. Many moralist opponents of women's novels either did not or would not see this dimension of fiction. Elizabeth Fox-Genovese has argued that a later fictional character, Scarlett O'Hara, did not understand it either: "Scarlett's tragedy lies in her inability to understand the meaning of being a lady . . . Scarlett fails to realize that the prevailing etiquette represents a social effort to codify, institutionalize, and reproduce the deeper qualities of the lady in the fabric of the entire society. Having never grasped the depth and meaning of the informing spirit, she confuses it with its forms." See Fox-Genovese, "Scarlett O'Hara: The Southern Lady as New Woman," *American Quarterly* 33 (1981): 390–411.

43. Schoolcraft, "Black Gauntlet," 132–33; Graves, *Girlhood and Womanhood*, 51–52.

44. King, "Coquette," 292–93.

45. Ibid., 296–98.

46. Hentz, "Red Velvet Bodice," 102; "Beauty Transformed," 300. See also Tuthill, *Reality*, 230–34.

47. Southworth, "Sybil," 116–17; *Love's Labor*, 75; *Retribution; or, the Vale of Shadows. A Tale of Passion* (New York: Harper & Brothers, 1849), 14; see also Hentz, "Pet Beauty," 65–67. The phrase "inordinate affection" was used frequently by moralists, who warned against it, and by novelists, who admired it.

48. Caroline Lee Hentz, *Linda; or, The Young Pilot of the Belle Creole: A Tale of Southern Life* (Philadelphia: Parry & McMillan, 1850), 143–44. This novel went through thirteen editions in two years.

49. King, "Coquette," 309; Hentz, *Linda*, 143; Hentz, "Red Velvet Bodice," 105; Tuthill, *Reality*, 67–68; King, *Lily*, 89.

50. Graves, *Girlhood and Womanhood*, 73, 71.

51. Ibid., 51–52; Hentz, "Red Velvet Bodice," 98; Tuthill, *Reality*, 68.

52. It is begging the question to see women as simply victimized by courtship, or to see them as older histories often do, as beautifully transformed by love into "an indefinable composite of many attractions," in Arthur Calhoun's hazy words. Rather, as Nina Auerbach observes, "Victorian women were an essential part of a complex and capacious milieu, not a separate and beleaguered class or nation. As such, like all citizens, women were fortified by the dreams of their culture as much as their lives were mutilated by its fears." See Calhoun, *History of American Family*, 2:311; Auerbach, *Woman and Demon*, 34.

53. Robert Q. Mallard to Mary Jones, November 3, 1856, in Robert M. Myers, *The Children of Pride: A True Story of Georgia and the Civil War* (New Haven: Yale University Press, 1972), 259.

54. Augustin Taveau to "Cousin," February 26, 1854, Augustin L. Taveau Papers, William Perkins Library, Duke University, Durham, N.C. (hereafter cited as Duke).

55. Samuel Leland diary, July 14, 1853, South Caroliniana Library, Univer-

sity of South Carolina, Columbia (hereafter cited as SCL); Marion Singleton to Angelica Singleton, November 20, 1834, Singleton-Deveaux Papers, SCL; Julia [Pickens] to Eliza Mira Lenoir, May 15, 1834, Lenoir Papers, Southern Historical Collection, University of North Carolina, Chapel Hill (hereafter cited as SHC).

56. Henry Townes to George Townes, July 24, 1837, Townes Papers, SCL; H. A. Jones to William Augustus Townes, October 5, 1846, Townes Papers, SCL. See also Oscar Lieber to Francis Lieber, December 27, 1847, Lieber Papers, SCL.

57. Joseph Cumming to Harford Cumming, June 6, 1855, Hammond-Cumming-Bryan Papers, SCL.

58. Louis Wigfall to John Manning [ca. March 23, 1840], typed copy, Williams-Chesnut-Manning Papers, SCL; Thomas J. Withers to James H. Hammond, November 10, 1826, Hammond Papers, SCL; J. A. Gadsden to Augustin Taveau, May 20, 1845, and February 17, 1844, Taveau Papers, Duke; H. W. Hilliard to James H. Hammond, June 15, 1826, Hammond Papers, SCL. See also Leland diary, March 9, 1853, SCL.

59. Thomas J. Withers to James H. Hammond, September 24, 1826, and May 15, 1826, Hammond Papers, SCL. See also Hattie Lane to Emma Ross, January 24, 1860, Ross Papers, SHC; James H. Hammond commonplace book, 1825–1844, passim, Hammond Papers, SCL (see also Hammond's diary for the 1820s, Library of Congress); Oscar Lieber to James H. Hammond, December 3, 1859, Hammond-Bryan-Cumming Papers, SCL; Maria Bryan to Julia Cumming, April 5, 1830, Hammond-Bryan-Cumming Papers, SCL; Hattie Lane to Emma Ross, January 2, 1861, Ross Papers, SHC.

60. Mary Townes to William Augustus Townes, September 17, 1837, Townes Papers, SCL.

61. James H. Hammond to Harry Hammond, December 20, 1852, Hammond-Bryan-Cumming Papers, SCL.

62. Thomas J. Withers to James H. Hammond, August 28, 1827, Hammond Papers, SCL.

63. Louis Wigfall to John Manning, [ca. March 23, 1840], typed copy, Williams-Chesnut-Manning Papers, SCL.

64. For a typical account of resort activities, see Matilda Lieber to Hamilton Lieber, August 20, 1848, in Lieber Papers, SCL. See also Lawrence F. Brewster, *Summer Migrations and Resorts of South Carolina Low Country Planters* (Durham: Duke University Press, 1947).

65. Oscar Lieber to Francis and Matilda Lieber, May 12, 1861, Lieber Papers, SCL; J. S. Green to Gaston Meares, September 11, 1849, DeRosset Papers, SHC; Delle Mullen Craven, ed., *The Neglected Thread: A Journal from the Calhoun Community, 1836–1842* (Columbia: University of South Carolina Press, 1951), 25–26 [entry for February 20, 1837].

66. Ella C. Thomas diary, May 15, 1851, Duke.

67. Egbert Ross to Emma Ross, April 20, 1860, Ross Papers, SCL.

68. Samuel Leland diary, January 17, 1854, SCL.

69. Ibid.

70. Ibid., November 10, 1853, and November 3, 1852, SCL; James Gwyn, Jr., to Mary Ann Lenoir, October 7, 1838, typed copy, Lenoir Papers, SHC.

71. Emily Cumming to Harry Hammond, [October 1859]; Henry Cumming to Julia Cumming, October 9, 1824, Hammond-Bryan-Cumming Papers, SCL; see also Samuel Leland diary, September 12, 1855, SCL.

72. Samuel Leland diary, September 12, 1855, SCL; Maria Bryan to Julia Cumming, August 14, 1839, Hammond-Bryan-Cumming Papers, SCL; Katherine DeRosset to "Geneva," September 7, 1849, DeRosset Papers, SHC. See also Anna C. White to [Augustin Taveau], January 17, 1848, Taveau Papers, Duke.

73. Emily Cumming to Harry Hammond, September 30, 1859; Maria Bryan to Julia Cumming, April 19, 1830, and December 13, 1829, Hammond-Bryan-Cumming Papers, SCL.

74. Samuel Leland diary, 1851, September 26, 1855, March 20, 1856, April 12, 1856, SCL. Janet G. Altman, writing about the epistolary novel, comments on lovers' letters: "As a mediator of desire . . . the letter functions on two figurative levels. On the one hand . . . the epistolary situation in which one writes to an absent lover fosters the generation of substitute images of the lover. . . . On the other hand . . . the letter as a physical entity emanating from, passing between, and touching each of the lovers may function itself as a figure for the lover." Altman, *Epistolarity: Approaches to a Form* (Columbus: Ohio State University Press, 1982), 19. On the change in the rhetoric of letters, see Lewis, *Pursuit of Happiness*, 220-29.

75. For the value placed on candor in northern love letters, see Rothman, 108-12.

76. Robert Q. Mallard to Mary Jones, January 20, 1857, in Myers, *Children of Pride*, 295 (see also August 25, 1856, 234); Elizabeth McCall to Benjamin F. Perry, February 1, 1837, Mrs. Benjamin F. Perry Papers, SCL.

77. Robert Q. Mallard to Mary Jones, December 29, 1856, in Myers, *Children of Pride*, 283-84; Elizabeth McCall to Benjamin F. Perry, January 16, 1837 (see also Benjamin F. Perry to Elizabeth McCall, February 14, 1837), Perry Papers, SCL; Tristrim Skinner to Eliza Harwood, November 6, 1848, November 14, 1848; Eliza Harwood to Tristrim Skinner, November 14, 1848, and August 2, 1849; Skinner Papers, SHC.

78. Altman, *Epistolarity*, 186-87.

79. [Catherine Fitzsimons?] to James H. Hammond, November 4, 1829, Hammond Papers, SCL.

80. Robert Q. Mallard to Mary Jones, August 11, 1856, in Myers, *Children of Pride*, 231-32.

81. Emmie Roberts to Robert Sams, February 16, 1864, Sams Papers, SCL.

82. Ibid.; Elizabeth McCall to Benjamin F. Perry, February 21, 1837, Perry Papers, SCL.

83. Robert Q. Mallard to Mary Jones, August 11, 1856, in Myers, *Children of Pride*, 231; Campbell R. Bryce to Sarah M. Henry, July 1, 1840, October 1, 1840, Bryce Papers, SCL.

84. Campbell R. Bryce to Sarah M. Henry, October 1, 1840, Bryce Papers, SCL.

85. Ibid.

86. Robert Q. Mallard to Mary Jones, September 4, 1856, and November 3, 1856, in Myers, *Children of Pride*, 234, 259; Emmie Roberts to Robert Sams, March 5, 1864, Sam Papers, SCL.

87. See Rothman, *Hands and Hearts*, chap. 3, for northern lovers.

88. "Geneva" to Katherine DeRosset, October 7, 1849, DeRosset Papers, SHC; Egbert Ross to Emma Ross, April 20, 1860, Ross Papers, SHC; Rebecca Haigh to Katherine DeRosset, 1849, DeRosset Papers, SHC.

89. Lucretia Townes to George Townes, June 28, 1837, Townes Papers, SCL;

J. A. Graves to William Augustus Townes, April 30, 1848, Townes Papers, SCL; Katherine DeRosset, to "Geneva," September 7, 1849; Katherine DeRossett Meares to Eliza DeRosset, February 28, 1857, DeRosset Papers, SHC.

90. Samuel Townes to Rachel Townes, November 2, 1834; Henry Townes to George Townes, January 16, 1834, Townes Papers, SCL.

91. Henry Townes to William Augustus Townes, February 8, 1846, Townes Papers, SCL; Rebecca Cameron to Margaret Mordecai, December 6, 1860, Cameron Papers, SHC; Henry Cumming to Julia Cumming, October 4, 1828; Maria Bryan to Julia Cumming, January 22, 1827, Hammond-Bryan-Cumming Papers, SCL.

92. Samuel Leland diary, March 24, 1853, SCL; Samuel Townes to George Townes, June 6, 1833, SCL; Eliza DeRosset to Katherine DeRosset Meares, February 28, 1857, DeRosset Papers, SHC; Augustin Taveau to Rosalie Simons, March 1846, Taveau Papers, Duke; Maria Bryan to Julia Cumming, August 14, 1839, Hammond-Bryan-Cumming Papers, SCL; Thomas Lenoir to Selina Lenoir, December 26, 1835; Thomas Lenoir to William Lenoir, December 28, 1835, Lenoir Papers, SHC.

93. H. A. Elbert to John B. Miller, November 14, 1848, and July 19, 1849, Miller-Furman-Dabbs Papers, SCL; Rebecca Singleton to Marion Singleton, May 16, 1830, and June 15, 1830, Singleton-Deveaux Papers, SCL.

94. Aldert Smedes to Katherine DeRosset, February 26, 1850, DeRosset Papers, SHC.

95. Mary C[hilds?] to Katherine DeRosset, May 13, 1850, DeRosset Papers, SHC.

96. Robina Norwood to Selina Lenoir, January 21, 1836, and March 16, 1836, Lenoir Papers, SHC.

97. Waddy Thompson to John Jones, September 14, 1846, Thompson-Jones Papers, SCL.

98. John Taylor to Franklin H. Elmore, October 17, 1826, Elmore Papers, SCL.

99. Franklin H. Elmore to John Taylor, October 24, 1826, Elmore Papers, SCL.

100. Franklin H. Elmore to Harriet Taylor, October 24, 1826, Elmore Papers, SCL.

101. Henry Townes to George Townes, December 15, 1838, Townes Papers, SCL; Eliza Rivers to William J. Rivers, December 2, 1852, Rivers Papers, SCL; Robert Q. Mallard to Mary Jones, October 20, 1856, in Myers, *Children of Pride*, 252; Emmie Roberts to Robert Sams, March 5, 1864, Sam Papers, SCL; Mary Ann Lenoir to Selina Lenoir, March 28, 1836, Lenoir Papers, SHC; see also Francis Lieber to Clara Lieber, December 2, 1849, Lieber Papers, SCL.

102. Henry Cumming to Julia Bryan, March 7, 1823, January 15, 1824, August 4, 1823, Hammond-Bryan-Cumming Papers, SCL; all citations for the Cumming-Bryan courtship are from this collection.

103. Ibid., January 15, 1824.

104. Ibid., August 4, 1823, April 9, 1823, June 5, 1823.

105. Ibid., November 26, 1822, September 18, 1823, August 4, 1823, August 23, 1823, September 18, 1823.

106. Ibid., May 17, 1823, August 4, 1823, March 7, 1823, November 26, 1822, May 17, 1823, January 24, 1824.

107. Penelope Skinner to Tristrim Skinner, February 26, 1840, Skinner Papers, SHC; all citations for Penelope Skinner's courtship are from this collection.

108. Ibid., September 4, 1837.

109. Ibid., October 21, 1838.

110. Ibid., November 5, 1838.

111. Ibid., December 8, 1838; Joseph B. Skinner to Tristrim Skinner, December 4, 1838.

112. Penelope Skinner to Tristrim Skinner, January 29, 1839; Joseph B. Skinner to Tristrim Skinner, January 30, 1839.

113. Tristrim Skinner to Joseph B. Skinner, February 22, 1839, February 8, 1839; Penelope Skinner to Tristrim Skinner, March 13, 1839; Tristrim Skinner to Joseph B. Skinner, April 7, 1839. Tristrim thought that French's vanity was rooted in his being the author of a book. It made a man vain, Tristrim remarked, "to see a large quantity of type put together knowing that it was his own composition." Tristrim Skinner to Joseph B. Skinner, February 8, 1839.

114. Penelope Skinner to Tristrim Skinner, March 13, 1839, April 5, 1839.

115. Ibid., January 15, 1840.

116. Ibid., January 31, 1840.

117. Ibid., February 26, 1840. She added, "We are to have no wedding *at all* not *even our* relations. Pa says that he disapproves of weddings."

118. Rothman, *Hands and Hearts*, 109.

119. Harry Hammond to Emily Cumming, April 7, 1859, Hammond-Bryan-Cumming Papers, SCL; all citations for the Hammond-Cumming courtship are from this collection. Neither Harry nor Emily was given to dating letters, but they often noted the day of the week. Most of the citations here follow their notations or whatever internal evidence helps distinguish one letter from another. A few of the letters have been included in Carol Bleser, ed., *The Hammonds of Redcliffe* (New York: Oxford University Press, 1981), 71–83. Also of interest is an edited volume of writings by Emily Cumming's sister-in-law, W. Kirk Wood, ed., *A Northern Daughter and a Southern Wife: The Civil War Reminiscences and Letters of Katherine H. Cumming, 1860–1865* (Baton Rouge: Louisiana State University Press, 1951).

120. Harry Hammond to Emily Cumming, July 15, 1859, [ca. July 1859] (see also "Sunday morning and Sunday afternoon," [1859] and "Friday morning," [1859]); "Thursday night," [October 1859]; Emily Cumming to Harry Hammond, [1859]; Harry Hammond to Emily Cumming, May 21, 1859 (see also July 11, 1859, "Saturday morning," [1859], "Tuesday morning," [1859]).

121. The definitive biography of James H. Hammond and his times is Drew Gilpin Faust, *James Henry Hammond and the Old South: A Design for Mastery* (Baton Rouge: Louisiana State University Press, 1982); see chap. 15 for Harry Hammond's relation with his father.

122. Harry Hammond to Emily Cumming, "Monday and Tuesday," [1859] and July 5, 1859; Emily Cumming to Harry Hammond, [1859]; Harry Hammond to Emily Cumming, "Saturday night," [1859]. On their meetings, see also Harry Hammond to Emily Cumming, "Friday morning," [1859].

123. Harry Hammond to Emily Cumming, "Monday and Tuesday," [1859].

124. Emily Cumming to Harry Hammond, September 30, 1859; Harry Hammond to Emily Cumming, [May 1859].

125. Harry Hammond to Emily Cumming, "Madison C[ourt] H[ouse] Mon-

day morning," [1859], [May 1859], "Thursday morning," [probably September 1859]; see also May 21, 1859.

126. Ibid., "Saturday night," [1859], July 5, 1859.

127. Ibid., [1859].

128. Emily Cumming to Harry Hammond, [probably October 1859].

129. Harry Hammond to Emily Cumming, "Wednesday morning," [probably October 1859].

130. Ibid., "Wednesday night," [1859]; see also Harry's accounts of his social awkwardness, April 7, 1859, and his irritation with his work, "Tuesday night," [1859]; Emily Cumming to Harry Hammond, [1859]; Harry Hammond to Emily Cumming, "Friday morning," [1859].

131. Harry Hammond to Emily Cumming, "Saturday morning," [1859]; Emily Cumming to Harry Hammond, [October 1859]; Harry Hammond to Emily Cumming, "Wednesday morning," [October 1859]; Emily Cumming to Harry Hammond, [October 1859] and September 30, 1859; Harry Hammond to Emily Cumming, [probably September 1859], and September 26, 1859.

132. Harry Hammond to Emily Cumming, "Monday and Tuesday," [1859], "Tuesday morning," [1859], [ca. October 1859], [September 1859] (see also September 25, 1859, "Friday morning," [1859], and Emily Cumming to Harry Hammond, September 30, 1859); Harry Hammond to Emily Cumming, "Wednesday night," [1859]. Five years after their marriage, Harry wrote to Emily from a Confederate army camp in Virginia about his "spells of hopeless weariness which . . . made me, you know, a most unhappy person before I knew you." See Harry Hammond to Emily Cumming, June 30, 1864.

Chapter 3. Coming of Age: Duty and Satisfaction

1. Histories of the family on which I have drawn are discussed in the Bibliographic Essay. Although Bertram Wyatt-Brown emphasizes the role of the father more than I do, I agree that in southern families the heroic authority of forefathers and child-rearing practices "subjected the young to flawed prescriptions of shame and humiliation and the ideals of heirarchy and honor, a mode in sharp contrast to the conscience-building techniques of pious Yankees." These were part of deeper tensions in American family life during the antebellum years because of the absence of men from the home, the moral elevation of women, and the sentimentalization of childhood. See Wyatt-Brown, *Southern Honor: Ethics and Behavior in the Old South* (New York: Oxford University Press, 1982), 118.

2. John B. Grimball diary, March 10, 1850, Southern Historical Collection, University of North Carolina, Chapel Hill (hereafter SHC); Elisha Hammond to James H. Hammond, December 21, 1827, James H. Hammond Papers, South Caroliniana Library, University of South Carolina, Columbia (hereafter SCL); Louis Wigfall to John Manning, [1840], typed copy, SCL. See also Jasper Adams, *Elements of Moral Philosophy* (Cambridge: Folsom, Wells & Thurston, 1837); Mary Howard Schoolcraft, *Plantation Life: The Narrative of Mrs. Henry Rowe Schoolcraft* (1860; New York: Negro Universities Press, 1969); for moral advisers with a cautious view of marriage, see Virginia Cary, *Letters on Female Character, Addressed to a Young Lady, on the Death of Her Mother* (Richmond, Va.: A. Works, 1828) and Margaret Coxe, *The Young Lady's Companion: In a Series of Letters* (Columbus, Ohio: I. N. Whiting, 1839); for novelists, see Caroline Lee Hentz, *Love after Marriage and Other Stories of the Heart* (Philadelphia: T. B.

Peterson & Brothers, 1870) and E.D.E.N. Southworth, *Retribution; or, the Vale of Shadows: A Tale of Passion* (New York: Harper & Brothers, 1849). Nina Baym remarks that she found "only one thoroughly good man" in fourteen of Southworth's novels. See Baym, *Woman's Fiction: A Guide to Novels by and about Women in America, 1820–1870* (Ithaca: Cornell University Press, 1978), 115.

3. Wyatt-Brown, *Southern Honor*, 273. For an emphasis on affection in marriage, see Daniel Blake Smith, *Inside the Great House: Planter Family Life in Eighteenth-Century Chesapeake Society* (Ithaca: Cornell University Press, 1980), 159–60; Anne F. Scott, *The Southern Lady: From Pedestal to Politics* (Chicago: University of Chicago Press, 1970), 25; Catherine Clinton, *The Plantation Mistress: Woman's World in the Old South* (New York: Pantheon Books, 1982), 69–70; Jane Turner Censer, *North Carolina Planters and Their Children, 1800–1860* (Baton Rouge: Louisiana State University Press, 1984), 72–74; Wyatt-Brown, *Southern Honor*, 223. For the counterpoint of conflict in marriage, see Clinton, *Plantation Mistress*, esp. 74–76; Smith, *Great House*, 165–73; Wyatt-Brown, *Southern Honor*, esp. 270–75.

4. Campbell Bryce to Sarah Bryce, October 6, 1851, Bryce Papers, SCL; Henry Cumming to Julia Cumming, April 10, 1836, Hammond-Bryan-Cumming Papers, SCL; Elizabeth Perry to Benjamin F. Perry, December 6, 1851, Benjamin F. Perry Papers, SCL; Henry Cumming to Julia Cumming, June 4, 1826, Hammond-Bryan-Cumming Papers, SCL; J. T. Coles to Mrs. R. M. Deveaux, December 16, 1835, Singleton-Deveaux Papers, SCL; Hugh S. Ball to Isaac Ball, January 1, 1823, Ball Papers, SCL.

5. Alice Izard to Margaret I. Manigault, July 28, 1811, Manigault Papers, SCL; Maria Bryan to Julia Cumming, March 7, 1824, August 12, 1833, Hammond-Bryan-Cumming Papers, SCL. Women's loneliness after marriage, and their fear of losing other relationships, is also noted in Scott, *Southern Lady*, esp. chap. 2; Clinton, *Plantation Mistress*, esp. chap. 4; and in Jean E. Friedman, *The Enclosed Garden: Women and Community in the Evangelical South, 1830–1900* (Chapel Hill: University of North Carolina Press, 1985), esp. chap. 2.

6. Henry Cumming to Julia Cumming, April 27, 1824, Hammond-Bryan-Cumming Papers, SCL; Samuel Leland diary, April 25, 1852, SCL; Henry Cumming to Julia Cumming, June 25, 1827, Hammond-Bryan-Cumming Papers, SCL; Katherine Meares to Gaston Meares, July 30, 1850, DeRosset Papers, Southern Historical Collection, University of North Carolina, Chapel Hill (hereafter cited as SHC); Henry Cumming to Julia Cumming, March 17, 1828, Hammond-Bryan-Cumming Papers, SCL; Elizabeth Perry to Benjamin F. Perry, [1837], Mrs. Benjamin F. Perry Papers, SCL. Historians of women in the South disagree fairly sharply about the marital happiness of planter women. Misery, and worse, marks the women in Clinton, *Plantation Mistress*, who often seem less able to grasp happiness or satisfaction than their slaves. On the other hand, Censer, *North Carolina Planters*, 72, finds that the "reality [of marriage] often approximated that ideal of domestic harmony." The problem may be a confusion of harmony with happiness—outer form with inner feeling.

7. Elizabeth Perry to Benjamin F. Perry, [1837], Mrs. Benjamin F. Perry, SCL; Eliza DeRosset to Armand DeRosset, April 18, 1845, DeRosset Papers, SHC; Penelope Skinner to Thomas Warren, August 8, 1840, Skinner Papers, SHC; Samuel Leland diary, June 20, 1852, SCL.

8. Planter men and women perceived the separation of spouses, rooted in

their different work, as implying different moral duties. See Wyatt-Brown, *Southern Honor*, 275–80; Clinton, *Plantation Mistress*, 8–10; Scott, *Southern Lady*, 40–43; Censer, *North Carolina Planters*, 7–8; Steven M. Stowe, "Intimacy in Planter Class Culture," *Psychohistory Review* 10 (1982): 141–64.

9. Anne Middleton to [husband], November 23, 1851, Middleton Papers, SCL; Eliza DeRosset to Armand DeRosset, April 15, 1845, DeRosset Papers, SHC; C. R. Woodbury to Katherine DeRosset, July 25, 1850, DeRosset Papers, SHC; Maria Bryan to Julia Cumming, March 20, 1833, Hammond-Bryan-Cumming Papers, SCL.

10. Henry Cumming to Julia Cumming, April 23, 1826, October 5, 1824, Hammond-Bryan-Cumming Papers, SCL; James H. Hammond to Catherine Hammond, January 12, 1834 (see also December 4, 1840, and August 8, 1845), Hammond Papers, SHC; cf. George Braxton in Smith, *Great House*, 42.

11. Henry Cumming to Julia Cumming, 1832, Hammond-Bryan-Cumming Papers; SCL; Elizabeth Perry to Benjamin F. Perry, May 2, 1842, Mrs. Benjamin F. Perry Papers, SCL; Elizabeth Perry to Benjamin F. Perry, December 4, 1842, December 6, 1841 (see also December 2, 1852), Benjamin F. Perry Papers, SCL.

12. Virginia Cary, *Female Character*, 101–2 is typical; see also Daniel Hundley, *Social Relations in Our Southern States* (New York: Henry B. Price, 1860), 74; Earl Thorpe, *Eros and Freedom in Southern Life and Thought* (Durham, N.C.: Seeman Printers, 1967), 32.

13. Adams, *Moral Philosophy*, 146 and passim. These ideals are ably discussed (though with a northern bias) in Bernard Wishy, *The Child and the Republic: The Dawn of Modern American Child Nurture* (Philadelphia: University of Pennsylvania Press, 1968); Nancy F. Cott, *The Bonds of Womanhood: "Woman's Sphere" in New England, 1780–1835* (New Haven: Yale University Press, 1977); Steven Mintz, *A Prison of Expectations: The Family in Victorian Culture* (New York: New York University Press, 1983); Mary P. Ryan, *Cradle of the Middle Class: The Family in Oneida County, New York, 1790–1865* (New York: Cambridge University Press, 1981).

14. Adams, *Moral Philosophy*, 146, 140, 143; Benjamin F. Perry to Elizabeth Perry, December 2, 1854, Benjamin F. Perry Papers, SCL. For a suggestive look at the religious idiom of planter life, see Elizabeth Fox-Genovese and Eugene D. Genovese, "The Old South Considered as a Religious Society," paper presented to the National Humanities Center, April 26–27, 1985.

15. William Muhlenberg, "Christian Education; an Address after a Public Examination of the Students of the Institute at Flushing, L.I.," n.p., [July 28, 1831], 21; Hundley, *Social Relations*, 75–76; Joseph F. Kett, *Rites of Passage: Adolescence in America 1790 to the Present* (New York: Basic Books, 1977), 14. Kett suggested that the often vague notions of "youth" in the antebellum years make a modern attempt to analyze developmental stages anachronistic. However, as Tamara Hareven notes, we should try to ascertain fully how "typical lives [were] 'timed' in the past, and how . . . these life-course patterns fit into their economic, institutional, and demographic setting. . . . A focus on timing enables us to see the point at which family members converge or diverge at different stages of their individual development and how such patterns relate to the collective experience of the family at different points in its development." See Hareven, "Family Time and Historical Time," *Daedalus* 106 (1977): 59–60. For views on young children, see William DeSaussure to J. B. Miller, May 20,

1825, Miller-Furman-Dabbs Papers, SCL; Louis Wigfall to John Manning, [July 17, 1839], typed copy, William-Chesnut-Manning Papers, SCL; Elizabeth Perry to Benjamin F. Perry, May 2, 1842, Mrs. Benjamin F. Perry Papers, SCL; Eliza DeRosset to Armand DeRosset, April 5, 1845, DeRosset Papers, SHC; Maria Bryan to Julia Cumming, July 2, 1840, Hammond-Bryan-Cumming Papers, SCL.

16. Almira Phelps, *The Female Student, or, Lectures to Young Ladies on Female Education* (New York: Leavitt, Lord & Co., 1836), 29; Francis Lieber to "a committee of the Euphradian Society," November 22, 1848, MS copy in Lieber's hand, Francis Lieber Papers, SCL; Paul C. Cameron to Duncan Cameron, September 27, 1865, Cameron Papers, SHC; Thomas Ruffin to Paul C. Cameron, December 6, 1865, Cameron Papers, SHC.

17. Margaret Coxe, *Young Lady's Companion*, 69; Cary, *Female Character*, 135; Joseph Skinner to Tristrim Skinner, May 30, 1838, Skinner Papers, SHC; Samuel Townes to Augustus Townes, November 29, 1842, Townes Papers, SCL. The absence of explicit references to mastery over slaves is striking, and raises the question of when and how (or if) youth of both sexes were systematically and plainly told of their duties as slave managers.

18. Caroline Gilman, *Recollections of a Southern Matron* (New York: Harper & Brothers, 1838), 57; see Gilman's reservations, however, regarding the isolation of boys' education, chap. 28; Hundley, *Social Relations*, 29, and see also chap. 4 on the cotton snobs, esp. 170–72, 184–86. Young southerners schooled in the North sometimes remarked on Yankee vigor in terms that emphasized the difference between urban and rural life. See, for example, William Elliott, Jr., to William Elliott, August [24?], 1847, Elliott-Gonzales Papers, SHC.

19. On the rise of academies and education in general see James McLachlin, *American Boarding Schools: A Historical Study* (New York: Charles Scribner's Sons, 1970); Wishy, *Child and the Republic*; Edgar W. Knight, *The Academy Movement in the South* (Chapel Hill: University of North Carolina Press, 1919); Carl F. Kaestle, *Pillars of the Republic: Common Schools and American Society, 1780–1860* (New York: Hill & Wang, 1983), esp. chap. 8; Rosser H. Taylor, *Antebellum South Carolina: A Social and Cultural History* (Chapel Hill: University of North Carolina Press, 1942), 108–12; Smith, *Great House*, 95–96; Wyatt-Brown, *Southern Honor*, 92–99; Ralph M. Lyon, "Moses Wadel and the Willington Academy," *North Carolina Historical Review* 8 (1931): 284–99; Phillida Bunkle, "Sentimental Womanhood and Domestic Education, 1830–1870," *History of Education Quarterly* 14 (1974): 13–30; Martha G. Waring, "Savannah's Earliest Private Schools," *Georgia Historical Quarterly* 14 (1930): 324–34; Ralph M. Lyon, "The Early Years of the Livingston Female Academy," *Alabama Historical Quarterly* 37 (1975): 192–205; Nancy Green, "Female Education and School Competition, 1820–1850," in *Woman's Being, Woman's Place: Female Identity and Vocation in American History*, ed. Mary Kelley (Boston: G. K. Hall & Co., 1979). For suggestive essays focused on the North, see William H. Pease and Jane H. Pease, "Paternal Dilemmas: Education, Property, and Patrician Persistence in Jacksonian Boston," *New England Quarterly* 53 (1980): 147–67, and Daniel H. Calhoun, "Eyes for the Jacksonian World: William C. Woodbridge and Emma Willard," *Journal of the Early Republic* 4 (1984): 1–26.

20. Gabriella Huger to Mrs. R. M. Deveaux, June 12, 1844; S. J. Snowden to Mrs. R. M. Deveaux, November 15, 1843, Singleton-Deveaux Papers, SCL; on

Ruffin see Avery Craven, *Edmund Ruffin, Southerner: A Study in Secession* (Hamden, Conn.: Archon Books, 1964), 22–23 and n. 18, p. 261; Alfred Cumming to Julia Cumming, January 23, 1839; see also November 30, 1839; Julien Cumming to Julia Cumming, January 28, 1841; Maria Bryan to Julia Cumming, February 1, 1838, Hammond-Bryan-Cumming Papers, SCL. Another young boy's account of home schooling is William DeRosset to Katherine DeRosset, July 26, 1845, DeRosset Papers, SHC. For samplings of advice regarding home education, see Charles Butler, *The American Lady* (Philadelphia: Hogan & Thompson, 1836), 38–40, 248–56; Lydia H. Sigourney, *Letters to Mothers* (Hartford: Hudson & Skinner, 1838), 107–10; Cary, *Female Character*, 166; Coxe, *Young Lady's Companion*, 179–81; Hundley, *Social Relations*, 72; see also Eleanor Thompson, *Education for Ladies, 1830–1860* (New York: King's Crown Press, 1947), 45–48.

21. St. Mary's Hall, "An Appeal to Parents for Female Education on Christian Principles" (Burlington, N.J.: J. L. Powell, 1837), 16–17; [Joseph G. Cogswell], *Outline of the System of Education at the Round Hill School* (Boston: N. Hale's Steam Power Press, 1831), 3–4; Muhlenberg, "Christian Education," 21; Phoebe Pinckney to Anne Elliott, August 8, 1833, Elliott-Gonzales Papers, SHC; Amory Dwight Mayo, *Southern Women in the Recent Educational Movement in the South* (1892; Baton Rouge: Louisiana State University Press, 1978), 43; J. B. Grimball diary, January 7, 1851, SHC. On academy circulars, see Katherine Batts Salley, ed., *Life at St. Mary's* (Chapel Hill: University of North Carolina Press, 1942), 3–4, 13–14; on the increasing sense of sectional tension in academy education see Almira Phelps, *Hours with My Pupils; or, Educational Addresses* (New York: Scribner, 1859), 115; Thompson, *Education for Ladies*, 68; for a variety of uses of the academy as a preparatory school and as an alternative to poor home tutoring, see, e.g., James H. Hammond to Catherine Hammond, August 25, 1840, Hammond Papers, SHC; Robert Rogers to William J. Rivers, December 19, 1850, William J. Rivers Papers, SCL; Frances Griffin, *Less Time for Meddling: A History of Salem Academy and College, 1772–1866* (Winston-Salem, N.C.: J. B. Blair, 1979), 200.

22. See the Williamston Academy Records, January 17, 1865, SHC. This collection is composed of the school's minutes of the board of trustees, 1817–1890, Williamston, Martin County, N.C. For other evidence of academies' importance even in the stress of war and after, see William Bingham to Paul Cameron, January 4, 1865, Cameron Papers, SHC and Caroline Sams to Lewis Sams, July 13, 1867, Sams Papers, SCL. For a typical student list published by many academies, see Episcopal School of North Carolina, Raleigh, N.C. "Report on the State of the School," (Raleigh, 1834–1835), New York Public Library (NYPL). For the significant number of southerners at certain northern institutions in the early antebellum period, see Cogswell, *Outline of the System*; it lists 92 students from southern states in a total student body of 294 at his Northampton, Mass., academy; see also McLachlin, *American Boarding Schools*, 71–104. See also St. Mary's Hall Annual Catalog (Burlington, N.J.: J. L. Powell, 1838, and Powell & George, 1839), NYPL; for the summer term, 1838, fourteen of the sixty-six female students were from the South; for the winter term, six of fifty-two. In the summer term of 1839, twenty-three southerners were among a student body of sixty-nine. For tuition and other costs in schools popular among southerners, see, e.g., Muhlenberg, "Christian Education," 18; St. Mary's Hall [Burlington],

"An Appeal," 21–22; Madame Chegaray's Boarding School for Young Ladies [New York City], circular, [hand dated October 2, 1832], in William Gaston Papers, SHC; Williamston Academy Records, SHC, passim; School for Boys, Barnwell C[ourt] H[ouse], S.C., circular, 1859, in James H. Cornish Papers, SCL; St. Mary's [Raleigh], 1847, invoice, in DeRosset Papers, SHC; William Bingham to Paul Cameron, invoice, 1864, Cameron Papers, SHC. John B. Grimball regularly noted expenses for his children's schooling in his diary, e.g., entries for October 3, 1837, January 7, 1848, SHC. Less straightforward financial arrangements, such as schools assuming the cost of boarding certain students or allowing special terms for ministers' children, are sometimes glimpsed in the records; see, e.g., M. E. Jones to Mary N. Steele, April 14, 1832, John Steele Papers, SHC; Benjamin Reuchel to Elizabeth McNair, February 10, 1830, Miller-Furman-Dabbs Papers, SCL. On typical curricula, see Madame Chegaray's Boarding School for Young Ladies circular, [1832], in Gaston Papers, SHC; class report card for Norman Lieber, May 18, 1850, Francis Lieber Papers, SCL; Hester Chapone, *Letters on the Improvement of the Mind* (Boston: James B. Dow, 1834), 109–11; Muhlenberg, "Christian Education," 21; Episcopal School [Raleigh, N.C.], "Report," n.p., 1835; Cogswell, *Outline of the System*, 11–12; Adams, *Moral Philosophy*, table of contents. See also, Thompson, *Education for Ladies*, 58.

23. William McNeil to William Gaston, September 30, 1834, Gaston Papers, SHC; Oscar Lieber to Francis Lieber, September 18, 1851, Lieber Papers, SCL. For the variety of Newbern Academy applicants, see, e.g., Robert Rose to William Gaston, September 26, 1834; William Hulbert to William Gaston, September 27, 1834; Robert B. Smith to William Gaston, October 1, 1834; Henry L. Davis to William Gaston, September 30, 1834; S. E. Parker to William Gaston, September 25, 1834, Gaston Papers, SHC. For accounts of teachers' duties and recommendations, see Emma Willard to William Gaston, October 7, 1836, Gaston Papers, SHC; Benjamin Reuchel to Elizabeth McNair, February 10, 1830, Miller-Furman-Dabbs Papers, SCL; Williamston Academy Records, August 14, 1818, SHC; Thomas Arthur to Caroline Sosnowski, November 23, 1853 Sosnowski-Schaller Papers, SCL; Griffin, *Less Time For Meddling*, 208–9. Some parents scrutinized teachers closely. William Elliott, in Charleston seeking to place his daughter in school, wrote of that city's noted Madame Ascelie Togno: "I . . . am highly pleased with her. She is very intelligent, kindly *and* firm. I think she is no humbug—her pupils obey and love her." William Elliott to Anne Elliott, January 1, 1855, Elliott-Gonzales Papers, SHC.

24. Salley, *Life at St. Mary's*, 29; Caroline Hentz, *Eoline, or Magnolia Vale*, (Philadelphia: A. Hart, 1852), 173; McLachlin, *American Boarding Schools*, 99; Salley, *Life at St. Mary's*, 10; Hentz, *Eoline*, 44; Henry D. Waller, *A Sketch of Flushing Institute* (New York: Bowne & Co., 1903), 5.

25. Mary Boykin Chesnut, "A Boarding School Fifty Years Ago," MS in Williams-Chesnut-Manning Papers, SCL, 305–7.

26. James McLachlin also stresses the academy's isolated environment, though rather than "transforming the young into adolescents" the academy attempted to transform them into adults; see *American Boarding Schools*, 125.

27. Salley, *Life at St. Mary's*, 16–17; Chesnut, "Boarding School," 319; St. Thomas Hall, circular, n.p., 1840. For rules and procedures making for a closed-in world, see, e.g., Chesnut, "Boarding School," 274; Salley, *Life at St. Mary's*, 27;

Cogswell, *Outline of the System*, 6–10; Hentz, *Eoline*, 92; Madame Chegaray's school, circular, [1832]; Muhlenberg, "Christian Education," 18; Griffin, *Less Time for Meddling*, 195. For a sense of the value placed on warm, familiar feeling see, e.g., Phelps, *Hours with My Pupils*, passim; Salley, *Life at St. Mary's*, 25; Anne Ayers, *Life and Work of William Augustus Muhlenberg* (New York: Harper & Brothers, 1880), 98–101.

28. [Round Hill School], circular, n.p., n.d. [1826?]. For other examples of the structured daily routine, see Griffin, *Less Time for Meddling*, 86–91, 198–99; Salley, *Life at St. Mary's*, 15–19, 25–26; Cogswell, *Outline of the System*, passim; St. Mary's Hall [Burlington], "Appeal," 16–19; Frank Schaller to Sophie Sosnowski, March 30, 1861, Sosnowski-Schaller Papers, SCL; Elizabeth Allston Pringle, *Chronicles of Chicora Wood* (New York: Charles Scribner's Sons, 1922), 123–36, 176–86.

29. Egbert Ross to Emma Ross, May 18, 1860, Egbert Ross Papers, SHC; Frank Schaller to Sophie Sosnowski, March 16, 1861, Sosnowski-Schaller Papers, SCL; Muhlenberg, "Christian Education," 6; Hentz, *Eoline*, 39; Louisa Tuthill, *I Will Be a Lady: A Book for Girls* (Philadelphia: Perkinpine & Higgins, [ca. 1848]), 27; Harriott H. Rutledge to Mrs. Edward C. Rutledge, June 18, 1841, Harriott Horry Rutledge Letters, William R. Perkins Library, Duke University, Durham, N.C. (hereafter Duke); Egbert Ross to Emma Ross, April 20, 1860, Ross Papers, SHC.

30. Chesnut, "Boarding School," 308–9; John Norwood to Thomas Lenoir, September 20, 1829, Lenoir Papers, SHC; [Aunt] H. P. H. to Mrs. Edward C. Rutledge, August 26, 1841, Rutledge Letters, Duke; W. J. Bingham to [Thomas Lenoir], June 26, 1838, Lenoir Papers, SHC. For examples of disciplinary procedures, see Cogswell, *Outline of the System*, 3–4; Williamston Academy Records, May 18, 1820, SHC.

31. Chesnut, "Boarding School," 340. Other accounts of parties, holidays, and outings showing the closeness among students are in Pringle, *Chicora Wood*, 129; Egbert Ross to Emma Ross, October 21, 1860, Ross Papers, SHC; Harriott H. Rutledge to Mrs. Edward C. Rutledge, June 7, 1841, Rutledge Letters, Duke; Eliza Lenoir to Mary Ann Lenoir, April 2, 1834; Louisa Lenoir to Selina Lenoir, in letterbook and commonplace book, 1819, Lenoir Papers, SHC, Frank Schaller to Sophie Sosnowski, February 24, 1861, Sosnowski-Schaller Papers, SCL; Hentz, *Eoline*, 79, 85–87; Salley, *Life at St. Mary's*, 26–27.

32. Hentz, *Eoline*, 33; Mary Ferrand to Mary Steele, July 15, 1831, John Steele Papers, SHC; Mary Ann Lenoir to Sarah Lenoir, December 28, 1835, Lenoir Papers, SHC; Charlotte Daly to Katherine DeRosset, February 10, 1847; "Beck" [Rebecca Haigh?] to Katherine DeRosset, July 27, 1848; Charlotte Daly to Katherine DeRosset, February 10, 1847, DeRosset Papers, SHC; Chesnut, "Boarding School," 350. Women wrote more at length about the happiness of academy life than did men. Teachers also wrote of the closeness among the inmates, e.g., Ayers, *Muhlenberg*, 106–11. For evidence of jealousy and conflict, especially regarding social standing, see, e.g., Phelps, *Hours with My Pupils*, 63; Chesnut, "Boarding School," 295–300; [Aunt] H. P. H. to Mrs. Edward C. Rutledge, June 18, 1841, Rutledge Letters, Duke.

33. Coxe, *Young Lady's Companion*, 71; Salley, *Life at St. Mary's*, 22; Chesnut, "Boarding School," 275. Almira Phelps advised her students that "it is well in *tête-à-tête* conversations, to avoid discussing our own faults or virtues,"

Hours with My Pupils, 205; but teacher-novelist Caroline Hentz shows her young women bringing flowers to each other, combing each other's hair at bedtime, and other behavior that invited intimate conversation; *Eoline*, 121, 137. See also Mary Ann Lenoir to Sarah Lenoir, October 26, 1835, Lenoir Papers, SHC.

34. Cogswell, *Outline of the System*, 9–10; Samuel Leland diary, [1851], 26. Descriptions of classroom work and routine are in Frank Schaller to Sophie Sosnowski, February 10, 1861, March 4, 1861, Sosnowski-Schaller Papers, SCL; Williamston Academy Records, May 18, 1820, SHC; Mary Ann Lenoir to Walter Lenoir, January 1836; Maria Bryan to Julia Cumming, March 14, 1838, Hammond-Bryan-Cumming Papers, SCL; Salley, *Life at St. Mary's*, 18. On the importance of public examinations, as symbol and as entertainment, see Griffin, *Less Time for Meddling*, 194–95; Round Hill School, "Round Hill Exhibition," n.p., n.d. [1826?], passim; Williamston Academy Records, November 23, 1819, SHC; Joseph Skinner to Tristrim Skinner, May 30, 1838, Skinner Papers, SHC; Rebecca Singleton to Marion Singleton, January 23, [1830], Singleton-Deveaux Papers, SCL; Maria Louisa Spear, "Report of the Hillsborough Female Seminary . . . ," June 23, 1838, Lenoir Papers, SHC.

35. See "memo of S. L. Lenoir's Books," 1834, Lenoir Papers, SHC; typical copies of poems, recipes, handwriting exercises are in James H. Hammond, copybook, 1820–1826, SCL; Mary Ann Lenoir copybook, [ca. 1835], Mary J. Welcker copybook, 1840, Julia A. M. Pickens commonplace book, 1830, George Welcker copybooks, 1831, 1831–1832, Lenoir Papers, SHC; see also Griffin, *Less Time for Meddling*, 198. The rote forms fall under Geraint Parry's observation that "for the traditionalist . . . education inculcates a person into an established discipline which is social as well as intellectual, and the code of which is to be discovered in the achievements of the relevant authorities." See Parry, *Political Elites* (New York: Praeger, 1969), 83.

36. The copybook pastiche of the classical, romantic, and colloquial ends up being evidence of what Clifford Geertz calls "local knowledge"—the ineluctable combination of idea and expression that characterizes a people and a place. If in this way academy education can also be said to have been a kind of political act, shaped by the push and pull of interests and bent on solving problems, then J.G.A. Pocock's observation on the rhetoric of politics is apt: "It is the nature of rhetoric and above all of political rhetoric . . . that the same utterance will simultaneously perform a diversity of linguistic functions. . . . Because factual and evaluative statements are inextricably combined in political speech, and because it is intended to reconcile and coordinate different groups pursuing different values, its inherent ambiguity and its cryptic content are invariably high." What appears on one level to be student recitation of timeless verities was on another level an inclusive vagueness—an intellectual roominess —that permitted more than one interpretation of what education ought to be. See Geertz, *Local Knowledge: Further Essays in Interpretive Anthropology* (New York: Basic Books, 1983), 4–6, and J.G.A. Pocock, *Politics, Language, and Time: Essays on Political Thought and History* (New York: Atheneum, 1971), 17.

37. Phelps, *Female Student*, 325; Butler, *American Lady*, 150–53, 187; *The New Universal Letter-Writer* (Philadelphia: D. Hogan, 1850), 15; Butler, *American Lady*, 152; *Universal Letter-Writer*, 1850, 32. For the affinity of women, language, and reading, in a moral and even sensual dimension, see Butler,

American Lady, 165-70. Coxe, *Young Lady's Companion,* 69, warns of novel-reading as "that state of luxurious self-indulgence"; Cary, *Female Character,* 131, depicts Madame de Staël infecting girls' imaginations with her "Corrinne" and "Delphine." For a representative list of books commonly recommended to youth, see Louisa Tuthill, *The Young Lady's Reader* (New Haven, Conn.: J. Babcock, 1839), iii-1v; Muhlenberg, "Christian Education," 14-15. For an excellent discussion of the power fiction was presumed to have over women, see Mary Kelley, *Private Woman, Public Stage: Literary Domesticity in Nineteenth-Century America* (New York: Oxford University Press, 1984), 115-26.

38. *Universal Letter-Writer,* 1850, 11; Sigourney, *Letters to Mothers,* 163-64; Louisa Tuthill, *The Young Lady at Home and in Society* (New York: Allen Bros., [1869]), 66; *Universal Letter-Writer,* 1850, 21.

39. *Emily and Charles; or, A Little Girl's Correspondence with Her Brother* (Boston: Samuel Coleman, 1837), 14, 18, 24. Most advice of this sort stressed the importance of learning to write a good letter early in life, because, as one educator warned, "all the injury of bad company may be done through the medium of letters." See Muhlenberg, "Christian Education," 23.

40. John C. Calhoun to Anna Calhoun, December 30, [1831], in Clyde N. Wilson, ed., *Papers of John C. Calhoun,* 15 vols. (Columbia: University of South Carolina Press, 1966) 11:531-32; M. I. Manigault to Charles Manigault, October 24, 1815, Manigault Papers, SCL; Matilda Lieber to Hamilton Lieber, March 3, 1850, Lieber Papers, SCL; Thomas Ruffin to Duncan Cameron, January 13, 1860, Cameron Papers, SHC; Mary Ann Lenoir to Selina L. Lenoir, July 20, 1835, Lenoir Papers, SHC; M. I. Manigault to Charles Manigault, October 24, 1815, Manigault Papers, SCL; Thomas Ruffin to Duncan Cameron, January 13, 1860, Cameron Papers, SHC; Eliza DeRosset to Katherine DeRosset, December 14, 1844, DeRosset Papers, SHC. Writing also was a chore, of course, and one nine-year-old told her older sister frankly, "Ma says I must write to one of you every Sunday night and I wrote to Brother last Sunday and now it is your turn," Alice DeRosset to Katherine DeRosset, December 7, 1845, DeRosset Papers, SHC.

41. John P. Richardson to Elizabeth Richardson, April 11, 1805, Richardson Papers, SCL.

42. Armand DeRosset to Katherine DeRosset, July 18, 1847, DeRosset Papers, SHC.

43. George Mordecai to Duncan Cameron, September 14, 1863, Cameron Papers, SHC; Henry Townes to Augustus Townes, August 18, 1841, Townes Papers, SCL; John Ball to Hugh Ball [MS copy], July 26, 1826, John Ball Papers, Duke. For examples of typical words of praise, see Thomas Cumming to Ann Cumming, September 6-9, 1803, Hammond-Bryan-Cumming Papers, SCL; Penelope Skinner to Tristrim Skinner, January 22, 1839, Skinner Papers, SHC.

44. Armand DeRosset to Katherine DeRosset, August 4, 1844, DeRosset Papers, SHC; John P. Richardson to Elizabeth Richardson, April 11, 1805, Richardson Papers, SCL; Eliza DeRosset to Katherine DeRosset, June 16, 1844, and July 29, 1844, DeRosset Papers, SHC; John P. Richardson to Elizabeth Richardson, March 9, 1809, Richardson Papers, SCL. Letters from both parents to daughters demonstrate parental concern with girls' education, and I see no evidence that "men thought of women as wife or mother but rarely as daughter," as Thompson, *Education for Ladies,* 47, declares.

45. Mary Ann Lenoir to Louisa Lenoir, June 13, 1835, Lenoir Papers, SHC;

Hugh S. Ball to Isaac Ball, January 1, 1823, Ball Papers, SCL; Mary Ann Lenoir to Louisa Lenoir, June 13, 1835, Lenoir Papers, SHC.

46. Walter Lenoir to Selina Lenoir, October 8, 1836, Mary Ann Lenoir to William A. Lenoir, March 15, 1836, Louisa Lenoir to Selina Lenoir [letterbook copy], 1819, William A. Lenoir to William Lenoir, October 16, 1835, Lenoir Papers, SHC; Anne Cumming to Henry H. Cumming, March 25, 1841, Hammond-Bryan-Cumming Papers, SCL. For youth who did not feel greatly in need of their parents' presence, conventional letters at least provided a structured way for them to "meet." For youth who did feel in need, the letter often became parental love itself, something that still occurs, particularly in times of stress. Saul Friedlander, to take an extreme example, recalls waiting to hear from his parents after they had been taken by the Nazis in pre–World War II Europe: "And the strange thing was that, as the presence of my parents began to become blurred in my mind, their letter, the one that never arrived, became more and more important, more and more laden with nostalgia and vain expectations. Dare I say it? I have the impression that, as time passed, the letter corresponded to a more immediate need than my parents' return; this symbol of love and attachment took the place of the persons themselves." Friedlander, *When Memory Comes* (New York: Farrar, Straus & Giroux, 1979), 119.

47. Mary Ann Lenoir to Selina Lenoir, June 13, 1835, Lenoir Papers, SHC; Katherine DeRosset to Armand DeRosset, December 1, 1844, DeRosset Papers, SHC; Mary Ann Lenoir to Selina Lenoir, October 5, 1835, Lenoir Papers, SHC; William DeRosset to Armand DeRosset, July 14, 1846, DeRosset Papers, SHC; Julien Cumming to Julia Cumming, March 13, 1842, Hammond-Bryan-Cumming Papers, SCL; Tristrim Skinner to Joseph Skinner, December 5, 1835, Skinner Papers, SHC.

48. See Censer, *North Carolina Planters*, 48–53, 95–105, who stresses a lack of conflict.

49. The biographical information is from the Augustin Louis Taveau Papers, Duke.

50. Martha Taveau to Augustin Taveau, March 28, 1839, January 18, [1839], March 6, 1839, Taveau Papers, Duke.

51. Louis A. Taveau to Augustin Taveau, August 20, 1840, July 30, 1839, March 17, 1839, March 7, 1839, Taveau Papers, Duke.

52. Augustin Taveau to Caroline Rosalie Taveau, January 5, 1846; Louis A. Taveau to Augustin Taveau, August 20, 1840; Augustin Taveau to Louis A. Taveau, October 21, 1845; Louis A. Taveau to Augustin Taveau, May 15, 1845. See also Augustin Taveau to Louis A. Taveau [MS copy], September 13, 1847, Augustin Taveau to Martha Taveau, January 2, 1846, Taveau Papers, Duke.

53. Augustin Taveau to Louis A. Taveau, December 11, 1845; [Augustin Taveau marginal note in] Louis A. Taveau to Augustin Taveau, September 26, 1848, Taveau Papers, Duke.

54. James H. Hammond diary, August 1855, James H. Hammond Papers, Library of Congress (hereafter LC).

55. James Chesnut, Sr., to James Chesnut, Jr., September 11, 1834, Williams-Chesnut-Manning Papers, SCL; Samuel Townes to George Townes, January 17, 1830, Townes Papers, SCL; Elisha Hammond to James H. Hammond, March 4, 1827, Hammond-Bryan-Cumming Papers, SCL; James H. Hammond diary, August 2, 1839, Hammond Papers, LC; James H. Hammond copybook, 1820–1826,

41, Hammond Papers, SCL. For examples of sons relying on their fathers for career advice and help, see Henry Cumming to Thomas Cumming, June 30, 1820, Hammond-Bryan-Cumming Papers, SCL; Tristrim Skinner to Joseph Skinner, January 16, 1838, and May 13, 1838, Skinner Papers, SHC; Thomas Lenoir, Sr., to Thomas Lenoir, Jr., November 16, 1835, Lenoir Papers, SHC.

56. Henry Townes to Augustus Townes, November 18, 1845, Townes Papers, SCL; Louis Wigfall to John Manning, [ca. March 23, 1840], typed copy, Williams-Chesnut-Manning, SCL; James H. Hammond diary, June 15, 1839, Hammond Papers, LC; Elisha Hammond to James H. Hammond, June 13, 1826, Hammond Papers, SCL; James H. Hammond, diary, June 1, 1839, Hammond Papers, LC.

57. H. W. Hilliard to James H. Hammond, April 21, 1826, Hammond Papers, SCL; William Lenoir to William A. Gant, March 31, 1834, Lenoir Papers, SHC; Samuel Leland diary, [1851], SCL; Thomas J. Withers to James H. Hammond, June 8, 1826, Hammond Papers, SCL. For many young men this was the first intimation of the loneliness that would bedevil them throughout their lives and, as noted in chapter 1, formed a strong undercurrent in their social and political dealings.

58. Louisa Tuthill, *Young Lady at Home*, 174; Charles Butler, *American Lady* 257. See also Cary, *Female Character*, 43; Phelps, *Hours with My Pupils*, 47, 101, 177–79.

59. Louisa Lenoir to "Elizabeth," Lenoir letterbook, 1819, Lenoir Papers, SHC; Charlotte Daly to Katherine DeRosset, November 4, 1848, DeRosset Papers, SHC; Sarah Dillard to Sarah Lenoir, January 25, 1840, Lenoir Papers, SHC.

60. Delle Mullen Craven, ed., *The Neglected Thread: A Journal from the Calhoun Community, 1836–1842* (Columbia: University of South Carolina Press, 1951), 10; Ella G. Thomas diary, September 29, 1848, Duke; see also entries for October 9, 1848, and May 4, 1852; Charlotte Daly to Katherine DeRosset, February 10, 1847, DeRossett Papers, SHC.

Chapter 4. The Gastons: The Treasure of Offspring

1. William Gaston to Hannah Gaston, August 16, 1828, William Gaston Papers, Southern Historical Collection, University of North Carolina, Chapel Hill, N.C. (hereafter SHC; all manuscript citations are from these papers unless otherwise noted).

2. William R. Taylor's description of "Southern mugwumps" suits Gaston well: "They were children of the Enlightenment—men of broad experience and tempered provincialism. They were apt to be conservative both in politics and in their personal lives, relying heavily on the precept and example of the Founding Fathers. They were inclined to look upon their lives as a never-ending procession of duties and responsibilities which were to be undertaken as a public service and discharged in a spirit of *noblesse oblige.*" These were the men, of course, who were most discomfited intellectually by the surge of romantic, democratic sentiment after 1830. See Taylor, *Cavalier and Yankee: The Old South and American National Character* (New York: Anchor Books, 1963), 32. For a biography of Gaston, see J. Herman Schauinger, *William Gaston, Carolinian* (Milwaukee: Bruce Publishing Company, 1949).

3. This biographical information is derived from Schauinger, *William Gaston*, and from my reading of the Gaston papers.

4. About the only way Gaston could be said to have indulged himself was the pride he took in his public character, displaying it quietly but steadily to "the world." John Fraser, writing of Henry Canby and a later time, nevertheless fittingly characterizes this pride "wherein small things as well as large became charged with significance and every social occasion could 'seem a little more than it was.' " See Fraser, *America and the Patterns of Chivalry* (New York: Cambridge University Press 1982), 203.

5. For William Byrd, see Michael Zuckerman's excellent "William Byrd's Family," *Perspectives in American History* 12 (1979): 255–311, and for Landon Carter see Jack P. Greene, *Landon Carter: An Inquiry into the Personal Values and Social Imperatives of the Eighteenth-Century Virginia Gentry* (Charlottesville: University Press of Virginia, 1965). See also Jan Lewis, "Domestic Tranquility and the Management of Emotion among the Gentry of Pre-Revolutionary Virginia," *William and Mary Quarterly*, 3d ser., 39 (1982): 135–49.

6. For Gaston and courtship, see his classicly formal letters to Eliza Worthington throughout the spring and summer of 1816. For Gaston's defense of his honor, see L. D. Henry to William Gaston, December 30, 1831, James Wyche to William Gaston, January 1831, and William Gaston to Susan Gaston, April 3, 1831.

7. William Gaston to ?, October 25, 1832; William Gaston to Thomas Devereux, August 19, 1833; A. Henderson to William Gaston, January 15, 1836.

8. William Gaston to Susan Gaston, October 2, 1826; William Gaston to Alexander Gaston, July 1, 1828. Gaston's correspondence contains many letters from neighbors, constituents, even strangers, asking for various favors from him. See, e.g., S. M. Chester to William Gaston, September 18, 1830, and James Robertson to William Gaston, July 31, 1832. A close study of planter-class drinking and alcoholism has yet to be written, although many have suggested the need for it. See Francis P. Gaines, *The Southern Plantation: A Study in the Development and Accuracy of a Tradition* (New York: Columbia University Press, 1924), 160–63; Philip Alexander Bruce, *Social Life in Old Virginia* (1910; New York: Capricorn Books, 1965), 38–44; Avery Graven, *Edmund Ruffin, Southerner: A Study in Secession* (Hamden, Conn.: Archon Books, 1964), 9–11; Eugene Genovese, *Roll, Jordan, Roll: The World the Slaves Made* (New York: Vintage Books, 1976), 641–46. For heartfelt letters to Gaston from drinking men, see H. C. Jones to Willam Gaston, July 2, 1828, and John Manning to William Gaston, July 15, 1832, and October 24, 1832.

9. William Gaston to Mrs. John L. Taylor, August 16, 1826; William Gaston to Susan Gaston, July 3, 1826; William Gaston to Hannah Gaston, January 13, 1827; William Gaston to Susan Gaston, June 13, 1829.

10. William Gaston to Joseph Hopkinson, August 26, 1823, and March 1, 1823, Joseph Hopkinson Papers, SHC.

11. Ibid., January 4, 1823, Joseph Hopkinson Papers, SHC.

12. Ibid., September 21, 1823, Joseph Hopkinson Papers, SHC.

13. The quality of Gaston's love for Susan reveals how problematic is the picture of the affection-steeped, "child-centered" family that historians see emerging in this period. Gaston expressed his affection to Susan, but much more frequently expressed it *about her* to others. His words were loving, for all of their conventionality, yet there is no denying that he was distant in more ways than one, and that he considered himself the final judge of Susan's best inter-

ests. His almost reflexive control of her ritual coming of age must modify the view that affectionate parents were parents who valued their children's autonomy above other concerns.

14. William Gaston to Susan Gaston, July 3, 1826, September 12, 1827, September 11, 1826.

15. Ibid., October 2, 1826.

16. William Gaston to Robert Donaldson, June 2, 1827.

17. William Gaston to Susan Gaston, September 12, 1827.

18. Ibid., September 21, 1827; see also April 1, 1828. These exchanges between Gaston and his daughter are the most emotionally laden in all of his correspondence, bespeaking the charged relationship between fathers and daughters that frequently appears in family letters. Philip Greven, drawing upon many southern sources for the eighteenth century, saw "unconscious oedipal ties" in daughters' love for father and Heavenly Father; see Greven, *The Protestant Temperament: Patterns of Child-rearing, Religious Experience and the Self in Early America* (New York: New American Library, 1977), 134. Catherine Clinton, *The Plantation Mistress: Woman's World in the Old South* (New York: Pantheon Books, 1982), 44, takes note of the typical "intense and warm relationships" between planter fathers and female offspring, and Bertram Wyatt-Brown remarks upon the same matter in *Southern Honor: Ethics and Behavior in the Old South* (New York: Oxford University Press 1982), 272–73. John C. Calhoun's daughter Anna wrote him frequently of her love. Soon to be married, Anna wrote to her friend Maria Simkins in 1838 referring to her father as "the cherished object" of her life who might fit awkwardly in her married state. "You who know my idolatry for my father, can sympathize with my feelings," she wrote. Even after eleven years of marriage to Thomas Clemson, Anna could still write of love and loss, telling her father, "I am so afraid sometimes, you will yet used to doing without me and miss me less. Love me I know you always will." Quoted in Ernest M. Lander, Jr., *The Calhoun Family and Thomas Green Clemson: The Decline of a Southern Patriarch* (Columbia: University of South Carolina Press, 1983), 6, 115. Such feelings reached a literary apotheosis in postwar books; Susan Dabney Smedes's extended eulogy of her father raises him to such heights that he is disposed of as well as acclaimed. See her *Memorials of a Southern Planter* (1887; Jackson: University Press of Mississippi, 1981).

19. See William Gaston to Susan Gaston, January 13, 1828.

20. Ibid.; William Gaston to Hannah Gaston, June 24, 1826, and July 27, 1828; see also September 30, 1826.

21. William Gaston to Hannah Gaston, June 24, 1826, and October 6, 1826.

22. Ibid., June 29, 1828, and August 16, 1828.

23. Ibid., June 24, 1826.

24. William Gaston to Joseph Hopkinson, August 26, 1823, Joseph Hopkinson Papers, SHC; William Gaston to Hannah Gaston, June 24, 1826; William Gaston to Mrs. John L. Taylor, July 31, 1826. Gaston's desire that his son excel in the display of right principles and manly skills was tied to no profession aside from law, and Gaston's wish that Alexander settle in a law office somewhere derived from a desire to see Alexander use law as a route to civic leadership. Divisive tensions between sons and fathers are incisively explored in Wyatt-Brown, *Southern Honor*, esp. chaps. 6 and 7, in which he also observes that

fathers and sons were drawn together by "a passion for the hunt, a loyalty to family honor, and a mistrust of women." Drew Faust ably depicts the uneasiness between the young James H. Hammond and his demanding, almost taunting father, in *James Henry Hammond and the Old South: A Design for Mastery* (Baton Rouge: Louisiana State University Press, 1982), 21–25, 33–34. Downplaying conflict and relying more on paternal than filial sources are Daniel Blake Smith, *Inside the Great House: Planter Family Life in Eighteenth-Century Chesapeake Society* (Ithaca: Cornell University Press, 1980), esp. chap. 3, which emphasizes the dutifulness of most sons, and Jane Turner Censer, *North Carolina Planters and Their Children, 1800–1860* (Baton Rouge: Louisiana State University Press, 1984), esp. chap. 3, which stresses fathers' loving interest in the growth and education of sons.

25. William Gaston to Susan Gaston Donaldson, March 9, 1828, and April 1, 1828.

26. William Gaston to Robert Donaldson, May 30, 1828; William Gaston to Susan Gaston Donaldson, August 20, 1828.

27. This kind of judgment was close to the center of the planters' familial common sense, and shows how seamless and self-fulfilling the authority of such common sense can be. As Clifford Geertz remarks, "Common sense is not what the mind cleared of cant spontaneously apprehends; it is what the mind filled with presuppositions . . . concludes. . . . As a frame for thought, and a species of it, common sense is as totalizing as any other; no religion is more dogmatic, no science more ambitious, no philosophy more general." See Geertz, "Common Sense as a Cultural System," in his *Local Knowledge: Further Essays in Interpretive Anthropology* (New York: Basic Books, 1983), 84.

28. See W. W. Worthington to William Gaston, October 8, 1830; William Gaston to Susan Gaston Donaldson, February 24, 1833. For other evidence of Gaston's preoccupation with the schooling of Eliza and Catherine, see, e.g., Susan Gaston Donaldson to William Gaston, April 30, 1829, July 8, 1830, May 4, 1831, January 9, 1833; William Gaston to Susan Gaston Donaldson, October 23, 1830, November 16, 1831, February 24, 1833.

29. Susan Gaston Donaldson to William Gaston, April 29, 1830, and August 17, 1830; William Gaston to Hannah Gaston Manly, February 3, 1833; William Gaston to Susan Gaston Donaldson, February 24, 1833. Strain in family relations was apparent when Hannah did not schedule her wedding to allow Susan to attend; see Eliza Gaston to William Gaston, January 28, 1832.

30. William Gaston to Susan Gaston Donaldson, October 23, 1830, and July 10, 1830.

31. Susan Gaston Donaldson to William Gaston, April 30, 1829, July 8, 1830, [n.d., 1832], January 9, 1833.

32. Ibid., April 3, 1830, March 7, 1831, July 20, 1835; see also October 19, 1830. Like her father, Susan used her letters to bridge time as well as distance; they calmed her. Putting words to paper invented the continuity she craved. The critic Richard Gilman notes: "We live in a succession of . . . temporary fulfillments" and "language is one force that works to obscure this. Its own continuity seems absolute, and we borrow this seeming permanence." See Gilman, *Decadence: The Strange Life of an Epithet* (New York: Farrar, Straus & Giroux, 1979), 25.

33. William Gaston to Eliza Gaston, June 4, 1833; William Gaston to Eliza

and Catherine Gaston, March 17, 1833; William Gaston to Eliza Gaston, June 19, 1834, and June 9, 1832.

34. Eliza Gaston to William Gaston, July?, 1829, and January 18, 1831.

35. Ibid., October 29, 1832, and December?, 1830.

Chapter 5. The Lacys: The Thing, Not Its Vision

1. Drury Lacy to Williana Lacy, May 24, 1845; Drury Lacy to Williana Wilkinson, June 22, 1823, Drury Lacy Papers, Southern Historical Collection, University of North Carolina, Chapel Hill, N.C., hereafter SHC; all manuscript citations are from the Lacy Papers, unless noted otherwise. For the social context of evangelical Presbyterians, see Anne Loveland, *Southern Evangelicals and the Social Order, 1800–1860* (Baton Rouge: Louisiana State University Press, 1980).

2. Drury Lacy to Bessie Lacy, June 13, 1845.

3. Ibid., and August 8, 1845.

4. Drury and Williana Lacy to Bessie Lacy, January 10, 1845; Drury Lacy to Bessie Lacy, August 6, 1845; see also Bessie Lacy to Williana Lacy, September 22, 1845; Horace Lacy to Bessie Lacy, August 23, 1845. Throughout, Drury Lacy shows a familiarity with the moral and pedagogical literature discussed in chapter 3, as would be expected of a clergyman with a literary bent.

5. Williana Lacy to Bessie Lacy, January 10, 1845; Drury and Williana Lacy to Bessie Lacy, January 10, 1845; Williana Lacy to Bessie Lacy, August 30, 1845, November 28, 1845, August 30, 1845. Despite recent attention to planter-class social history, there is surprisingly little comment on mother-daughter relations. Catherine Clinton briefly notes maternal advice to daughters, but without explicit comment. Jane Turner Censer tends to speak of parent-child relations without drawing many distinctions between mothers and fathers, sons and daughters, and Anne F. Scott's path-breaking study has almost nothing to say about mothers and daughters as such. Bertram Wyatt-Brown's able discussion of family alliances does not linger on the mother-daughter dyad in particular. See Clinton, *The Plantation Mistress: Woman's World in the Old South* (New York: Pantheon Books, 1982), 40–44, 60–62; Censer, *North Carolina Planters and Their Children, 1800–1860* (Baton Rouge: Louisiana State University Press, 1984), 48–60; Scott, *The Southern Lady: From Pedestal to Politics, 1830–1930* (Chicago: University of Chicago Press, 1970), passim; Wyatt-Brown, *Southern Honor: Ethics and Behavior in the Old South* (New York: Oxford University Press, 1982), 230–35. As for Williana Lacy and her daughter Bessie, their relationship was typical in that it was more candid but less playful than Bessie's with her father. Williana could speak with authority from within the woman's sphere, but at times was more didactic than even her husband.

6. Williana Lacy to Bessie Lacy, July 10, 1845, November 28, 1845, August 23, 1845. Here Williana echoed moral advisers, but her direct characterization supplies an edge to feminine modesty. Williana wishes Bessie not to be *un*exciting, but *more* exciting for her subtlety; cf. the relatively pallid Virginia Cary: "The perfection of feminine excellence, consists in an [*sic*] union of firmness and consistency in the practice of virtue, with meekness, gentleness, and modesty, in outward demeanor. There is something indescribably repulsive in a boisterous, passionate, blunt, coarse female." See Cary, *Letters on Female Character, Addressed to a Young Lady, on the Death of Her Mother* (Richmond, Va.: A. Works, 1828), 77–78.

7. Williana Lacy to Bessie Lacy, July 10, 1845, July 28, 1845, November 28, 1845, September 19, 1845, August 30, 1845. See also November 26, 1845, and December 6, 1845.

8. Ibid., November 26, 1845, February 1, 1846, January 2, 1846, February 23, 1846. Jean Friedman notes that many women used tree imagery for their lives, and indicates that the image also filled their dreams. See Friedman, *The Enclosed Garden: Women and Community in the Evangelical South, 1830–1900* (Chapel Hill: University of North Carolina Press, 1985), 35–36.

9. Bessie Lacy to Drury Lacy, September 19, 1846.

10. Bessie Lacy to Horace Lacy, March 16, 1847. See Drury Lacy's similar feelings in a letter to Bessie, August 6, 1845.

11. Drury Lacy to Horace Lacy, May 16, 1847, September 12, 1847, October 8, 1847, March 30, 1848. Drury's anxiety, inspiring urgent, abstract exhortations to manliness, places him squarely in the male culture of education described in chapter 3.

12. Drury Lacy to Horace Lacy, February 5, 1848; see also March ?, 1847, and Bessie Lacy to Drury Lacy, April 24, 1847.

13. Drury Lacy to Horace Lacy, May 16, 1847.

14. Bessie Lacy to Drury Lacy, Jr., January 12, 1847; Bessie Lacy to Drury Lacy, December, 1846; Bessie Lacy to Horace Lacy, October 11, 1847; Bessie Lacy to Drury Lacy, September 21, 1847; Bessie Lacy to Horace Lacy, January 12, 1847; Bessie Lacy to Drury Lacy, [1847], September 5, 1846, March 30, 1848; see also July 25, 1846.

15. Bessie Lacy to Drury Lacy, February 12, 1848.

16. Ibid., February 11, 1847.

17. Bessie Lacy to Horace Lacy, August 15, 1847; Bessie Lacy to Drury Lacy, January 27, 1848.

18. Maggie Morgan to Bessie Lacy, January 12, 1849.

19. Ibid., January 13, 1849.

20. Ibid., September 15, 1849.

21. Bessie Lacy to Drury Lacy, June 16, 1851, and March 25, 1851.

22. Bessie Lacy to Thomas Dewey, "Christmas," 1851.

23. Ibid., May 10, 1852.

24. Ibid.

25. Ibid., and, May 7, 1852, February 22, 1853, June 30, 1852.

26. Ibid., May 7, 1852. Without much effort to conceal, Bessie was trying out the masks courtship permitted—or compelled—lovers to wear. A reader of novels, Bessie found her own rhetoric shaped by fictional prose, but she was not therefore being duplicitous or consciously manipulative. As Anne Jones points out, the fictional device of giving female characters masks to wear was extended to both evil and good characters. Like a character in one of these novels, Bessie seems to have moved "not toward unmasking, but toward, first, self-awareness, and, second, ethical 'policy'—that is, the conscious and responsible choice of masks." Jones remarks of Augusta Evans's popular 1859 novel *Beulah*: "Only two or three times in 440 pages does a sentence tell the reader what Eugene or Guy actually felt and thought. Almost always the reader is told only what they *seem* to feel—that is, one is shown only the mask." See Jones, *Tomorrow Is Another Day: The Woman Writer in the South, 1859–1936* (Baton Rouge: Louisiana State University Press, 1981), 72, 74.

27. Bessie Lacy to Thomas Dewey, June 30, 1852, May?, 1852, June 30, 1852, July 26, 1852.

28. Thomas Dewey to Drury Lacy, November, 1852.

29. Bessie Lacy to Thomas Dewey, January 19, 1853, February 8, 1853, [undated, 1853].

30. Ibid., [undated, 1852], February 4, 1853, [undated, 1853], [undated, late 1852], March 4, 1853, March 18, 1853. In this struggle, Bessie and Thomas continued to watch closely and count letters, and to have their conflict shaped by them. Bessie, in particular, perceived that correspondence could let down as swiftly as it could build, and that letters could strike as they could caress. Janet G. Altman, writing of the epistolary novel, observes of lovers "meeting" through letters: "In seduction correspondence [it] is an intermediate step between indifference and intimacy; on the other side of seduction it is an intermediate step between conquest and abandonment. The same seducer who uses the letter to engage his victim at the beginning of a relationship may substitute the letter for his actual presence when he wishes to disentangle himself." See Altman, *Epistolarity: Approaches to a Form* (Columbus: Ohio State University Press, 1982), 42-43.

31. Maggie Morgan to Bessie Lacy, February 4, 1853.

32. Bessie Lacy to Thomas Dewey, August, 1853; B. T.[ucker] Lacy to Bessie Lacy, June 6, 1853.

33. Alexander McPheeters to Thomas Dewey, July 26, 1853; Mary R. Lacy to Thomas Dewey, [undated, 1853]; Mary Dewey to Thomas Dewey, July 11, 1853.

34. Sarah Dewey to Thomas Dewey, August 29, 1853; Drury Lacy to Thomas Dewey, October 7, 1853. The intense feelings of loss expressed by Thomas's sisters was a mark of the high-strung relations between sisters and brothers. I tend to agree with Bertram Wyatt-Brown that though such relations were not singularly southern they found particularly fertile ground in southern family life. See Wyatt-Brown, *Southern Honor*, 251-53.

35. William Lacy to Bessie Lacy Dewey, October 10, 1853; Bessie Lacy Dewey to Drury Lacy, October 28, 1853; "Priscilla" to Bessie Lacy Dewey, November 30 [1853].

36. Drury Lacy to Bessie Lacy Dewey, March 8, 1854.

37. Mary R. Lacy to Bessie Lacy Dewey, June 17, 1854; Bessie Lacy Dewey to Thomas Dewey, July 8, 1854 and July 24, 1854; see also Thomas Dewey to Bessie Lacy Dewey, July 30, 1854.

38. Bessie Lacy Dewey to Thomas Dewey, August 3, 1854, August 13, 1854, [undated, late 1854], November, 1854, August, 1854.

39. Mary R. Lacy to ?, September 14, 1854; Bessie Lacy Dewey to Thomas Dewey, September 17, 1854; Drury Lacy to Thomas Dewey, September 29, 1854.

Chapter 6. The Kings: Waiting for Father

1. Biographical information is drawn from the Thomas Butler King Papers, Southern Historical Collection, University of North Carolina, Chapel Hill, N.C., hereafter cited as SHC; all manuscript citations are from these papers, unless otherwise noted. I have also made use of Edward M. Steel, Jr., *T. Butler King of Georgia* (Athens: University of Georgia Press, 1964) for information regarding King's political career. This biography includes little about King's family or personal life.

2. Stephen Elliott to Thomas Butler King, December 15, 1841. For other correspondence regarding education, see Joseph Storey to Thomas King, January 17, 1841, Josiah Quincy to Thomas King, January 18, 1841, Henry McKean to Thomas King, July 3, 1842. On King's "biblious habit," see his allusion to it in his letter to Anna King, October 6, 1841.

3. Thomas King to Anna King, October 24, 1842; Anna King to Thomas King, June 2, 1842; Georgia King to Thomas King, August 15, 1842. For an early letter in which Anna wishes her husband home, see hers to Thomas, July 26, 1842.

4. John Dunham to Thomas King, July 29, 1841, and May 1, 1841; Andrew King to Thomas King, September 16, 1842; Anna King to Thomas King, August 11 and 12, 1842, and August 15 and 16, 1842; William P. Mollett to Anna King, October 16, 1841; Anna King to Thomas King, August 9, 1842. Cousin Mollett, though not involving himself formally in the Kings' finances, apparently sent Anna some money for her personal use; see his letter to her, January 7, 1843.

5. For a sampling of Thomas King's political correspondence, see Thomas King to R. R. Cuyler, January 3, 1843; Thomas King to "Dear Sir," October 7, 1844; W. P. Mollett to Anna King, November 24, 1845; Henry King to Thomas King, July 25, 1845. In 1846 King received many requests for copies of his "The Oregon Question" speech of that year; these requests are good examples of planter-class male flattery and politics. King's correspondence throughout 1842 to 1844 contains many invitations to speak or officiate which also give the flavor of his political dealings. Before 1850 King seldom mentioned slavery as a political issue, but he indirectly alludes to "southern interests" several times, as did most slaveowners.

6. Thomas King to Anna King, December 26, 1842.

7. Ibid., February 12, 1843.

8. Ibid., May 11, 1844.

9. Ibid., September 28, 1841, and October 6, 1841; Charles Floyd to Thomas Bourke (MS copy in Floyd's hand), January 8, 1845; R. R. Cuyler to Thomas King, January 16, 1846.

10. Anna King to Thomas King, August 5, 1842, December 27, 1844, April 7, 1848; Lou[isa] King to Anna King, July 31, 1847; Anna King to Thomas King, June 8, 1849.

11. Anna King to Thomas King, May 23, 1848.

12. Anna King to Lord King, September 5, 1848.

13. Ibid., September 28, [1848]; Lord King to Thomas King, April 7, 1848; Florence King to Lord King, September 18, 1848. Lord King to Thomas King, May 3-14, 1849, reveals Lord as a political student and confidant of his father.

14. Butler King to Thomas King, January 10, 1848, January 25, 1848, February 25, 1848; Butler and Lord King to Anna King, June 1847; Butler King to Anna King, April 23, 1849; Butler King to Thomas King, May 11, 1847.

15. See Steel, *T. Butler King*, esp. chap. 2, 3.

16. Butler King to Anna King, May 20, 1849. Regarding King's trip to California, see Steel, *T. Butler King*, 70-89. For Butler and Anna managing Retreat plantation, see Butler King to Anna King, October 16, 1849, October 17, 1849, November 23, 1849; Anna King to Thomas King, June 8, 1849.

17. On King's second trip to California, see Steel, *T. Butler King*, 84-97. On the financial irregularities, see ibid., 184n. and the bond dated May 31, 1854, in the King Papers, SHC.

18. Georgia King to Thomas King, June 28, 1849; Thomas King to Anna

King, September 15, 1851, and April 4, 1852; Thomas King to Florence King, April 17, 1852. See also Thomas King to Anna King, April 4, 1852.

19. Thomas King to Lord King, March 8, 1856; Thomas King to Anna King, March 25, 1856, April 4, 1852, June 28, 1849. King's distance from his family, and his imagining it in abstract terms of duty and self-sacrifice, paralleled the drift of the "men of mind" in Drew Gilpin Faust's study of antebellum intellectual elites. These men, searching "to establish their mundane relevance" defined themselves "not in terms of social location or affiliation, but in relationship to transcendent conceptions of duty and mission." In addition to being an armor against disappointment, the reliance on higher duty and hard political work deflected family tensions. In Bertram Wyatt-Brown's summary these included the "ambivalences of mothers toward their young sons, their dependents and their future masters; the latent hostilities of boys toward their fathers, their models and their rivals; and the mixed emotions of fathers toward their sons, their replications and their future replacements." See Faust, *A Sacred Circle: The Dilemma of the Intellectual in the Old South, 1840–1860* (Baltimore: Johns Hopkins University Press, 1977), 145; Wyatt-Brown, *Southern Honor: Ethics and Behavior in the Old South* (New York: Oxford University Press, 1982), 174.

20. Anna King to Thomas King, July 11, 1848 and [June] 19, [1849]; Anna King to Lord King, March 10, 1851; Anna King to Thomas King, May 20, 1849. See also Anna King to Butler King, August 1849, and Butler King to Anna King, January 29, 1851.

21. Anna King to Thomas King, June 20, 1849, February 21, 1850, April 11, 1850.

22. Butler King to Anna King, July 3, 1850, November 25, 1850, January 1, 1852, January 15, 1852. See also Butler King to Anna King, May 3, 1852.

23. Ibid., November 15, 1851, October 15, 1851, September 30, 1851. See also October 13, 1852, for Butler on himself and Lord as courters of women.

24. Ibid., May 11, 1851, September 30, 1852, March 30, 1851. On Butler preferring planting, see also his letter to Anna, August 14, 1851.

25. Ibid., January 1, 1852; Anna King to Thomas King, November 28, 1853; Butler King to Anna King, September 30, 1852. The characterization of an individual slave is rare in the Kings' letters, as in most elite correspondence. Once, however, Anna was moved to write about a slave, Annie, who died despite Anna's best efforts and close attendance. Anna King was deeply affected, writing to Thomas on October 6, 1858, "I had raised that child from a little girl, and loved her much."

26. Butler King to Anna King, July 15, 1851, May 16, 1852, February 18, 1852.

27. Ibid., May 18, 1852.

28. Ibid., October 31, 1851, January 15, 1852, July 15, 1852.

29. See Virginia King to Thomas King, November 8, 1854; Richard King to Anna King, November 4, 1854.

30. Butler King to Anna King, February 8, 1853, and November 20, 1853.

31. Anna King to Butler King, February 20, 1855; Anna King to Thomas King, December 12, 1853; Anna King to Lord King, May 22, 1854. See also Anna King to Butler King, January 15, 1855; Anna King to Thomas King, July 17, 1854.

32. Anna King to Thomas King, February 17, 1855.

33. Anna King to Thomas King, April 16, 1855; Anna King to "Dearest Children," October 9, 1857; Anna King to Thomas King, April 23, 1855. On October 1,

1857, Anna similarly wrote her husband: "Our dear Buttie writes rather de-spondently of his matrimonial prospects. It will be *truly unfortunate* if he is disappointed. It is full time dear Buttie should be at work for *himself*—if he can marry the woman he loves, your own name will be perpetuated in him."

34. Anna King to Thomas King, October 16, 1857; Thomas King to Lord King, March 8, 1856, and August 10, 1856. The letters of both Anna and Thomas can be seen, in Kafka's stark expression, as part of the "terrible dislocation of souls in the world" produced by the "feasibility of letter writing." Depending upon letters "is truly a communication with spectres, not only with the spectre of the addressee but also with one's own phantom, which evolves underneath one's own hand in the very letter one is writing or even in a series of letters, where one letter reinforces the other and can refer to it as a witness." Many times, in the later years of the Kings' marriage, they seem to be talking to ghosts. (Kafka is quoted in Janet G. Altman, *Epistolarity: Approaches to a Form* (Columbus: Ohio State University Press, 1982), frontispiece [p. 2].

35. Anna King to Thomas King, July 26, 1857; Butler King to Thomas King, September 4, 1857.

36. Thomas King to Anna King, December 22, 1858; Anna King to Floyd King, March 18, 1859; Anna King to Thomas King, April 6, 1859; Georgia King to "Tip" [Richard King], October 18, 1859. See also Anna King to Thomas King, March 2, 1857, and October 1, 1857.

Conclusion

1. Eugene D. Genovese remarks upon the elite planters' efforts to "make their class more conscious of its nature, spirit, and destiny," observing that "the class as a whole must be brought to a higher understanding of itself—trans-formed from a class-in-itself, reacting to pressures on its objective position, into a class-for-itself, consciously striving to shape the world in its own image" in *Roll, Jordan, Roll: The World the Slaves Made* (New York: Vintage Books, 1974), 27.

2. C. Vann Woodward, *American Counterpoint: Slavery and Racism in the North-South Dialogue* (Boston: Little, Brown & Co., 1971), 40.

BIBLIOGRAPHICAL ESSAY

The aim of this essay is to highlight certain studies in method and interpretation that I have found helpful, and to tie them to histories of southern family life and culture. I hope to be suggestive rather than exhaustive, to sharpen discussion for future work in this field.

Much of the recent history of planter-class culture begins with U. B. Phillips's work, a watershed. He chose, however, for the most part to emphasize the elite's mannered style, concern with money, and love of education, with luminaries like Thomas Jefferson as his mainstays. Phillips says comparatively little about what the gentry made of their daily lives. Some thirty years later, Clement Eaton was concerned that the South be taken as a civilization and also gave little attention to what ordinary inhabitants of white culture said about it. See Phillips, *Life and Labor in the Old South* (1929; Boston: Little, Brown & Co., 1963 and Eaton, *The Growth of Southern Civilization, 1790–1860* (New York: Harper Torchbooks, 1961), esp. chapts. 1, 8, and 13. Other essential works that tackle the general nature of plantation society are Francis P. Gaines, *The Southern Plantation: A Study in the Development and Accuracy of a Tradition* (New York: Columbia University Press, 1924); Rosser H. Taylor, *Ante-Bellum South Carolina: A Social and Cultural History* (Chapel Hill: University of North Carolina Press, 1942); William H. Freehling, *Prelude to Civil War: The Nullification Controversy in South Carolina, 1816–1836* (New York: Harper Torchbooks, 1965); James L. Roark, *Masters without Slaves: Southern Planters in the Civil War and Reconstruction* (New York: W. W. Norton, 1977); J. Mills Thornton III, *Politics and Power in a Slave Society: Alabama, 1800–1860* (Baton Rouge: Louisiana State University Press, 1978); James Oakes, *The Ruling Race: A History of American Slaveholders* (New York: Alfred Knopf, 1982); Eugene D. Genovese, *Roll, Jordan, Roll: The World the Slaves Made* (New York: Vintage Books, 1976); Bertram Wyatt-Brown, *Southern Honor: Ethics and Behavior in the Old South* (New York: Oxford University Press, 1982).

Studies about white elite experience in terms of formal intellectual life and "national character" include Wilber J. Cash, *The Mind of the South* (New York: Alfred Knopf, 1941); Rollin G. Osterweis, *Romanticism and Nationalism in the Old South* (Baton Rouge: Louisiana State University Press, 1949); C. Vann Woodward, *American Counterpoint: Slavery and Racism in the North-South Dialogue* (Boston: Little, Brown & Co., 1971); Drew Gilpin Faust, *A Sacred Circle: The Dilemma of the Intellectual in the Old South, 1840–1860* (Baltimore: Johns Hopkins University Press, 1977); Michael O'Brien, *The Idea of the American*

South, 1920–1941 (Baltimore: Johns Hopkins University Press, 1979); Fred Hobson, *Tell about the South: The Southern Rage to Explain* (Baton Rouge: Louisiana State University Press, 1983); William R. Taylor, *Cavalier and Yankee: The Old South and American National Character* (New York: Anchor Books, 1963).

Comment on the planters' cultural life in histories of slavery has been patchy, and often revolves around a discussion of white paternalism. This concept, and the muddled definitions that surround it, deserves a study of its own. Paternalism is a common-sense fact of life in the work of Phillips, who usually alludes to it as a kind of inclusive, public kindliness extended from master to slave. But in *Life and Labor*, 196–97, he also sees paternalism as shaped by "the customary human forces, interchange of ideas and coadaptation of conduct. . . . In so far as harmony was attained—and in this the plantation mistress was a great if quiet factor—a common tradition was evolved embodying reciprocal patterns of conventional conduct." This focus on reciprocity between owner and slave was not pursued by Phillips's chief critic, Kenneth S. Stampp, who stressed the equation of paternalism with kindliness, seeing paternalism as so much "legend" except for a "kind of leisure-class indulgence of . . . domestics." See Stampp, *The Peculiar Institution: Slavery in the Ante-bellum South* (New York: Vintage Books, 1956), 322, 326. Stanley Elkins, too, tended to be caught up in how kindly paternalism may have been, noting that "for all the system's cruelties there were still clear standards of white patriarchal benevolence inherent in its human side, and . . . such standards were recognized as those of the best Southern families[.]" See *Slavery: A Problem in American Institutional and Intellectual Life* (Chicago: University of Chicago Press, 1959), 104. Elkins, however, did not have much else to say about the human side of slavery, and indeed portrayed masters and their culture in only a sketchy way. It was Eugene Genovese who took the focus off benevolence by looking at the reciprocity Phillips perceived, albeit far more analytically. Paternalism was a social situation born of a set of relationships, always problematic and changing: "Paternalism's insistence upon mutual obligations—duties, responsibilites, and ultimately even rights—implicitly recognized the slaves' humanity," *Roll, Jordan, Roll*, 5.

As I have tried to show, paternalism's rituals informed relations among whites as well as those between the races. I have expressed my debt on the historical meaning of ritual to the work of Clifford Geertz, Mary Douglas, Victor Turner, and others in the notes. A helpful perspective on the usefulness of anthropologic studies to history is Ronald Walters, "Signs of the Times: Clifford Geertz and Historians," *Social Research* 47 (1980): 537–56; Israel Scheffler, "Ritual and Reference," *Synthese* 46 (1981): 421–37. For ethnography, see Rhys Isaac, "Ethnographic Method in History: An Action Approach," *Historical Methods* 13 (1980): 43–61; John L. Caughey, "The Ethnography of Everyday Life: Theories and Methods for American Culture Studies," *American Quarterly* 34 (1982): 222–43; a classic still worthy of mention (though excessively given to jargon) is Peter L. Berger and Thomas Luckmann, *The Social Construction of Reality: A Treatise in the Sociology of Knowledge* (New York: Anchor Books, 1966). Related, but still largely unexplored, are essays on the history of perception; for example, Donald M. Lowe, *History of Bourgeois Perception* (Chicago: University of Chicago Press, 1983). Also suggestive are Basil Bernstein, "Some

Sociological Determinents of Perception," *British Journal of Sociology* 9 (1958): 159–74; James Fulcher, "Context and Formula," *Intellectual History Group Newsletter* 5 (1983): 26–30. These lead into a wide field of culture and personality studies; I found useful Anthony F. Wallace, *Culture and Personality* (New York: Random House, 1961); Robert A. LeVine, *Culture, Behavior, and Personality* (Chicago: Aldine Publishing Co., 1973); Silvan Tomkins and Carroll Izard, eds., *Affect, Cognition, and Personality* (New York: Springer Publishing Co., 1965); Robert A. LeVine, "Culture, Personality, and Socialization: An Evolutionary View," in *Handbook of Socialization Theory and Research*, ed. David A. Goslin (Chicago: Aldine Publishing Co., 1969).

Two broad, incisive works that raise issues in the historical re-creation of culture are E. D. Hirsch, *Validity in Interpretation* (New Haven: Yale University Press, 1967) and Daniel Lerner, ed., *Parts and Wholes* (New York: Free Press, 1963). Quentin Skinner's skepticism regarding the reconstruction of past intellectual life is illuminating; see his "Meaning and Understanding in the History of Ideas," *History and Theory* 8 (1969): 3–53 and "The Limits of Historical Explanations," *Philosophy* 41 (1966): 199–215. For challenging replies, see Margaret Leslie, "In Defence of Anachronism," *Political Studies* 18 (1970): 433–47 and Bhikhu Parekh and R. N. Berki, "The History of Political Ideas: A Critique of Quentin Skinner's Methodology," *Journal of the History of Ideas* 24 (1973): 163–84. Some of the best recent writing on the methods and means of cultural history has centered on the nature of historiography, especially the way narrative and the chronological relation of "fact" shape one's sense of what counts as evidence. For a sample, generally admiring of narrative, see Paul Hernadi, "Re-Presenting the Past: A Note on Narrative Historiography and Historical Drama," *History and Theory* 15 (1976): 45–51; Richard T. Vann, "The Rhetoric of Social History," *Journal of Social History* 10 (1976): 221–36; David A. Hollinger, "Historians and the Discourse of Intellectuals," in *New Directions in American Intellectual History*, ed. John Higham and Paul K. Conkin (Baltimore: Johns Hopkins University Press, 1979), 42–63; Hayden White, "The Question of Narrative in Contemporary Historical Theory," *History and Theory* 23 (1984): 1–33; Robert H. Canary and Henry Kozicki, eds., *The Writing of History: Literary Form and Historical Understanding* (Madison: University of Wisconsin Press, 1978); Dominick LaCapra, *Rethinking Intellectual History: Texts, Contexts, Language* (Ithaca: Cornell University Press, 1983), esp. chaps. 1, 2, and 10.

An instructive essay into problems of culture and class dominance is T. J. Jackson Lears, "The Concept of Cultural Hegemony: Problems and Possibilities," *American Historical Review* 90 (1985): 567–93. A novelist's view, with brilliant if brief reflections on the narrative unity of history and fiction, is E. L. Doctorow, "False Documents," *New American Review* 26 (1977): 215–32. Reconstructing the richness of past life has been a historical biographer's problem as well; a suggestive collection is Marc Pachter, ed., *Telling Lives: The Biographer's Art* (Washington, D.C.: New Republic Books, 1979). Also useful, and different in approach and method, are William M. Runyan, *Life Histories and Psychobiography: Explorations in Theory and Method* (New York: Oxford University Press, 1982) and the far more positivist collection, Daniel Bertaux, ed., *Biography and Society: The Life History Approach in the Social Sciences* (Beverly Hills, Calif.: Sage Publications, 1981). Two wide-ranging works which raise many interpretive issues in a broad, social-historical context of method and analysis are Fred Weinstein and Gerald M. Platt, *Psychoanalytic Sociology: An Essay on the Interpretation of Historical Data and the Phenomena of Collective Behavior* (Baltimore: Johns Hopkins University Press, 1973) and Robert F. Berkhoffer, Jr., *A Behavioral Approach to Historical Analysis* (New York: Free Press, 1969).

For landmark yet accessible studies in general linguistics, see Ferdinand deSaussure, *A Course in General Linguistics*, trans. Wade Baskin (1915; New York: McGraw Hill, 1966); Benjamin Lee Whorf, *Language, Thought, and Reality*, ed. John B. Carroll (Cambridge: MIT Press, 1956); Edward Sapir, *Culture, Language, and Personality: Selected Essays*, ed. David G. Mandelbaum (Berkeley and Los Angeles: University of California Press, 1949). For a rather donnish critique of both Whorf and Sapir and the focus on specific cultures, see Max Black, *Models and Metaphors: Studies in Language and Philosophy* (Ithaca: Cornell University Press, 1962). Useful are studies of social life and literary or linguistic forms, including the always insightful Kenneth Burke, especially *Language as Symbolic Action* (Berkeley and Los Angeles: University of California Press, 1968); Walter J. Ong, *Rhetoric, Romance, and Technology: Studies in the Interaction of Expression and Culture* (Ithaca: Cornell University Press, 1971); Mary Kay Ritchie, *Male/Female Language: With a Comprehensive Bibliography* (Metuchen, N.J.: Scarecrow Press, 1975); Dan Ben-Amos, "Analytic Categories and Ethnic Genres," *Genre* 2 (1969): 275–301; Robert C. Post, "A Theory of Genre: Romance, Realism, and Moral Reality," *American Quarterly* 33 (1981): 367–90; J. Christopher Crocker, "The Social Functions of Rhetorical Forms," in *The Social Use of Metaphor: Essays on the Anthropology of Rhetoric*, ed. J. David Sapir and J. Christopher Crocker, (Philadelphia: University of Pennsylvania Press, 1977); B. N. Colby, "Ethnographic Semantics: A Preliminary Survey," *Current Anthropology* 7 (1966): 3–32; Basil Bernstein, "A Public Language: Some Sociological Implications of a Linguistic Form," *British Journal of Sociology* 10 (1959): 311–26.

For particular historical studies focusing on language forms, see Nancy S. Struever, *The Language of History in the Renaissance: Rhetoric and Historical Consciousness in Florentine Humanism* (Princeton: Princeton University Press, 1970); Carolly Erickson, *The Medieval Vision: Essays in History and Perception* (New York: Oxford University Press, 1976); Sandra S. Sizer *Gospel Hymns and Social Religion: The Rhetoric of Nineteenth-Century Revivalism* (Philadelphia: Temple University Press, 1978); Peter N. Moogk, " 'Thieving Buggers' and 'Stupid Sluts': Insults and Popular Culture in New France," *William and Mary Quarterly*, 3d ser., 36 (1979): 524–47; Drew Gilpin Faust, "The Rhetoric and Ritual of Agriculture in Antebellum South Carolina," *Journal of Southern History* 45 (1979): 541–68; Joseph J. Hemmer, Jr., "The Charlston Platform Debate in Rhetorical-Historical Perspective," *Quarterly Journal of Speech* 56 (1970): 406–16.

For recent surveys of the history of the family that at least touch upon some of these issues, see Glenn Elder, "History and the Family: Discovery of Complexity," *Journal of Marriage and the Family* 43 (1981): 489–519; Lawrence Stone, "Family History in the 1980's," *Journal of Interdisciplinary History* 12 (1981): 51–87; Louise Tilly and Miriam Cohen, "Does the Family Have a History?" *Social Science History* 6 (1982): 131–79; Virginia Tufte and Barbara Myerhoff, eds., *Changing Images of the Family* (New Haven: Yale University Press, 1979), esp. "Introduction"; Daniel Blake Smith, "The Study of the Family in Early America: Trends, Problems, and Prospects," *William and Mary Quarterly* 3d ser., 39 (1982): 3–28. A particularly thoughtful consideration of the difficulty of interpreting the meaning of family life is Jane Flax, "The Family in Contemporary Feminist Thought: A Critical Review," in *The Family in Political Thought*, ed. Jean Bethke Elshtain (Amherst: University of Massachusetts Press, 1982), 223–53.

For views of the workings of southern family life in the eighteenth century, see Michael Zuckerman, "William Byrd's Family," *Perspectives in American History* 12 (1979): 255–311 and his "Penmanship Exercises for Saucy Sons: Some Thoughts on the Colonial Southern Family," *South Carolina Historical Magazine* 84 (1983): 152–66; Rhys Isaac, *The Transformation of Virginia, 1740–1790* (Chapel Hill: University of North Carolina Press, 1982); Jack P. Greene, *Landon Carter: An Inquiry into the Personal Values and Social Imperatives of the Eighteenth-Century Virginia Gentry* (Charlottesville: University Press of Virginia, 1967); Daniel Blake Smith, *Inside the Great House: Planter Family Life in Eighteenth-Century Chesapeake Society* (Ithaca: Cornell University Press, 1980); Jan Lewis, *Pursuit of Happiness: Family and Values in Jefferson's Virginia* (New York: Cambridge University Press, 1983), an excellent bridge to the nineteenth century.

For recent work on the history of women and the family in the antebellum years, see Anne F. Scott, *The Southern Lady: From Pedestal to Politics, 1830–1930* (Chicago: University of Chicago Press, 1970); Catherine Clinton, *The Plantation Mistress: Woman's World in the Old South* (New York: Pantheon Books, 1982); Jane Turner Censer, *North Carolina Planters and Their Children, 1800–1860* (Baton Rouge: Louisiana State University Press, 1984); Jean Friedman, *The Enclosed Garden: Women and Community in the Evangelical South, 1830–1900* (Chapel Hill: University of North Carolina Press, 1985); Russell L. Blake, "Ties of Intimacy: Social Values and Personal Relationships of Antebellum Slaveholders" (Ph.D. diss., University of Michigan, 1978). For collections of family letters, see Robert Manson Myers, ed., *The Children of Pride* (New Haven: Yale University Press, 1972) and Carol Bleser, ed., *The Hammonds of Redcliffe* (New York: Oxford University Press, 1981).

INDEX

Academies: Academy of the Visitation, 184; and adolescence, 130; class consciousness in, 139–40; and coming of age, 133, 136–42, 196; compared to home schooling, 171, 177, 196; conflict in, 139; discipline in, 139; Edgeworth Female Seminary, 193–94, 198–99, 201–6; and family relations, 122, 142–50; and family values, 137; fees and expenses, 134; Hillsborough Military Academy, 85, 134, 138, 199; and homesickness, 148, 194, 196, 236; as a homosocial world, 137–42, 148–50, 196; and letter-writing, 142–50; Madame Chegaray's school, 134, 185; Madame Greland's school, 134; Madame Sigoignes's school, 171, 177; Madame Talvande's school, 134–37, 141; manners in, 138; Montpelier Female Institute, 134, 225; organization of, 134; and planter class power, 142; planter class support for, 132; religious origins of, 132; rise of, in South, 132–33; routine in, 137–42, 201–3; and rural life, !33–34; St. Mary's Episcopal School, 101, 134, 140; as setting for courtship, 84, 109–10; and sexual spheres, 138; subjects of study in, 134, 141, 202; and teachers, 130, 135, 202–3; and womanhood, 133, 202–3, 225. *See also* Coming of age; Education

Adams, Jasper, 123, 128–29

Adolescence: and academies, 130; and education, 122; and family harmony, 129–30; and moral advice, 130. *See also* Coming of age

Affair of honor: averted, 24–30, 168; and circular letters, 33–34; and coming of age, 155; compared to courtship, 78, 89; and cowardice, 19; cultural themes in, 11–14; and death, 10, 38; and emotion, 22, 34, 229; equality in, 21, 36, 41–46;

and family values, 10–11; and fighting, 20; and insult, 29; and language, 6, 10, 11, 17–20, 29–31, 44–45, 168; letters in, 18–19, 23, 32, 40–42; and manhood, 5–6, 10, 22–23, 46–49; and men's relations, 23–28, 42, 229; origins of, 6; and paternalism, 38, 49, 168; and planter class power, 21–22, 32–33, 47; and political life, 21–22, 34, 168, 229, 230; and rage, 11, 14, 43–44; role of friends in, 12–13, 21–22, 32, 35–36, 41, 44, 48, 229; rules of, 21, 46–47; and self-control, 11, 22; and self-esteem, 14, 17, 22, 46–48, 168; and social order, 14–15, 45, 168; stages of, 9–10; as story, 47, 49; weapons in, 36, 43. *See also* Code of honor; Dueling; Honor

Alcoholism, and planter class men, 169, 225

Altman, Janet, 92, 271n.74, 290n.30

Ambition, and manhood, 155–57, 227–29

Auerbach, Nina, 269n.52

Aunt Polly (slave), 140

Balandier, Georges, 258n.1

Ball, Hugh, 125

Bonham, Milledge Luke, affair of honor with Preston Brooks, 30–33

Brenan, Ellen, 79

Brice Creek plantation, 166, 170, 180

Brooks, Preston, affair of honor with Milledge Luke Bonham, 30–33

Brother-sister relations. *See* Men, and relations with sisters; Women, and relations with brothers

Bryan, Joseph, 100

Bryan, Maria, 87–88, 99, 125, 127, 133

Bryce, Campbell R., 94–96, 124

Butler, Charles, 55, 57–58, 143, 158

Caldwell, D. F., and affair of honor with Charles Fisher, 33–38

BOOKS IN THE SERIES